Praise for

WE HAVE THE WAR UPON US

"Cooper suggests Lincoln might have forestalled the march toward secession by speaking out before his inaugural, but he refused and was as firmly opposed to compromise as the rest of his party.... The book gains momentum as the crisis deepens and Cooper describes the enormous pressures on Lincoln as he agonized whether to reinforce beleaguered Fort Sumter in Charleston Harbor." —*Seattle Times*

"Cooper leaves no stone unturned as he explores the hard decisions and compromises leading up to the war, beginning with the way Lincoln's election changed the face of American politics. . . . Cooper's research is thorough and unbiased, assigning credit and blame on all sides. . . . Civil War buffs will appreciate the expert examination of the period." —*Publishers Weekly*

"Written from the perspectives of Americans who experienced the efforts to forestall disunion and war during the five months between November 1860 and April 1861 and could not know the full consequences of their actions, this book captures the drama and tensions of those perilous times. Especially noteworthy is Cooper's treatment of William H. Seward, whose struggles to patch together a compromise form the main thread running through this important book." —James M. McPherson, author of *Tried by War: Abraham Lincoln as Commander in Chief*

"The book reads like a Shakespearean tragedy played out on the national stage, where everything is converging toward a point of catastrophe, and the one thing that could avert disaster at the last minute (in this case, some kind of compromise) fails. . . . There are moral implications here, as well as historical." —*The Daily Beast*

"*We Have the War Upon Us* is the best survey of the secession crisis published in a generation. There is no more important question than how the Union fell apart in the wake of Abraham Lincoln's election in November 1860. Cooper answers it with a clarity that comes only after years of research and thought. This is a book for scholars to ponder, but for all interested readers to enjoy." —James Oakes, author of *Freedom National: The Destruction of Slavery in the United States, 1861–1865*

"William J. Cooper's superb new book reminds us that whatever the influence of vast political, social, and economic forces, history is ultimately the story of human beings making decisions based on flawed perceptions and imperfect knowledge. This powerful narrative will keep readers enthralled even though they know the outcome. Here moderates such as John J. Crittenden and William H. Seward share the stage with Abraham Lincoln, Jefferson Davis, radical Republicans, and southern fire-eaters. Rejecting an irrepressible conflict interpretation, Cooper shows how the partisan, ideological, and sectional interests of political leaders gradually drove the nation toward the abyss. This sobering work recaptures the anguish of the nation's greatest crisis and surely holds lessons for our own time."

—George C. Rable, author of *God's Almost Chosen Peoples: A Religious History of the American Civil War*

"Written with characteristic panache, deeply researched, and replete with shrewd judgments and welcome fresh perspectives, Cooper's richly detailed study of the secession crisis should delight fellow scholars and general readers alike. It's a gem of a book." —Michael F. Holt, author of *By One Vote: The Disputed Presidential Election of 1876*

William J. Cooper

WE HAVE THE WAR UPON US

William J. Cooper is a Boyd Professor at Louisiana State University and a past president of the Southern Historical Association. He was born in Kingstree, South Carolina, and received his A.B. from Princeton and his Ph.D. from Johns Hopkins University. He has been a member of the LSU faculty since 1968 and is the author of *The Conservative Regime: South Carolina, 1877–1890*; *The South and the Politics of Slavery, 1828–1856*; *Liberty and Slavery: Southern Politics to 1860*; *Jefferson Davis, American*; *Jefferson Davis and the Civil War Era*; and coauthor of *The American South: A History*. He lives in Baton Rouge.

ALSO BY WILLIAM J. COOPER

Jefferson Davis and the Civil War Era

Jefferson Davis, American

The American South: A History
(with Thomas E. Terrill)

Liberty and Slavery: Southern Politics to 1860

The South and the Politics of Slavery, 1828–1856

The Conservative Regime: South Carolina, 1877–1890

EDITOR

In the Cause of Liberty:
How the Civil War Redefined American Ideals
(with John M. McCardell)

Jefferson Davis: The Essential Writings

Writing the Civil War: The Quest to Understand
(with James M. McPherson)

A Master's Due: Essays in Honor of David Herbert Donald
(with Michael F. Holt and John M. McCardell)

Social Relations in Our Southern States
(by Daniel R. Hundley)

WE HAVE THE WAR UPON US

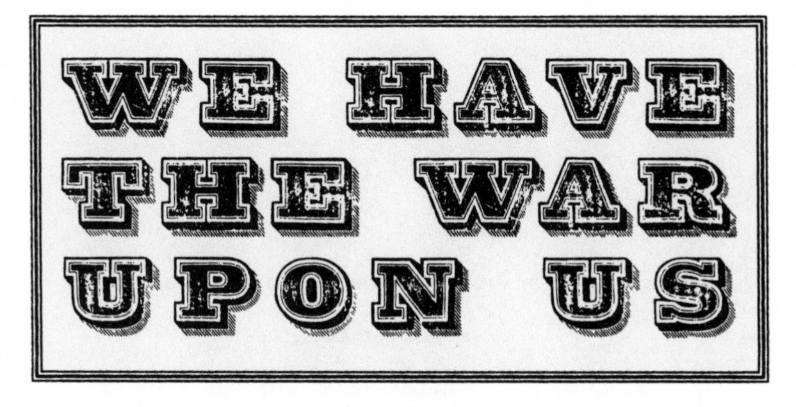

THE ONSET OF THE CIVIL WAR,

November 1860–April 1861

William J. Cooper

VINTAGE CIVIL WAR LIBRARY
Vintage Books
A Division of Random House, Inc.
New York

FIRST VINTAGE CIVIL WAR LIBRARY EDITION, JUNE 2013

The Library of Congress has cataloged the Knopf edition as follows:
Cooper, William J. (William James)
We have the war upon us : the onset of the Civil War, November 1860–April 1861 / William J. Cooper.—1st ed.
p. cm.
Includes bibliographical references and index.
1. United States—Politics and government—1857–1861.
2. United States—History—Civil War, 1861–1865—Causes.
3. Secession—Southern States.
4. Lincoln, Abraham, 1809–1865. I. Title.
E440.5.C77 2012
973.7'11—dc23 2012019675

VINTAGE ISBN: 978-1-4000-7623-9

Author photograph © Michael Lionstar
Book design by Robert C. Olsson
Maps by Gary D. Joiner

www.vintagebooks.com

Printed in the United States of America
10 9 8 7 6 5 4 3 2 1

For My Grandchildren

Michael and John Cooper
and
Clover and Catherine Cooper

CONTENTS

ILLUSTRATIONS

MAPS

PREFACE

The cataclysm of the Civil War is the defining moment in the history of the United States. At the cost of more than 750,000 dead and that many more wounded, it guaranteed the preservation of the Union and abolished the institution of racial slavery. Even with that frightful human toll, the outcome made it a good war for the United States. These generalizations are well known and shared by most Americans of our time.

Yet the men who made the fateful decisions leading to that massive conflict did not share our perspective. The great historian David M. Potter commented on the difficulty, but necessity, of understanding the perspective of those we study. "The supreme task of the historian," he wrote, "and the one of most superlative difficulty, is to see the past through the imperfect eyes of those who lived it and not with his own omniscient twenty-twenty vision." Recognizing the arduousness of his assigned task, Potter concluded, "I am not suggesting that any of us can really do this, but only that it is what we must attempt."[1]

In this book I have tried to adhere to Potter's charge. In the months between the election of the Republican Abraham Lincoln as president in November 1860 and the outbreak of hostilities in April 1861, no one knew whether war would occur, or if it did, no one could foresee the price, course, or result of that war. Even those who did expect armed conflict, a few excitedly, more fearfully, had no conception of its magnitude.

Slavery and the political issues surrounding it occupy a central place in my account. Yes, the war ended slavery, and to most Americans of today it was fought for that cause. The war was not begun to eradicate slavery, however. Even the leading Republican policymakers understood that a war started to kill slavery could not command united northern support and could quite possibly destroy their party.

This judgment was based on the reality that Americans, Republicans included, overwhelmingly believed that the Constitution protected slavery in the states where it existed. Moreover, except in extreme antislavery circles, owning slaves did not make a person a moral ogre or persona non grata in civil society. Additionally, the racial character of American slavery was of cardinal importance. In the mid-nineteenth century almost all white Americans and Western Europeans believed in the supremacy of the white race. I will not keep pointing out that this outlook is different from mine and that of our own era. I should not need to.

Before the Civil War, white southerners constantly talked about liberty—its preciousness and their commitment to it. They perceived no contradiction between their faith in liberty and the existence of slavery. From at least the period of the American Revolution, white southerners defined their liberty, in part, as their right to own slaves and to decide the fate of the institution without any outside interference. In their view, living in a slave society made them no less American than their fellow citizens in the free states. While such a concept is foreign to our thinking, it was fundamental to white southerners until 1865.

Writing a book about the coming of the Civil War, even one so chronologically restricted as mine, I place myself in a long line of historians who have grappled with the causes of the war. I owe an enormous debt to my predecessors, who have illuminated so many facets of the sectional struggle from abolition to secession. Answering the question of why the war came is not my aim. My goal is not so grand. I want to tell the story of those whose action and inaction brought the country to the precipice and finally over it.

I concentrate on the five months between Lincoln's election and the commencement of fighting. During those weeks the attention of Americans became increasingly riveted on the great crisis of the Union. The southern states threatened to break up the Union. The immediate crucial issue was the place of slavery in the national territories; the longer-term question concerned the character of the Union and who would wield power in it.

At the outset, many Americans assumed that a political compromise fashioned in Congress would settle the dispute. Compromising sectional disagreements had been a hallmark of the nation since the Constitutional

Convention of 1787. The precedent set there had been followed on several volatile occasions during the succeeding three-quarters of a century.

But not all Americans wanted another compromise. In the South, radical secessionists saw this moment, the election of a northern president heading a northern party by northern voters, as their opportunity to disrupt the Union. The North had its own segment that spurned any compromise with the South. These vigorous partisans of the triumphant Republican party were determined to celebrate their victory without any deal with an alarmed, uneasy South.

Between these extremes, Americans in both sections ardently desired to reach an equitable settlement between North and South. Although this pro-compromise sentiment could be found in the Deep South and in the Republican party, it flourished among northern Democrats and in the Upper South and Border. A fact often overlooked is that pro-compromise forces included men both antislavery and proslavery.

My book focuses on why the pro-compromise legions lost, or why the American tradition of sectional compromise failed. In the past few years, several scholars have investigated different parts of this story, most notably the success of the secessionists and the dynamics within the Republican party. But no one has treated North and South, Republican and Democrat, sectional radicals and sectional conservatives in the same place. I have done that.[2]

WE HAVE THE WAR UPON US

PROLOGUE

"Is This Not a Remarkable Spectacle?"

IN THE EARLY evening of Sunday, March 3, 1861, the white-headed gentleman stood once more among his fellow senators. Of medium height, spare and erect, with a face deeply lined, almost craggy, John J. Crittenden commanded attention. With a long commitment to his country and an unsurpassed reputation for integrity, he was foremost a man of character. But Crittenden's audience consisted of more than his Senate colleagues. Spectators jammed the galleries long before he spoke at 7:00 p.m. In this assembly sat Abraham Lincoln, to be inaugurated president the next day.[1]

For the past three months, during the entire span of the Second Session of the 36th Congress, Senator Crittenden had striven to get his colleagues to address the crisis that convulsed the nation. The Union he cherished was coming apart. Since December 1860, seven southern states, from South Carolina west to Texas, had severed their relations with the United States. In mid-February these seceders had created a new polity, the Confederate States of America. Furthermore, turmoil and uncertainty about their future course dominated discussion in most of the remaining eight slave states. Recognizing his inability thus far to secure any congressional action to prevent this dismemberment, Crittenden on that Sunday made a final plea for his beloved Union.

John Jordan Crittenden is not a name remembered today. But in 1860 and 1861 he was a consequential man, with admirers in both North and South. A native Kentuckian, born in 1786 and trained in the law, he had spent most of his life serving his state and nation in various offices: state legislator, governor, twice a cabinet officer, and on four separate occasions a United States senator. Since the 1830s he had always been a Whig, the party formed to oppose Andrew Jackson's Democratic party. The Whigs generally believed in active government to facilitate the material growth and cultural progress of the country. Moreover, Crittenden was a political disciple and protégé of one of the giants of antebellum American politics, Henry Clay, a fellow Kentuckian. Even though the Whig party as an organized force disappeared in the mid-1850s, a victim in large part of increasing sectional tension, Crittenden in 1860 still called himself a Whig.

In the Second Session, Crittenden worked to emulate Clay, who had gained fame as the Great Compromiser or the Great Pacificator. On three occasions when sectional strife had endangered the stability, even the continuation, of the Union, Clay, as congressman or senator, had assumed a major role in finding a legislative settlement. In 1820, when a dispute over the admission of Missouri as a slave state caused a national crisis, Speaker of the House Clay was central in fashioning the Missouri Compromise. Then, in 1832 and 1833, during the Nullification Crisis, which brought South Carolina and the administration of Andrew Jackson to the brink of armed conflict, Clay, now in the U.S. Senate, was instrumental in crafting the Compromise of 1833 and defusing the explosive situation. Finally, toward the end of his life, again a senator, he initiated a drive to settle the struggle between North and South over slavery's future in the Mexican Cession, territory that came to the United States following the Mexican War—California and the modern Southwest. The resulting Compromise of 1850 thwarted what could have become a full-blown secession crisis. In 1860 and 1861, Crittenden wanted to replicate Clay's achievement.[2]

The same subject that underlay the political clash of 1850 occupied the country and Senator Crittenden in 1860 and 1861—the future of slavery in the territories belonging to the United States, or, more fundamentally, the future of slavery in the nation. Southerners and many northerners disagreed. Overwhelmingly, southerners asserted their right as Americans to go into the national territory with their property, including slave property. In 1860, southerners based their claim not only on the general southern understanding of their constitutional rights, but also on a recent ruling of the U.S. Supreme Court. In its *Dred Scott* decision of 1857, the Court declared that southerners enjoyed a constitutional right to carry slaves into the territories, a right that Congress could not proscribe.

That judicial conclusion directly contradicted the main tenet of one of the two major parties—the Republican party, which had grown in the North from the rubble of the old Whig party and from Democrats disaffected by what they perceived as an increasingly pro-southern bias in their former political home. With its single-minded commitment to the North, the Republican party had barely a footprint in the South, and that only in the Border slave states. From the very inception of their party, Republicans had preached no slavery in the territories as their gospel. Even in the face of *Dred Scott* they refused to back away. In 1860, the Republican candidate for president, Abraham Lincoln, running on a platform that trumpeted territorial prohibition, was elected president of the United States without a single electoral vote from a slave state.

Lincoln's triumph overturned American politics. A new party with a solely northern constituency would take control of the executive branch of the federal government. That had never happened before; previously, all victorious parties had had a southern connection. Republicans were exuberant, though inexperienced in governing. The defeated Democrats confronted their own problem. Many in the South, the base of the party's strength, were distraught, even fearful; they foresaw a Republican administration threatening their most basic interests. In the slave states, sectional radicals called fire-eaters cheered the Republican victory as the catalyst for their chief goal, breaking up the Union. Although southerners were certainly not unified on secession, tumult wracked the South. Yet while Republicans basked in the glow of victory and southerners debated their course, the nation turned its eyes to Congress. The Second Session of the 36th Congress would convene in early December, less than a month after the election.

When Congress met, however, no clear statement signaled that it would settle the sectional dispute that had rapidly ascended to the level of national crisis. No person, group, or party immediately stepped forward to calm the excitement. In fact, leadership appeared alarmingly absent. Turning to the Bible, a reporter wrote, "Babel was not in a more confused condition than is Congress at this time." This witness found "the gabbing, gibbering, many who have nothing to lose, and some hope that they may gain by disorder and dissolution, and who laugh, cackle and gossip over the general conflagration." The tradition of Congress grasping and handling major crises was seemingly in jeopardy. Southern fire-eaters strutted; Republicans crowed. In contrast, anguished men on both sides of the Mason-Dixon Line struggled to find a way toward reconciliation.[3]

Senator Crittenden came forward with proposals, chiefly to settle the territorial question by extending the old Missouri Compromise line westward to California and embedding the division in the Constitution. Between December and March he pushed, at times altering the specifics of his plan to attract support. Other senators and congressmen floated additional suggestions; none went anywhere. The judgment of a close observer in mid-January described the plight of the would-be compromisers: "Things look dark here today. The utter inactivity of Congress stupefies those who would otherwise have some hope." Most Republicans were fundamentally obdurate in opposing any compromise touching the territories, even in permitting either House or Senate to vote on any such measure. Their strength increased in both houses as congressmen and senators from seceded states left the capital. Despite his arduous efforts, Crittenden never even succeeded in getting the Senate to say aye or nay to his plan.[4]

Now, with the session coming to a close and no congressional action on his or any other proposal, the venerable lawmaker gave his final assessment. It was also his valedictory, for his term expired with the 36th Congress. Crittenden spoke the language of failure, but even more of incomprehension. Addressing his fellow senators, Crittenden asked, "Is this not a remarkable spectacle?" He wanted to know why "when the country trusted to our hands is going to ruin," the Senate has been unable "to devise any measure of public safety." "We see the danger," he announced; "we acknowledge our duty." Yet, he sorrowfully noted, "we are acknowledging before the world we can do nothing; acknowledging before the world, or appearing to all the world as men who do nothing." "The saddest spectacle," he deplored.[5]

Denying accusations hurled at him that he acted as if he had a special commission to make peace, Crittenden heaped praise upon colleagues who had also worked for settlement. He had done no more, he declared, than those others. He also made clear that he was no evangelist for slavery, announcing, "I appear here as the advocate of Union." Borrowing from Shakespeare, he told senators their role "must be to do something, or to do nothing."

For a man who professed no allegiance to an active party, Crittenden's cry for patriotism to country over party loyalty posed no difficulty. Still, recognizing the power of party on professional politicians, he insisted that the Senate no longer confronted "a question of party," but "a question of country and Union." He went on to affirm the equality of all Americans under the Constitution.

Thus, in his view the South did have constitutional rights in the common national territory. And these rights, in his mind, included taking slave property into that territory. He even admitted that the South had "some plausible reason to be discontented" because Republicans repeatedly maintained that they would bar southerners from the territories, taking all for the North. For Crittenden solving this problem was simple—a compromise, extending the Missouri line westward to California. This was more than an equitable division, he informed Republicans, for it gave the North fully two-thirds of the national domain. Furthermore, because of the inhospitable climate and terrain below that line, he foresaw little chance of slavery taking hold there. As a result, he defined Republican insistence on the total prohibition of slavery as "a mere question of abstract right."

Crittenden said he would never waver in his great goal to halt any future secession and then aim for reconstruction of the Union. From Republicans he solicited compromise, "giv[ing] to the nation breathing-time" to get past the alarm pervading the country. But he admitted despite that single request "this is refused." He pointed out to Republicans that they would control the executive branch, that the northern population and economy were outpacing the southern. Over time, northern power would only increase. Thus, offering the South now what he termed "a little boon" in order to save the country he saw as wise policy, not craven compromise. He chided the Republicans for their commitment to the shibboleth "woe to the conquered; no compromise," comparing it to the proclamation of Roman emperors, "*vae victis*." Simply put, it was not American. Moreover, he insisted that a large portion, "if not a majority," of the northern electorate rejected Republican obduracy. Crittenden based this estimate on petitions and memorials flooding Congress. He specified that no less than a quarter million northern voters had signed petitions submitted to Congress. He also noted that legislatures had "memorialized, and, in fact, petitioned Congress in the name of the people of their States." Even executives of railroad lines traversing the North testified to widespread backing for compromise and expressed their wishes for settlement along the lines of his proposals, Crittenden added. Given the "assurances" proclaimed by all these citizens and his "confidence in the intelligence and public virtue of the people, [which] is greater than it is in any body of their representatives," Crittenden professed his conviction "that right will eventually be done."

Identifying himself as a southern man, though one utterly attached to the Union, he urged southerners to recognize the moment as "a time of high party excitement by one Congress." This emotional spasm would pass, he asserted. New elections would result in more balanced views in Congress. To buttress his case he emphasized the same petitions and memorials he used to appeal to Republicans. Reasonable and fair adjustment of even the territorial issue, he assured southerners, would result from their patience.

Although he tried hard to dam the torrent of disunion, Crittenden left no doubt about his personal position. "I am not for secession. No, sir," he announced. Whatever came he would stand by the Union, and he urged his state, Kentucky, to do likewise. Nothing that secession could promise, he declared, could match the glory of the Union. Only "an imperious necessity" that he could not envision would legitimize Kentucky's seceding. Kentucky, the Constitution, the Union—together they comprised the rock of Crittenden's conviction and patriotism.

While Crittenden made clear his personal stance, he had no illusions. Realizing that Congress would not pass his propositions, he still clung to "every word I have said." But he warned Republican senators not to feel triumphant, for "I tell you now that, whatever security the apparent peace that surrounds us may induce you to suppose exists in the country, it is a delusion." His reading of the future was foreboding: "To-morrow, after to-morrow, and each to-morrow brings with it new fears and new apprehensions to my mind." In his view, "rebellion, revolution, seem to be epidemic in the land." Facing his fellow senators, he lamented, "I thought we could do something to stay it." Crittenden and those like him failed, for when Congress adjourned the day after his speech, no settlement had been embraced.

"Restoration," his major object, had not been achieved. No one at that time could tell whether the Union would again be whole or be engulfed by bloodshed.

CHAPTER ONE

"The Future Is . . . Shrouded in the Very Blackness of Darkness"

JUBILATION, EXCITEMENT, JOY—all reverberated through the great body of the Republican party. One stalwart captured the moment: "I want to live more than I have done for years; to see the future of this great nation under its new impulse of regeneration." The Republican candidate for president had won the election of 1860. In only its second try for the nation's highest office the party had triumphed.[1]

While this impressive showing thrilled the Republican faithful, the uniqueness of the victory matched their delight. In the mid-nineteenth century, the United States had both slave and free states, a division that had obtained since the beginning of the country. By 1860, the nation had grown from the original thirteen states to thirty-three, with eighteen free and fifteen slave. There was also a sectional divide, with the former in the North, the latter in the South. The Republican party was a sectional party, with its roots and voting strength in the free states. It barely had a presence in any of the slave states, and none at all below the Border slave states that adjoined the free states. Never before in American history had a party with no southern connection won a national election. For the first time, a party would control the executive branch of the federal government that had no constituency in and no political obligation to a vast portion of the country.[2]

This state of affairs neither surprised nor alarmed Republicans, for they proudly displayed their sectional colors. The political movement that became the Republican party grew out of the wreckage of what had become known as the second American party system, the competition between Democrats and Whigs that had dominated the nation's politics from the early 1830s until the mid-1850s, when the Whig party expired.

Although no single political disease ravaged the Whigs, the bitter sectional fight over slavery, its future in the country, and, specifically, its expansion into the national territories, was particularly virulent. National parties existed when northerners and southerners could agree on basic issues, or, at least, on how to handle them. With the demise of the Whigs, Democrats alone enjoyed such an agreement, for they had in their fold those northerners willing to cooperate with southerners demanding both constitutional equality for slaveowners and recognition of their slave institution as American.

Overwhelmingly, northern Whigs refused to meet these southern demands, but ex-northern Whigs alone could not build a party to compete with the Democrats. Another critical component of the new political alliance came from a minority of northern Democrats disaffected from their party because of what they perceived as its increasingly pro-southern stance. Mostly associates of former president Martin Van Buren of New York, these Democrats hated the South. In their view, southerners had literally stolen their party from them. To their fledgling political force also came strident antislavery men who had operated outside both the Whig and Democratic tents. They brought idealism, visceral hatred of political deals with the South, and a powerful indictment of slavery as un-American.

The full history of the rise of the Republican party is not my subject. For my purpose it suffices to note that by the middle of the 1850s these former adversaries had joined together to form a new party, distinctly sectional in identity. They designated it Republican to emphasize that only they could save the country, the republic inherited from the founding generation, from the machinations of the southern politicians and their northern friends who had disrupted and corrupted their political universe.

This new Republican party was a northern party with its own defining cornerstone, made of antisouthern granite. That foundation was absolutely essential, for the coalition included ex-Democrats and Whigs who still disagreed over economic issues like the tariff and over the proper attitude toward new immigrants, especially those professing the Roman Catholic faith. "Anti-South" provides a more accurate description of the Republicans and their message than the narrower and balder term "antislavery." Although Republicans counted antislavery zealots among their number, a substantial majority believed that the Constitution granted states

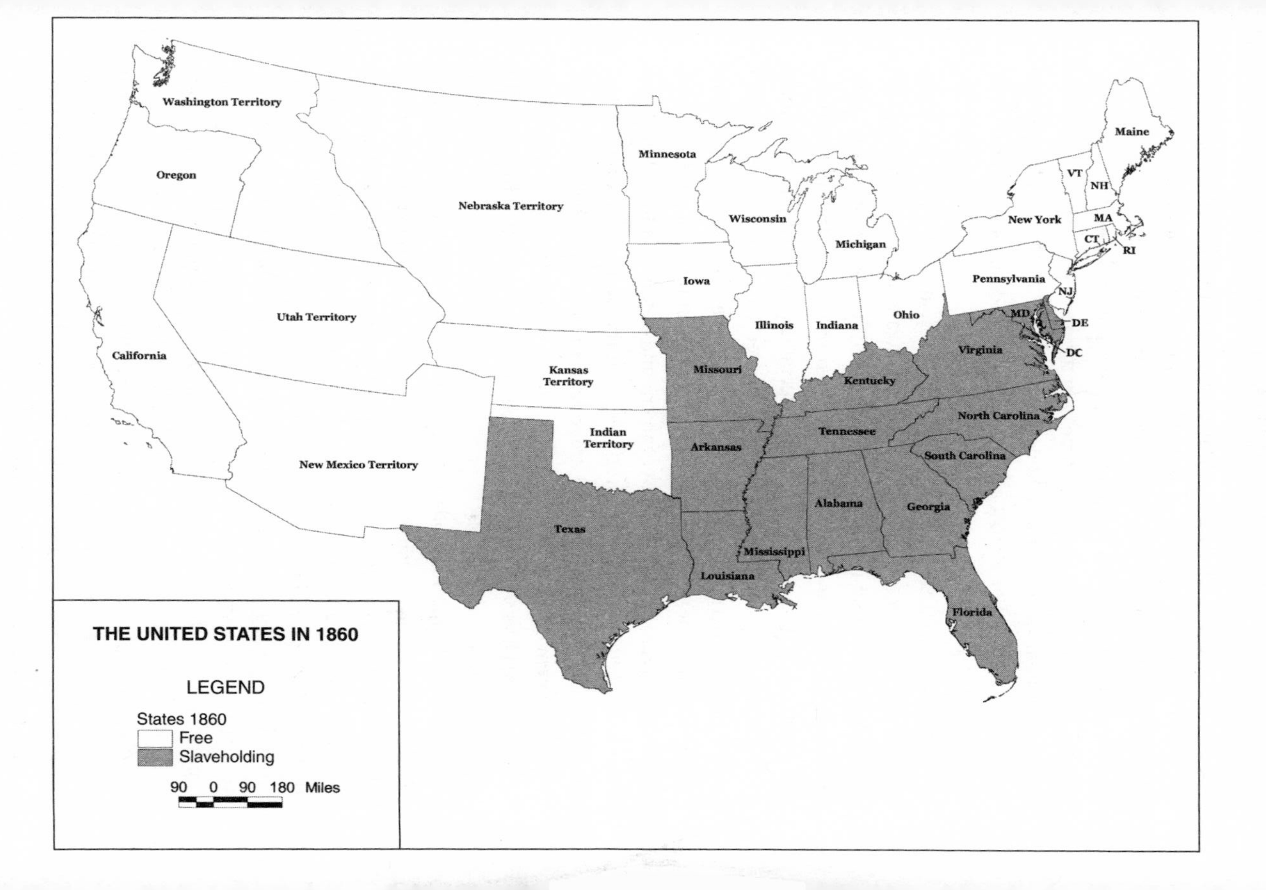
THE UNITED STATES IN 1860
LEGEND
States 1860
Free
Slaveholding
90 0 90 180 Miles
Washington Territory
Oregon
California
Utah Territory
New Mexico Territory
Nebraska Territory
Kansas Territory
Indian Territory
Texas
Minnesota
Iowa
Missouri
Arkansas
Louisiana
Wisconsin
Illinois
Michigan
Indiana
Ohio
Kentucky
Tennessee
Mississippi
Alabama
Georgia
Florida
South Carolina
North Carolina
Virginia
Pennsylvania
New York
Maine
VT
NH
MA
CT
RI
NJ
MD
DE
DC

control over slavery within their borders and that the federal government could not legitimately interfere with the institution in states that permitted it. At the same time, this majority embraced two critical propositions: first, the Constitution gave the federal government power through Congress to control, or to permit or prohibit, slavery in the national territories; second, the government of the United States could never recognize slavery and freedom as equals. For almost all Republicans freedom must predominate, and at some point slavery would cease to exist.

Republicans shaped their assault on the South around a powerful symbol, the Slave Power. For Republican politicians the Slave Power provided a powerful rallying cry more than a critique of the human tragedy of slavery that ardent abolitionists agonized over. That the Slave Power possessed, in the view of Republicans, excessive power within the national government irked them more than the power slaveowners exerted over their human property. In Republican rhetoric the Slave Power embodied the unholy influence exercised by slaveowners acting through the Democratic party over the national government and national policy. This Slave Power, advised Republicans, interfered with the basic rights of northerners. "The liberties of our country are in tenfold the danger they were at the commencement of the American Revolution," shouted a Republican editor in New Hampshire. "We then had a distant foe to contend with. Now the enemy is within our borders."[3]

According to the Republican script, only nefarious and unscrupulous manipulation could explain why the South, the Slave Power, had so much influence at the federal level. With America a democracy, Republican leaders proclaimed, the free states should be directing national affairs because their population far exceeded that of the South. On the numbers, they were certainly correct. In 1860 the free states counted more than 18.8 million people while the slave states had but 8.3 million free people along with almost 4 million slaves. Republicans constantly cried that the North had to assert itself to take its rightful role in leading the country.

Yet a particular provision of the Constitution rankled Republicans even more—the three-fifths clause that for representation counted a slave as three-fifths of a free person. In 1860 that calculation meant that the slave states had a population of 10.7 million for representation, notably increasing their strength in both the House of Representatives and the Electoral College. The actual increase was twenty-five additional congressmen and electoral votes. For Republicans, the Slave Power depended upon this unsavory formula.[4]

Despite what they regarded as a constitutional blemish, Republican politicians believed they could wrestle control from the Democrats, whom they depicted as pledged to "execute all the designs of the slave holders." Consolidating the North could defeat the political handmaiden of the hated Slave Power. With their substantially larger population the northern states dominated the Electoral College, which named presidents. There the free states had 183 electoral votes, the slave states, even with the three-fifths clause, but 120. Thus, by sweeping the North, a Republican presidential candidate could win a national election without a single southern electoral vote. Accordingly, Republicans aimed their message solely at the North, working assiduously to unify the northern electorate while proclaiming that only a North united behind the Republican party could save the republic from the Slave Power.[5]

The Republican national platforms of 1856 and 1860 made unequivocal declarations about the plight of the country. Although those documents did not specifically speak about the Slave Power, their language describing the dangers facing the nation spoke of its manifestations. In 1856 nothing so endangered the republic as "attempts to violate [the Constitution] for the purpose of establishing Slavery in the Territories. . . . " Slavery itself was condemned as a "relic of barbarism." Four years later no talk of "relic" appeared, but the platform declared that only the Republican party could protect the country from the "measureless subserviency to the exactions of a sectional interest" as practiced by the Democrats. That "subserviency," in the Republican view, led to policy "revolutionary in its tendency, and subversive of the peace and harmony of the country." Republicans especially decried what they termed efforts to permit slavery in any new territory as the most heinous evidence of Democratic perfidy. In the Republican interpretation, those attempts violated the principles of the Declaration of Independence and the provisions of the Constitution.[6]

Not only a new party with unprecedented organization and outlook, the Republicans in 1860 also presented an untried, inexperienced leader, Abraham Lincoln of Illinois. He had not held any state or national office since the 1840s, when he served a single term as a representative in the 30th Congress. When Republicans met in Chicago in May 1860 to nominate a presidential candidate, they did not act as most observers thought they would. The leading contender, Senator William Henry Seward of New York, famous for the declarations of a "higher law" than the Constitution and of an "irrepressible conflict" between North and South, between freedom and slavery, was set aside.[7]

Seward lost because many Republican politicians feared he could not win the presidential election. Specifically, they worried that voters in the lower portions of states like Illinois, Indiana, and Pennsylvania—states essential for a Republican triumph—would spurn Seward as too radical. Far more prominent than any other Republican in 1860, Seward had been the preeminent spokesman for antislavery politics for a decade. Condemning any territorial compromise as far back as 1850, he had called on a higher law than the Constitution. For Republicans hungering for victory, Seward had simply been in the public eye for too long. He was passed over. The convention eventually chose Lincoln, a man widely seen as less radical than Seward, and thus more electable.

The Republican decision to jettison Seward and go with Lincoln might well have been the major reason for the party's performance in the presidential election. Lincoln carried all the critical states on the way to a virtual sweep of the free states, only failing in New Jersey, where he shared the electoral vote. In the nation he won 180 electoral votes, a clear majority, though he received none in any of the fifteen slave states. But the popular vote was another matter; he managed only 39.8 percent. In ten slave states he received no votes at all. Since the widespread adoption of popular voting for president three decades earlier, no previous candidate had won with such a small percentage of the popular vote.[8]

Not only was Lincoln distinctly a minority president, he had little national political experience. When the 30th Congress adjourned, in early 1849, Lincoln's time in office also ended. Yet, he was a key figure in building the Republican party in Illinois. A good Whig, he had held on to that party for its lifetime. Upon its disappearance he went to work in earnest for the new organization. Illinois Republicans recognized Lincoln's contribution; no other Republican in the state stood above him. Although he failed in his two tries for the United States Senate, in 1855 and 1858, the latter election was critical for him despite his loss.[9]

That defeat propelled him beyond Illinois borders, for he had challenged the most prominent northern Democrat, United States Senator Stephen A. Douglas. Their widely reported joint speaking tour through the

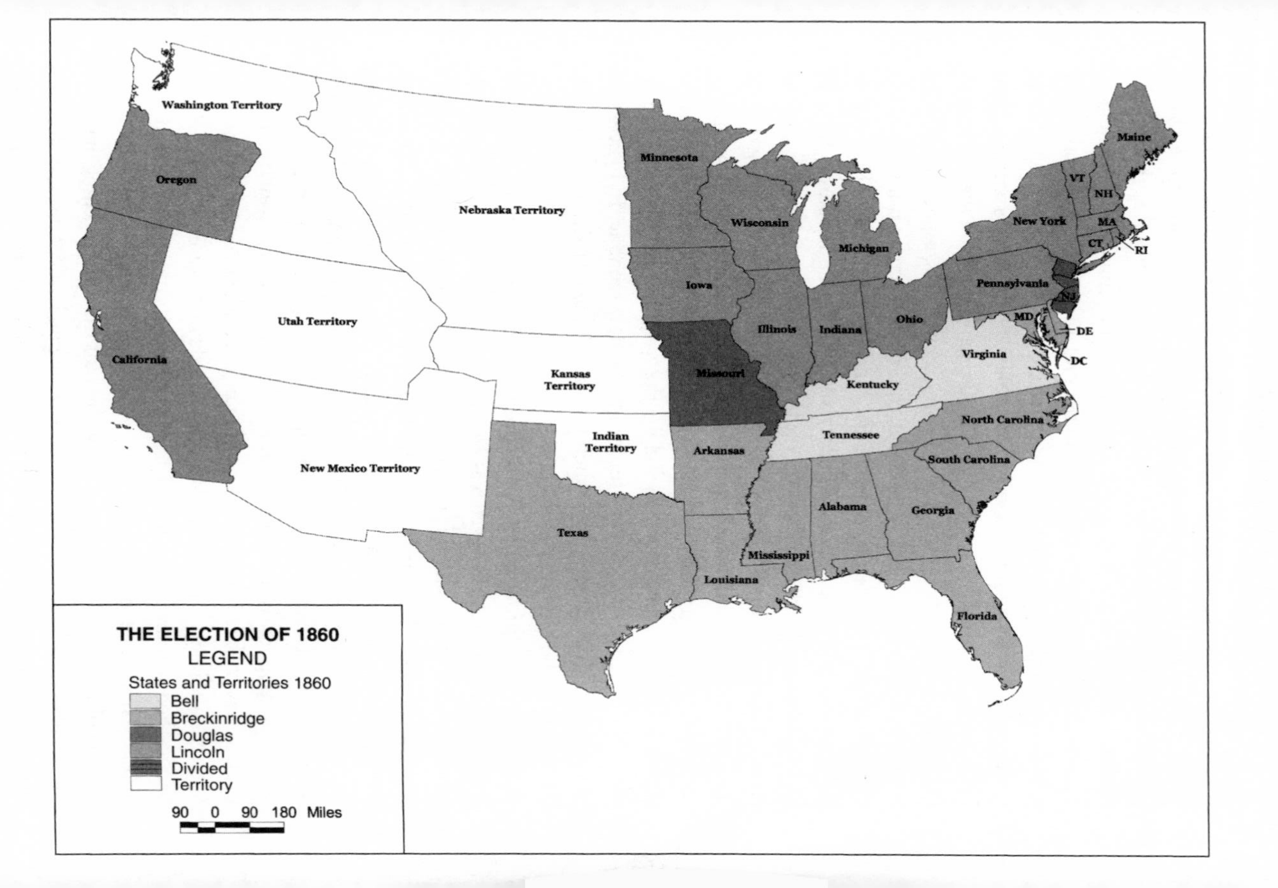
THE ELECTION OF 1860
LEGEND
States and Territories 1860
Bell
Breckinridge
Douglas
Lincoln
Divided
Territory
90 0 90 180 Miles
Washington Territory
Oregon
California
Nebraska Territory
Utah Territory
New Mexico Territory
Kansas Territory
Indian Territory
Texas
Minnesota
Wisconsin
Iowa
Missouri
Arkansas
Louisiana
Illinois
Michigan
Indiana
Ohio
Kentucky
Tennessee
Mississippi
Alabama
Georgia
Florida
South Carolina
North Carolina
Virginia
Pennsylvania
New York
Maine
VT
NH
MA
CT
RI
NJ
MD
DE
DC

state had carried Lincoln's name, his speeches, and his position on national issues, chiefly the territories, across the North. That he stood up to Douglas in their demanding political journey impressed many Republicans far beyond Illinois. But always, and certainly in his contest with Douglas, Lincoln had been in opposition. From the mid-1850s on he had constantly attacked individuals and the party in power.

Then, in February 1860, he traveled to New York City for what resulted in his famous speech at Cooper Union. His performance on the evening of February 27 really impressed northeastern Republicans, especially those in New York opposed to Seward. Although this speech may not have made Lincoln president, it certainly propelled him toward the top of the list of serious contenders for the Republican nomination. In this address Lincoln strove to make Republican opposition to slavery in the territories and the power of the federal government to enact such a policy direct legacies of the Founding Fathers. Focusing on a discrete group of that generation, the men who actually signed the Constitution, Lincoln argued that they were overwhelmingly antislavery, including the southerners. They intended, Lincoln insisted, an antislavery future for the new republic. In his version of history that noble goal had somehow been shunted aside. To restore its primacy was the duty of Republicans.[10]

As a political pronouncement to promote himself and to galvanize the Republican faithful, the speech was enormously successful. As a legal brief, it was indeed effective. But as history, and Lincoln defined his remarks as history, always emphasizing "the facts," it was decidedly one-sided. The Founding Fathers had not circumscribed slavery. For three decades after the ratification of the Constitution, slavery and freedom had marched westward side by side. That simultaneous expansion had occurred with powerful support from some notable Founding Fathers. New territories open to slavery had been acquired or organized under every president from George Washington to James Monroe. On slavery the Founding Fathers bequeathed a more complicated legacy than Lincoln reported and evidently wanted to believe.

Lincoln's political activity during the half decade preceding his election as president had centered on campaigning and ardent partisanship. He had no experience in governing, even on the state level. The only politicians he knew really well were his fellow Republicans in Illinois, who, for their entire existence, had battled against the powerful figure of Douglas.

Even though they knew occasional success, they were fundamentally men in opposition. They felt that standing united and holding fast to party doctrine were imperative for survival against the titan in their midst.

Just as its newly elected leader found himself thrust into a new role, the Republican party had to adopt a different national posture. Previously, it had been on the outside attacking Democratic administrations while arousing its adherents. Not only had the party never before elected a president, it had never controlled Congress. Although Republicans in the House of Representatives had a plurality and had chosen the speaker in the First Session of the 36th Congress, they did not come close to having a majority, and had had to give the nod for speaker to one of their most conservative members. In the Senate, Democrats far outnumbered Republicans thirty-seven to twenty-six, with three self-declared Whigs or Union men who usually voted with Democrats on sectional issues.

The election for members of the 37th Congress, which would come into being with Lincoln's inauguration on March 4, 1861, gave Republicans little reason for optimism that basic power relationships would change. Because in the mid-nineteenth century there was no single national election day, the final lineups for the 37th Congress remained unknown. But the results tabulated by December 1860, along with projections for 1861 elections, made clear that the Republicans would remain a minority. In the House they would fall more than twenty short of a majority while the Senate division would basically replicate that of the 36th Congress. The party would have to change gears from outsider to insider, from campaigning to governing, never an easy task. And this difficult shift would have to occur without control of either house of Congress and with an inexperienced, minority president.[11]

While the excited Republicans relished their triumph, the Democrats faced losing the presidency they had held for almost a decade. But the defeat had not come as a surprise. Professional politicians in both North and South had anticipated that outcome because the party had come apart during its national convention back in the spring. Unable to agree on either a candidate or a platform, the nation's oldest party split along basically North-South lines, with each side naming its own candidate and adopting its own platform. Northern Democrats nominated Stephen A. Douglas, while southern Democrats chose John C. Breckinridge of Kentucky, the sitting vice president.[12]

The dissolution of the Democratic party dated from Douglas's defection from the party line back in 1858. The issue was slavery in the territories, specifically in Kansas. Proslavery forces in that territory had called for the selection of delegates to a constitutional convention, an election boycotted by free-soil settlers. Then they fashioned a constitution allowing slavery, even though all involved knew that a majority of Kansans opposed legalizing the institution within their borders. Moreover, the proslavery men set up an approval process that denied Kansas voters the ability to reject or accept the constitution completely. When their creature, known as the Lecompton Constitution, which would have made Kansas a slave state, reached Congress, the southern Democrats and President James Buchanan stood behind it. They correctly maintained that in Kansas all legal technicalities had been followed by its writers and backers. Yet both the president and the southerners knew that the Lecompton Constitution did not enjoy the approval of a popular majority in Kansas. For the southerners, the chance to add another slave state overcame that hurdle. The president went with the major leadership of his congressional party, believing that with Kansas a state, the combustible, divisive territorial issue would fade.

Senator Douglas refused to follow his party and his president, however. For Douglas, who had staked his political reputation on popular sovereignty—the doctrine declaring that territorial settlers in a free vote could decide aye or nay on slavery—Lecompton was simply unacceptable. He accurately denounced Lecompton for making a mockery of popular sovereignty. Being pressed hard in Illinois in his own reelection year by Republicans pushing their total prohibition doctrine, he could not do otherwise. Falling in line on Lecompton in Washington meant political suicide for him in Illinois. Douglas's stance combined with Republican opposition defeated Lecompton. The administration and the southerners prevailed in the Senate, but fell short in the House, where Douglas loyalists joined with Republicans to stop it.

In the aftermath the president and the party leadership in the Senate waged political war on Douglas, wielding the patronage club and stripping him of his cherished chairmanship of the Committee on Territories. Despite these heavy blows, Douglas stood his ground. After a hard-fought contest he won reelection to the Senate, defeating Lincoln. In 1860, Senator Douglas, not President Buchanan, was undoubtably the most popular northern Democrat.

In the Democratic convention of 1860, which met in Charleston, South Carolina, in April, the South desired both the rejection of Douglas and a platform acknowledging the constitutional rights of slaveowners in the territories, a right affirmed by the United States Supreme Court in its *Dred Scott* decision of 1857. Douglas's stalwarts would give on neither, demanding the senator's nomination and refusing on the territorial issue. As a result, the convention dissolved, with an agreement to regroup in Baltimore in June. But with both sides holding firm, the second conclave provided no resolution on either candidate or platform.

Thus the party broke into two parts, fielding two tickets—one northern, the other southern. Although each side truthfully claimed that it had supporters in the other section, in reality the divided party had two campaigns, one in each section. Douglas lost the North to Lincoln, gaining electoral votes only in New Jersey, though he won more than 1,380,000 popular votes throughout the country. Breckinridge, on the other hand, carried eleven of the fifteen slave states, though nationally he managed only 848,356 popular votes.[13]

Defeated and divided, the Democrats found themselves in opposition, with the task of putting their party back together. Loss might spur former combatants, but provided no guarantee. Douglas remained ascendant in the North and anathema to the southerners who dominated the party in Congress. The Democrats were not powerless, however. They controlled the Senate, and signs pointed to increased Democratic numbers on both sides of the Capitol in the 37th Congress. Making effective use of that strength of course depended on restoring party unity. Some Democrats in each section did begin calling on their comrades in the other to come together to stifle the Republicans. In the words of an editor in Albany, New York, a reunited Democracy would mean a Republican party "stricken down within a single year, as if by paralysis."[14]

Yet, the most immediate menace to a party already in disarray were the voices of disunion in the Cotton States. In the South, particularly in the Deep South, or the Cotton States as they were called, stretching from South Carolina westward to Texas, some men nominally connected to the Democratic party also preached disunion. These secessionists commonly held office as Democrats, including governorships and seats in Congress, though they were not committed to the Democratic or any other party. Contemporaries often termed these men fire-eaters, highlighting the incendiary language and dire pronouncements they customarily employed. These fire-eaters had only one fundamental commitment—to break up the Union. "The South can never know peace and security again in the Union," cried one of them.[15]

The fire-eaters' most fervent message centered on slavery. They insisted that an antislavery Republican party would take control of decisions regarding slavery from the South. This message resonated with many southerners, for since at least the time of the American Revolution white southerners had defined their liberty, in part, as their right to own slaves and to decide the fate of the institution without any outside interference. Losing that right, then, meant losing liberty, their most precious possession. For the white South, liberty and slavery had become inextricably intertwined.[16]

Slavery formed the core of southern society and the southern economy. In 1860 some four million slaves populated the fifteen states that permitted the institution, though they were not evenly dispersed through the region. More than half lived in the Deep South, and the numbers decreased as slave country approached the free states. The slave population had quadrupled since 1800. Its value in 1860 totaled some three billion dollars, exceeding the combined sum of national investment in manufacturing and railroads plus bank capital by some 600 million dollars. In sum, by a wide margin slaves were the most valuable investment in the country.[17]

White southerners could not imagine a world without slavery. With slavery whites controlled a race they believed distinctly inferior to their own in basic intellect and promise. White southerners were not unique in their racial outlook; in the mid-nineteenth century almost every white American and Western European believed that whites were superior to blacks. According to southern whites, the end of slavery would mean either race war or amalgamation, equal horrors to them—or, even worse, both. In addition, slavery formed the backbone of the economy. The massive investment in the institution made it central. Moreover, southerners could not envision how their agricultural economy could function without slaves. All the major crops from the Lower to the Upper South depended upon their labor. Furthermore, as the southern states began to industrialize, slaves were utilized effectively in iron and textile mills, on railroads, and in other enterprises. Southerners found slave labor flexible and considered it essential to their growing, prosperous economy. Thus, for southerners an assault on the institution became an attack on their way of life and deepest values.[18]

The fire-eater call for action to protect the South and slavery condemned political parties for dulling southern perception of an imminent peril. The leading fire-eater journal, the *Charleston Mercury*, asserted, "The truth is 'that party activities' are more or less, fraudulent in their incipiency and practices." They certainly did not serve the best interest of the southern people. The fire-eaters, to overcome what they defined as the party-induced torpor that made southerners indifferent to danger, took as their mission awakening others to what they saw as the life-or-death southern predicament.[19]

In the midst of the presidential contest of 1860, the secessionist Edmund Ruffin of Virginia sent to the governors of the slave states pikes he had obtained from John Brown's cache of weapons. Back in 1859, Brown, a self-proclaimed God-ordained avenger of abolition, had led a failed raid to rouse slaves against their masters. Captured at Harpers Ferry, Virginia, by United States forces, tried and executed by Virginia, Brown became at once a martyr in extreme antislavery circles and a terrorist to white southerners. On each pike Ruffin affixed a label: SAMPLE OF THE FAVORS DESIGNED FOR US BY OUR NORTHERN BRETHREN. Fire-eaters constantly thundered their gospel—southerners must "organize for themselves a separate and independent Confederacy."[20]

Through their public onslaught the fire-eaters promulgated two important ideas. Their solution to all southern problems was secession, and they continually and forcefully preached its necessity. Although other southerners spoke about secession, its possibility and its legality, the fire-eaters gave form, emphasis, and attractiveness to the concept. In 1860, few southerners denied the legitimacy of secession, though many disputed its need. Turning to the reason for secession, fire-eaters constantly warned southerners that the Union held great danger for them. Their pamphlets—with ominous and pressing titles like *The Doom of Slavery . . .* and *The South Alone Should Rule the South . . .*—circulated widely, stirring emotions and fears.[21]

Yet if the fire-eaters succeeded in driving or pushing southern states out of the Union, the result would be devastation for the Democratic party as well as for the country. By 1860, the South had become the bastion of the party. With any significant number of southerners out of their seats, the party would dwindle into an insignificant minority in Congress. Any hope of a presidential victory would disappear.

For the fire-eaters, Lincoln's triumph meant their crucial moment had arrived. Theirs was an especially difficult task—to persuade southerners to leave the Union. There were two principal reasons. First, southerners overwhelmingly revered the Union. They counted themselves good, loyal Americans, who cherished the nation's history and treasured national leaders from George Washington forward who were southerners and Americans. Additionally, the fire-eaters asked southerners to march into the political unknown. No one knew what the world outside the United States would be like, though the fire-eaters promised a political and economic Garden of Eden. Even if unhappy with specific events and certain trends within the Union, like John Brown's raid and the growth of the Republican party, southerners knew it and had powerful ties to it. They did not find it easy to give up familiarity and pride for uncertainty.

But Lincoln's ascension signaled that the unknown of secession was now matched by another, the prospect of a Republican administration. No one had any certainty about what a Republican heading the executive branch would mean for the South. Fire-eaters defined that latter unknown as one filled with potential horrors the South simply could not risk. The *Mercury* left no doubt: "The Southern States are now in the crisis of their fate."[22]

Fire-eaters were convinced that the South must act promptly. They fulminated against any talk of delay. To move the South out of the Union required action as well as words. Fire-eaters had to push, to pull, to lead. They had to decide on the strategy that would permit them to reach their goal of disunion. Whatever the precise steps, they must be immediate.[23]

Between the Republicans and the Democrats and at the far end of the political spectrum from the fire-eaters were the self-styled conservatives who mostly supported the Constitutional Union party in the presidential election. Concentrated heavily in the Upper and Border South, these people had been overwhelmingly Whig. The demise of their traditional partisan home had left them in the political wilderness. They could abide neither the sectional, anti-South Republicans nor their long-term enemy, the Democrats. From the mid-1850s they kept themselves alive in a variety of state and local parties through which they maintained influence. The prospect of a presidential election in 1860 provided them an opportunity to try to construct another party that transcended state, even sectional lines.

They called their handiwork the Constitutional Union party, to affirm the glories of the Constitution and the Union. Choosing a ticket of former Whig mainstays—John Bell of Tennessee for president and Edward Everett of Massachusetts for vice president—these political wanderers denounced both Democrats and Republicans for putting partisanship and sectionalism above patriotism and the Union. With practically no organization, they had no chance of winning the presidency, yet the Bell-Everett ticket gained more than 590,000 popular votes, just over 12.5 percent. The party performed respectably in the slave states, carrying three—Kentucky, Tennessee, and Virginia—and amassing at least a third of the popular vote in all the rest save Alabama, Delaware, and Texas. In the free states, though, the performance was miserable, failing to reach that one-third mark in any of them.

That result told an unmistakable story. In the South, old Whigs remained a force and had the potential to influence southern politics. In the North, however, by 1860, few old Whigs had resisted the lure of the Republicans. They added an essential element to the victorious Republican coalition largely camped on the right wing.

In the aftermath of the election, the Constitutional Unionists clung to the hope that somehow a new national Union or Conservative party could rise on their foundation. At the same time they recognized that "there is too much heat and too little cool and patriotic reflection . . ." in both North and South. They saw no option in the Republicans, for that party in its current form was simply too sectional. The Democrats not only represented their former antagonists, but these veteran Whigs also found them too extreme on southern questions. Their hope was that as the Republicans had to shift to governing and the Democrats had to try reconstructing themselves, possibly one or the other would extinguish the "bad passions" that both had aroused. Then, the welcome sign would greet these pro-Union political nomads. Whether or not a new institutional home awaited them, they would advocate a Conservative course that emphasized the maintenance of the Union over any partisan or sectional platform.[24]

While most of the nation was consumed with assessing the meaning of Lincoln's triumph, several southern states acted. Within a month of the election the South was in motion, hastening formal deliberation on whether or not to remain in the Union. In November, the governors of Louisiana, Mississippi, South Carolina, and Virginia either urged their legislatures to remain in session or called special sessions to confront what all saw as an emergency. Arkansas, Florida, and Georgia legislatures in their regular meetings during that month debated the issue. Back in February, Alabama lawmakers had authorized the governor to call for election of delegates to a secession convention should a Republican win the presidency; on December 6 he issued such a call. In that month, Texas also joined the parade, scheduling an election. Thus, even before Republicans had time to finish congratulating themselves, nine slave states had begun the process of deciding whether they wanted a future in a Union governed by a Republican administration.

In the seven Deep South states, where the fire-eaters had their greatest strength, chief executives and legislatures were moving promptly to calculate the value of the Union. This unity did not signify, however, that all citizens in those states embraced the fire-eater gospel of immediate secession. Yet, almost all of them believed that the Constitution permitted secession. They heeded the states'-rights interpretation of the Constitution widely accepted in the South before 1861. Initially formulated by Thomas Jefferson and James Madison in the 1790s and pushed further by John C. Calhoun in the 1820s and 1830s, this exposition argued that the states, through their ratifying conventions, created the Constitution and thus the federal government. The states, the creators, were sovereign, not the federal government, the created. Carried to its logical conclusion, this thesis asserted that just as states had decided individually to come into the Union, each could decide individually to leave it. Even so, in late 1860 belief in the constitutional right of secession did not necessarily lead to a conviction about either its need or its efficacy.

The advocates of delaying or postponing secession generally found themselves defined as cooperationists. That designation differentiated them from the fire-eaters, also called immediatists, as they clamored for the immediate secession of single states. Cooperationists were not all of one mind, however. Some urged a southern convention where the slave states would come together and present an ultimatum to the North. Only with rejection of those demands would secession be appropriate. Others called for their own states to hold back, to await the secession of one or more sister slave states. Still others maintained that until the future Lincoln administration took some overt action against slavery or the South, such as prohibiting slavery in the territories or interfering with the interstate slave trade, the southern states should remain in the Union. No matter their particular views, cooperationists recognized that they needed to slow the rush to disunion. "*Time* is everything to us," wrote an Alabamian, "and if we fail to gain that we are lost."[25]

Fire-eaters understood the need for haste. They wanted to strike while southern outrage and fear were most intense. An opponent understood: "We are in the midst of a Revolution which is advancing with unprecedented rapidity." A convention would take time; it would put off the day of decision, especially if the Upper South and Border slave states participated. The fire-eaters wanted to leverage those states, not to be leveraged by them because of delay. No direct attack could come from Lincoln and the Republicans before March, when Lincoln took office. For fire-eaters the prospect of waiting for several months heightened the likelihood that secession would never occur.[26]

Yet, individual state action had its drawbacks, for no one knew what would happen if only a single state seceded. In most of the Deep South anxiety over that unknown meant probable delay. Secessionists focused on South Carolina, the most radical state on sectional issues. Fire-eaters considered the Palmetto State their citadel, the stronghold where they exercised enormous influence. Moreover, the legislature had extended its regular session so that it could decide upon its response should Lincoln win. South Carolina seemingly could go out quickly.

Even though the state enjoyed a well-earned reputation for radicalism, its penchant for extremism had a complicated history. In 1832 and 1833, during the Nullification Crisis, South Carolina challenged federal authority and the administration of Andrew Jackson by threatening to nullify the tariff law passed by Congress. In doing so the state found itself uncomfortably alone; no other state joined the crusade. The situation became exceptionally tense when President Jackson declared that he would send the United States Army to enforce the law in South Carolina. While menacing the militant state, Jackson also became part of an effort in Congress to find a compromise on the tariff that would defuse the explosive situation.

A compromise was reached, which led to a peaceful outcome. In fact, some of the nullifying Carolinians took as the chief lesson of the crisis that they had faced down the federal government.

Not quite two decades later, during and after the struggle over slavery in the territory added to the country after the Mexican War ended in the Compromise of 1850, South Carolina's fire-eaters agitated for secession. Remembering the loneliness of the Nullification episode, leaders secretly searched for some other state that would go out first. Then, South Carolina would take the step. Forthwith, the governor of Mississippi made such a commitment, but proved unable to deliver his state. Facing the likelihood of once again standing alone against the federal government, South Carolina decided against direct action. That decision so incensed United States Senator Robert Barnwell Rhett, Sr., the state's most visible fire-eater, that he resigned from the Senate, denouncing his fellow Carolinians for their refusal to resist "aggression of the General government" and for spurning his cherished disunion. There was no repeat of 1832 and 1833. Still, that inaction did not smother talk of secession or the eagerness of men like Rhett to lead their state out of the Union.[27]

Even before the votes had been cast in November 1860, fire-eater chieftains had begun plotting their path. In October, Governor William Gist of South Carolina contacted his counterpart in every Deep South state but Texas, home of the self-proclaimed Unionist governor Sam Houston, as well as in neighboring North Carolina, asking about the possible meeting of legislatures and their likely decisions. He assured his gubernatorial brothers that South Carolina would surely secede, if only some other state would lead the way. In the event that none would take that step, Gist went on to say, he thought South Carolina would go first "if she had any assurance that she will soon be followed by another or other States." Without such a guarantee, Gist confessed, he doubted his state would move. The responses did not cheer him. Even though several of his fellow governors said they sincerely desired disunion, no one would place his state in the vanguard. Most agreed with pro-secessionist Joseph Brown of Georgia that their states really wanted a southern convention that would take "common action." Should South Carolina go alone and war result, however, they did pledge their assistance. Only the governor of Florida, in a late reply, indicated that his state would stand with South Carolina, war or no war.[28]

Later that same month, Robert Barnwell Rhett, Jr., son of the former senator, who shared his father's policies, sent to a few Deep South politicians a secret inquiry asking about the possibility of immediate secession based on separate state action. The younger Rhett's query commanded attention, for all knew his name; moreover, he edited the *Charleston Mercury,* his family's paper. Although it is known that Rhett received more than one response, only one is extant. From United States Senator Jefferson Davis of Mississippi, one of the most influential men in the Senate, Rhett got little encouragement. In fact, Senator Davis urged Rhett to wait. Davis did not think any other state, including his own, would follow South Carolina out of the Union unless the federal government resorted to coercion. But he did not foresee "that act of usurpation folly, and wickedness. . . ."[29]

From Gist's and Rhett's covert questioning it appeared that the South Carolina fire-eaters could depend on no one else embracing their doctrine of immediate, separate secession. Too many southerners, even in the Deep South, were wary of rapid movement by individual states. They preferred, in Davis's words, "to bring these [Deep South] states into cooperation before asking for a popular decision"—or, put another way, no elections for conventions until the Deep South states could reach common ground. Additionally, they wanted to ascertain how the victorious Republicans would react to southern concerns. They looked for signs of what the Republicans intended to do with their new power.[30]

Even though the Republicans who so concerned southerners would not take charge of the executive branch until early March, they remained the focus of southern anxiety and possible action. Republicans did not respond to southern fears and threats with unity, however. Many considered secessionists no more than "noisy blusterers" engaged in "brag and bluster." " 'Fire-Eating' is practiced by jugglers as well as Politicians," noted a Republican editorialist, who amplified: "The great point of the tricks, in the performance of both, is not really to eat the fire, but only to seem to the public to eat it." Acknowledging the excitement in the South, the enormously popular antislavery minister Henry Ward Beecher chose the kitchen for his analogy: "But I also know these ebullitions of feeling are somewhat of the nature of the boiling pot which extinguishes the fire by boiling over." These observers were all "convinced that the agitation raised in the South would gradually and surely subside into peace."[31]

Then, some Republicans said they did not really care if one or more slave states left the Union. Secession to an Ohio Republican looked like a "farce," causing less excitement than a fire or a storm on Lake Erie. A Boston constituent of Congressman Charles Francis Adams reported a growing feeling to let all the slave states go. In his diary, Adams himself wrote that he wanted secessionists to succeed, at least long enough "to enable the Republicans to establish their authority in the federal government. . . ." Even the vehemently antislavery and anti-South senior senator from Massachusetts, Charles Sumner, stated that he would willingly let the Deep South go.[32]

As for the state leading the cry for dismemberment, a number of Republicans rejoiced to be "well rid of South Carolina, if we are wise enough to count it a riddance. . . ." A Republican newspaper in Maine found the source of South Carolina's extremism in the "Tory blood" that "filled" the veins of her people. This editor urged the government to buy the land in the state, then follow the example set with the Creek and the Cherokee and force the Carolinians west, all the way to Mexico. Senator Zachariah Chandler of Michigan raged, "But as God is my judge I would rather see every traitor in South Carolina hanged & *Charleston burned* than to see one line from Mr. Lincoln to appease them. . . ."[33]

From the outset, a minority of Republicans took seriously the possibility of disunion and thought the potential division of the country ruinous. The "irrepressible conflict" is upon us, noted one Republican loyalist. To these Republicans their party would have to respond with equal seriousness. The question was, in what manner. Some asserted that the Union must be preserved at all hazards, even with force, calling "Peaceable Secession an Absurdity." The youthful, exuberant Henry Adams, son of Charles Francis, minced no words: "South Carolina has got to eat dirt; yea repent in sack-cloth and ashes." Still other party faithful wanted calming statements from their leaders that would temper southern excitement and bridle the rush to secession.[34]

Despite the range of reactions among Republicans, few could conceive of secession as a popular movement. Republicans constantly described the plans of fire-eaters as a "conspiracy." They perceived no popular uprising against the Union, even in the Deep South. Rather, they spoke of "a well concerted and deeply laid conspiracy." Republicans fixated on the conspiracy thesis, for they envisioned themselves giving "no just cause" for jeopardizing the Union. Republicans, they repeatedly intoned, had never attacked state authority or state control over slavery and never would.[35]

The two most important Republicans reacted quite differently. The man who had been the most notable figure in the party prior to the nominating convention of 1860 changed sharply in November. On November 2, in a speech in New York City, William H. Seward refused to take seriously all the southern rhetoric portending disunion should Abraham Lincoln win the presidency. The men who crowded in to hear Seward saw a slouching, slender figure, a beaked nose and shaggy eyebrows prominent on his visage. Though slight and standing only five feet six inches, the fifty-nine-year-old Seward had a presence that commanded attention. He had twice served as governor of New York and had been a United States senator since 1849, initially as a Whig, then reelected in 1855 as a Republican. With this pedigree and his national standing, Seward in 1860 had expected the Republican nomination for president, but political fortune decreed otherwise. Despite his deep disappointment in that loss, Seward took to the campaign trail for Lincoln, traveling and speaking widely in the North.

In that address, almost on election eve, Seward defined threats to secede the way he had throughout the campaign—as political bombast such as had emanated from the South so often in the past. Once the election was over, he predicted, no matter who won, the volatile language would simply fade away. The Union would stand firm in 1860 and "for forty presidential elections afterward," he declared.[36]

Seward's opinion would carry considerable weight among Republicans, for even after Lincoln's win many of them still thought of Seward as their natural party leader. Statements such as "I regard you as the champion and head of the North" filled his mail. These correspondents told Seward that he occupied a special place and had an uncommon responsibility. Seward basically shared that opinion; Lincoln's lack of experience in national politics concerned many.[37]

Seward also pondered his role with a Republican administration taking office on March 4, 1861. He could certainly remain in the Senate. There was the possibility of the most prestigious diplomatic assignment, minister to Great Britain. Or, he could accept an anticipated place in Lincoln's cabinet, probably the prime slot, secretary of state. Finally, he could decide on an entirely different option and retire, "to rest and look on" as he told a fellow Republican senator.[38]

Seward did not consider the last option seriously for very long, if at all. In 1860, he had been a major player on the national stage for more than a decade. He would not likely depart just as his party was about to take power. As Seward calculated the political possibilities, he determined that he could exert the greatest influence on the new president and, thus, national policy, in the cabinet. If the expected offer came to join Lincoln's official family, he would embrace it. In the meantime, he was still a United States senator from New York. In a national crisis, William Henry Seward would not be on the sidelines.[39]

Seward quickly decided one was coming. As he surveyed the political landscape after the election, he rapidly jettisoned the dismissive attitude toward secession that had marked his preelection speeches. Events as well as reports from the South changed his mind. On November 12, the South Carolina legislature set an election on December 6 for delegates to a secession convention and the convention itself for December 17. Seward also had correspondence from the Deep South affirming the inflamed passion raging in those states.[40]

A letter he wrote on November 18 to his longtime political partner, really political alter ego, Thurlow Weed, confirmed his new outlook. A dominant force in New York Republicanism as he had been in the state's Whiggery, Weed also edited the *Albany Evening Journal*, where a Seward son worked as an assistant editor. Since the 1830s, Weed had managed and won elections for others, preferring to remain a power broker behind the scenes rather than an officeholder. Weed had asked when Seward intended to head for Washington and the Second Session of the 36th Congress, scheduled to convene on December 3. Replying, Seward said that he had originally contemplated remaining at home in Auburn, New York, until after Christmas, but had changed his mind. What he termed "the Southern demonstrations" caused the shift. Now he expected to be in the capital on opening day because, he believed, his absence "even for a day" would result in "dissatisfaction somewhere." Although he denied being able to foresee the future or having a particular plan in mind, he had become convinced a national crisis loomed, one that necessarily and by his own choice would involve him.[41]

Realizing that the appeals for secession were not mere gasconade, Seward concluded that the country could come apart. To prevent that result he believed Republicans would have to take seriously the potential for disunion and strive to mollify distraught southerners. What Seward could or would do was constrained by his imagination and judgment about the politically possible as well as by the president-elect. How Lincoln reacted to this turn of events would have an enormous impact on both Seward and the party. At this point no one could predict the relationship that would develop between the experienced old hand and the relative novice. No one could be sure which man would end up as the dominant force among Republicans.

Abraham Lincoln did not share the New York senator's views. In Springfield, Lincoln experienced the adulation bestowed upon the presidential victor. Congratulatory missives cascaded in; visitors besieged him. As a temporary headquarters he adopted the governor's office on the second floor of the state Capitol, just a few blocks from his house. Those who found their way to this small space faced a man tall, six feet four inches, slim, with uncombed dark hair. He had a long neck and arms, with huge hands and feet. Observers commented on his naturally inexpressive face with dull gray eyes; when animated, however, his face brightened and his eyes sparkled. By the time he had become president-elect, Lincoln had begun growing a beard, famously responding to a letter from an eleven-year-old girl who told him that because his face was so thin, whiskers would improve his looks. Lincoln welcomed all with an easy informality. Treating everyone as a fellow citizen, he chatted about a multitude of subjects, told some of his famous stories, and shook hand after hand. Many even followed him home.[42]

Some of the incoming letters did more than congratulate him. "Your problems have just commenced," wrote an old associate. Another correspondent "pray[ed] to God that you may be enabled manfully to bear up under the weight and skillfully to pilot the vessel through the breakers of the threatened storm." None struck Lincoln more than the epistle from the man who had been his closest friend, Joshua Speed. Now living near Louisville, Kentucky, Speed confided, "As a friend, I am rejoiced at your success." Even though Speed and Lincoln had separated politically, Speed took pains to say that his old comrade's triumph did not disappoint him. But Speed did not dodge the political crisis which that victory had spawned, concluding, "How to deal with the combustible material lying around you without setting fire to the edifice of which we are all so proud and of which you will be the chief custodian is a difficult task." In a response that highlights Lincoln's respect for Speed, the president-elect asked him to bring his wife and join the Lincolns in Chicago, with the admonition to keep their meeting secret.[43]

Lincoln himself seemed to react in two different ways. First, testimony makes clear that he took his elevation to the presidency quite seriously. He certainly paid close attention to the correspondence that poured in. Upon his election, Lincoln reported, "I then felt, as I never had before, the responsibility that was upon me." Greeting friends and neighbors at the governor's office, he commented, "Well, boys, your troubles are over now, but mine have just commenced."[44]

At the same time, Lincoln averred that the noise about secession did not distress him. Asked by a visitor whether he thought the South would secede, he answered, "I do not think they will." Another who journeyed to Springfield found the future president "well, and in fine spirits. The threats of secession do not alarm him." Lincoln came to this conclusion based on two key convictions—one about the South, the other about himself.[45]

Lincoln identified southerners as fellow Americans. That belief persuaded him that all the talk about secession was simply part of the election barrage, which would give way to a more "politic" mood. He informed "a gentleman" that because the South had always been so loyal to the Union, he could not imagine southerners seriously contemplating breaking it up even before he took office. To him, the South wrecking the Union just made no sense.[46]

Second, Lincoln thought of himself as a conservative. His conservatism precluded any rash action in any area. Repeatedly he declared, "I do not wish to interfere with them [southerners] in any way, but protect them in everything they are entitled to." Calm, reasonable southerners, in his mind, would "find no cause to complain of me." Lincoln noted that southerners who came through Springfield and spoke with him "seem to go away apparently satisfied." All he desired, Lincoln privately declared, was that the South give him the opportunity and he would show them the groundlessness of their fears. In office he would prove to the South that it had no call for concern.[47]

Only two days after the election, Lincoln read a thoughtful letter from Truman Smith, a man who had been a Whig colleague in the House of Representatives and then a Whig senator from Connecticut. Like Lincoln he had migrated to the Republican party. Smith was delighted with Lincoln's election, but worried about the South. "Many of our friends speak lightly of the threatened disorder of the South," he wrote, thus confirming Lincoln's own opinion. Smith went on, however, "But I shall not be surprised should we meet with very serious difficulties from that quarter." Then Smith suggested that the moment had arrived for the president-elect to make public "some exposé of views to counteract falsehood and allay excitement, particularly at the South." In his judgment, Lincoln needed to "allay causeless anxiety" and "induce all good citizens" to "judge the tree by its fruit."

In a prompt reply marked "Private and confidential," Lincoln communicated his "most profound appreciation of your motive, and highest respect for your judgment too." Despite those accolades, Lincoln rejected Smith's advice. In one of his most momentous postelection decisions, Lincoln stated, "I feel constrained, for the present, at least to make no declaration to the public." That present would last for more than three months, until Lincoln's preinaugural journey from Illinois to Washington. To those who chorused Smith's call for a public statement, Lincoln iterated and reiterated that he had nothing to add to the positions already part of his public record. Additionally, as president-elect he had no real power, and would possess none until his inauguration on March 4, 1861. While Lincoln clung to those explanations, he was the only president-elect in the nation and in that role the apparent head of the Republican party, which would take control of the executive branch for the first time. These two positions conveyed enormous influence. No matter what he said or did not say in public, Lincoln would have to decide how and for what purpose to use that influence.[48]

The president-elect might dismiss the danger of secession, but the sitting president had no doubts about its seriousness. Though a lifelong Pennsylvanian, James Buchanan was a man absolutely attuned to the South. Throughout his long career in national politics, in Congress, in the cabinet, as a diplomat, and, finally, in the presidency, he had a number of close southern friends. As president, his policies had clearly been pro-southern, from advocating acceptance of the *Dred Scott* decision to championing the failed attempt to obtain the admission of Kansas as a slave state. He lined up behind a slave Kansas even though it meant sundering his party because many northern Democrats, including the most influential, Senator Stephen A. Douglas, refused to go along. Buchanan felt deeply that the South did have legitimate grievances against antislavery agitators and politicians. His secretary of the treasury, the Georgian Howell Cobb, did not exaggerate when he described Buchanan as "the truest friend to the South that ever sat in the presidential chair."[49]

President Buchanan also knew that he had executive responsibility for the next five months. Any threat to the Union was a threat to the country he presided over. Upon Lincoln's election, Buchanan began his attempt to keep the country together, at least until he left office. A cautious man, whom critics called timid, he was unlikely to make bold moves, but because he was president, whatever he did, or did not do, would have a significant impact.

Buchanan did not have to look beyond the Executive Mansion for concrete evidence of a crisis that could strike at the vitals of the Union as well as the different responses to it. Meetings of his cabinet witnessed considerable "wrangling," as opinions of his "official family" members delineated the treacherous political terrain. Howell Cobb, the real leader of the cabinet, who was extremely close to the president, and Secretary of the Interior Jacob Thompson of Mississippi espoused the constitutionality of secession. A third southerner, Secretary of War John Floyd of Virginia, was not a secessionist, but opposed any moves that might result in a confrontation between secessionists and the federal government. The navy secretary, Isaac Toucey of Connecticut, agreed with Floyd. Vigorously opposing any constitutional sanction for secession, Attorney General Jeremiah Black of Pennsylvania and Secretary of State Lewis Cass of Michigan also maintained that the federal government had the right and the duty to defend its property even in a seceding state. Lastly, Joseph Holt of Kentucky, the postmaster general, counted as a firm Unionist.[50]

Despite these diverse opinions, Buchanan wanted a harmonious cabinet backing administration policy in the face of the crisis. Two separate matters preoccupied the president and his ministers in the initial postelection weeks. First, the administration had to decide how to deal with federal property, chiefly military posts, in the states with secessionist fever. Most of these were forts located near seaports from Virginia all the way around Florida to Louisiana; all were undermanned, some with no garrison at all. While the question posed to the leadership was clear—would strengthening these bastions hasten or quell secession—the answer was murky, with proponents on both sides. Then, the president had to decide how he would personally respond. He could promptly issue a proclamation announcing his views or he could wait until early December and spell out his position in his annual message to Congress.

The matter of the southern forts had come up even before Lincoln's election. Aware of the fiery rhetoric accompanying the campaign in the South, in late October the commanding general of the United States Army, Winfield Scott, had urged the secretary of war and the president to bolster the forts from Hampton Roads in Virginia to the mouth of the Mississippi River in order to preclude any surprise strike against them by the secessionists. Buchanan's southern advisers in the cabinet and out remonstrated that such movement would serve no good purpose. Instead, it would lend credence to fire-eater cries that the federal government intended to harm the South. The president ended up on their side; he decided against any general reinforcement, believing such action would only inflame southern opinion.[51]

Even though Buchanan rejected Scott's proposal to strengthen all the southern forts, he recognized that among all the locations one stood out: Charleston, South Carolina, home to four installations, two of them tiny and inconsequential. But in the case of conflict the two others would indeed be consequential—Fort Moultrie, on Sullivan's Island, just over five miles as the crow flies from the city, guarded the entrance to the harbor, while the partially completed Fort Sumter occupied a man-made shoal at the mouth of the harbor, around four and a half miles from the city. With South Carolina the most likely state to secede, the status of these forts was critical. If Carolinians made a surprise move, the tiny garrison of a few dozen men at Moultrie stood no chance. Sumter, even more precarious, had only a lieutenant overseeing some construction workers.

The day after the election, Buchanan instructed Secretary of War Floyd to ensure that the federal commander in Charleston had the men and matériel necessary to hold his position. As the president put it to his secretary, "If those forts should be taken by South Carolina in consequence of our neglect to put them in defensible condition, it were better for you and me both to be thrown into the Potomac with millstones about our necks." Floyd assured his chief that the situation was in hand. He had sent an army officer to make a special inspection, and on November 15 a new commander had been ordered to Charleston—Major Robert Anderson, a Kentuckian. Still, with rumors flying that the Carolinians would strike, the president wanted reinforcements dispatched. Floyd temporized, even though upon his arrival at Fort Moultrie, Major Anderson had asked for additional troops.[52]

Pressure now squeezed Buchanan from two sides. His southern cabinet members, Holt excepted, along with major southern congressional leaders and confidants, like Senator Jefferson Davis, insisted that South Carolina would consider any reinforcing a hostile act leading to the possibility of armed conflict—the result Buchanan least wanted. At the same time Attorney General Black and Secretary of State Cass, with Black in the lead, maintained that the government needed to show its resolve by "sending at once a strong force into the forts at Charleston harbor, enough to deter if possible the people from any attempt at disunion." They implored the president to stand firm behind his soldiers on the scene in order to guarantee that the Carolinians would not snatch an easy victory, humiliating both president and country.[53]

The imbroglio was settled by an uneasy and unofficial truce. Wanting to assist if possible their friend the president and simultaneously avoid any shooting between South Carolina, still a state in the Union, and the federal government, southern leaders in Washington got Governor William Gist to guarantee the safety of federal property in his state. With Gist's pledge in hand, the constant pressing of his southern allies, and his own determination to escape armed conflict, Buchanan decided against buttressing Anderson's force. Black protested, to no avail. Although the president held back on reinforcements, he kept the flag flying in Charleston harbor. November ended with the patched-up armistice keeping the situation in Charleston explosive, but not exploding.

While Buchanan deliberated about his options in Charleston, he also decided on the form and content of his personal response. The president considered which venue the more appropriate to present his views—immediately issuing a presidential proclamation or waiting for his annual message upon the convening of the Second Session of the 36th Congress during the first week in December. As always on consequential matters, Buchanan brought the question before his cabinet. In the official family no doubt existed about the seriousness of the crisis. "We are probably in the middle of a revolution, bloodless as yet," observed Attorney General Black. All worried that "this great country is to be dismembered." In this highly charged atmosphere, Buchanan wanted the opinion and advice of the cabinet, but he especially desired unity among his formal advisers, if at all possible.[54]

When the president met with these men, they witnessed a veteran politician trying to cope with not only the most serious crisis of his career but also the greatest threat to the nation in at least a generation. Six feet tall, with a full head of white hair and a heavy physique, Buchanan presented a hearty guise. But it was not quite the forceful figure one might think at first glance. His eyes created a problem. They had different colors, one hazel, the other blue. With myopic vision, he had a peculiar way of focusing, which appeared as a squint. That made him lean his head toward the left, a tendency accentuated by a surgical scar that pulled his neck farther off. An observer described "one of the most quizzical faces I ever saw." Buchanan attempted to overcome "these blemishes" by invariably wearing a large collar and expansive neckwear, always stark white. His appearance connoted age more than vigor.[55]

Even before conferring with the cabinet, the president wanted a clear understanding of his constitutional powers facing the prospect of disunion. To this end he requested from Attorney General Black a written opinion detailing executive authority. To make sure that the attorney general's response addressed precisely the information the president desired, Black helped prepare the questions he would answer.[56]

Black's memorandum of November 20, 1860, conformed to the interpretation of the Constitution and executive authority accepted generally by Democrats and undoubtably by a large number of antebellum Americans. He began by declaring the Union perpetual and emphasizing that the federal government had unquestioned power to confront with arms any entity that challenged it with force. At the same time, Black maintained that the federal government could not obliterate a state. In sum, he argued that the president could not use the military to prevent secession. No law gave that permission, for the framers of the Constitution never contemplated such an occurrence. Because he had to enforce the law, however, the president could legally collect revenues, in the form of tariff duties, on board ships if no federal officer remained in the ports of any state. While the federal government, according to Black, had no constitutional purview for any offensive action, both the Constitution and statutes mandated defense of any attacked federal property. The conclusion: a president could only wield power to enforce and defend.[57]

Black's opinion did not provide an outline for unity. Cobb and Thompson would never accept the condemnation of secession, the idea of a perpetual Union, or any thought of resorting to force. Black and Cass would never agree to any right of secession and stood firm on the legality of using defensive force. Among the ministers, a presidential proclamation commanded no consensus. Therefore, the president decided his perspective would appear in his annual message. And no matter how much he wanted unanimity, no matter how hard he strove to obtain it, the division in his cabinet illustrated not only the impossibility of unity within his official family, but also the extraordinarily complex task of crafting a response that would deal effectively with the crisis and simultaneously unite the country.

Sent to Congress on December 3, Buchanan's message left no doubt about the struggle taking place in the mind and heart of its author. It put in prose the competing views of secession and Union that had characterized debates in the cabinet and among other presidential advisers. The president tried to hack his way through a constitutional and political thicket without any clear markers from a trail that no one had previously used.[58]

The president's message had real strengths. It proclaimed to Congress and country that the nation confronted an unprecedented crisis. To resolve it would require "the good name and patriotic forbearance" of all Americans. Buchanan did not hold his head in his hands. Urging the South to stand fast, he insisted that nothing had yet happened so horrible as "to justify the immediate destruction of the noblest system of government ever devised by mortals." He went on to point out that Lincoln, elected "by a mere plurality" and restrained by the Constitution, could do little damage to the South, even if he so desired. Moreover, Buchanan noted that "under this free government there is an incessant ebb and flow in public opinion." According to the president, that truth meant that every issue "will have its days." In his judgment, anti-South and antislavery opinion had "reached and passed the culmination point."

Then, he called for action, even specifying a plan. He wanted Congress to adopt an amendment to the Constitution that would "restore harmony" and forward it to the states for ratification. His proposed amendment would have three provisions: state unequivocally the right of property in slaves; declare the right to hold slaves in a territory, until the territory became a state, when it could decide for or against the institution; make clear the right of a master to have a runaway slave returned to him. He believed that all states would act favorably on these measures, which, he noted, either the Constitution itself or the Supreme Court had already affirmed.

Although his proposals were surely pro-southern, he stood on solid constitutional and legal ground. The Constitution certainly accepted slavery and explicitly provided for the return of fugitive slaves, while the Supreme Court in *Dred Scott* had ruled that slaveholders had constitutionally guaranteed rights in the territories. Buchanan contended that his plan should be tried. He was undoubtedly overly optimistic in anticipating that every state would accept such an amendment, but whether enough of the states to reach the constitutionally mandated three-fourths would have is another and unknown matter. Clearly, however, for this proposition to have any chance, Congress would have to act promptly, which the president pressed it to do. Thus far, Buchanan was exerting leadership. Yet, he did not continue with a focus demanding that all lovers of the Union come together and force a settlement with a concurrent condemnation of all radicals, North and South.

Instead, he went awry. Rather than remain concentrated, he wandered. He found a villain in the story, the Republican party with its vehement anti-South campaign. This assault was politically normal, for the Republicans were the political enemy. Additionally, in his own mind the continuous Republican assault on the South spawned disunion sentiment. But by slamming the political opposition so directly, he practically destroyed all hope that any Republicans, even the most conservative, might come to his side.

When the president dealt with secession directly in his message, he created a conundrum, stemming directly from the impossible choices that he told himself he faced. He argued with the South over the constitutionality of secession, averring that the framers of the Constitution "never intended to implant in its bosom the seed of its own destruction, nor were they at its creation guilty of the absurdity of providing for its own dissolution." He put it directly: "Secession is neither more nor less than revolution."

But literally on the same page in his message he asserted that he possessed no constitutional prerogative to stop a state from seceding. He repeated once more that his power was strictly defensive, to repel attacks on the government, its property or agents. Only further legislation from Congress could give him the authority to act. Even so, he gave his opinion that the Constitution had not delegated to Congress the power to make war on a state. In his view the idea of using armed might to keep a state in the Union was utterly repugnant to the spirit of the Constitution.

Announcing his powerlessness, the president passed the initiative to Congress, stating that only the legislative branch could enact the statutes spelling out how the federal government would deal with the actual secession of a single state or several states. Only Congress had that power, just as it had the authority to begin the amending process. The president clearly wanted lawmakers to do something, preferably adopt his proposal to amend the Constitution. Just as surely he hoped to maintain the status quo, without armed conflict, until the Republican takeover of the presidency on March 4.

Not surprisingly, the annual message displeased many, especially southerners and Republicans. The latter understandably dismissed it as nothing more than partisanship. They vehemently rejected the president's depiction of them as the men wearing the black hats. Congressman Charles Francis Adams damned the message as "timid and vacillating in the face of the Slaveholding rebellion," while castigating it for being "bold and insulting towards his countrymen [Republicans] whom he does not fear." Nothing in Buchanan's administration, according to Adams, "deserve[d] respect."[59]

Recognizing that the message would be "violently denounced" by Republicans "because it justly charges all our troubles on them," Howell Cobb still admitted it would please few in his section even though it contained no word of "rebuke" for the South. Yet, despite Cobb's admission of its pro-southern "spirit and temper," he and other southern leaders could not accept it because the president emphatically denied the constitutionality of secession. The southern Democratic chieftains had been Buchanan's loyalists and friends. They had believed that that friendship and loyalty would be returned in his unwavering support of their position. Particularly, they had thought he stood with them on the Constitution and secession. Disappointed and frustrated, they began turning against him.[60]

The president did have his champions, however. Northern Democrats who backed him approved of the message for its "comprehensive" vision and for its "statesman like view" of the situation. Some even found a "manly tone." A longtime Buchanan supporter wrote, "I think this is the general sentiment." Defining the message as a success, he expressed the opinion, which the president surely hoped for, that it pleased "all moderate men." Applause was not limited to Buchanan's most ardent backers. Upper South Conservatives who wanted most to avoid any kind of confrontation between the federal government and any state deemed that the chief executive had struck the proper chord. "It is moderate and sensible," commented the prominent Marylander John Pendleton Kennedy, an ex-Whig, who closely followed the crisis. Although Kennedy objected to the president's tortured constitutional logic, which he attributed to Buchanan's congenital "caution and timidity," he concluded that those characteristics were "wise just now."[61]

Kennedy spoke for Border state Conservatives who would be at the center of trying to resolve the crisis. Almost without exception former Whigs, these men had generally backed John Bell in the presidential election. His defeat had not altered their commitment to the Union above all else. Providing a specific name for these Union lovers is difficult, for the Constitutional Union party disappeared even more rapidly than it had appeared. It did not survive the election. But neither their ancient enemy, the Democrats, with their ties to southern extremists, nor the Republicans, with their hard sectionalism, appealed to its adherents. They clung to the Constitution and the Union, as they understood them. "Border Conservatives" seems the best and most accurate designation. Although these Unionists congregated in the Border states, they had consequential allies in Virginia, North Carolina, and Tennessee, with a few staunch partners in the North.

As individuals largely situated literally on the border between North and South, in what one termed "the temperate zone of politics," they saw themselves as uniquely positioned to broker or sponsor a solution to what they could see was a rapidly escalating conflict between the Deep South and the Republicans. Living overwhelmingly in slave states, with a number actually owning slaves, they understood the apprehension that the Republican victory spread through the South. At the same time, residing in states actually touching free states and sharing almost daily interaction with northerners, they were confident that few of their neighbors, including Republicans, either advocated or intended harm to the South or slavery.[62]

These Border Conservatives feared one great political monster—radicalism. They characterized the secession movement as a "wicked frenzy"; "the tide of passion" they felt roiling the South frightened them. Looking northward they found mightily distressing "the declaration of unceasing warfare against slavery as an institution, as enunciated by the

Representative men" of the Republican party, for it unsettled the political world. To bridle the Republicans they begged the president-elect to jettison those they called "the fanatics of the North." Lincoln's doing so they were certain would dampen "the very many men who are now inflamed and who are led to believe through Demagogues that they are about to pass under the yoke of an enemy."[63]

These Conservatives, and they relished that identification, discerned themselves trapped in a political vise. The inexorable pressure pushing upward from the southern secessionists and downward from northern Republicans caused great emotional and psychological swings. John Pendleton Kennedy searched for a "good temper on both sides [that] *must* bring about a better state of things." In contrast, a political compatriot lamented, "The future is to me shrouded in the very blackness of darkness." Yet, while acknowledging, in the words of a like-minded New Yorker, "the condition of the country fills my mind with heavy forebodings," as self-defined reasonable men, they hoped that "folly is a fever and has its cycle."[64]

CHAPTER TWO

"We Need a Statesman of Nerve to Meet the Terrible Crisis"

CONGRESS CONVENED ON December 3 with a torrent of emotions cascading over the solons. That the session would be "more crowded with excitement and passion than fruitful in good work, it requires no prophetic voice to foretell," noted one observer. Yet even in this time of "unusual emotion," Representative Charles Francis Adams reported, "the decorum was remarkable." It struck an Iowa congressman that "every appearance of Courtesy and Kindness seemed to be exchanged among members of all parties." At the same time, many recognized "the threatened storm" heading toward them. That tempest menaced party and country, for as Senator Seward understood, "the ultra-Southern men *mean* to break up the Union," while "the Republicans who come here are ignorant of the real design in danger."[1]

Fundamentally, Seward was on the mark, though a number of his comrades realized "We will have trouble this winter." Despite this recognition by Seward and some others, Republicans did not all stand in the same place. Senator Salmon Chase of Ohio urged his party to steer clear of all issues relating to the Union, to the sectional question. Welcoming "the present condition of affairs," Senator William Pitt Fessenden of Maine declared that renewed quiet demanded facing down "the Slave Power" by demolishing its attempted intimidation of Republicans by talk of disunion. In contrast, Congressmen Schuyler Colfax of Indiana and Samuel Curtis of Iowa believed that "our Republicans shall and should be conciliatory and forbearing." Connecticut's Senator James Dixon captured the range of Republican attitudes and feelings: "Some talk of concession—some of coercion—but all seem bewildered by the magnitude of the great event approaching." Everyone, however, expressed concern about comity in the party and the reaction of the party to the crisis.[2]

The most important congressional Republican, Senator Seward, assessed the situation with the eye and sensibility of an experienced, careful, and crafty veteran of political upheaval. Arriving in Washington convinced that the country and his party would confront a real crisis, his immediate observations only confirmed that view. To dinner companions he spoke of "the eruption of the body politic in a sea of change." He made clear that in his judgment the radical southerners, whom he dubbed "mad-caps," were in earnest. He also discovered that they desired nothing more than for the Republicans to adopt policies that would annoy the South. To his political alter ego, Thurlow Weed, he admitted that some Republicans wanted most to inflame; those he deemed "as uncompromising as the Secessionists in South Carolina."[3]

Seward moved immediately. First, his activities and conversation made absolutely clear that he intended to place himself at the center of his congressional party. To fellow Republicans, both in and out of Congress, he "preach[ed] quiet moderation, cheerfulness, graciousness to all." While he wanted his party to avoid both a contentious posture and antagonizing words, he insisted that "influence must not be sullen, as last year, but respectful and fraternal." His initial test came on December 3, when unexpectedly he was summoned to a conference of Republican senators in the antechamber of the Senate.[4]

There he learned that the antislavery firebrand John Hale from New Hampshire had called the meeting partly because he wanted to give a speech. At that moment, "this immature time," in Seward's words, he managed to curb Hale. But his success was short-lived, for on the fifth Hale took the Senate floor to flay the South as "a dictatorial oligarchy," warning that if the South should "refuse to submit" to Lincoln's election, war was inevitable. Serious compromise he spurned.[5]

A verbal explosion like Hale's not only violated Seward's intentions for his party, it also jeopardized his wish for a calming period. According to Charles Francis Adams, Seward hoped "that with prudence every thing might go right." Ultimately, Seward wanted "to reconcile the factious men who are bent on division, reckless of civil war, to the ascendency of an Administration based on the principles of justice and humanity." For the present, reaching that goal demanded his own public quiet, for he perceived neither southern "mad-caps" nor Republicans yet prepared for any substantive agreement. He did not want to move too quickly. But he did convey his opinion that, in time, "the temper [would] be favorable on both sides for consultation." His buoyant confidence remained in place. "I have faith that my good angel won't desert me," he wrote to his wife.[6]

While Republicans confronted their uncertainty and internal division, Democrats had to deal with their own disunity. Somehow they had to overcome the sectional division that had wrecked the party. Hoping to get past that preelection disruption, Democratic leaders knew they had no easy task. The conservative New York banker August Belmont put the matter directly to Stephen A. Douglas: "What is the feeling and danger at the South?" With that reference to danger, Belmont underscored that northern Democrats recognized the seriousness of southern fire-eaters. Checking the temper of southerners in Congress, northern observers noted confusion and perceived the real threat of radical influence. An Illinois congressman worried about "fanaticism and infatuation" seizing his southern colleagues.[7]

The most important northern Democrat had arrived in Washington on December 1 amid great fanfare. Aware of the political capital his almost a million and a half voters had given him, Douglas avowed his primary goal, preservation of the Union. Even though the vast bulk of his presidential support had been northern, he asserted that pro-Union strength remained sufficiently strong in the South to save the country. He had campaigned through the region, and letters from southern supporters poured in to him. Stressing that all party considerations should be shelved until the safety of the Union was assured, Douglas declared that he wanted to "lay aside our party feuds until we had saved the country."[8]

Douglas announced on the floor of the Senate, "I am ready to act with any party, with any individual of any party, who will come to this question with an eye single to the preservation of the Constitution and the Union." To his colleagues he professed, "I am as good a party man as anyone living, when there are only party lines at stake. . . . " He continued, "I do not desire to hear the word party, or to listen to any party appeal while we are considering and discussing the question upon which the fate of the country now hangs."[9]

Making such remarks publicly and privately, Douglas intended to take a leading role in the congressional session. To contemporaries he seemed akin to a tyro. Only five feet four inches tall, he had a large head, broad shoulders, and a powerful body. Politically astute, exuding energy, and relentless in pursuit of a goal, Douglas was at once a powerful friend and a formidable foe. His enjoyment of food, spirits, and cigars knew few bounds. Because of his force and his appetites, his purist Republican opponents condemned him as "a brute." Henry Adams penned a caricature: "gross, vulgar, demagogic, a drunkard." No matter the diatribes of Adams and his coterie, Douglas would have influence.[10]

Although Douglas believed the Union in genuine peril, he emphasized that the South had no legitimate reason to threaten disunion. In his estimation, the grievances aired by fire-eaters had no real substance. He correctly identified them as only interested in destroying the Union. To southerners he insisted that they had no need to fear Lincoln as president. First, Lincoln was a conservative. Second, having to contend with a Democratic Congress, Lincoln could not harm the South. Even if he were foolhardy enough to try an antisouthern move, the Senate with Douglas in the forefront would block him. Douglas underlined that both the Constitution and political reality protected the South. At the same time, he committed himself to fight the constitutional and political battle with the South; he made clear, however, that he would never recognize separate state secession without consent from the remaining states. The whole Union he held dear.[11]

Other leading northern Democrats joined Douglas in imploring southerners to resist the fire-eaters. Belmont told southern correspondents that Lincoln would be ineffectual. Moreover, he attributed Lincoln's election not to strong antislavery feeling among northern voters but rather to their disgust with the "misrule & corruption" of the Buchanan administration. Many conservative men voted simply to throw out the Democrats. Belmont urged southerners to "pause before leaving the field to their enemies, and abandoning their faithful allies to the mercy of a ruthless victor." With that plea he voiced the northern Democratic fear that the secession of many southern states would doom the party to minority status, even impotency, in their section.[12]

To allay that unpleasant prospect, southerners were assured that a conservative reaction was already occurring in the North. "Powerful agencies are at work in all the Northern states," Belmont informed the Georgian Herschel Johnson, "which must result in complete vindication of the rights of the South but this will require time." Democratic newspapers from New England to Iowa documented the theme that at the same time a united Democracy would secure southern rights and rout the Republicans. One editor asserted that within a year fanaticism would have burned out. The South could obtain all its constitutional rights, Belmont wrote, only if it acted "firmly and manly but without precipitation."[13]

More than anything else, northern Democrats wanted southerners to give them time. Southerners must spurn hasty action. The conservative reaction in their section the northerners so confidently described would take time, as they admitted. Yet, in early December they pointed to recent municipal elections, even in Massachusetts, in which Democratic triumphs took place where Lincoln had won. Likewise, they publicized what they called Union meetings in cities like Trenton and Philadelphia. In the telling of northern Democrats, these events presaged a powerful surge in the northern electorate that would absolutely guarantee southern rights and equality. If only the South held fast, the Democracy would quickly aright its political ship, a mighty vessel that would demolish the Republican craft.[14]

In this script, disruption of the Union would not only upset the party, but would also signal "the death bell of human liberty" by dismembering the country. Thoughtful northern Democrats understood that southern anxiety over Lincoln's triumph went far deeper than one man's victory in a single election. An editorial writer decried "the bitterly hostile feeling which has been mused into existence by designing politicians." Chorusing that view, another asserted, "Let the Southern people be treated as friends and neighbors, not as aliens and enemies." At a public meeting in New York City, Daniel Dickinson, a former United States senator from New York, asserted that the Republicans did their real damage by whipping up antisouthern feelings in the northern population. Dickinson feared for a country without "fraternal feelings and common motives." Yet, "upon proper consideration," he expressed confidence that "a returning sentiment of fidelity and justice in the Northern States" would accompany a renewed Union.[15]

While northern Democrats pledged their fervent support for their southern comrades—to gain equal rights for the South—they simultaneously made clear their devotion to the Union. Secession was not an acceptable option; they would lend no assistance to disunion. They understood that in the politics of the free states if they could frame the contest as one between the constitutional rights of the South and the Republicans, they occupied a powerful position. In contrast, should the issue become secession versus the Union, they had no realistic choice. They must embrace the Union. For the vast majority of northern Democrats, practical reality dictated that decision. Early on they recognized what a few weeks later an Illinois congressman stated bluntly: "If we become entangled with disunionism we will be lost as a party." But even among the most conservative there was more. "Of course we who are in the Union cannot seem to aid, encourage or even countenance their trying to go out," observed Sidney Webster, who had been former president Franklin Pierce's private secretary. "That," he said, "would be disloyal and unpatriotic."[16]

Regular southern Democrats found themselves in a frightful place. They had to face insistent pressure from fire-eaters, who demonized any attempt to delay and censured compromise as "a dodge, a plot set on foot to entrap the South once more into submission, which is but another name for dishonor and disgrace." And these secessionists, as depicted by an experienced Georgia politico who opposed them, were "active and noisy—disgustingly blatant." The regulars had contributed significantly to their own predicament because they had constantly railed against the Republican threat, especially during the presidential campaign, when they predicted ruin for the South should the Republicans win. In short, they had helped stoke the fiery opinion that fire-eaters were striving to fan into a conflagration.[17]

In Congress the fire-eaters did not let up. The two South Carolina senators had already resigned. An acute observer noted the "unparalleled" pressure exerted by the radicals upon their more conservative colleagues. A congressional opponent described their sole purpose: "To increase the excitement by discussion here, and to force disunion." In the Senate, the Texas agitator Louis T. Wigfall boldly announced, "If this government does not suit us, we will leave it." Senator Alfred Iverson of Georgia extolled the rush toward disunion. "The time is rolling rapidly to the consummation of the great objects," his description of the secession of the southern states read. Men like Iverson and Wigfall eagerly anticipated the secession of their own states and spoke confidently of others following.[18]

Although not every notable southern Democrat in Congress belonged to the fire-eater band, they all had to contend with its message that the

South was in mortal danger. "I am a Southern man and no one can feel a deeper interest in the preservation of the constitutional rights of the South," wrote Senator Robert M. T. Hunter of Virginia. For Hunter, the question was whether they could be preserved in the Union. He spoke for many southern party regulars.[19]

Senator Jefferson Davis arrived in Washington hoping to avert disunion, but he knew full well the force of radicalism. In 1860, the tall, slender, fifty-two-year-old Mississippian stood not only as the foremost politician in his state, but as a major force in the Senate and a respected figure in the nation. Many Democrats in North and South had spoken of him as a presidential prospect for 1860. The famous Mathew Brady photograph of that year presents a well-groomed and composed man, with hair and fringe beard permeated with gray. Moreover, the worn, tension-filled face reveals the scars from a ravaging physical illness that had afflicted him in 1858 and the enormous political pressure enveloping him. That pressure was unrelenting. Even before the election, Robert Barnwell Rhett, Jr., the fire-eater and editor of the *Charleston Mercury*, asked for Davis's opinion of South Carolina's acting alone, a cause Rhett advocated. Replying just after the election, Davis counseled against haste, saying that he doubted Mississippi would take such action. Shortly thereafter, Davis attended a meeting of the congressional delegation called by the governor of Mississippi, who wanted advice on the appropriate action he and his state should take in view of Lincoln's election. Davis found himself alone in advocating delay, in wanting to hamper the bolt for disunion. He fully realized that to withstand the powerful force propelling secession he had to demonstrate the continued safety of the South in the Union. The temper of Congress, especially the Republican stance, would be crucial for him.[20]

In early December one man who had been a regular of regulars made the decision Davis did not want to make, a choice portentous for the future of his fellow Democratic loyalists. Amiable, even jolly, heavyset, with a full head of black hair, the forty-five-year-old Howell Cobb stood out in Buchanan's cabinet. Back in the early 1850s he had been a staunch proponent of the Compromise of 1850 and a successful opponent of sectional radicalism in his state. During the decade he became a highly regarded, solid Democratic leader.[21]

James Buchanan invited him into the cabinet; president and minister became fast friends. Cobb called his chief "the truest friend to the south that ever sat in the presidential chair." He also thought his presence in the cabinet important for the South. In addition, he anguished over leaving the president in "the hour of his greatest peril. . . . " At the same time, political allies in Georgia implored him to come home to reinforce "the friends of Resistance." Cobb's counsel was essential, for "men are confounded." "The ordeal through which I am now passing is the most trying of my life," he confessed. When the president in his message denied the constitutional right of secession, Cobb concluded he must resign. Finally, on December 8, he submitted his resignation, telling Buchanan, "The evil has now passed beyond control, and must be met by each and all of us under our responsibility to God and country."[22]

Cobb addressed a pamphlet to the people of Georgia that spelled out his rationale for his personal action and for secession. He told Georgians that a majority of northerners, former Whigs and Democrats, had united in hostility to the South. Republican campaign materials, he proclaimed, made the "most bitter and malignant approach to the antislavery sentiment of the North." Republicans denied all constitutional protection to slavery, he charged, while they castigated the institution as a moral and political evil. Noting the prediction that the Republican party, even in the presidency, could not harm the South and would soon come apart, Cobb responded, perhaps, but the South was not at a safe distance from such an inveterate enemy, whose hostility toward slavery composed its political glue. He then emphasized that remaining in the Union with a Republican administration meant for southerners risking their property and their society. A potential solution did exist, he admitted, one recommended by President Buchanan: making explicit with amendments guarantees in the Constitution. But Cobb asserted that the Republicans rejected such measures. Thus, southern security mandated secession.[23]

Cobb's decision painted in the broadest possible strokes the dilemma confronting Deep South politicians like Davis. Put simply, they could not unite with northern Democrats to derail the Republican administration unless they commanded a weapon that would neutralize the fire-eaters. Cobb's pronouncement that no cooperation from the Republicans would be forthcoming struck at their most vulnerable spot. That a party stalwart like Cobb had assumed this position signaled that fire-eating had spread from the periphery into the center. To dam the secessionist surge, the regulars had to show that they had a strategy that would protect the South. Doing so meant they had somehow to gain what Cobb said could not be obtained—Republican agreement to or acquiescence in a settlement or compromise that acknowledged what southerners defined as their constitutional rights as Americans.

While Republicans and Democrats encountered the crisis with one eye cocked toward partisan concerns, no politically active group focused more intently on keeping the Union whole than Upper South and Border Conservatives. While they decried "the confusion of the times," they did not think the extant evils sufficient to justify the destruction of the Union. Their watchwords: "Patriots, pure men, must stand up and beat back the power of darkness." They wanted to believe that such men would prevail. "So much good temper on both sides," John P. Kennedy reasoned in his journal, "*must* bring about a better state of things."[24]

Yet these Conservatives fully appreciated the potential damage by those they branded as extremists — men North and South who did not care whether the Union survived or who worked actively to dismember it. The presidential candidate of most of these self-identified moderates, John Bell, pointed directly to the potential power of a small group, able and dedicated. He informed a colleague, "I need not explain to you how a *talented and active* minority may prompt a *majority* of the people into measures which would not be approved by the majority, if allowed to express their opinion directly, at the polls."[25]

On the second day of the congressional session, the attitude and goal of the Conservatives were forthrightly recommended in the Senate by the man who became their champion, John J. Crittenden. Anointing Crittenden as "the bosom friend of the immortal Clay," Governor Thomas Hicks of Maryland had charged him "to go forward in the important work of saving the country." "An angry debate" must become no part of their discussion, Crittenden told his fellow senators. He continued, "This Union was established by great sacrifices; this Union is worthy of great sacrifices and great concessions for its maintenance." With more yearning than confidence, he pled, "I trust there is not a Senator here who is not willing to yield and to compromise much in order to preserve the government and the Union of the country." He made absolutely clear his own intention to "search out, if it be possible, some means for the reconciliation of all the different sections and members of this Union, and see if we cannot restore again that harmony and that fraternity and that union which gave so much of blessing and so much of benefit to us all."[26]

From the ranks of these men came the initial congressional response to the crisis. On December 4 in the House of Representatives, just after the reading of the presidential message, Congressman Alexander Boteler of Virginia proposed a special committee to consider the portion of the message "as it relates to the present perilous condition of the country." He wanted thirty-three members, one from each state. Immediately, John Sherman of Ohio, a rising Republican star known as a moderate, countered with a membership of fifteen or some other number. Sherman did not like representation by states; he asserted that the House had never before set up a committee of one from each state. After a brief discussion centering on a flurry of offered and withdrawn amendments, the House passed Boteler's proposition by a comfortable margin of 145–38.[27]

Such a prompt and substantial victory for what became known as the Committee of Thirty-three seemingly revealed a substantial House majority desiring to look carefully for a settlement of the crisis. Two caveats require attention, however. Sixteen southerners abstained, all from states that had already called secession conventions, though six of their compatriots voted aye. That abstention indicated to some Deep South representatives, at least for the moment, the decision for disunion had already been made. Moreover, some denigrated "the stupidity of such an effort," while expressing "mortification" that the idea for the committee originated with a southerner. A press report commented on a caucus of secessionists held to bring pressure on other Deep South congressmen to reject serving. Two even demanded to be excused from service, one of them terming the committee "the Grecian horse introduced into Troy."[28]

Even more important, more than three dozen Republicans cast ballots against creating the committee. Although Republicans did say yes by 62 to 38, from the very beginning a goodly number made unmistakably clear their opposition to any serious discussion of a settlement. In contrast, every northern Democrat and every voting southerner placed themselves on the opposite side.[29]

The very next day the Republican speaker of the House, William Pennington of New Jersey, appointed the committee members. In the chair he placed the veteran politician Thomas Corwin of Ohio. The tall, heavyset

Corwin, now sixty-six, had served as a Whig in both houses of Congress, in the cabinet, and as governor of his state. On the national stage since the 1830s, Corwin brought lengthy experience, a national outlook, and perspective to the task. He was a thoughtful moderate who, unlike many in his party, fully comprehended the scope of the crisis. To Abraham Lincoln he wrote that in his judgment northern opinion was not "well informed on the excitement prevailing in the South." Even though in his mind "it seem[ed] to border on madness," he took it quite seriously. "I have never in my life seen my country in such a dangerous position," he continued. Despite his "great alarm," he "resolved not to be paralyzed by dismay." He saw safety only ensured by "looking the danger full in the face and acting with calm dignity in such way as if possible we may ride out the storm." This man wanted to find a solution.[30]

The partisan makeup of Corwin's committee conformed to the alignment in the House. Pennington put on it sixteen Republicans, fourteen Democrats, and three southerners who remained in opposition to the Democrats. The membership included Republicans who had voted against forming the committee and southern Democrats who had abstained. Still, overwhelmingly the members had as their goal finding a settlement. One of them, Charles Francis Adams, thought that "conservativism" marked the membership.[31]

Pennington's choices left one notable group most unhappy, however. Northern Democrats protested that they had been shortchanged, with one congressman depicting the speaker's action as an "insult to the Northern Democracy," for which he should be "scourged." Only two had been appointed, the representatives from California and Oregon, states without a Republican congressman. All the other sixteen free states were represented by Republicans, a fact also noted by southerners. The evidence does not reveal clearly why Pennington shunned northern Democrats, but two explanations seem probable. First, with the Democratic domination of southern delegations, he had limited alternatives from the slave states. That meant that he could fill the Democratic roster with slave-state men. Second looms the figure of Stephen A. Douglas. Republicans saw him as their chief antagonist on their home ground. More northern Democrats on the committee would give him additional influence and voice in its deliberations. Keeping them off would ensure less.[32]

The committee began on an apparently positive note. It met initially on

December 11 and during the first two days speeches ruled the day, including traditional sectional recrimination. Then, on the thirteenth, Albert Rust of Arkansas introduced a resolution stating that southerners had cause for their "existing discontents." He wanted "just concessions and additional and more specific and effectual guarantees . . ." of southern rights. Northerners did not reject Rust's proposal out of hand. In fact, some Republicans came toward him, though without embracing any justification for southern distress. On that very day William M. Dunn of Indiana proposed a substitute proclaiming that whether or not southern unrest had any legitimacy, "any reasonable, proper and constitutional remedies, and additional and more specific and effectual guarantees of their peculiar rights and interests as recognized by the Constitution, necessary to preserve the peace of the country and the perpetuation of the Union, should be promptly and cheerfully granted." Although he did not admit that the South had cause for complaint, Dunn declared unequivocally that Congress should act to address southern grievances. Dunn's substitute so favored the South that Rust withdrew his initial resolution. An attempt by more hard-line Republicans to displace Dunn's with a milder measure failed. The Dunn solution promptly came to a vote. Republicans split evenly, with eight, including Corwin, for and eight against. These eight positive Republicans added to the fourteen non-Republicans resulted in a majority of twenty-two to eight for Dunn's proposal. The more extreme Republicans failed.[33]

Explaining why Dunn acted as he did and why seven of his colleagues joined him poses a problem, for the available evidence does not provide a complete answer. A Mississippi secessionist accused them of duplicity, making promises they had no intention of keeping. Perhaps, but pressures were intense to find a way to hold the Union together. Republicans felt them just as others did. Even Charles Francis Adams, who had voted against Dunn's resolution, concluded that some kind of "remedial course" would have to be found. Moreover, many Republicans, like Corwin, had conservative Whig backgrounds. To them the Union was dear indeed.[34]

While the House moved promptly, the Senate lagged. Its dilatoriness did not result, however, from lack of effort. Like Representative Boteler, Senator Lazarus Powell, Crittenden's colleague from Kentucky, acted quickly with a proposal. On December 6, in the aftermath of the reading of the presidential message, he suggested that the Senate refer the portion of the message relative to the "distracted condition of the country, and the grievances between the slaveholding and the non-slaveholding States to a special committee of thirteen members." But, unlike on the other side of the Capitol, debate and delaying tactics held up action. Neither Republicans nor southern radicals wanted the committee. Finally, on December 18, after almost two weeks, the Senate adopted Powell's resolution without a recorded vote.[35]

No group was more eager for a settlement than the northern business community, especially in the major seaport cities. Of course, many of these businessmen in financial, mercantile, and shipping enterprises relied heavily on southern connections. Financing crops, providing supplies of all kinds, transporting commodities—chiefly cotton—comprised the major activity of a substantial portion of northeastern commercial interests. Southern agricultural products, with cotton taking the lead, were almost as important to these northerners as to southerners. Threats of secession not only endangered future transactions with the South, they also rattled financial markets. As one Philadelphian wrote President-elect Lincoln, "The commercial pressure precipitated by the madness of the South" had created enormous "strife." He and others like him wanted Lincoln's aid in lifting "*this galling pressure*." Panic gripped some. "IN CONSEQUENCE OF THE PANIC! PANIC!! PANIC!!!," one firm offered customers its "VERY LARGE STOCK OF FALL IMPORTATIONS . . . AT SUCH PRICES AS MUST COMMAND IMMEDIATE SALE."[36]

These worried men did what they could to generate support for a conciliatory stance. They had two major goals—to slow the southern rush to secession and to get a Republican commitment to conciliation. They implored their southern trading partners to recognize that Lincoln's election did not mean that anti-South sentiment dominated in the North. Making that point, they asserted that many businessmen had voted for Lincoln because of their disgust with corruption in the Buchanan administration, not because of any antisouthern or antislavery convictions. They called for mass meetings in cities and lobbied legislatures to repeal the statutes obstructing the return of fugitive slaves that aroused southern ire. Without question this desire originated mostly with Democrats, or at least non-Republicans. At the same time, some Republicans clearly signed on, though rarely in leadership positions.[37]

The most notable effort became known as the Pine Street meeting, which took place at 33 Pine Street in New York City, the business address of the well known, pro-southern merchant Richard Lathers. Called by a self-defined Committee of Fifteen, this gathering was designed to highlight the breadth of support for compromise or conciliation. Some two thousand merchants and bankers appeared, requiring a couple more buildings to handle the crowd. Only a few Republicans attended, and Republican newspapers condemned it, though numerous Republican businessmen agreed with its thrust. Organizers did try to go beyond the city, reaching out to notable men like former president Millard Fillmore.

Most in attendance declared that the crisis of the Union could be satisfactorily solved. Speakers repeated what had been said before: Lincoln's election did not signify a rising anti-South tide; a conservative reaction was already under way in the North, signaling a growing pro-compromise opinion; the South should not act hastily. They urged southerners to heed this appeal of "their truest friends." The speeches and resolutions did emphasize that blame for the crisis rested with the Republican party, whose overt sectionalism, they said, caused southern fears and triggered talk of secession.[38]

Some Republicans took settling the crisis as their chief end. What they feared most was fratricidal conflict. A New York correspondent quoted the great English commander the Duke of Wellington to Lyman Trumbull, the Republican senator from Lincoln's state: "Anything is better than civil war. I have seen it and know what it is." No one took this dictum with more fervor and even political daring than Thurlow Weed, editor of the *Albany Evening Journal*.[39]

Weed was not simply another newspaperman. Long a prominent figure in New York State politics, he had been a Whig leader, a position he easily shifted to the Republicans. He was dedicated to politics, becoming the consummate backstage manager. Never an elected official, he exerted enormous influence through his massive sway over patronage in New York State. Because of his success, his political enemies inside as well as outside his party damned him as an amoral manipulator. Weed's main entrée to national politics came through his intimate association with William Seward. Seward, the public man, had been a governor and was now a senator, while Weed remained content to wield his power through his organizational skill. Each man required the other to achieve his political goals.

Weed was a tall, strong man, physically and mentally. His personality fit his role. One who knew him described him as "the most confidential man in manner I ever encountered," always conversing in "a subdued tone." "His tone was very expressive," another remembered, "expressive of shrewdness and intellectual force." But the key was his nose, "the most expressive feature of his face—long, sagacious, penetrating & commanding." With his omnipresent cigar, Weed greeted all "as a confidant, whispering in their ears."[40]

Confronting the crisis, Weed had a single objective. He strove for a peaceful, nonpartisan settlement. From his Republican compatriots he desired "concession, not surrender." As he told a Republican senator, he wished "to soften the tone of the Republican press. . . . " To this end, as early as November 24, he publicly broached the possibility of jettisoning a cardinal Republican shibboleth, no slavery in the territories. In his newspaper he suggested undermining secessionists and defusing the crisis by extending the Missouri Compromise line westward to California.[41]

In a long editorial on November 30, Weed more fully developed his argument that Republicans should compromise. Noting his previous suggestion to extend the Missouri Compromise line, he said it had accomplished his purpose "in awakening and discussion." He knew bringing up that topic would distress many of "our own most valued friends" (read fellow Republicans, for whom the Missouri extension had become a bête noire). "But unfortunately," Weed countered, "the pending issue is to be decided irrespective of its merits."[42]

Weed declared that the South had been convinced by its leaders and the northern Democratic press that Republicans were political jackals who intended to rip apart southern interests and institutions. Those tirades, he went on, would not cease before March 4 and Lincoln's inauguration. Republicans, Weed insisted, had to demonstrate the error in such charges. To his comrades "who will not question our devotion to Freedom, however, they may mistrust our judgment, we submit a few earnest admonitions." Weed contended that the consequences that could result from the crusaders of disunion in the South and the "fanatic zeal" of abolitionists in the North could be "averted" only by bringing together and strengthening the Union sentiment in the entire country.

He pointed out that secessionist attitudes seemed dominant in the seven Deep South states and fractious in the other slave states. Asserting that Republicans had to accept the reality that many southerners were "blinded by passion," Weed maintained that by exercising "moderation and tolerance" Republicans would nourish southern Unionist sentiment. "The

Union," he stated bluntly, "is worth saving." He emphasized his point with an analogy—when a house is on fire, people do not try to ascertain the cause before putting it out. "A Victorious Party can afford to be tolerant," he concluded, "not, as our friends assume, in the abandonment or abasement of its principles or character, but in efforts to correct and disabuse the minds of those who misunderstand both."

Weed called for a convention of delegates from all states. Such a gathering would precede any call to action. He admitted that some Republicans would say they had done no wrong and had nothing to offer. Even if true, Weed argued, that was precisely why Republicans should "*propose* and *offer* whatever may, by possibility, avert the evils of civil war and preserve the blessings of the Union."

He closed by stating that should the slave states secede, the North would lose much. United, the country was strong; divided, it would be weak. The duty of the Republican party "dare not consist in folded arms, or sealed ears, or closed eyes."

Weed's message did not unite his party. Some Republicans agreed while others did not. Compiling a comprehensive census of where all Republicans lined up on a possible territorial compromise is impossible. The historical record does not permit such accuracy. Working from imperfect and imprecise sources, the historian can only point to the range of opinion and then on the available evidence make a judgment about the depth and extent of divergent views.

Although not every Republican rallied around Weed's call, it did resonate with a substantial portion of his party. In New York City both the *Times* and the *Courier and Enquirer* followed Weed's lead in promoting a sectional division of the territories. Additionally, major party newspapers in Cincinnati, Detroit, Indianapolis, Pittsburgh, and Springfield, Massachusetts, did likewise. Letters affirming his viewpoint filled Weed's mail; fellow Republicans told him his editorials were "right in temper and spirit."[43]

For backers of compromise, their victorious party should move to meet southern demands. Doing so "would have an instantaneous & great effect on such of the Southern people as honestly believe we meditate aggression upon their rights." J. Watson Webb, editor of the New York *Courier and Enquirer*, wrote Lincoln that Republicans could afford to be "magnanimous." In their minds the party had "even a duty" to demonstrate that a

Republican administration would in no way threaten southern interests. In the words of a New York merchant, Republicans should not be obstinate, but rather "show a disposition to bring back quietude and peace to the country."[44]

According to this thinking, dividing the national domain with the slave states entailed giving up nothing tangible. It emphasized that the rapidly growing northern economy and population were outpacing the South. In the future the slave states could not compete as equals. The free states would dominate the country. Thus, insulting the South by denying any access to the national territory served no real purpose. In Weed's language, Republicans needed to "come off the stump" and relinquish the "spread-eagle style of argument." Let "common sense" reign, he cried. Additionally, as one of Charles Francis Adams's constituents noted, the Missouri Compromise had kept the peace for a generation. Reinstating it might very well accomplish the same for another generation.[45]

Republicans taking this stance generally equated compromise with the preservation of the Union. Taking the push for secession quite seriously, they maintained that nothing else, platform or policy, compared to the preservation of the Union. Without some compromise arrangement, they predicted not only the dissolution of the Union but also the likelihood of civil war, the worst possible outcome. The correctness of a party or sectional stance, in the view of these men, did not have "much consequence at such a time." They reported that the kind of arrangement Weed proposed would settle the matter. Republicans mentioned particular southern politicians, even from the Cotton States, who indicated they could accept such a plan.[46]

Pro-compromise Republicans also discussed practical politics. Weed believed the territorial issue had done its work in electing Lincoln. In a letter to Seward's senatorial colleague from New York, Weed used direct language: "The views of the late campaign are obsolete." An Indiana senator agreed, asserting, "If our Republican leaders don't learn wisdom we should be scattered to [illegible] the very next election." The party needed new views. A relative of the governor of New York explained what he saw as political necessity: "A moderate majority of the northern people only are with the Republican party, and the South are all against us." Then, he asked the fundamental question: "How can the Republican party grow or maintain its persistence by sacrificing the Union for the sake of maintaining opinions upon questions abstract, and non-essential compared to the preservation of the Union?" This political calculus particularly impressed pragmatists like Weed, who declared that "the normal proclivities of the American people are Democratic" and who foresaw in the near future a reunited Democratic party confronting the Republicans. To provide the requisite boost for his party, he wanted to reach out to southern Unionists, especially in the Upper South and Border slave states—in other words, the Constitutional Unionists. Republican obduracy on the territories or any other prominent slavery issue would preclude that possibility.[47]

Weed and his allies did not underestimate the obstacles they faced within their own party. They constantly spoke of difficulties with "our friends," the euphemism everyone used for fellow Republicans. A supporter warned Weed that his editorials would turn away "some hitherto good friends." To these men their friends either placed the party first or simply did not comprehend the stakes. In the forefront of the unyielding stood the extreme antislavery men who preferred destruction of the Union to any deal with the South. Refusing to bend, as the former governor, congressman, and senator Hamilton Fish, of New York, put it, "soon they will find neither party nor country to call their own." "Our friends are almost as inane as the traitors who desire to destroy the government," observed the prominent Indiana Republican John D. Defrees.[48]

For these Republicans, devotion to the Union, confidence in northern strength, fear of civil war, along with practical political necessity, resulted in a clarion call for compromise. What they desperately wanted was a major elected party official publicly to take this position. A correspondent of Pennsylvania's senator Simon Cameron exclaimed that someone must step forward to save the party, the Union, and Lincoln. That person must possess "undaunted moral & physical courage." "Be bold," another cried. In a letter to Weed, John Defrees blared the bugle: "We need a statesman of nerve to meet the terrible crisis. Oh for a Henry Clay!"[49]

From the other end of the Republican spectrum, denunciation of the "timidly cowardly" assailed anyone who advocated or even spoke positively about territorial compromise. No generally accepted label exists for these men. Two described themselves as Republicans of "the first water." A historian has used "stalwart," which is surely not inaccurate, but many conservatives certainly thought of themselves as stalwart for the party. Most assuredly on sectional questions they were hard-liners or, in modern parlance, the left of the party. In my judgment both "hard-liners" and "the left" are accurate, and I will use them interchangeably.[50]

Republican hard-liners gave no legitimacy to southern concerns. "I am unwilling to surrender an iota of ground to the Southern demands," wrote one. "The day of Compromise has past," declared Senator Ben Wade of Ohio. If southerners did not like that fact, he did not care, roaring, let them "howl and rave, like so many devils, tormented before their time." Wade's senatorial colleague Zachariah Chandler had more in mind than wild wailing: "*Individually*, I do want a little shooting or hanging done before this matter is ended if we have a decent excuse for it." These men termed the southern insistence on compromise "Bullying the Free States." That image was used by Weed's journalistic and political rival in New York State Horace Greeley. Editor of the *New York Tribune*, the most widely circulated of all Republican newspapers, Greeley crusaded against any thought of compromise, which he depicted as "a wasted and absolute surrender of our sacred principles."[51]

Any indication toward compromise the hard-liners hailed as "cowardly" or "weak-kneed." "It will never do to let our opponents suppose with any justice that Weakness is a Republican failing," one of them asserted. They upheld as their standard the Republican platform, adopted at the convention in Chicago, which, in their definition, had become more than a broadside designed to spur the party faithful and win an election. It became a secular Ten Commandments. In fact, the platform allowed for some policy flexibility—stating, for example, that while freedom was "the normal condition" in the territories, Congress should legislate against slavery in them only when "necessary." The hard-liners overlooked the political origins of the platform and any possible ambiguity in it. Instead, they presented it as an inflexible moral document, a political catechism.[52]

For these Republicans on the left, turning a campaign platform into a moral treatise underscored their sense of their party's victory as a triumph of virtue. Decrying talk of compromise, a Pennsylvanian stated, "Our sympathetic prayer and labors are with the right & against the wrong." They identified themselves with "the cause of humanity and civilization." As one said, "It is too late in the day for [us] to yield right for wrong. This is a day of progressivism & of reformation[.] It won't do to retrograde."[53]

The hard-liners placed slavery at the heart of the political contest. The spirit of the party is "*hostility* to *slavery*," a constituent informed Lyman

Trumbull. "Liberty & slavery are absolute antagonists," avowed Lincoln's law partner William H. Herndon. Compromise could not be contemplated, as a critic of Weed told him, because it would mean "young robust liberty asking quarters of Slavery! Shame! Shame! Never!" These Republicans believed literally in irrepressible conflict. In their view, the country had finally found the correct path. The hard-liners exulted in the moral clarity of the Republican stance, a posture they admitted could not have been attained as long as Henry Clay, Daniel Webster, and their disciples prevailed, for they placed the Union first.[54]

This conviction did not place all the hard-liners in the abolitionist camp. Again, the historical record does not permit an accurate breakdown. Without question the abolitionists in the party demanded an immediate end to slavery, and some wanted the federal government to lead the assault against the hated institution. But just as assuredly, their gang was a small minority. The great majority on the Republican left wanted to see the United States as a country committed to freedom, without the embarrassment of slavery, which they saw as a holdover from less progressive times. Seward's senatorial colleague made the outlook quite clear in countering Weed's case for compromise. Preston King asked Weed, "Is it possible you do not see the magnitude of the evil to spring from such a proposition . . . ?" Stating that he was not going to argue, King concluded, "But I beseech you to consider what you are doing."[55]

While proud of their professed moral purity, this wing of the party contained committed partisans, whether officeholders, activists, or simply enthusiastic voters. To a man they maintained that backing compromise "would disband the Republican party." They were convinced that, as one said, any concession on the turbulent issue would "break us all into pieces—I mean our party." These men foresaw cataclysm, and offered descriptions of destruction and annihilation. Unlike Weed and the other conservatives, the left did not think nationally, only sectionally. With the Republican party constituted as solely a northern organization the hard-liners perceived that they ensured for themselves an influential voice within it. When they spoke of annihilation, they meant that many of their like-minded compatriots would fall away or bolt from the party—not that the professional officeholders would take such a drastic step, but that activists and voters would. Thus, for the hard-liners maintenance of the party in its 1860 configuration was central. This priority meant the party had to keep anti-South and antislavery, at least total firmness on the territorial issue, at its core. Compromise would place the Union first. That eventuality they would resolutely fight.[56]

The hard-liners believed their unyielding stand would have one of two outcomes. As soon as the South realized its "bullying" would not yield compromise, it would back down. According to this view, the South only made demands or insisted on compromise when confronting a weak North. Thus, a stern Republican stance would force a southern retreat, maybe even in "ignominy and disgrace." Simply, it was a matter of strength in victory versus weakness in defeat.[57]

But if the South did not meekly accept its diminished status, the left announced its preparedness. Rather than compromise, they indicated their "willing[ness] that the whole South may go out of the Union." A correspondent of Seward said the South's leaving the Union would leave Republicans even stronger. Thus, again, their vision of a Republican-dominated Union overrode the Union they had inherited.[58]

In this version of the crisis, secession had a peaceful result. Of course, in the process of states leaving the Union events could get out of control, a possibility the hard-liners recognized. Recognition did not lead to any altered opinion, however. "War is a fearful calamity," one of them wrote, "*but we had better fight than yield our point.*" Horace White, of Chicago, announced to the president-elect that many would "writhe in the bitterness of grief" should any territorial compromise take place. Then, his verb changed: "to defend unblemished Republican victory, there are multitudes here who will plunge into blood to the horse's bridle."[59]

With the party divided, the stance of the leaders became vital. In addition to the staunch conservatives and entrenched hard-liners, many loyal Republicans had not yet made an ironclad commitment to either side. Congress contained a number of those concerned though yet uncommitted Republicans. For the most part, they comprehended the seriousness of the crisis, even if they had arrived in Washington unaware of its depth. Conveying that recognition, on December 9 Congressman Elihu Washburne informed his fellow Illinoisian the president-elect that "sectional feeling has assumed proportions of which I had but a faint conception when I saw you at Springfield. . . . " Washburne went on to say that he did not believe western Republicans had a sense of "the imminent peril" now upon the country. He considered it "folly to attempt to shut one's eyes as to what is transpiring all around us."[60]

Recognizing the situation as Washburne described it to Lincoln, congressional Republicans acknowledged that some steps should be taken to forestall secession and save the Union. The hard-liners, of course, rejected any such sentiment. On the floor of his chamber, Wade staked out their position in bold language rejecting any legitimacy for southern concerns. But at that moment it is doubtful that he spoke for a majority of Republican members, though absolute precision is impossible. Senator James Dixon of Connecticut and Congressman Samuel Curtis of Iowa were representative of Republicans who admitted both the existence of a secession crisis and the division in their party. They thought, as did Indiana's Schuyler Colfax, that Republicans "should be conciliatory and forbearing." Yet these men, in the words of a New York congressman, were "fundamentally passive and in doubt as to what should be done." They all looked to their leadership.[61]

The two men who mattered most were the senior senator from New York and the president-elect. Their decisions and actions would have a massive influence on all Republicans, in and out of Congress. Two key questions predominated. First, would Seward and Lincoln agree on the appropriate response to the crisis? Second, whether agreeing or disagreeing, who would lead and who would follow, or would some dual leadership arrangement emerge?

Even though Lincoln's election had inaugurated the crisis, Seward at that time still stood as the more widely known and respected figure in both party and nation. William Henry Seward was a professional politician as well as a careful and wily veteran of partisan struggle. Sensible that back in the spring he had failed in his bid for the Republican presidential nomination, he also knew that the man who had bested him would head up the executive branch of the federal government. At the same time, however, he was aware that his closest confidant, Thurlow Weed, was suggesting a far-reaching territorial compromise that violated Republican doctrine.

Because of their intimate political relationship, it is implausible to think that Weed acted without Seward's agreement. Yet, Seward heedfully kept himself apart from his partner's initiative. Likewise, in his editorials Weed never implicated Seward as a coauthor of his suggestions. They had agreed to keep the latter's name out. In a caucus of Republican senators called by the hard-liners when Congress opened, some tried to attach Seward to Weed, asking him directly about his involvement in Weed's suggestion. Just as directly, albeit somewhat disingenuously, Seward replied that he knew nothing about it. Writing Weed he said, "I told them they would know what I think and what I propose when I do myself."[62]

At this early moment Seward's strategy required his public silence. He came forth with no bold announcements or challenging proposals. In fact, he took no speaking role in the Senate. He did, however, converse with a wide variety of political people from both parties and sections. While claiming to have no specific plan, he confided to his wife, "I begin to see my way through, without sacrifice of principle." He did strive quietly to keep his party's left from openly brandishing its hostility to the South. He thought the hard-liners just as "convulsed" and impossible as the South Carolina fire-eaters.[63]

Seward wanted a moderate Republican face before Congress and the public. Experienced in the Senate, with many friendships crossing sectional as well as partisan boundaries, his goal was to maintain all possible alternatives. He was convinced, as he informed Weed on December 2, that "if we keep peace and quiet for a time, the temper will be favorable on both sides to consultation." He made one great exception, however. He felt that nothing could deter South Carolina from seceding. No matter, avoiding "collision and bloodshed" was his fervent wish.[64]

His fellow Republicans noted his demeanor and tried to decipher his policy. While "puffing at his everlasting cigar," he kept his own counsel. To close observers he seemed almost inscrutable. His admirer Charles Francis Adams, in whose home he often visited, confided to his diary that he found the New Yorker "enigmatical," though "hopeful that with prudence everything will go right." They saw him holding to a public silence while trying to keep his more confrontational colleagues in check. Despite Seward's effort Senator John Hale of New Hampshire opened the Senate session with a blistering anti-South diatribe. Still, Seward's toil was not entirely futile, for most Republicans did not adopt Hale's belligerent posture.[65]

Perhaps Seward did operate in the shadows, but he was not invisible. On December 18, the Senate finally managed to create its own version of the House Committee of Thirty-three, an outcome held up by Republicans and fire-eaters, both of whom wanted chiefly to avoid direct consideration of the crisis. Known as the Committee of Thirteen, after the number of its members, it was in one way quite unlike its House counterpart. The Committee of Thirteen included the major luminaries in the Senate, Democrat and Republican, southern and northern, with Seward, of course, among its members. Even though he was not in the capital at the moment, Seward surely expected to have his voice heard when basic decisions regarding the crisis were being made, or not made.[66]

Before Seward went public with any plan or program, he understandably wanted to find out where the president-elect stood and where he stood with the president-elect. As the major party figure he knew himself to be, he could reasonably expect a request to join the cabinet. And it came in a confidential letter from Lincoln dated December 8, offering the first cabinet chair, secretary of state. Though not unexpected, the invitation was flattering. Yet, Lincoln's missive contained no information about either potential colleagues or whether Seward would have any influence in their selection. At this point, Seward decided he needed to confer back in New York with his ally Weed.[67]

Moreover, because Lincoln had maintained a conscious public silence on the crisis, Seward did not know the incoming chief executive's views on the threat of secession or the possibility of compromise. Although his wished-for conference with Lincoln could not take place at that time, he anticipated answers. When he met with Weed in Albany during the weekend of December 15 and 16, he learned that the editor had received a rather urgent message asking him to visit Springfield. Lincoln's close advisers had praised Weed's work in the campaign and had committed to listening to him, although with the caveat that they could not speak for the president-elect. After an exchange of letters, word came to Weed that Lincoln desired to see him in Springfield "immediately." This meant patronage and probably policy.[68]

When Seward left Washington, on December 13 or 14, for his meeting with Weed and his western New York home, he said that politics did not prompt his journey. But as Henry Adams, who often saw and heard about Seward in his father's home, noted to his brother, "W.H.S. is not to be sounded by ordinary lines." From Washington, a Republican operative told Lincoln that Seward had departed the capital "mum as an oyster." "Some of our friends," he continued, "say he is badly frightened."

Concluding his letter, he underscored how successful Seward had been in masking his point of view: "I know not how it is."[69]

Seward expected to learn from Weed exactly how it was. On the sixteenth, he wrote Lincoln that he and Weed had discussed "the condition and prospect of public affairs," which Weed could relay to the president-elect. As he prepared for his western trip after his deliberations with Seward, Weed in his *Albany Evening Journal* renewed his call for compromise, for extending the Missouri line. It is inconceivable that this renewed plan occurred without Seward's knowledge and concurrence. He and Weed obviously hoped to lure Lincoln while disguising Seward's involvement. Weed left for Springfield with high aspirations for his and Seward's vision for the Republican party.[70]

On December 20, the day South Carolina seceded, Weed met for several hours with Lincoln in the president-elect's home, joined by two of Lincoln's confidential advisers with whom Weed had corresponded, David Davis and Leonard Swett. By all accounts Lincoln and Weed got along well. According to Weed's recollections, he brought up secession, which initially Lincoln seemingly wanted to avoid. Explaining his position on the issue, Weed maintained that Republican control of the executive branch would effectively block slavery in the territories. Thus, Republicans could agree to extending the Missouri line without defaulting on party principle. Doing so would mollify the South, get around the quagmire of compromise, and pay a big political dividend, rallying the North on the issue of the Union behind a conciliatory Republican party. From Weed's perspective no one could doubt Republican patriotism if the party conceded on what appeared to be a critical measure. Then, if southerners objected, they would become the obstinate obstructionists. Of course, for Weed the concession was practically meaningless, for in his mind Lincoln's victory had relegated the territorial issue to the political dustbin.[71]

Then Weed moved to the cabinet. He had a single goal, to get Lincoln's commitment to appoint mostly former conservative Whigs, including two southerners; such a lineup would ensure Seward's influence, and primacy, in the president's official family. Lincoln deftly parried Weed, however. Despite a friendly conversation about the cabinet, including Lincoln's agreement that he would appoint at least two southerners, the president-elect did not divulge his prior dealings on cabinet appointments. Furthermore, Lincoln made no commitment that the final group would meet Weed's criteria. Even more important, Lincoln sent Weed away without giving one iota on the crisis in general or on territorial compromise in particular. Commenting on Weed's pro-compromise editorial, Lincoln remarked, "This is a heavy broadside. You opened your fire at a critical moment." Without praise or criticism he observed, "It will do some good or much mischief." He did say he "hoped that by wisdom and forbearance the danger of serious trouble might be averted, as such dangers had in former times."[72]

Lincoln gave Weed written proposals for compromise that he wanted Seward to present to the Committee of Thirteen. What Lincoln thought of as compromise was indeed lame compared with Weed's suggestion. Lincoln set forth three propositions; two dealt with the fugitive slave matter and the third simply called for the preservation of the federal Union. Lincoln understood perfectly what he had done and had not done. Describing his proposals in a letter to Lyman Trumbull written upon Weed's departure, Lincoln observed, "They do not touch the territorial question." To a friend a few days later, Lincoln pointed to Weed's utter failure to move him on cabinet appointments or policy using a homey image—Weed headed east with "an extra large flea in his ear."[73]

It also seems indisputable that orally Lincoln added another proposition. In a letter to Lincoln on December 26, Seward wrote of Weed's giving him "verbally the substance of the suggestion you proposed for the consideration of the Republican members [of the Committee of Thirteen]." Seward then referred specifically to a proposed constitutional amendment that would make impossible any congressional interference with slavery in the states where it existed. At this time Lincoln never spoke publicly about his "suggestion." Doing so would, of course, have broken his vow of public silence on the crisis. But he never even mentioned it in subsequent letters to Seward. That he refused to put it in writing and remained quiet also suggests he feared that identifying himself with this measure would harm him with the hard-liners.[74]

When Weed's train east reached Syracuse, Seward boarded. On the rest of the ride back to Albany Seward learned what Lincoln had earlier made clear to close associates, but not to Seward: that he implacably opposed extending the Missouri line or any other proposition that could even theoretically permit slavery in any territory. Seward also found out that he would not have a truly influential voice in selecting other cabinet members. In short, Abraham Lincoln occupied a different political space from William Seward. By the time the train reached Albany, Seward had moved toward Lincoln's space. As the historian David Potter noted many years ago, on that journey the leadership of the Republican party transferred indisputably from Seward to Lincoln.[75]

There would be no more contest or doubt about which Republican headed the party. Seward became the subaltern. And from that December day until the outbreak of hostilities almost four months later, Seward would remain loyal to Lincoln while at the same time never stopping his attempts to moderate both his party and his new chief.

When Lincoln welcomed Weed to Springfield, the New Yorker really did not know where the president-elect stood on the questions that mattered most to him and Seward—Lincoln had shared his views with only a handful of trusted associates. He had kept publicly silent on territorial compromise as well as political issues generally. In deciding on silence, he certainly did not lack for advice. Many Republicans urged him not to open his mouth and praised him for keeping it closed. A New Yorker wrote "that the opinion is unanimous that *now* any explanation as to your public policy would be taken for weakness & satisfy neither side. . . . " "I hope you will not say one word to the South . . . ," asserted a firm Republican. Another predicted "any attempt at Explanation would only in my judgment dishonor the cause of Freedom and inflame rather than constrict the pretensions of the South."[76]

In contrast, other Republicans implored him to speak out. Even though Lincoln's political career was mostly a matter of public record, these advisers noted that a fundamental alteration had occurred. No longer just an Illinois politician and private citizen, not even just a party nominee for president, Lincoln was now president-elect, with a responsibility to the entire country. He needed to speak from that pedestal and with that authority. These correspondents, overwhelmingly conservative, told Lincoln that he had a "golden opportunity" to calm the storm. Supporting this outlook, Henry Raymond, the editor of *The New York Times,* tried to attach it to partisan advantage. "The main thing, you will note," advised Raymond, "is to have you say that *the South misunderstands the Republican Party*, and that a *Republican administration can alone correct the error*." A journalist in

Washington reported that a number of congressional Republicans wanted Lincoln to announce his moderate views in hopes of "allaying, if possible, the excitement existing throughout the South."[77]

Simultaneously Lincoln received conflicting advice on the territorial question. Any possibility of Lincoln's even leaning toward compromise appalled an Ohioan: "For heaven's sake do not be guilty of such a piece of flunkerism!" The North would "despise" it. Be firm; do not compromise; these cries filled Lincoln's mailbag. According to Carl Schurz, a German immigrant and leading Republican operative, party members wanted no "lowering of the Republican standard." The president-elect must not falter, ordered Schurz.[78]

Most of the same men who counseled Lincoln to make a moderating public announcement also approved his endorsing some kind of territorial compromise. In their minds such a move would assuage the crisis, torpedoing fire-eaters without damaging the Republican party. An Episcopal rector reminded Lincoln that in the past the Lord had raised up "pacificators"; in this instance, he wanted Lincoln to accept that charge.[79]

Lincoln was also getting eyewitness accounts of congressional affairs, both from members of Congress and from visitors to the capital. Contradicting his earlier opinion, he received news that secessionists were in earnest and real danger threatened the Union. Southern fear of a Republican administration and determination to act surprised some observers, and they told Lincoln so. He also learned that many "friends" were unsure about what to do. Hard-liners were anxious that some "friends" might respond positively to pressures for compromise.[80]

Contending with this torrent of advice and news, in addition to conversing with a multitude of visitors, Lincoln made crucial and far-reaching decisions—and he held to them with a powerful tenacity. Asserting that all his positions on political matters had been widely reported in newspapers and other publications, he rejected any public declaration of his intentions. That avowal he repeated time and again to any and all who suggested he should make some kind of announcement.[81]

The one time he deviated from this conviction had only confirmed his belief that it was better not to speak before he took office—in mid-November, Lincoln had made his sole attempt at a public pronouncement. In a speech Lyman Trumbull gave in Springfield only two weeks after the election, he incorporated a contribution from the president-elect, who sat on the stage. Secessionists were "in hot haste to get out of the Union," Lincoln wrote, because they knew they could not much longer frighten southerners with a Republican administration. As soon as southerners recognized that he and Republicans posed no threat to the South, unionists there would arise and overthrow the disunionists. Lincoln even included a sentence, omitted by Trumbull, that the southern unionists would use their opponents' military preparation to defeat them.[82]

The reaction to Trumbull's effort matched Lincoln's expectations. Friends liked it; foes did not. Lincoln thought the trial just as disastrous as he feared, and he pledged not to do it again. Privately, he asked if any previous opposition newspaper used the speech "to quiet public anxiety?" A disgusted Lincoln noted what should not have surprised him. Partisans used Trumbull's remarks for partisan purposes. "These political fiends," Lincoln roared, "are not half sick enough yet. 'Party malice and not public good' possesses them entirely. 'They seek a sign and no sign shall be given to them.'" Henceforth, Lincoln said nothing publicly.[83]

On the territories he maintained a similar silence before the public, but in private he did not camouflage his position. To political confidants he left no doubt. To his private secretary he made it clear that he would consider no measure that even hinted at expanding slavery. "Let there be no compromise in the question of *extending* slavery," he instructed Senator Trumbull. The same admonition went to Congressman William Kellogg of Illinois: "Entertain no proposition for a compromise in regard to the extension of slavery." The thought that any Republican would even contemplate territorial compromise appalled him. To do so would mean "demoralizing themselves."[84]

Defending his adamant stance, Lincoln repeated two basic points. First, he insisted that territorial compromise would upend the Republican triumph. Victory would become defeat. Douglas would once more bring forth his popular sovereignty; both man and doctrine Lincoln bugaboos. Then, he contended, Republicans would have to confront a revival of filibusters, pro-southern adventurers who mounted extralegal military ventures in foreign countries, invading places like Mexico, Central America, and the Caribbean islands. Second, such a compromise, Lincoln preached, "acknowledges that slavery has equal rights with liberty." That eventuality he could never accept. Thus, his command to his congressional troops: "Stand firm. The tug has to come, & better now, than anytime hereafter."[85]

Thus, early on Lincoln made his stand, and from it he did not budge. Lining up with his party's hard-liners, he rejected the legacy of his political hero, Henry Clay, the Great Pacificator. Lincoln always praised Clay extravagantly, declaring him "my beau ideal of a statesman."[86]

Perhaps Lincoln's best-known remarks on Clay came in the eulogy he delivered in Springfield on July 6, 1852, only a week after Clay's death. In it, Lincoln praised the Kentucky statesman for "his leading and most conspicuous part" in devising sectional compromise. At the same time Lincoln underscored that "as a politician or statesman no one was so habitually careful [as Clay] to avoid all sectional ground. Whatever he did he did for the country." Showering adulation on Clay for his willingness and ability to work with political opponents as well as allies, Lincoln highlighted his main point, that Clay "engaged his whole energies" on behalf of the Union. As late as February 1861, Lincoln professed, "During my whole political life, I have loved and revered [Clay] as a teacher and leader."[87]

In his acclamation at Springfield, Lincoln also noted Clay's opposition to slavery. For Lincoln that antislavery stance was vital, for as a sincere opponent of slavery, he could never embrace as his hero any man identified as proslavery. Several times thereafter Lincoln took care to point to Clay's detestation of slavery and particularly his opposition to the institution's spread. Although Lincoln did not invent an antislavery Clay, he overlooked and downplayed his paladin's willingness to moderate his stance.[88]

Without doubt Clay, though a slaveowner, did detest the institution, even striving unsuccessfully for Kentucky to adopt gradual emancipation. Clay also said he could never support forcing slavery into any area where it had not previously existed. Yet in 1850, referring specifically to the Mexican Cession, he declared that if the citizens there placed slavery in their constitutions, he would honor their choice. And Clay did back the Compromise of 1850, which left open the possibility of slavery in the New Mexico and Utah territories. For Clay no other moral issue, slavery included, matched in importance the maintenance of the Union.[89]

Lincoln, too, spoke about compromise, and initially did not turn from it. By his own account he treasured the Missouri Compromise, and he publicly stood for the Compromise of 1850. In fact, in his first major address attacking the Kansas-Nebraska Act for overturning the Missouri Compromise, Lincoln sounded very much like Henry Clay himself. Announcing, "I, too, go for saving the Union," he avowed "much as I hate slavery, I would consent to the extension of it rather than see the Union dissolved, just as I would consent to any other evil, to avoid a greater one." In the late 1850s, however, such declarations disappeared, though as late as 1858 he indicated his acquiescence in the Compromise of 1850.[90]

Lincoln received the Republican nomination for president in 1860 in large part because he was perceived as more conservative, thus more electable, than Seward. Yet a closer look would have cast considerable doubt on this assumption. In his widely distributed "House Divided" speech of 1858, Lincoln had explicitly pronounced that the country "cannot endure permanently half *slave* and half *free*." In substance, the "house divided" and the "irrepressible conflict" closely tied to Seward meshed perfectly; they were synonymous. One great difference did exist, however. Far more prominent in 1860 than Lincoln, Seward had been the eminent spokesman of antislavery politics for a decade. As far back as 1850 he had condemned any territorial compromise, calling on a higher law than the Constitution. For Republicans hungering for victory, Seward had simply been in the public eye for too long. He was passed over.[91]

When the crisis that erupted after Lincoln's election led to a discussion within the Republican camp on how to respond, Lincoln unequivocally opposed compromise even as the Union came apart. He absolutely did not adopt a Clay-like stance. Why he broke so sharply from Clay's heritage does not have a simple answer. Yet, the historical record does permit reasonable explanations. That evidence leads to three central motives: his ignorance of the South, his vigorous partisanship, his visceral antislavery commitment.

Lincoln's lack of understanding about the South was formative. Dismissing the seriousness of secession and looking on it as a conspiracy plotted by a small band of radicals soon to be put down by sensible Union men like himself. Lincoln found no other explanation possible. As he saw it, the drive for secession certainly had nothing to do with anything he or his party had said or done. That conclusion leads one inescapably to two observations. First, he clearly rationalized his House-Divided declaration, for in it he bluntly told southerners that the Union of the future had no place for their central economic and social institution. Moreover, the irrepressible-conflict scenario embraced by the Republican left did likewise. Could Lincoln have been tone deaf to how southerners would hear such assertions? He must have been, for he told a Kentuckian that neither he nor any other "prominent Republican had justly made himself obnoxious to the South by anything he had said or done."[92]

Lincoln evidently never stopped to think how he would have reacted to a responsible southern leader publicly maintaining that free states had no place in a future Union. Yet, he did react forcefully to what he claimed was a plot to nationalize slavery. In his rhetoric that goal was part of the Slave-Power conspiracy. Even though on the stump Lincoln struck out against this specter, even suggesting that the United States Supreme Court intended to make Illinois a slave state, no important southern politician ever advocated such a cause.[93]

It also appears indisputable that he assumed such a stance because he knew so little about the South. Yes, at nineteen and twenty-two he had taken brief trips down the Ohio and Mississippi rivers to New Orleans. Additionally, he was born in Kentucky and his wife came from a slaveowning family in that state as did his best friend, Joshua Speed. But that part of the Border South was all that he knew. After his two youthful journeys to New Orleans, he never traveled in the South beyond Kentucky. Aside from a few Kentuckians, he really did not know any southerners, certainly not any southern politicians. He had in the late 1840s served one term in the United States House of Representatives where he surely met southerners, became friendly with a few, and participated with an informal group known as the Young Indians, dominated by five congressmen from the South, that backed General Zachary Taylor for the Whig presidential nomination. But that was almost a decade and a half before the crisis he faced following his victory in 1860. In the interval he had kept up with none of those men. Fundamentally, he had no friends who could educate him about the South and southern politics.[94]

The record indicates that Lincoln's image of the slave South basically matched the common abolitionist and fervent antislavery depictions. In this South, rich planters dominated society and politics, in 1860–1861 agitating for secession and cowing non-slaveholding whites. Lincoln appears to have had no understanding either of the widespread ownership of slaves among whites or how deeply slavery had become embedded in southern society. Instead of comprehending that the overwhelming majority of southern whites were committed to their slave society, it seems that Lincoln thought of them as conservative Unionists with little attachment to slavery. In other words, they were like him, though probably without his moral outrage at slavery. Perhaps the mass of southern whites could not or would not act against slavery, but he could imagine them neither proslave nor on their own acting against the Union. A South where non-planters, even non-slaveowners, had an influential voice, feared Republicans, and actively supported secession was both foreign and unknown to Lincoln. When a visitor in November urged Lincoln to reassure southerners honestly alarmed by the Republican triumph, his reply spoke volumes—"There are no such men."[95]

When referring to the famous epistolary exchange between Lincoln and Alexander H. Stephens of Georgia in November and December 1860, writers have often described them as friends. This is surely an exaggeration, for the two men only saw each other during the sessions of the 30th Congress and had not been in touch since early 1849. In his request on November 30 for a copy of Stephens's address to the Georgia legislature, Lincoln stated that he had seen newspaper accounts. Responding, Stephens said they were substantially correct.[96]

One wonders how carefully Lincoln had read the speech. Yes, Stephens did deplore the rush to secession just because Lincoln had been elected. At the same time, however, he left no doubt about his opinion of the Republican party. "If the policy of Mr. Lincoln and his Republican associates shall be carried out," he announced, "no man in Georgia will be more willing or ready than myself to defend our rights, interest, and honor at every hazard and to the last extremity." Defining that policy, Stephens highlighted a congressional prohibition of slavery from the common territory. Of course, for Lincoln, that restriction was the primary Republican mission. Stephens urged Georgians to delay, not because he found the Republican program acceptable or because he would acquiesce in it, but because, he argued, the Congress, controlled by Democrats, along with the federal judiciary would thwart Lincoln. He predicted an enfeebled Lincoln presidency that could do the South no harm.

The four letters the men exchanged certainly have a civility about them, with each assuring the other of his respect. Stephens drew empathetic attention to Lincoln's massive burden, telling him, "No man had heavier or greater responsibility resting upon him than you have in the present momentous crisis." Trying to be conciliatory and reasoning, Lincoln, on December 22 in a letter marked "For your eyes only," stated that he "appreciat[ed] the present peril." He also told Stephens that the South had nothing to fear from him or a Republican administration. Word even came to Stephens indirectly that Lincoln called him "a great man." Still, Lincoln did recognize that he and Stephens differed on the "right" and "wrong" of slavery.

In his second letter, on December 30, Stephens emphasized, "Personally, I am not your enemy—far from it. . . . " He then called on Lincoln to do what he could "to save our common country." But Stephens was also pointed. Southerners worried, he wrote, that the Republicans' "leading object seems to be simply, and wantonly, if you please, to put the institutions of nearly half the states under the ban of public opinion and national condemnation." He connected that object to "the influence of fanaticism," which he saw influencing the Republican party. Yet the Georgian concluded that "a word fitly spoken by you now would be like 'apples of gold in pictures of silver.' " To this entreaty Lincoln did not reply.

With no firsthand knowledge of the South and having no real friends or even serious acquaintances among the southern politicians, Lincoln unsurprisingly did not acknowledge the distinction between fire-eaters, the zealous advocates of secession, and men like Stephens and even Jefferson Davis who were fundamentally conservative with no relish for disunion. Lincoln appears not to have understood the political force pressed by the fire-eaters on southern conservatives and regulars.

While Lincoln's ignorance of the South powerfully influenced his adamant opposition to compromise, his actions also made clear that he approached the crisis not as president-elect of the United States, but as leader of the Republican party. Moreover, by November 1860 he had spent but a few months as party chief. That brief tenure left him unsure about the security of his leadership and anxious about party unity. During the crisis many Republicans and non-Republicans alike urged him to make a public statement addressing the issues, reassuring southerners of their rights and his determination to be president of all Americans, southern as well as northern. Time and time again Lincoln refused.[97]

Responding to this cascade of requests, Lincoln embraced a mantra: "I could say nothing which I have not already said, and which is in print, and open to inspection to all." "*Repetition*," as he phrased it, could only harm his political position. In his inflexibility, he seemed not to fathom that the most vigorous rhetoric in some of what he had already said could terrify the South. Additionally, never did Lincoln acknowledge that every one of those statements had been made as a Republican partisan, not as the next president of a country. Furthermore, none of those declarations had been made when the country faced a monumental crisis.[98]

No group begged more for Lincoln to speak out than Border-state Conservatives. Facing the emotion-laden tidal wave generated by disunionists, they lamented that they had "no foothold to fight the Secessionists." One urged a close friend of Lincoln to remind the president-elect (and Lincoln did get this message) that unless "something [was] done within the next thirty days to avert the tide of passion in the South, he will be inaugurated on the 4th March as the Prest of a divided empire." These pleaders entreated Lincoln to come before the public while he could still do some good. "In heaven's name," a Kentuckian cried, "in the name of & for the salvation of our common, beloved Country, *can* you not do, say, *Something* to calm the storm now threatening us all."[99]

No one made a more thoughtful plea than an antisecessionist congressman from North Carolina, John A. Gilmer. Like most of his comrades a former Whig, Gilmer was a successful attorney, had served in his state legislature, and upon reaching Congress in 1857 rapidly became a leader of the southern opponents to the Democrats. Of medium height, with "a full round face," "strong compact form," and engaging personality, Gilmer had a knack for winning friends. Even some Republicans found him persuasive and sympathetic.[100]

On December 10, Gilmer wrote Lincoln. Admitting that he and his constituents had tried to defeat Lincoln, he invoked "the present perilous condition of the Country—threatening the destruction of the Union must be my excuse for the unusual liberty I take in writing this letter." "If by any fair measure possible," he wanted to maintain the peace and secure the constitutional rights of all Americans. His chief goal was "to have allayed, if possible, the apprehension of real danger and harm to [southerners] and their peculiar institution which have seized the people of my section."[101]

To that end Gilmer posed a number of specific questions. He wanted to know Lincoln's opinion on matters ranging from the Fugitive Slave Law to the admission of new slave states. He even asked about Lincoln's intentions regarding the agitation of the slavery issue through either policy or appointments. Finally, Gilmer came to the most contentious issue. How would Lincoln recommend settling "the disturbing question of slavery in the territories?"

Closing, Gilmer wrote, "I address you from pure motives." He hoped "a clean and definite exposition of your views" would "go far to quiet, if not to satisfy all reasonable minds." Gilmer confided that he believed "more misunderstanding than difference" separated Republicans and southerners. He was certainly convinced that the differences were "more abstract than useful." "A generous and patriotic yielding on the part of your section, now so largely in the majority," Gilmer pled, "would, on the one hand, be a mere sacrifice of opinion, and, on the other, the preservation of the best Government that has ever fallen to the lot of any people."

Lincoln took Gilmer seriously. That he replied at some length confirms that conclusion, though because his response went through an intermediary, it took extra time to reach Gilmer. At the same time, Lincoln marked the letter "Strictly confidential"; it was not, as Gilmer wished, for public distribution. The president-elect simply repeated that his positions on important political matters were already before the public. To Gilmer, however, Lincoln was direct. He answered the queries in a manner that could only have pleased Gilmer. He said he would not recommend the abolition of either slavery in the District of Columbia or the interstate slave trade. Additionally, he declared that he had no problem with employing slaves in federal arsenals and dockyards. He also indicated that he had no plan as a matter of policy to exclude slaveowners from patronage appointments. On the fugitive slave question, he gave no support to state laws that conflicted with the fugitive slave provision of the Constitution.

There was, however, a critical exception to these satisfying responses, one which Lincoln termed "the only substantial difference between us." "On the territorial question," Lincoln answered, "I am inflexible." He pointed to the Chicago platform and the published record of his 1858 debates with Stephen A. Douglas. He would agree to no extension of slavery. Yet, "for this," Lincoln reflected, "neither has any occasion to be angry with the other."[102]

As his letter to Gilmer showed, Lincoln obviously never stepped forward publicly in an effort to conciliate alarmed southerners. If he had, given his unmatched gift for crafting the befitting phrases for a particular political moment, one might imagine his theme, if not his words. Such an address could have noted his recognition that he was not one of them and that he represented a party perceived by the multitude of southerners as their enemy. He would have quickly countered, however, we are all still

Americans, and during his presidency neither he nor his party would in any way try to harm the South. Not once did Lincoln ever say publicly that he would be president of all Americans. In wedding himself to the Republican platform and claiming he could never deviate from it, he acted like a partisan's partisan, not the leader of a country.

The critical question focuses on the why underlying his rigidity. The evidence strongly suggests that he feared alienating his party's most fervent antislavery zealots, the hard-liners. Lincoln constantly expressed concern that any serious compromise would fracture the party; he meant drive off the left. If that segment bolted because of sectional compromise, Lincoln worried the Republican party would disintegrate. That group did not, of course, encompass the Republican party. Undoubtedly, it was a minority, albeit an articulate, vigorous minority. The right and the center of the party clearly outnumbered the left.[103]

A suggestive approach to assess Lincoln's course concentrates on Seward, who looked favorably on compromise. Early on, considerably before Lincoln, Seward perceived the Union to be in mortal danger. Above all, he wanted to prevent its dissolution, if possible. Having been in Washington for the entire decade of the 1850s and knowing many southern politicians, he had a much better grasp than Lincoln of the political force of secession and the political reality facing moderate southerners. Then, he, along with Weed, believed the territorial issue had done its work, elected a Republican president. To them it was chiefly a political matter. With all the territory controlled by the United States already covered by existing law, they thought any chance of adding new land remote and certainly not taking place without Republican concurrence.[104]

Additionally, the two New Yorkers saw the Republican victory in no small part as a result of Democratic division. Because they judged, "the normal proclivities of the American people are Democratic," as well as "the issues of the late campaign are obsolete," they regarded new issues mandatory to maintain the Republicans in power. In 1864, a reunited Democratic party would cause trouble for the Republicans unless the party could expand. Seward wanted to reach out to the Unionists in the South, especially in the Upper and Border slave states. He identified with the very men begging Lincoln to help them fend off the secessionists. To Seward, bringing them into the Republican tent was not only possible but essential. Without question, a number of them, overwhelmingly former Whigs and

Constitutional Unionists in 1860, made clear their willingness to come into a party that focused on the Union, not sectional antagonism. No evidence suggests that Lincoln at the time conceived of a Republican future beyond the border of the 1860 party.[105]

As for the unity of the newly triumphant Republican party, Seward occupied different ground than Lincoln. Since the inception of the party and even before that Seward, as the major spokesman for antislavery northern Whigs, had been the evangelist of the irrepressible conflict. He had the standing to repel an assault from the Republican left, which would surely have come. Moreover, if a party opting for sectional compromise really distressed the hard-liners, where could they go? And even if the most radical bolted, the adherence of southern Unionists would offset their loss. Thus, for Seward the Republican party would become the great Union party, with a solid presence in the South, particularly in the Upper and Border slave states. Lincoln did turn to the Union party idea, but only after the shooting had begun. Before hostilities he absolutely did not.

Yes, Lincoln was ignorant of the South, and he viewed the crisis from a partisan perspective, but a third fundamental reason underlay his rejection of serious compromise. The evidence suggests that he had a much deeper, more visceral hatred of slavery than did Seward. Seward did abhor slavery, never giving it moral equality with freedom. Convinced, however, that the rapid population growth and geographic expansion along with the burgeoning economic power of the free states would naturally overpower slavery, he was willing to let the institution and the southern political strength based on it become casualties of America's inevitable progress. Thus, after the territorial issue had accomplished its purpose in 1860, Seward was quite willing to shelve it.

Not so Lincoln—to him the territorial issue was never just about politics. To him it spoke about the nation, even if primarily as symbol. In his mind the nation must be about freedom, never slavery. That certitude had informed his important and well-known Cooper Union speech in February 1860. During the crisis itself in his confidential letters to John Gilmer and Alexander Stephens, Lincoln maintained that he could find no serious disagreement with them, except on one fundamental matter. Both southerners thought slavery right, and he considered it wrong. And he used the words "right" and "wrong."[106]

Those expressions had powerful antecedents. As early as 1850 Lincoln told a former law partner that "the slavery question can't be compromised." That was a logical statement for a man who described the sight of shackled slaves as "continual torment to me." He compared slavery and freedom to "two wild beasts in sight of each other, but chained and held apart. Some day," he predicted, "these deadly antagonists will one or the other break their bonds, and then the question will be settled." A key reason for his adamant opposition to Stephen A. Douglas, he avowed, was that Douglas "don't care whether slavery is voted up or down, but God cares, and humanity cares, and I care." To his Springfield pastor, Lincoln described slavery as "the evil out of which all other national evils and dangers have come." "It must be stopped," he vowed. Thus, faced with a decision to accept a compromise that would in his mind attach slavery even more securely to the country by permitting even its theoretical expansion, he said never.[107]

Lincoln's stance did not signify that he aligned with the abolitionists. He never advocated any move against slavery in states; time and again he declared that the federal government possessed no such power. With his deep commitment to the Constitution, he could say nothing else, for he believed the Constitution left the power over slavery to the states. For the vast majority of northerners to move against the institution in a state was both unlawful and unconstitutional. As a man with an abiding faith in the law, he simply could not countenance any direct assault on slavery where it existed. But by equating the territorial issue with the institution of slavery, Lincoln found a way past that constitutional barrier. Slavery, he pronounced, must remain within its borders. In that fashion he could place the evil in a permanent stockade.[108]

CHAPTER THREE

"The Prospects for the Country Are Gloomy"

ALTHOUGH DETERMINING HIS response to the secession crisis occupied his attention, Lincoln also devoted considerable time and energy to building a cabinet. Because the Republicans had never controlled the executive branch, the jockeying and lobbying for a seat at the president's official table had a special intensity. For Lincoln, cabinet making did not take place in a separate political universe from deciding about compromise, because both were intimately involved in how he viewed the Republican party and its future. Moreover, in each instance he confronted contrary advice, often from the same different party perspectives. He did not complete his final lineup in December, but he did make fundamental decisions.

Seward and Weed wanted a cabinet in which Seward would have the dominant influence. When Seward received Lincoln's confidential offer of the State Department, he did not accept at once, telling the president-elect he needed to think about it. That statement really only marked time, however. Although Seward desired to know more about the makeup of the cabinet before he accepted or rejected the proffered first seat among the ministers, he had little choice. If his goal remained to exert substantial influence in the first Republican administration, and it surely did, he had to become part of it. Retaining his seat in the Senate would not provide equal access to the president or even to his inner councils.[1]

Discussing Lincoln's intentions regarding the cabinet was a major goal of Weed's mission to Springfield in mid-December. He also wanted to press for Seward-friendly appointees. He and Seward hoped for two results—a body predominantly Whig, almost to the exclusion of ex-Democrats, and preferably one with two southern Unionists.[2]

The first objective posed no mystery. Seward would have more sway with men who shared his Whig background than with those who did not, most of whom detested him. For Seward, the southern Unionists would serve two purposes. Chiefly, they would surely look to him for advice; additionally, their appearance would underscore the legitimacy of Seward's vision of a future Republican party.

The two New Yorkers considered John A. Gilmer an appropriate choice, but they also mentioned additional names to Lincoln. Other Republicans and some southern Unionists wrote directly to Lincoln, feeling no need for an intermediary. The numerous names mentioned included John Minor Botts and William C. Rives of Virginia, William A. Graham of North Carolina, Balie Peyton and Emerson Etheridge of Tennessee, and Randall Hunt of Louisiana. Even John Bell, who had been a presidential candidate, had champions.[3]

Seward's Republican enemies also pressed Lincoln. Even while they recognized the likelihood of his inclusion in the cabinet, they wished for his exclusion. This group included the hard-liner Senator Salmon P. Chase, a former antislavery Democrat; and Francis P. Blair, Sr., of Maryland, another ex-Democrat, patriarch of an influential family, including his sons Francis, Jr., a former congressman from St. Louis, and Montgomery, also of Maryland. Joining these ex-Democrats was Horace Greeley, editor of the *New York Tribune*. Although he had been a Whig and a former ally of Seward and Weed, by 1860 Greeley counted himself among their ardent antagonists. Greeley battled Weed for Republican supremacy in New York, though unsuccessfully. This anti-Seward group championed Chase and wanted a cabinet made up entirely of Republicans, overwhelmingly hard-liners, and strove to block any southern Unionists.[4]

Lincoln heard from all. Looking at his behavior from the time of the election two points became quite clear. First, he would make his own decision; he would be no man's agent. In Springfield, Weed found himself rebuffed, with no Seward-dominated cabinet forthcoming. Second, the president-elect decided upon an official family that would represent the party, with no one faction or wing controlling, but with hard-liners certainly included. Abraham Lincoln would stand at center.

Regarding the possibility of a southerner or southerners, Lincoln appeared open. Shortly after the election he confided to his law partner William Herndon that he wanted to place a southerner there "by way of placation." He discussed various possibilities with Weed and others. Lincoln worried, however, about whether a respectable southerner would accept his positions on controversial issues, stating unequivocally that he would not give on policy. He also wondered what an appointee would do if his state seceded. He indicated that he thought either Edward Bates, a conservative from Missouri, or Montgomery Blair of the hard-liner Blairs would suffice for the Border states, signifying that he saw no overriding political reason to placate Unionism on the Border. Yet after lobbying not only from Seward and Weed, but also from his close Illinois associate David Davis, Vice President–elect Hannibal Hamlin of Maine, and Senator Trumbull, he decided to appoint a southerner. Finally he settled upon John Gilmer, though the offer did not come with dispatch. Although Lincoln made certain decisions in December, he would not settle upon his official family until much nearer his inauguration. In the intervening weeks cabinet concerns as well as lesser patronage matters never went away; he dealt with them constantly.[5]

To Lincoln and other party chieftains, in policy choices on compromise and cabinet decisions the matter of power assumed centrality, power in both the party and the nation. Who would control the party and in what direction would he lead? By mid-December, Lincoln answered these questions with indisputable clarity. He would hold and wield power in the party, aiming it in the direction of his choice. Just as he did in the nominating convention in Chicago back in May, the junior Lincoln would supersede the senior Seward.

Thus, Seward had to decide on his own course, personal and political. To have any chance of influencing administration policy, he had to take the secretaryship of state. Moreover, he still thought that he could manage the crisis to salvage the Union, or, if not all of it, most of it. He feared nothing could hold the Deep South, certainly not without meaningful territorial compromise. But those seven states did not account for even half of the slave states. He was convinced a sane, steady hand, his own, could maintain an equilibrium that in a reasonable time and without armed conflict would have the Union whole once more. Doing so would require placing himself in a position where he could possibly sway Lincoln and tug on policy.[6]

At the same time, going into Lincoln's cabinet meant moving into a seemingly subordinate position. The cabinet Lincoln was constructing did not please him. A majority of his colleagues, though not all were yet known, would not be men who looked up to him. Moreover, on sectional compromise, he would have to support openly, at least for the time, a policy he had not chosen. Yet he had no other realistic choice. To break with Lincoln, the first elected Republican president, on the eve of the party's ascending to national power meant turning himself into a political outcast. No Republican would respect or follow a man who had willfully undermined the great victory. Moreover, Seward was no political zealot or ideologue. He would nail no ninety-five theses to any doors. He had always been an insider, able to find a way to get his hands on the lever of power. To make his vision for party and country reality he would have to sit by Lincoln, slowly, even indirectly, trying to win the president-elect/president to his side.[7]

When Seward left for Washington after his train ride with Weed, the editor reported to Lincoln that he could absolutely count on Seward. Acknowledging that the two leaders had not originally been in the same place politically, Weed underscored Seward's shift and new loyalty. "His thoughts have been so long and with such intensiveness in one direction that it requires a little time to avert the momentum of his Engine!," Weed wrote. "But he entirely concurs in the necessity of getting right, in all respects, ourselves, and then of holding others to the duty of obeying the laws." Seward had become a Lincoln man.[8]

The maneuvering for leverage and jockeying for power within the Republican party exemplified the struggle taking place within the country. All Republicans rejoiced in what Salmon Chase termed "the overthrow of the slave power." They congratulated themselves that Lincoln's victory signified the slipping away of the massive influence the South had wielded over the national government.[9]

Congressman Charles Francis Adams perceptively identified the powerful southern reaction to the Republican triumph dramatized in the sectional clash. "The question is one of *power*," he avowed. Recognizing political power in the nation as the central issue, Adams identified its loss as the South's "only true grievance." The South, as he so aptly put it, "want[ed] to continue to rule." Adams could perceive no effective palliative, for, in his judgment, "the true difficulty is incurable." The South had already fallen behind in population and economic might and now could not match the

North in political strength. To Adams this cosmic shift in national power "doomed" the South because it had forever lost its primacy.[10]

Although not every Republican shared Adams's certainty about the permanence of their success, everyone certainly intended to grasp their new authority. They had no intention of sharing it with their defeated political enemy. But, all did not agree on how to manage the transition to their reformed Union. Even though they disagreed on particulars, Adams, Lincoln, Seward, and the great majority of their compatriots in the party leadership hoped to guide the country through the crisis without armed conflict, while even that possibility did not phase a minority of hard-liners. All Republicans, though, insisted on a Union in which the South would now be politically subordinate.

Southern political leaders confronted a staggering turnabout. For the first time in the country's history, they had to face the reality that an essentially alien political party would control the executive branch of the national government. Moreover, during the previous generation every president from Andrew Jackson to James Buchanan had been either a southern slaveholder or a northerner with a network of southern friends and heavily dependent upon the South politically. Used to holding power themselves or having close confidants who did, southerners had no experience as an opposition or a minority. With the accession of Lincoln and the Republicans, the southerners suddenly had to adjust to both those conditions. For the fire-eaters this political state was a godsend. They could now proclaim that a political force not only non-southern but antisouthern directed things. They could not have devised a more favorable environment for their mission of breaking up the despised Union.

But many regular Democrats, especially in the Deep South, found the climate unnerving. In their states they had to deal with fire-eaters newly galvanized with a potent message emotionally delivered. Then they had to decide whether they could adjust to opposition, which really meant taking a defensive position to obstruct a Republican administration and Republican policies. They were not powerless, for with their northern colleagues they dominated the Senate and remained formidable in the House. Moreover, they could count the Supreme Court in particular and the federal judiciary in general as allies. Yet they would have to accept a political subordination they had never before experienced.

Additionally, they had to decide whether the Republican triumph heralded their permanent political demotion. Perhaps, as their northern comrades tried to assure them, the election of 1860 was an aberration, but perhaps not. If the former, they had to accept only a brief recess from power, but if the latter, permanent exclusion. They worried that 1860 flashed a North determined to keep them down. In this scenario, they read "of an active and dangerously hostile sentiment in the North, which threaten[ed] them with perpetual disturbance and possible destruction." They were aware of the Republican newspapers that *The New York Herald* described as "becoming more and more bitter in the tone of their belligerent manifestos, and in their vituperative advocacy of extremist measures to reduce the slave States to submission to the doctrines laid down in the Chicago platform."[11]

But there was even more. Should the future hold permanent subordination, what would that condition mean for Republican intentions and southern prospects? The offer of patronage from a Republican president could attract some southern whites, especially non-slaveowners. Some southern leaders feared an adverse impact on white southern unity on slavery. Officeholders beholden to a Republican president could result in what a number of southern politicians dreaded, "a free labor party in the whole South." The next step in this gloomy forecast could be an antislavery movement in the South.

In a message to his legislature, Governor Joseph Brown of Georgia was blunt. Should the Republicans gain control of the federal government, he predicted catastrophe. He foresaw "a portion of our citizens" bribed to accept patronage or "a hungry swarm of abolitionist emissaries" roaming through the countryside to disrupt slavery. Brown went on to envision the white South's greatest horror. These "inflammatory" evangels would "do all in their power to create in the South, a state of things which must ultimately terminate in a war of extermination between the white and black races."[12]

On the national level these men also had to contemplate what their relative powerlessness might mean. Surely a decline would occur in southerners' ability to protect their vital interests. Legislation to prohibit slavery in all territories, to restrict the interstate slave trade, to increase tariffs, could be forthcoming, as could a more active and interventionist federal government. Over time, the South would have less and less ability to stop or even to deter measures that it considered deleterious.

In mid-November this struggle for the southern heart and mind played out in a small Georgia town, the state capital. A sleepy rural hamlet in the state's old cotton belt, Milledgeville stirred with activity only when the legislature met. It was in session when news of Lincoln's election reached the village. Legislators spoke out on their sense of its meaning. Additionally, a legislative committee requested members of Georgia's political elite to come to the Capitol and during the evenings discuss the import of the Republican triumph. Their remarks spoken and written highlighted the fundamental choices southerners saw themselves encountering.[13]

Those in attendance included the luminaries of Georgia politics, with only Howell Cobb, who was in Washington, missing. Along with Cobb, Robert Toombs, the senior United States senator, and Alexander Stephens, recently retired from the House of Representatives, had dominated the state during the 1850s. Back in 1850 and 1851, they had been allies in steering Georgia away from sectional radicalism. Behind them came influential men like former governor Herschel Johnson and the sitting chief executive, Joseph Brown.

This time the triumvirate of Cobb, Stephens, and Toombs failed to agree on their state's proper course. At this early date Cobb, still in Buchanan's cabinet, did not take a public side in the Milledgeville debate, though his younger brother, the widely respected Thomas R. R. Cobb, gave a ringing pro-secession speech. The younger Cobb led off for the secessionists; then Toombs followed with a veritable blast for disunion. On the other side, Stephens spoke eloquently against hasty action and for careful thought. Herschel Johnson reinforced Stephens's appeal with a public letter.

Toombs and his allies made the vintage cry of immediatists: Republican victory signaled cataclysm for the South. Standing over six feet with broad shoulders, thick black hair atop a sturdy, reddish face, testifying to his affection for strong drink, an emotional Toombs tore into his subject. Never known for moderation in language or anything else, Toombs called for immediate secession. "Nothing but ruin will follow delay," he bellowed. The free states, he declared, had committed numerous acts of aggression against the slave states. Regarding Lincoln, Toombs had no doubt but that "he is elected by the perpetuators of these wrongs with the purpose and intent to aid and support them in wrong-doing." As for himself and his role, Toombs cried, "I ask you to give me the sword; for if you do not give it to me, as God lives, I will take it myself."[14]

Taking the entirely opposite tack, Stephens and his supporters emphasized what opponents of immediatism did everywhere. On the rostrum, Stephens was Toombs's antithesis. Although close personal friends, they differed sharply in appearance and approach. Physically Stephens seemed almost freakish; five feet seven inches tall but weighing under ninety-five pounds, he was practically skeletal. He had a small head with large ears, pallid skin, and straggly hair. Because of almost constant shivering, he wrapped himself in heavy garments. His appearance approached spectral. But his blazing black eyes contradicted any thought of an invalid. His powerful intellect, which helped him become an accomplished public speaker, overcame his disconcerting physical appearance.[15]

In his address Stephens stressed two points—first, that Lincoln had not yet done the South any harm; and second, that even if he wanted, he was powerless to do so. Southern power in Congress and the pro-southern and proslave federal judiciary would bar him. Stephens foresaw a weak, harmless Lincoln presidency. At the same time, he made clear his identity with the South in his utter rejection of the Republican program, specifically the prohibition of slavery in the territories. Moreover, he professed that should Lincoln actually try to move against southern rights and slavery, he would stand in the first line of defense. For him resistance was surely legitimate, but should come only when called for.

The rhetorical fireworks in the Capitol in Milledgeville did not immediately answer the question of whose lead Georgia would follow, Toombs's or Stephens's. Yet, the legislature did deem the circumstances sufficiently dire that the citizens of Georgia must make the ultimate decision in the only appropriate venue, a state constitutional convention. Then, the legislators set the convention for January 16, 1861, with elections for delegates to take place two weeks prior, on January 2.[16]

Those in Milledgeville and elsewhere who shouted about mortal danger had one overriding goal—immediate secession. Clearly, Georgia was not going to act promptly; the convention to decide what to do would not even take place until mid-January. Moreover, the palpable division on display at the Georgia capital left murky what course the state would eventually take. As a result, the eyes of Georgia secessionists focused on their eastern neighbor, South Carolina. If South Carolina would act promptly, then secession might become a reality in Georgia.

In their capital, Columbia, some hundred and fifty miles east of Milledgeville, the South Carolina fire-eaters angled for action. That the preelection explorations of Governor Gist and Robert Barnwell Rhett, Jr., had failed to turn up significant enthusiasm for immediate secession did not deter the Carolina radicals. With their legislature also in session, they hoped the emotional thunderbolt of Lincoln's election would spark their state to act. Even moderates commented on "the political passion of the people" aroused by the victory of "the awful abolition party." The postmaster in Charleston reported to the postmaster general in Washington, "We are in the midst of a Revolution which is advancing with unprecedented rapidity." In his judgment, it had already raced "far beyond the reach of any human influence." Still, the fire-eaters did not confront an unimpeded path to secession.[17]

While firm Unionists were practically nonexistent in the Palmetto State, many Carolinians remained chary of any rash move. Aware of a past leap that a generation earlier had left their state exposed, they demanded more concrete evidence that should South Carolina secede immediately and unilaterally, she would not once again end up isolated. Initially these cautionary men blocked rapid action. Vows by the fire-eaters that secret letters promised support from elsewhere failed to move them. Even public revelation of these missives failed to ignite them. The legislature seemed on the verge of foiling the radicals. The constitutional provision that required a two-thirds legislative majority for calling conventions of the people gave the minority of the wary a way to block the immediatists. And in the legislature they beat back the efforts of the Rhetts and their compatriots who wanted to hold a secession convention at the soonest possible moment, before the end of the year. In fact, the legislature took initial steps to follow the same path as Georgia, calling for a convention on January 15, 1861, with the election for delegates set for a week prior. The Senate and a House committee passed such a resolution. Postponing the secession convention for that long could have several different results: allow time for passion to cool, permit the opinion to take hold that the South should act as a unit, or even afford time for the possibility of a congressional settlement.

To South Carolina fire-eaters all these possibilities were anathema. They wanted immediate secession by their state, recognizing it as pivotal. Only South Carolina could move promptly. Any delay by their home state could mean the death of their great goal, destruction of the Union. They were convinced, and rightly so, that for secession to succeed, a single state must strike first. As Christopher Memminger, who would soon serve in the Confederate cabinet, made clear, "Our great point is to move the other Southern States before there is any recoil." To wait for a united South, even for a solid front of the Cotton States, they feared, meant to wait forever. They correctly believed that such unity would never occur without some overt act by the Republican administration. And that they never contemplated; they had always portended a more insidious course by the hated Republicans. Getting South Carolina out, however, meant to them that others would surely follow.[18]

When the legislature pushed the convention back to the new year, the radicals redoubled their efforts. First, they insisted that South Carolina had to secede or become a joke. William Henry Trescot, still in Buchanan's State Department, reminded his fellows that many in the national capital "laughed at little South Carolina," designating the state as "almost as large as Long Island, which is hardly more than a tailfeather of New York." According to Trescot, they depicted her like "a child who sulks and won't play." Congressman William Porcher Miles of Charleston declared that his state must not become disgraced, but rather demonstrate that "our pride is enlisted to prove" ourselves "not so poor, weak and destitute that we cannot hold" our "own in the great community of nations." These cries helped push undecideds and fence-sitters. On election eve the formerly equivocal United States Senator James Chesnut, Jr., announced for immediate secession should Lincoln win. Other doubters and straddlers, including congressmen, fell into line. In Charleston, on the day after Lincoln triumphed, Andrew Magrath, the federal district judge, removed his silken judicial robe, declaring his loyalty solely to his sovereign state. Immediately thereupon, the other leading federal officeholders, the collector of customs, the district attorney, the marshal, did likewise.[19]

Of the prominent political Carolinians, only United States Senator James H. Hammond kept his counsel. Brilliant, erratic, almost tortured by his own demons, Hammond had delivered a powerful speech favoring the Union back in 1858. Fire-eaters worried about his course. On November 6 one of them, a legislator and confidant of Hammond's, asked for the senator's opinions. Assuming his views would be requested, Hammond had been preparing a lengthy reply, which he addressed to the legislature but sent privately to his friend. That epistle frightened the radicals. Hammond declared, "I do not regard our circumstances in the Union as desperate." He insisted that a united South could as before protect itself in the Union.

He foresaw a failed Lincoln presidency, which would not harm the South and would send Lincoln back to Illinois after a single term. He inveighed against an "impolitic, unwise, and unsafe" effort by one state to break up the Union. This ringing pronouncement, which could have had a momentous impact, did not leave its recipient's possession.[20]

With a balking legislature, the radicals did not want Senator Hammond's bombshell before the public. They strove to show that if only South Carolina would secede, then others, especially Georgia, would follow. Georgia's participation was critical, for even if Alabama, Florida, and Mississippi went out, without Georgia, South Carolina would find herself fundamentally alone, cut off geographically from any other seceded state. Trying to assure waverers that Georgia would come through, the immediatists brandished news that Governor Brown had issued an enthusiastically received call for a convention. Additionally, word raced through Columbia that federal officials in Milledgeville and Savannah had resigned. Then even more exciting, if erroneous, information arrived that Senator Robert Toombs had tendered his resignation.

Following these thrilling reports and rumors, a fortuitous episode provided the radicals the igniter for their fervently desired explosion. On November 9, a distinguished delegation from Savannah arrived in Charleston to celebrate the long-awaited completion of the railroad linking the two cities. Following an extravagant banquet, leading Charleston fire-eaters invited some of the visiting dignitaries to address a large crowd. These Georgians, former Whigs and Unionists notable among them, aroused the already charged throng with denunciations of Yankees and cries for independence. Telegraph wires crackled with the tidings that the Georgians had pledged their state to join their sister state outside the Union. The next morning a special train carried a group of prominent Charlestonians headed by the just-resigned federal officeholders to Columbia. They traveled to urge legislators to hurry and act, emphasizing the raging popular "fire in the rear." They declared all danger had now fallen away; doubters could no longer doubt. Any doubters now automatically became Republican sympathizers, or even worse, abolitionists.[21]

In an astonishing turnabout the legislature unanimously embraced secession. Even those who still preferred delay kept silent. Only twenty-four hours after opting for a delayed convention, the solons voted to hold it a month earlier than planned, on December 17, with the election for del-

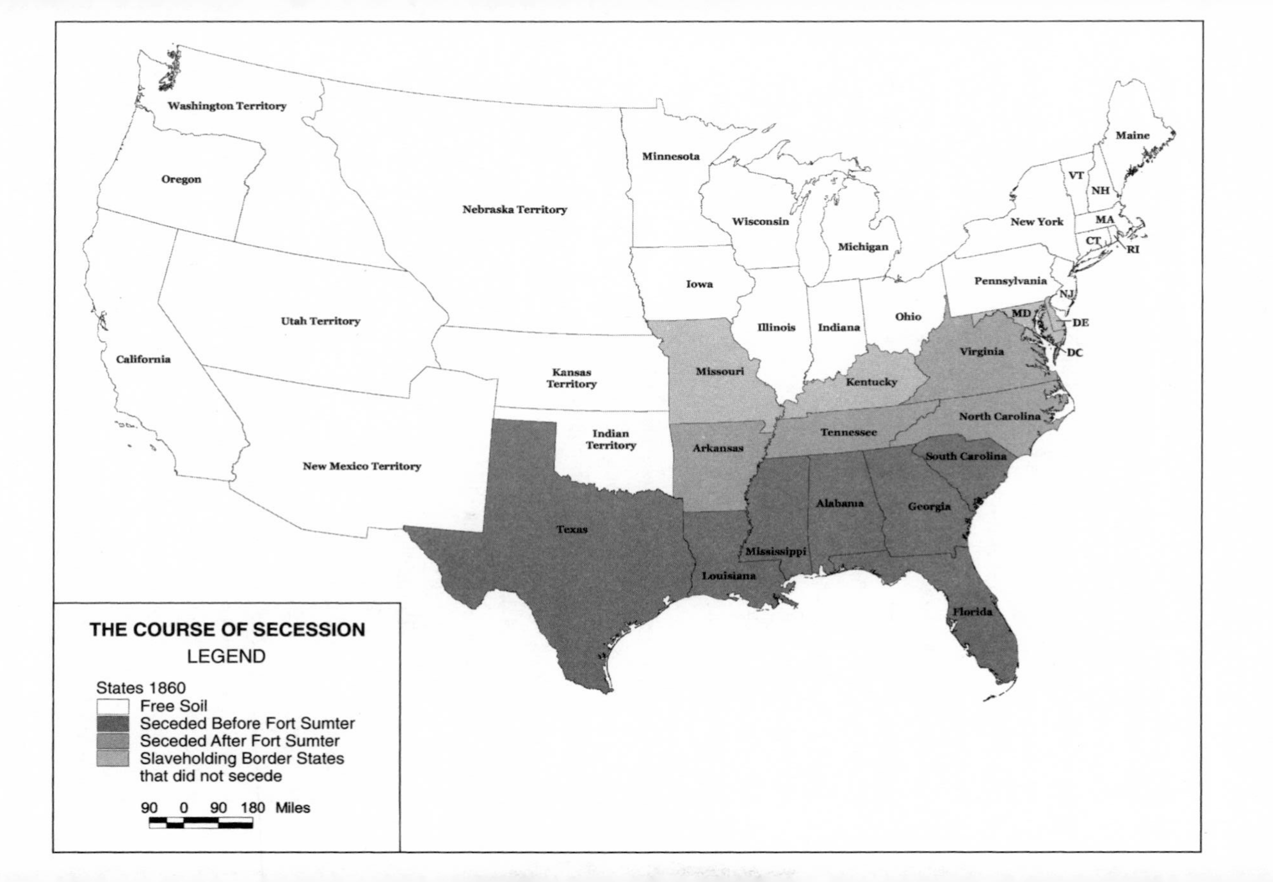
Washington Territory
Oregon
California
Utah Territory
Nebraska Territory
Kansas Territory
Indian Territory
New Mexico Territory
Texas
Minnesota
Iowa
Missouri
Arkansas
Louisiana
Wisconsin
Illinois
Michigan
Indiana
Ohio
Kentucky
Tennessee
Mississippi
Alabama
Georgia
Florida
South Carolina
North Carolina
Virginia
Pennsylvania
New York
Maine
VT
NH
MA
CT
RI
NJ
DE
MD
DC
THE COURSE OF SECESSION
LEGEND
States 1860
Free Soil
Seceded Before Fort Sumter
Seceded After Fort Sumter
Slaveholding Border States that did not secede
90 0 90 180 Miles

egates on the sixth. The tally underscored the triumph of the radicals—the House 117–0; the Senate 42–0. Two days later all the legislative procedures had been cleared. Neither did a political one remain. At the behest of a prominent legislator, Senator Hammond agreed to the embargo of his letter. Additionally, he immediately resigned his Senate seat. The state stood united. The radicals had conquered. The *Mercury* cried, "Gentlemen, hats off!—hip, hip, hip, hurrah! and hip, hip, hip, hurrah!—hurrah, hurrah, hurrah for the home we love!"[22]

The decision for an early convention, especially the unanimity behind it, signaled that South Carolina would almost certainly secede, and before Christmas. But elsewhere in the Deep South the signs were not so clear. To be sure, election and convention dates had been set, but all would occur in the new year. Reports of secessionist fervor cheered the fire-eaters. But, they remained anxious that before their goal of taking all the Cotton States out of the Union could be achieved, congressional action would stymie them. They feared Republicans would agree to a sectional compromise that would make reaching their objective of disunion beyond South Carolina much more difficult, if not impossible.

The fire-eaters thrived on their ability to portray Republicans as bestial hordes straining to stampede through the South. They applauded when Republicans like Hale and Wade hurled rhetorical broadsides at the South. There were no southern Republicans to counter such tirades. The future president and his congressional leaders did not match their own firebrands, but their idleness did nothing to mollify nervous southerners. They gave the fire-eaters a largely clear field.

In the Upper South and Border states "the greatest excitement and anxiety" captured the public mind. The general absence of fire-eaters, except in Virginia, meant less pressure for immediate secession. Still, the prospect of the Deep South seceding and the uncertainty of what Republican rule would mean stirred the region. A North Carolina Conservative decried "the confusion of the times" that precluded confidence in the proper course to follow. He described events moving so fast "that our most far seeing cannot penetrate the veil which shuts out from view the future."[23]

No Americans pushed harder for settlement of the national crisis than the Conservatives in the Upper South and along the Border. Leaders like John Pendleton Kennedy, as he informed the governor of Kentucky, saw their region as especially well positioned to be a "mediator" in adjusting the "disputed questions." In December, Kennedy even penned a lengthy pamphlet detailing why and how the Border should address the situation. He wishfully wrote that the Border states would "become the authoritative and controlling power to devise and establish the foundations of a secure and durable settlement." While men like Kennedy disliked secession, most rejecting it altogether, they wanted "the North to treat us with equality and justice."[24]

To that end they called directly on Republicans to adopt a policy that would mollify their states. "Much depends upon the Republicans," they told Republican partisans. They begged Republican leaders to understand that southerners needed reassurance because they genuinely feared Republicans' using their antisouthernism to rally the North against the South. In a letter the president-elect saw, a Kentuckian urged a close friend of Lincoln's to get him to act in such a manner as would "avert the tide of passion in the South." From Tennessee came direct advice to Lincoln. He should place a "card" in southern newspapers spelling out his position on matters critical to the South and declaring that he would be a national, not a sectional, president. Acknowledging that Lincoln had made many speeches, this correspondent said they would not suffice. He detailed why—some were too long; others were not readily available; many had been refracted through extra eyes. Now Lincoln needed a brief, powerfully worded statement.[25]

These Conservatives feared that Republican obduracy would have them in an untenable political position. "Conservative men are fast disappearing," a Virginian informed Senator Douglas. He continued, "The *defiant* position of the Republicans has scattered their forces, indeed driven them, or the most of them, into the ranks of the disunionists." Although he may have exaggerated the rush to the secessionist camps, he hit on a pervasive fear.[26]

With the Deep South seemingly on the independent tack led by South Carolina, the critical question confronting the Upper South and Border changed fundamentally. It was no longer whether to secede but whether to aid fellow southerners. Theoretically this question could stand forever without an answer, but realistically one would ultimately be required. On Christmas Day, a former Whig governor of North Carolina put to a friend the question that preoccupied so many: "Can it be possible that we shall never eat another Christmas dinner in the *United States*?"[27]

If in any way a seceded state and the Union came into confrontation, a decision would be forced upon the Upper South and the Border, a decision they did not at all relish. Condemning what he called "the ultra South" for "treating us badly," a Tennesseean lamented, "They go recklessly on regardless of our wishes, determined to precipitate themselves out of the Union and then to *drag* us out." "We entertain toward South Carolina the most bitter resentment," railed an antisecessionist Virginia newspaper. The Charlottesville *Review* accused South Carolina of "precipitately throw[ing] down the bulwark of the Union . . . with the full knowledge—aye, the intention—to hold Virginia and the border states between her and the Storm, and to carry out her caprices . . . while relying on them." In such an occurrence, all feared that civil war would be imminent. This alarm impelled the Upper South and the Border to reach out to Congress.[28]

In the House, after an auspicious start, the Committee of Thirty-three sputtered. The conciliatory Republicans could not use Dunn's resolution as an impetus. Several attempts were made to push forward, but all ran into the obstacle presented by a substantial Republican majority unwilling to budge on the territorial issue.

In December, the committee concentrated on two areas: fugitive slaves and the territories. Border members wanted Congress to induce northern states to repeal all laws hindering the enforcement of the fugitive-slave provision of the Compromise of 1850. After considerable discussion, on December 18, the committee decided to refer all matters relating to fugitive slaves to a subcommittee of five, all from the Border. Chairman Corwin appointed the group, four slave-state men along with Congressman William Kellogg of Illinois. Following this action the committee did not again bring up the fugitive-slave issue before the end of the year.[29]

On December 17, one of the two northern Democrats on the committee, John Burch of California, laid out a review of six measures, ranked by order of importance, that he said demanded the committee's attention in order "to restore peace to the country." These propositions, with congressional power over slavery in the territories listed first and the next two also dealing with the territorial question, only stated that the committee must address these matters, not that it approved them. Yet with Republicans unanimously opposed, Burch's proposal failed, 17 to 14.[30]

Slave-state members also strove to get the committee to adopt specific territorial compromises. Thomas A. R. Nelson of Tennessee and others rushed to get resolutions passed extending the Missouri Compromise line. Along with the extension they added what became a controversial phrase, specifying not only the lands already owned by the United States, but in addition, any the country might "hereafter acquire."[31]

It is easy to understand why southerners pressed on this point. In 1860, all other United States–owned territory aside from a portion of the Mexican Cession lay above the Missouri Compromise line, a considerably larger area than that to the south. That, of course, gave the North a great advantage. Moreover, from the colonial era to the mid-nineteenth century massive geographical expansion had marked the American experience. Most Americans did not expect their country's physical growth suddenly to stop. The South had taken part in the march to the Appalachians, to the Mississippi, and beyond. As Americans they wanted, even demanded, continued participation in that anticipated journey. Doing so was essential to maintain their political power and even more important to affirm their equality as American citizens.

Nelson's effort as well as all others was futile. They came to the same end as Burch's resolutions. By similar close votes, with the Republican majority unanimously opposed, they failed. Time and again the journal of the committee recorded the statement "without definite action the subject was postponed for future considerations."

Republicans ended up arrayed against any stratagem to settle the territorial question. In addition to their phalanx of opposition to territorial adjustment, they made several suggestions that would surely have complicated any additional territorial acquisition. One would have required two-thirds of the states registering approval; another stipulated two-thirds of the states in the Senate favoring and in the House two-thirds of the members. Yet, they never offered these qualifiers as negotiating points; instead they simply stated them.[32]

While stalwart in opposition, committee Republicans had difficulty uniting behind any positive measure. Although a moderate who had indicated a willingness to strive for an equitable solution to the crisis, Chairman Corwin provided little leadership. Despite his experience he did not step forward to advance either his own plan or anyone else's. He received no direct guidance from his party's two most notable leaders, for both Lincoln and Seward clung to their public silence. Moreover, the record contains correspondence from neither man to Corwin during the period.

In a December 11 letter Lincoln did warn Congressman Kellogg against any compromise, an admonishment that Kellogg could have passed on to Corwin.[33]

Within the committee some Republicans worried about "pale faces in our ranks," who might respond to pressures for compromise. Others said they feared their constituents' ire should they relent and accept a deal. Wavering did occur. On December 17, Kellogg presented a set of resolutions that essentially embodied popular sovereignty, but they went no-where. Four days later Republicans convened in a fruitless attempt to agree on policy. On that very day the committee adjourned for the Christmas holiday, not to reconvene until the twenty-seventh. Despite South Carolina's secession on December 20, the Republican majority clearly felt no sense of urgency.[34]

The single affirmative approach that generated almost unified Republican support came on Charles Francis Adams's resolution guaranteeing protection for slavery in the states where it existed, stating that any constitutional amendment designed to interfere with slavery in those states had to originate with one of them and that it could not become valid without the assent of every state in the Union. That limited step came after more than two weeks of deliberation. It did not even brush the most contentious case, slavery in the territories. Backing improbable procedures and embracing delay seemingly satisfied most Republicans.[35]

Even Adams, who, when the session opened, thought some kind of meaningful gesture warranted, changed his mind. He began to worry that too many of his colleagues might heed the blandishments of the compromisers. His opinion mattered, for he had assumed a leadership role on the committee, filling a void created by Corwin's lack of force. Although a first-term congressman and despite his reserved and charmless personality, Adams's name, as the son and grandson of presidents, his diligence, and his apparent moderation led to his prominence. Astute congressional observers like Senator Crittenden noted his growing influence.[36]

While Adams had no intention of supporting any territorial compromise, he did have two goals. As an Adams, the historical record mattered to him. In his view the Republicans must not rest on obstructionism. They must not be perceived as permitting the Union to break up over slavery. He also wanted to demonstrate that the Lower South desired to have the expansion of slavery "nailed to the Constitution," and if that failed, to dissolve the Union. Seeing no way he could meet that particular demand, he wanted to separate the Lower South from the remaining slave states. "I am yet in hope," he wrote, "that moderation and firmness may stay the border states."[37]

Adams believed he had found the issue he needed with New Mexico. New Mexico Territory had been carved out of the Mexican Cession as part of the Compromise of 1850. Regarding slavery, it had been created with popular sovereignty governing, meaning that it could either adopt or prohibit slavery. By 1860, although involuntary servitude had been legal for a decade, allegedly only a handful of slaves lived and worked there. That fact and discussions with a longtime resident of New Mexico convinced Adams that slavery had no viable future in the territory because New Mexico was geographically so inhospitable to the institution. Still, if promptly admitted to the Union, New Mexico would come in as a slave state, a status Adams was certain would be temporary.[38]

Thereupon, on December 29, Adams proposed the admission of New Mexico as a state, knowing that it would join the Union as a slave state. For him, this move would become his wedge to divide the slave states. Adams's initiative was not the first time statehood for New Mexico had been broached in the committee. Eight days earlier, Henry Winter Davis, a Know-Nothing from Maryland inclining toward the Republicans, had offered resolutions that would bring in New Mexico and Kansas as states, with the assumption that the former would enter slave, the latter free.

Although the committee adjourned for Christmas prior to any vote on Davis's submission, Adams saw it as "a cannon shot through the line" of the South. According to him, most southerners wanted a slave New Mexico with the extension of the Missouri line, which would put Congress on record affirming the expansion of slavery, rather than simply admitting New Mexico as a slave state. But, he was persuaded that the Border southerners looked with more favor upon the immediate admission of New Mexico with slavery. That action with Republican support would signify congressional willingness to admit a new slave state, signaling national acceptance of slavery, at least partially. The initial response did not confirm Adams's opinion. On first consideration Adams's resolution did pass, by 13 to 11, but four of the six slave state members voting said nay. Henry Winter Davis and Francis Bristow of Kentucky voted aye. Adams could hope that number would increase.[39]

By coming forward with New Mexico, Adams realized that he might alienate his stalwart antislavery constituents. "But," as he confided to his diary, "all public life is made of great hazards on trying occasions." And he did receive stacks of mail opposing any conciliatory gesture toward the South. Still, he felt sacrificing himself worthwhile if New Mexico could halt or even slow the rush to secession. Even while calculating the potential personal cost of New Mexico, however, Adams told a fellow Republican that he would not be "tenacious" on New Mexico. To him it was a ploy, which he would jettison if it threatened the unity of his party.[40]

Adams's stance on New Mexico, though by his own admission feeble, highlighted a sharp divergence on the expansion of slavery, not only in Adams's case, but also in many other Republicans'. If they were convinced slavery had no future in New Mexico, which took up much of the Mexican Cession east of California, and were willing to assist in its becoming a slave state, why did they take such an adamant position against extending the Missouri line? They continually spoke of allegiance to the Chicago platform, but it appears they genuinely feared giving the South something the South really wanted. Moreover, to them agreeing to territorial expansion entailed more significance for the future. Finally, a substantial number were clearly anxious about the health of the party. They worried that without powerful leadership behind it territorial compromise would fracture the party. Even to Adams, New Mexico was but a maneuver which he would abandon, if it endangered the party.

In their opposition to territorial compromise, Republicans fastened upon southern efforts to include any future territory acquired in the area below the Missouri line, which included Mexico, Central America, and the Caribbean islands. Objecting to any mention of future acquisitions, they denounced attempts to make a contentious issue of territory not belonging to the country. Yet, eliminating that particular element did not alter their stance.[41]

Republicans' professed distress about "hereafter" is difficult to understand. During the 1850s, under the Democratic administrations of Franklin Pierce and James Buchanan, when the South basically controlled national policy, no new territory was added, except for a small parcel bought from Mexico to improve a potential railroad route to the Pacific. Even extralegal efforts, known as filibusters, generally failed. If the South could not manage to secure new land under those conditions, no logical reason existed to believe southerners could succeed under a Republican administration. Additionally, Republicans in Congress were quite strong enough to block any treaty they disliked.[42]

The only reasonable conclusion is that focusing on "hereafter" provided Republicans a way to deflect their unwillingness to compromise on contemporary issues. "Hereafter" was not at all central. Republicans never indicated that dropping the provision would gain their backing for extending the Missouri line. At the time, congressional Republicans never bent on any territorial matter.

Republican tactics frustrated most southerners on the committee. The fire-eaters, of course, wanted no part of it. A Georgian spoke of "the stupidity of such an effort." Both William Boyce of South Carolina and George Hawkins of Florida requested the House to excuse them from service. Although the House turned them down, Boyce attended only one meeting and Hawkins none. Additionally, by the end of the month members from Alabama, Georgia, Louisiana, and Mississippi either departed or declined to participate further in committee deliberations. The Upper and Border South men, however, hoped for something, that Dunn's resolution would lead somewhere. They looked for what they never found—Republican agreement on a territorial deal, or at least movement toward one. They liked the amendment that essentially confirmed constitutional protection for slavery in the states where it existed, and New Mexico pleased some. But they really wanted a territorial settlement, which by late December seemed unlikely. Acknowledging committee inaction on that front, on the twenty-seventh Congressman Nelson withdrew his proposal to extend the line and offered the Crittenden Compromise, at that moment being discussed on the other side of the Capitol.[43]

On December 18 the Senate finally approved a resolution by Senator Lazarus Powell of Kentucky to create a select Committee of Thirteen to consider the crisis. Although Powell had introduced his proposal on the sixth, pointless and occasionally acrimonious debate, highlighted by Republican obstinacy, held up consent. Most Republicans wanted no special body. Speaking for the hard-liners, Senator Wade in lengthy remarks on the seventeenth had professed himself "totally unable to understand precisely what it is of which [southerners] complain." But on the next day, without a recorded vote, the Senate said yes to Powell's proposition, which directed the committee "to inquire into the present condition of the country, and report by bill or otherwise." Two days later Vice President Breckinridge as the president of the Senate appointed the members.[44]

Breckinridge's appointees included the most notable names in the Senate. Because Powell had written the resolution the vice president, following usual procedure, designated him chair. Likewise, because Democrats constituted a majority of the Senate, he chose more of them than Republicans. The most important northern Democrat, Stephen A. Douglas, led his region's Democrats, with William Bigler of Pennsylvania and Henry Rice of Minnesota. Southern Democrats included Jefferson Davis, probably the most influential man from his section, and Robert Toombs of Georgia from the Cotton States plus Robert M. T. Hunter of Virginia, and, of course, Powell from the Upper South and Border. William Seward headed the Republican contingent; joining him were Jacob Collamer of Vermont, James Doolittle of Wisconsin, James Grimes of Iowa, and Benjamin Wade of Ohio. Finally, there was John J. Crittenden, who shunned both parties, clinging to his revered Whiggery.

Crittenden's name became attached to the committee because he advanced the most comprehensive and far-reaching settlement. His package came as six amendments to the Constitution, chiefly because he wanted a permanent settlement of the "serious and alarming dissensions [that] have arisen between the northern and southern States, concerning the rights and security of the slaveholding States, and especially their rights in the common territory of the United States." Making his compromise part of the Constitution would remove the slavery question from partisan and electoral politics. In Crittenden's view doing so would "restore to the people that peace and good-will which ought to prevail between all citizens of the United States." Additionally, his territorial provisions, which would ban slavery in part of the national domain, contradicted the decision of the Supreme Court in the *Dred Scott* case, which held that Congress could not prohibit slavery in any territory.[45]

Crittenden tried to place a blanket over the slavery issue. First, he addressed the territories, specifying the extension of the Missouri line, with slavery prohibited north of it and "recognized as existing" south of it. Congress could not abolish slavery there during the territorial period. These provisions would also apply in any territory "hereafter acquired." When any territory attained the population required for a member of Congress, it could apply for statehood slave or free as it chose. And Congress could not deny admission to the Union because of that choice.

The second, third, and fourth resolutions dealt with the power of Congress in other venues. They declared that Congress could not abolish slavery on federal property within a slaveholding state, and that it could not end slavery in the District of Columbia as long as the institution existed in Virginia and Maryland, nor without the consent of the residents of the District or without the compensation to slaveholders who opposed any abolishment. Additionally, Congress could not interfere with the interstate slave trade whether conducted over land or water.

Number five addressed fugitive slaves. It empowered Congress to recompense slaveowners in cases where officers failed to capture fugitive slaves because of violence or intimidation. Furthermore, in the event Congress did pay, it could sue the county in which the forcible act occurred to recover the expended funds. Finally, the county had the right to sue those involved in preventing enforcement of the law.

The last resolution stipulated that no future amendment to the Constitution could affect the provisions of its five predecessors. Finally, it simply stated that the Constitution could not be amended to give Congress any authority to intrude on or abolish slavery in any state that permitted it.

To his suggested amendments, Crittenden appended four measures that he wanted Congress to adopt by joint resolution. Three dealt with fugitive slaves: affirming the constitutionality of the federal laws in place for the apprehension of fugitives; recommending that states repeal all statutes hindering the execution of the federal legislation; revising the fee structures of officials hearing fugitive slave cases so that no difference should exist whether they found for or against the claimant (as the law stood at the time, officials would receive five dollars if they found for the slave, but ten dollars if they found for the claimant). The final measure called for toughening the laws suppressing the international slave trade and their operation.

Despite the length and inclusiveness of Crittenden's constitutional and legislative bundle, one element absolutely overshadowed all else. As Crittenden knew, the territorial issue formed the core of the crisis. While debate and difference of opinion, both partisan and sectional, could and did occur in all other particulars, attention and intent concentrated on the territories. It was almost as if all other provisions disappeared. Handling the territories successfully would clear the road for all else. The Committee of Thirteen riveted its attention on the territories.

Before the Committee of Thirteen even began its deliberations, it adopted a critical procedural rule. For it to take any plan to the full Senate would require a majority not just of the committee but of both Republicans and other members. Jefferson Davis made the motion, which was accepted without discussion. Davis and other southerners felt this prescript essential, for Republican concurrence was critical for a meaningful agreement. Democrats by themselves could get legislation through the Senate, but not by the two-thirds majority necessary for constitutional amendments. Besides the arithmetic, for the southerners only a Republican commitment to a proposal they supported demonstrated Republican respect for southern rights.[46]

Senator Davis was central on the committee. Definitely a leader, the most respected and influential of the southern Democrats, his signing on to any measure coming out of the committee would have a powerful impact on the South, as would his opposition. Davis had not come to the committee enthusiastically. In fact, upon being named to it, he asked to be excused from serving. But then two days later he withdrew that request. The Senate again consented to his wish.[47]

Davis found the initial weeks of the session frustrating. He had arrived in Washington even before Congress convened, called to counsel President Buchanan on his message. He along with other southern confidants was dismayed when the president refused to countenance the constitutionality of secession. Then, in the Senate, Davis found little cause for hope that Republicans would recognize southern rights, as he and most other Cotton State Democrats understood them. A pessimistic Davis was quoted as saying, "No human power can save the Union." He even looked with disfavor upon his fellow Mississippian Reuben Davis (no relation) for agreeing to serve on the House's Committee of Thirty-three. On December 14, he joined other southerners in a public letter "To Our Constituents," proclaiming that "the argument is exhausted" because Republicans would "grant nothing that will or ought to satisfy the South." "The honor, and independence" of the South, these congressmen and senators continued, required secession by each state.[48]

When on the twentieth he declined appointment to the Committee of Thirteen, he seemed in step with his earlier position. But then two days later by his own request he was reinstated, recollecting his change of mind as "my willingness to make any sacrifice to avert the impending struggle." Davis was known as a stalwart champion of southern rights, but also as reasonable in sectional politics. A reporter for *The New York Herald* characterized him as "moderate, but firm." A Mississippi newspaper dubious about secession ran the headline "JEFFERSON DAVIS FOR MODERATION." Even a Republican congressman reported that his information did not locate Davis among the seceders.[49]

Davis surely did not want the Union dissolved, and he just as surely looked for some guarantee of southern rights. But the historical record does not permit an authoritative explanation for Davis's shift on serving on the Committee of Thirteen. Still, it appears that his hope for success in the search for something concrete from the Republicans stemmed from his relationship with William Henry Seward. Despite their partisan and ideological differences Davis and Seward had established a friendship based on mutual respect. In the winter and spring of 1858 when a devastating ophthalmological illness prostrated Davis for weeks, Seward visited the invalid every day and "sometimes oftener." Even in the aftermath of 1865, Davis's wife, Varina, commented on Seward's "earnest, tender interest," which she believed "unmistakably genuine." Furthermore, according to Varina Davis, Seward had told both her and her husband that much of what he said was for political effect. Specifically regarding slavery, Seward certified to the Davises that his antislavery rhetoric did not reflect his own views, but it was "potent to affect the rank and file of the North." That admission was not confined to the Davises, however, for in the midst of the crisis he made the same acknowledgment to the Virginia Conservative William C. Rives.[50]

Thus, with Weed angling for compromise and the uncertainty among the Republicans in Congress, it is logical that Davis would pin his hopes on Seward's guiding Republicans toward a settlement the Mississippian could accept. And Seward was on the Committee of Thirteen. Moreover, Seward had departed Washington for his fateful meeting with Weed, not to return until after the initial meeting of the committee. That Davis and Seward would have discussed the crisis seems most likely. That both men hoped Seward would come back willing to make a deal both could endorse is equally plausible.

Davis made it clear that he would support Crittenden or something comparable, as did the other non-Republicans on the committee. Senator Douglas had been working with Senator Crittenden to make compromise succeed. He backed Crittenden's proposal even though it did not include his cherished popular sovereignty. Even the avid secessionist Toombs said yes, not because he personally liked it, but because Georgians would accept it. With all seven Democrats on board along with Crittenden, the compromise had a clear majority of eight members of the Committee of Thirteen. Yet, for the committee to make a positive recommendation to the Senate required not that simple majority, but the agreement of a majority of Republicans as well.[51]

Before the committee got under way Crittenden had reason for optimism about his plan's chance for success, which did not lessen during deliberations. Not only did he have on his side Davis and Toombs from the Deep South, he also enjoyed the enthusiastic support of Border men and northern Democrats in Congress. They all seemed to agree with Governor Thomas Hicks of Maryland, who informed Crittenden that "in our extremity" Crittenden had an almost providential mission "to go forward in the important work of saving the country."[52]

Crittenden also received multitudinous signals of support from the North. Writing Crittenden that he had not met a single "conservative and Union-loving man" who did not back his resolutions, August Belmont went on to bemoan "the handful of Puritanical fanatics and selfish politicians" bent on destroying the country. Crittenden was told that three-quarters of the states would eagerly ratify his amendments. Even former president Martin Van Buren, who had conversed with Crittenden in New York City, affirmed his general support for the Kentuckian's propositions. From Boston, Crittenden's longtime friend the former Whig leader Robert C. Winthrop applauded his old comrade's advocating "such measures as were essential to rescue us from disunion and civil war."[53]

Crittenden's mail, however, did not contain choruses or pledges from any notable Republican figure. Uncertainty marked the Republicans in Washington. A number, albeit unknown, appeared amenable to a settlement. A hard-liner congressman and confidant of the president-elect told him, "We are not out of danger of a compromise." Writing Lincoln, a friend in Washington worried about the "great numbers of our friends afflicted with secession panic." Party members spoke about the possibility of embracing popular sovereignty for the territories. John Sherman in the

House broached the idea of admitting all territories immediately as states. In their unsettled environment the conclusion reached by yet another Lincoln correspondent struck by all the "excitement" pointed toward a great truth: "God only knows what a single day may bring forth under such influence." Yet, a New York representative relayed to Thurlow Weed a possible prognosis: "Should he [Lincoln] lead off on some reasonable and practical plan, it would have great weight and decide the course of many who are now passive and in doubt as to what should be done."[54]

While Republicans in Washington struggled for clarity in their murky surroundings, Lincoln, in Springfield, who knew of their predicament, awaited another important visitor. This caller was not another Republican notable, however. President Buchanan had decided to invite his successor to come to the national capital and join him in searching for a settlement or to agree on settling the crisis by amending the Constitution, not necessarily by accepting a particular compromise. The president had concluded that attempts to forge a congressional compromise would either come too late or fail entirely. He also did not think that Lincoln would suddenly announce that he favored the Crittenden Compromise or something similar. To deliver his invitation he sent sixty-nine-year-old Duff Green, a native Kentuckian and an experienced political hand who was also an acquaintance of Lincoln's. In fact, Green was married to a sister of a Lincoln brother-in-law. Politically, the tall, slender Green had been an ardent supporter of Andrew Jackson, editing the original Jackson organ in Washington, but as a John C. Calhoun loyalist and an in-law—a son was married to a Calhoun daughter—his allegiance to the Democratic party ended with the Jackson-Calhoun split. Later he sympathized with the Whigs and served in several diplomatic posts.

Green and Lincoln met on Friday, December 28. Following Buchanan's instructions Green asked the president-elect about amending the Constitution to pacify the South. On the night of his interview, Green reported to the president that Lincoln said, "The question on amendments to the Constitution and the questions submitted by Mr. Crittenden belonged to the people and states in legislatures and conventions, and that he would be inclined not only to acquiesce, but to give full force to their will thus expressed."

Lincoln requested Green to call again the next day for a written statement, which Green intended to telegraph to Washington. The president's emissary had interpreted Lincoln's initial remarks positively. Although Lincoln did pen a letter on Friday night, he did not hand it to Green on Saturday morning. Evidently he had changed his mind, or more likely his oral response had been more ambiguous than Green had recounted. Instead, he sent Green away with no written document. He had prepared a message for Green, but it was enclosed in a letter to Senator Trumbull.

In that reply Lincoln totally rebuffed the Buchanan-Green overture. He told Trumbull that Green had endeavored to draw a memorandum from him; he said he had prepared one that he was sending first to Trumbull and that he believed "could not be used to our disadvantage." Lincoln stated directly, "I do not want any amendment to the Constitution," though he hastened to add that if any of Crittenden's amendments ever reached the states, he would agree that the American people had the right to express their will. At this point Lincoln backed away from his earlier proposal to Weed regarding a constitutional amendment guaranteeing slavery. Even though he repeated that each state had the "inviolate" right to "control its own domestic institutions," he clearly did not want to be identified with any new constitutional sanction for slavery. Additionally, he denounced "lawless invasion, by armed force, the soil of any State or Territory, no matter under what pretext, as the gravest of crimes." Then, he informed Trumbull that he would only countenance publication of the epistle to Green if one half of the senators from Alabama, Georgia, Florida, Louisiana, Mississippi, and Texas also signed it. In closing, he added a potent qualification: "If, on consultation with our dearest friends, you conclude that it may do harm, do not deliver it." Trumbull killed it; Green never saw it. Nor did Buchanan ever get any word from Lincoln via Green or anyone else.

Although Green's journey and his meeting occurred in secrecy, early in January he made the entire episode public in a letter to *The New York Herald* detailing his mission and how it ended. To Lincoln, he wrote privately, "I regret your unwillingness to recommend an amendment to the constitution which will arrest the progress of secession."[55]

Lincoln, of course, had already made his fateful decision. Green's arrival did nothing to alter his adamant opposition to any far-reaching settlement. He had so instructed his allies in Congress just as he had sent Weed away empty-handed. By the time Seward returned to Washington, no Republican could doubt party policy as laid down by the president-elect. In his diary Charles Francis Adams underscored the new certitude. The clarity of

Lincoln's "declarations," he wrote, "have had the effect of perfectly consolidating the Republicans."[56]

The Committee of Thirteen sat for the first time on December 22, while Seward was still en route to Washington. After agreeing to Jefferson Davis's motion on double majorities, the senators turned directly to the Crittenden Compromise. Following several hours of discussion in which everyone took part, a vote was held. Republicans preferred to wait for Seward's return, but because no one knew exactly when he would appear, his colleagues finally agreed to an immediate ballot. For the first time in this session of Congress a territorial compromise came to a vote. The Republicans presented a solid front, all saying no.

When Seward showed up for the next meeting, on December 24, he made quite clear that his party would not yield on the territorial issue. Obtaining permission to record his position on the ballot already taken, he placed his negative alongside his colleagues'. Every Republican voted against every significant feature in Crittenden's Compromise. Then, Seward introduced three resolutions, though not those Lincoln had given to Weed, except for the unwritten one. Seward presented all as his own. The first, following the president-elect's oral guidance to Weed, would not permit the alteration of the Constitution to allow Congress to interfere with slavery in any state that sanctioned the institution; another would have Congress grant a jury trial to accused fugitive slaves; a third would request states to repeal all statutes obstructing enforcement of the Fugitive Slave Law of 1850. None of these even touched on the territories. In a letter home on that very day, Seward noted the import of the Republican stance: "We came to no compromise; and we shall not. We shall, therefore, see the fuller development of the secession movement." He had done Lincoln's work.[57]

That unified Republican standing did not mean, however, that the committee disbanded straightaway. The opposite occurred. Strenuous efforts were continued by those hoping to prove Seward's prediction wrong, with the Democrats, chiefly the northerners, leading the way. Immediately upon the demise of the Crittenden Compromise, Senator Douglas put forward resolutions highlighted by his long-cherished idea of popular sovereignty for the territories. Although he had striven to obtain aid from conservative southerners like Alexander Stephens and moderate northerners like his fellow Democrat August Belmont and former president Millard Fillmore, Douglas's overture moved neither southerners nor the Republicans on the committee. Robert Toombs and Jefferson Davis tried to get approval for southerners' property rights, including slavery, in the territories. Unsurprisingly, Republicans vetoed their attempt. From Senator Bigler came suggested constitutional amendments that would divide all territory on the Missouri line, with eight free territories north of 36°30' and four to the south. All would later be admitted as states. This offering went down without a recorded vote. Through all the ballots on the resolutions and amendments thereto, the Republicans formed an impenetrable square, repulsing any assault that even suggested the possibility of slavery moving into any territory.[58]

Then, on December 28, came a proposal from an entirely different direction. Henry Rice of Minnesota submitted a resolution that would separate all remaining territory into two states that would be promptly admitted into the Union. The one lying north of 36°30' would be called Washington, the one to the south Jefferson. Because of the immense size of these potential states, Rice made provisions for them to be subdivided into new states when the population reached 130,000 within any area of not less than 60,000 square miles. Rice defended his idea in a preamble: "Whereas the Territories of the United States, and the question of the admission of new states into the Union have caused most, if not all, the agitation of the question of slavery; and whereas it is desirable that the question should be forever abolished from the halls of Congress, and that it should cease to be a political element among the people."[59]

Rice's concept attracted more attention. At least some Republicans evinced interest, including Montgomery Blair, who would end up in Lincoln's cabinet. Upon its introduction Seward moved an amendment excluding the area contained in Kansas, whose statehood application was before Congress. The resulting poll revealed a tie, six on each side with partisan lineups largely holding. Only Douglas broke ranks to join the five Republicans on the aye side while all the southerners plus Rice said nay. Bigler did not vote. The tie defeated Seward's amendment. Then, Rice's plan also fell, with only three for it, Bigler, Davis, and Rice.

The demise of Rice's proposal ended the committee's attempt to cope with the crisis. The members decided to report that they could not agree upon any proposition to present to the full Senate. On the last day of the year Chairman Powell informed the Senate that the committee had been unable "to agree upon any general plan of adjustment." Upon Powell's call the committee did meet once more that same day. No southerners attended. The committee had foundered.

The failure of the Committee of Thirteen had momentous repercussions. Not until then did Jefferson Davis abandon reaching "an honorable peaceable settlement" that secured the Union with southern rights, as he understood them. His reliance on Seward had not worked out as he had hoped, for Seward had fallen in line with Lincoln's policy. From the moment of the committee's collapse no one could doubt that the secession of the Lower South would proceed apace. South Carolina had seceded on December 20, but the course of the other six states had been unsure before the hope of compromise from the committee crumbled. Although dates for elections and conventions had been set from Georgia to Texas, a compromise touted by Davis and Toombs would have hobbled secession in their states, and most likely also in the four remaining Cotton States. In that case, just as a generation earlier during the Nullification Crisis, South Carolina would have been left alone to confront the United States.[60]

The man whose name the major compromise package carried surely felt defeat, but not despair, sharing that outlook with his close ally on the committee, Senator Douglas. The determination of the Republicans to block any adjustment left John J. Crittenden "indignant and often times hotly denunciatory. . . . " While admitting that the scuttling of compromise distressed both men, they kept asserting that no one should give up on the Union. Writing to a supporter, Crittenden was honest: "I have to say that I think there is not a rational hope of preserving the Union." But in the very next sentence he urged, "Don't despair of the republic." Douglas echoed his older compatriot, admitting that "the prospects for the country are gloomy"; yet in almost the same breath he announced, "I do not entirely despair of the Union." Time remained, they claimed, to work through difficulties, to keep the country whole or, if necessary, to restore a partially severed Union.[61]

For Republicans, following the undeviating guideline of their new leader, the wreck of the committee should have caused no concern. After weeks of uncertainty the party's legislators found themselves arrayed atop the monument of the Chicago platform chanting the shibboleth of "no territorial compromise." The hard-liners provided the volume while the remainder at least hummed a chorus.

Only Crittenden's reputation and prestige, they averred, garnered his proposal the attention it got. That Republicans blocked it buoyed the hard-liners. Trumpeting the same no-territorial-compromise anthem, the *New York Tribune* proclaimed, "Let us retract nothing; let us not yield a single inch; let us be firm under every provocation and threat." Senator Charles Sumner declared he preferred war to any territorial deal. Sumner alarmed Charles Francis Adams by proclaiming he even "look[ed] forward to the violence of civil war, with the consequences of insurrection in the South almost with a grim satisfaction."[62]

Not every Republican took their devotion to party principle to such an extreme, though all remained committed to the faith. Some relished the political advantage from the secession of several slave states along with their Democratic solons, which meant the Republicans could control the Senate. Ever alert and perceptive, Seward recognized that the smashup of the Committee of Thirteen would propel the Lower South out of the Union. He also confessed to Lincoln that he did not know what the Upper South and Border would do. Only Crittenden's package, he informed the president-elect, would surely hold them, a condition Republicans would not accept. Yet, retaining at least a modicum of optimism, he opined that secessionist fervor would eventually dissipate. Others admitted worrying about what might occur before March 4 and Lincoln's inauguration and even after, in a Lincoln administration. Put simply, the committee explosion which brought Republican certainty left in its wake uncertainty.[63]

While Congress stumbled and South Carolina strode out of the Union, President Buchanan once again confronted the explosive issue of the forts in Charleston harbor. Earlier he had rejected General Winfield Scott's recommendation for reinforcements, fearing that such an action would result in a violent reaction in the South. Also, his cabinet was divided, with the southerners, led by Cobb, adamant against sending additional troops while the northerners, spurred by Jeremiah Black, wanted the president to follow Scott's advice.

Two critical events in mid- and late December had a major impact. One altered the political calculus; the other sparked a new crisis. Because of resignations the president had to rearrange his cabinet. Cobb and Thompson left because of their commitment to secession, while on December 15 Secretary of State Cass submitted his resignation to protest Buchanan's failure to add to the federal force in Charleston harbor. The resulting shuffle made Black secretary of state. From that post he persuaded an unenthusiastic

Buchanan to replace him as attorney general with Edwin M. Stanton, an able lawyer and staunch Unionist with antislavery views. As a result, the cabinet became more firmly pro-Union in conviction and determination, if not in number.[64]

At this point one prominent southerner remained in Buchanan's official family, Secretary of War John Floyd, who occupied a position of great strategic importance. Although the Virginian was pro-southern, he claimed he was no secessionist. Floyd's chief difficulties in December came not from his politics, but from his lax and indifferent administration of the War Department. Scandal became normal, and the worst erupted just before Christmas. Even though the president had instructed Floyd to desist from endorsing promissory notes from an army contractor, the secretary continued the practice. Then, it was revealed that the contractor had induced a government clerk to accept $870,000 in these bills for negotiable bonds in the Indian Trust Fund.

Floyd clearly had to go, but Buchanan lacked the will to fire him. The chief executive vacillated—unsurprisingly, given his indecisiveness and his proclivity to sidestep unpleasant situations. Floyd, who had always opposed any stronger federal pressure in Charleston harbor, refused to resign. He hoped somehow to vindicate himself, an impossibility. After some blustering he finally agreed to step down. His replacement, Joseph Holt, moving from the Post Office Department, was a notable addition to the Unionist contingent that by late December dominated the cabinet.

In Charleston harbor itself the recently appointed commanding officer, Major Robert Anderson, sparked a new crisis. As Anderson surveyed his command, he rightly concluded that with his small force he had no chance of successfully defending Fort Moultrie. He had only 101 men, including 8 musicians. No serious obstacles blocked the South Carolinians from approaching the fort. Anderson understood that if the state authorities decided to take it, he could not prevent their doing so.[65]

Concerned about an attack on his vulnerable command, Anderson understandably wanted specific direction from his superiors that detailed what they expected from him. The decision made in Washington would have Anderson remain on the defensive, but to defend himself if attacked. Secretary Floyd sent an officer to Charleston to deliver those orders personally and to inspect Anderson's situation.

At Fort Moultrie, Floyd's agent concurred with Anderson that defending the post was impossible. Then, seemingly going beyond his explicit authority, he penned written instructions repeating that Anderson was to assume a defensive stance, but "if attacked you are to defend yourself to the last extremity." In a critical addition, Anderson was given the discretion to transfer his men to Fort Sumter whenever he had "tangible evidence of a design to proceed to a hostile act." A copy of this directive went to the War Department where Floyd endorsed it before it landed in the department's files.[66]

The actual secession of South Carolina on December 20 only increased the tension in Charleston harbor. Rumors abounded that the Carolinians intended to assault Fort Moultrie, talk that reached Anderson, who became convinced he faced an immediate and dire threat. New orders arrived from Washington on the twenty-third. Although signed by Floyd, Secretary of State Black actually wrote them. They did not contravene Anderson's earlier instructions; in fact, they confirmed the previous ones while emphasizing the criticalness of Anderson's judgment. The commander must "exercise a sound military discretion." If attacked, he must defend, but not to the last extremity. He was not to make a "useless sacrifice" of his troops. If he judged the force against him as simply too powerful, he should secure the best possible terms before yielding.[67]

A West Point graduate, Major Robert Anderson had served in the U. S. Army for three and a half decades, compiling an excellent record. Fifty-five years old in 1860, he was of medium height, solidly built, with iron gray hair. He was deeply religious and invariably courteous. His narrow face had an almost soulful look. Both the army and his country required his devotion; his sense of duty permitted nothing less. A Kentuckian, his sympathies lay with the South in the political conflict consuming the country, yet he was at the same time a committed Unionist and a professional soldier. Anderson perceived his major mission as avoiding bloodshed, if at all possible. He believed the surest way to carry out his assignment was to make his position so strong that the Carolinians would never assault him. To that end, upon his taking command and recognizing his fundamental weakness, he called for reinforcements.[68]

Reinforcements never came. The president feared that sending them would only exacerbate the situation, even to the point of prodding the Carolinians to go on the offensive. And Buchanan wanted most of all to avoid armed conflict. Moreover, a so-called gentleman's agreement had been fashioned by southerners in the cabinet and Congress who got the endorsement of the governor of South Carolina—no additional soldiers would go to Anderson and South Carolina would not use force to remove him. Even so, to a delegation of South Carolina congressmen, the president would not make an explicit pledge never to reinforce Anderson. At the same time, his vague language left the Carolinians believing he had made such a commitment.[69]

But with the secession of South Carolina old agreements and understandings were obsolete. South Carolina no longer considered itself a state in the Union, but an independent republic. The new governor, Francis W. Pickens, promptly dispatched three commissioners to Washington to discuss the disposition of all the federal property in the Charleston area. Their charge: to get Anderson evacuated and to end the federal presence within the state's borders.

Meanwhile, Major Anderson made his fateful decision. While president and Congress vacillated, argued, debated, and obstructed, he acted. He decided that he would secretly transfer his entire command to Fort Sumter, sitting atop its man-made island at the mouth of the harbor. He had quickly assessed Sumter as "the key to the entrance of the harbor." Moreover, as he noted, "its guns command this work, Moultrie, and could drive out its occupants." On the night of December 26, he spiked the cannons at Moultrie and moved his troops. Secrecy held; the Carolinians did not discover his move until he was safely ensconced in Fort Sumter. He had made the shift without losing a man and without even a single shot being fired.[70]

Anderson did not conceive of his action as in any way offensive—far from it. He believed that Fort Sumter afforded him a powerful defensive bastion, one the Carolinians could not overcome. Thus he would postpone, possibly even prevent, what he most feared, armed conflict between South Carolina and the federal government. Although he shared that dread with his commander in chief, his move changed the political calculus governing the standoff in Charleston harbor. Federal forces now occupied a position of strength, not weakness.[71]

Anderson's presence in Fort Sumter sparked outrage in South Carolina. Governor Pickens immediately sent an officer to the fort to insist that Anderson return to Moultrie, asserting that the major had violated the gentleman's agreement between the president and the state. Anderson responded that although "he was a Southern man in his feelings upon

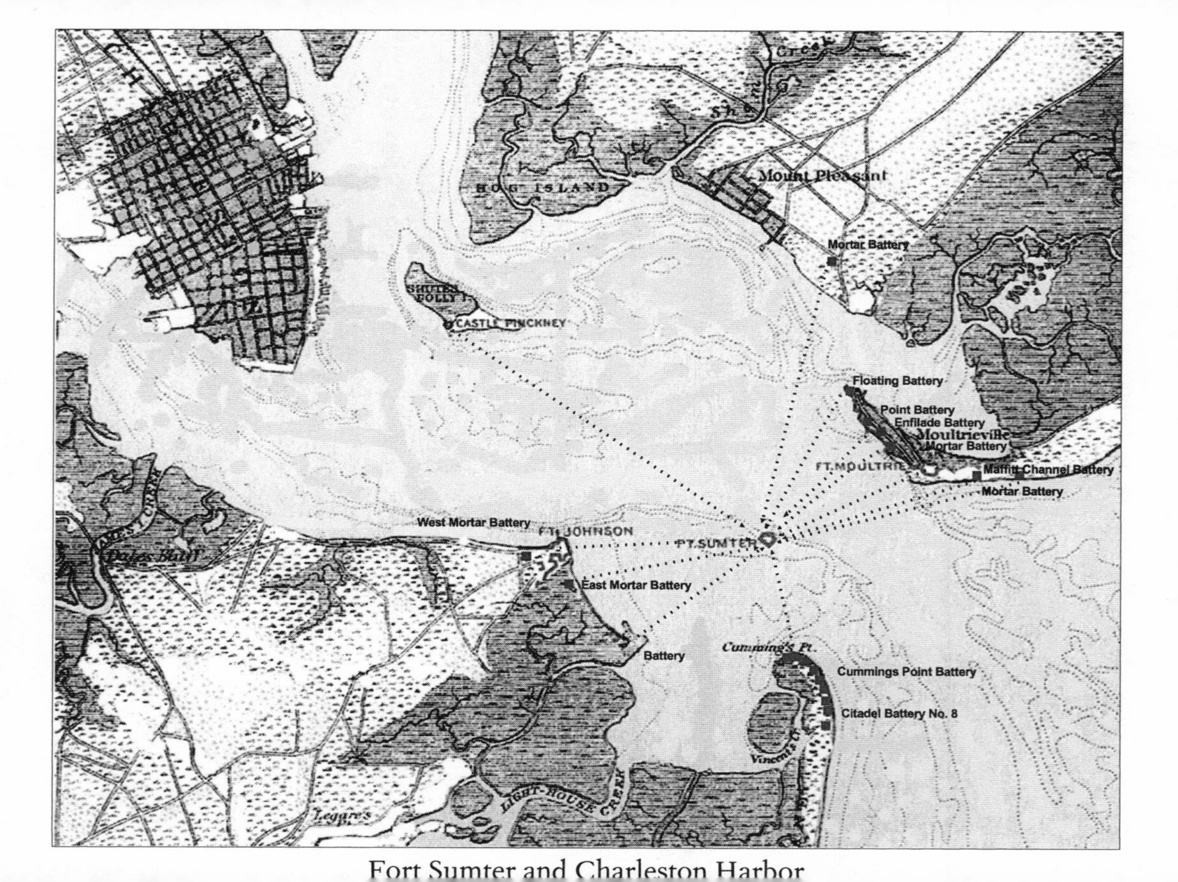

Fort Sumter and Charleston Harbor

the question at issue," he knew of no such arrangement, and he had conformed to his orders. Anderson refused Pickens's demand. In turn, Pickens ordered state forces to occupy all other federal installations in and around the harbor, including Fort Moultrie.[72]

In Washington, both the delegation from South Carolina sent to negotiate with President Buchanan and the president himeslf were caught off guard. Arriving late on the twenty-sixth, the three commissioners had just arranged through William Henry Trescot, a fellow South Carolinian, and until recently the assistant secretary of state, to see the president when word came via telegraph of what had transpired in Charleston harbor. The Carolinians expected Buchanan to rescind Anderson's move and send him back to Moultrie, to restore the gentleman's agreement. They informed him that the state had upheld the accord when it could have taken the remaining federal property, such as Fort Sumter.

Trescot looked for help to press Buchanan. Going to the Capitol, he enlisted Jefferson Davis and Robert M. T. Hunter to accompany him to the White House to remonstrate with the president. On the twenty-seventh, these men brought the news to Buchanan, who had not previously heard it. Insisting that the president had pledged his honor to them as well as to South Carolina that Anderson would remain in Fort Moultrie, they maintained that Buchanan must order Anderson's return to his former location. Disconsolate, the president, standing by the mantel, "crush[ed] up a cigar into pieces in his hand." Trescot remembered him crying out, "My God are calamities . . . never to come singly. I call God to witness—you gentlemen better than anybody know—that this is not only without but against my orders, it is against my policy."[73]

In part, he was right. His policy was to hold to the status quo, and he had given no direct order authorizing Anderson's move. To the War Department dispatch of December 23 the president had probably given little thought.

Now the president came under a ferocious bombardment. Southern senators, his allies and friends, argued forcefully that he must rescind Anderson's move. Secretary Floyd, after being sent for, arrived, asserting that he had not ordered the transfer, but he joined the senators in pressing Buchanan. They told him that his standing behind Anderson risked the possibility that South Carolina would garrison the remaining forts and assault Fort Sumter, initiating the bloodshed the president so desperately wanted to avoid. At first, the chief executive seemed ready to direct Anderson's return. But then he wavered, falling into his pattern of hesitancy. He concluded he could not condemn Anderson without hearing his side, and that he must call his cabinet together. Saying they understood his hesitation, the southerners told him they only wanted assurance that he would do as they requested if he learned that Anderson had not been attacked. This reassurance the president refused to give. Nor did he provide it to others who came later that day with the same plan. He did, however, postpone his meeting with the South Carolina commissioners until the twenty-eighth, after he had consulted with his cabinet.[74]

When his cabinet came together, Buchanan found himself in a vise. The Unionist bloc headed by Black pressed him not only to back Anderson, but also to send reinforcements. At this moment a blustering Floyd resigned. His departure only added to Black's strength in coming days, when Joseph Holt, a staunch Unionist, was appointed in Floyd's stead. General Scott, too, added his voice and prestige to Black's side. Still the president paused. Finally, on Sunday, December 30, he decided he must confirm Anderson at Fort Sumter. And on the next day he agreed to send reinforcements. It was close. Black told Trescot, "You nearly beat us but we had one card left and fortunately that was a trump, so we beat you." The trump was the threat of resignation by Black and his cabinet allies.[75]

The president's stance severed his long-standing and intimate personal and political ties with the southern leadership in Washington. The divorce was not amicable. The southerners displayed what the wife of a pro-southern California senator termed the "most violent" feelings against Buchanan. They judged that he had broken his word to South Carolina and, even more important, to them. Senator Davis used the word "perfidious." According to Davis, the president's "weakness has done as much harm as wickedness would have achieved." To the southerners, Buchanan had misled them and turned on them, not from maliciousness, but from weakness. In their minds pressure from his cabinet and fear of northern opinion had collapsed his promise. In short, they could not trust him. "Though I can no longer respect or confer with him and feel injured by his conduct," Davis explained, "yet I pity and would extenuate the offenses not prompted by bad design or malignant intent."[76]

Buchanan's backing of Anderson had massive significance; it matched in consequence the major's occupation of Fort Sumter. Together they fundamentally altered not only the military disposition in Charleston harbor but also the relationship between the state and the federal government. The vulnerability of Fort Moultrie left Anderson open to intimidation and even a swift overpowering onslaught. At Fort Sumter, he held an essentially impregnable position, which the Carolinians could not easily or immediately reduce. By supporting Anderson and withstanding the substantial pressure placed on him to countermand his officer, Buchanan retained options in Charleston for himself and potentially for his successor. If he had withdrawn Anderson, no federal presence would have been left in the city. Even an order sending Anderson back to Moultrie would have signaled notable weakness, for the president would have been caving in to southern demands. South Carolina would have had the upper hand militarily, politically, and psychologically. But the United States flag still flew over a powerful military installation in the state, or country, of South Carolina. Exaggerating the importance of that fact is impossible.

Buchanan's handling of this episode in the ongoing crisis has been vigorously criticized, and not only by southerners. Even friends were unsparing: "In truth his mind has lost its power of comprehending a complicated situation," one wrote. "He is nervous & hysterical, & I think completely unmanned." Republicans, of course, railed against him for colluding with secessionists and abetting traitors. He was derisively referred to as "the Old Public Functionary," who stood, as one put it, "lowest, I think, in the dirty catalogue of treasonable mischief-makers." Condemnations hurled at him harangued him for not following the example of Andrew Jackson in defying treason and threatening enemies of the Union with the sword. To these critics Jackson's confronting South Carolina in the Nullification Crisis of 1832–1833, in which he purportedly forced the state to back down, became the standard. And Buchanan failed to measure up.[77]

The two presidents were quite different men. The old soldier Jackson perceived his political enemies as he had his battlefield opponents, as unworthy, even evil foes, who must be destroyed. And Jackson with his iron will would see to their demise. In contrast, Buchanan had spent a lifetime as a professional politician and diplomat, always searching for some way around a hostile showdown. Moreover, without Jackson's unshakable sense of his own self-righteousness and his fierce willpower, Buchanan lacked the conviction that he alone could overpower any antagonist.

Aside from having sharply differing backgrounds and personalities, the two chief executives faced distinctly dissimilar situations. Jackson had to deal with one state still in the Union averring that it would not allow the enforcement of a single federal law, the protective tariff of 1832. In the initial Fort Sumter quandary, Buchanan also engaged but one state, even the same one, but this time South Carolina proclaimed that it no longer belonged to the Union. Furthermore, several additional states were in motion to join South Carolina outside the Union. And the president was convinced his use of force would surely drive them out, an outcome he desperately hoped to prevent. Thus, Buchanan had to contend with a much more complex case. Additionally, at the same time Jackson warned of employing armed might against South Carolina, he waited, watched, and assisted as Congress worked on a compromise that would settle the dispute. When Congress reached a deal, he signed on. The Compromise of 1833, which lowered the tariff while it put Congress on record backing the president's use of force if necessary, resolved the matter. In contrast, Buchanan had no hope of any assistance from Congress, a reality he recognized. In part, his lack of leadership helped hamstring the Congress, but Republican intransigence was the paramount obstacle.

Then, at the close of the Nullification Crisis, South Carolina had as legitimate a claim to victory as President Jackson. Yes, the attempt to nullify a federal law had been stymied, but that law was amended to lower the hated tariff, and the state suffered no political, much less military, harm. For many Carolinians the lesson was clear: they went head to head with the federal government, and they not only survived but came out ahead. A number of them were still around in 1860, as were even more of their children.

To be sure, James Buchanan was not Andrew Jackson, but almost in spite of himself he did make a stand that kept his flag flying in contested territory. That decision did not, however, end his crisis or that of his country.[78]

CHAPTER FOUR

"Up with Folly, Down with Wisdom Is the Order of the Day"

THE NEW YEAR began with the dissolution of the Union ongoing and collision between South Carolina and the federal government ranging between possible and probable. The failure of the Committee of Thirteen and with it the likelihood of serious compromise, at least for the moment, propelled secession forward in the Deep South. South Carolina would not long occupy a lonely outpost. There, in Charleston harbor, a presidential decision increased the odds of armed conflict commencing.

Following his successful move to Fort Sumter, Major Anderson became a hero in much of the North. Plaudits came from all quarters. On its front page *The New York Herald* ran a detailed map of Charleston harbor displaying Anderson's relocation. "The Lord bless your noble soul!" praised an exuberant correspondent. He assured the major, "Oh, my dear sir, the whole country will triumphantly sustain you." A constituent of Charles Sumner defined Anderson's action as the nation's finest moment since 1776. A longtime Democratic politico in New York wrote that Anderson's "conduct is approved here by all parties, even by the warmest advocate of Southern rights." By a resounding margin—more than two to one—the House of Representatives passed a resolution proposed by a Democratic congressman from New Jersey. It declared: "That we fully approve of the bold and patriotic act of Major Anderson in withdrawing from Fort Moultrie to Fort Sumter." Almost every northerner voted aye.[1]

Even President Buchanan stepped forward. Immediately upon his decision to confirm Major Anderson at Fort Sumter, he authorized sending reinforcements to the new hero. Debate over strengthening the federal military presence in Charleston had divided his administration since early fall. Previously the president had lined up with those who argued that augmenting the federal force there would only increase the risk of shots being fired. Now, however, he decided to follow up his affirmation of Anderson's action by sending additional resources. Long a proponent of this, Secretary of State Black pushed hard for it just as he had for his chief to ratify Anderson's move. Additionally, General Scott still advocated forwarding reinforcements. On December 28, he urged the secretary of war to do so; two days later he addressed the president himself, requesting permission to send additional troops in a sloop of war.

Scott's opinion carried weight, almost as much as his own, for he was the foremost soldier in the nation. Winning his initial plaudits on the battlefield during the War of 1812 and his first general's star at twenty-seven, Scott became the army's commanding general in 1841. His brilliant campaign in the Mexican War made him a national hero and the Whig presidential nominee in 1852. Though in 1861 still an imposing figure, with a huge reputation and an ego to match, the years were catching up with him. At seventy-five, he had become mountainous; his frame of over six feet four inches carried around three hundred pounds. He was afflicted with dropsy and could no longer sit on a horse.[2]

On the last day of the year Buchanan authorized added men and supplies. He entrusted the implementation of his directive to his secretaries of war and the navy along with General Scott. Initially, the plan was to use the warship *Brooklyn*, lying off Fort Monroe, in Virginia, with some two hundred men. Instead, the general wanted to employ a merchant ship with a lighter draft; he thought it more likely to get over the Charleston harbor bar and any other obstruction successfully. As a result, the government chartered a steamer in New York City called *Star of the West*. The mission was shrouded in secrecy—the ship's supposed destination was New Orleans, and she picked her load of soldiers up from tugs near Staten Island. On January 5, loaded with supplies and carrying some two hundred soldiers, *Star of the West* steamed out into the Atlantic and headed south.

President Buchanan knew full well that the expedition might precipitate what he most wanted to avoid—war. That same evening a friend reported that she had never seen the president "so solemn." He told her "nothing but the interposition of all-wise Providence could save our country." Anguish gripping him, he confessed that "he had despaired of being able to do anything himself." Then came news from Major Anderson that the state had erected batteries on Morris Island guarding the southern entrance to the harbor and the main ship channel. Moreover, he stipulated that he felt secure in Fort Sumter. A rescinding order went promptly by telegraph to New York, but it arrived too late. *Star of the West* had departed.[3]

Star of the West approached the entrance to Charleston harbor just after midnight, early in the morning on January 9. From several sources in Washington, South Carolina authorities had been made aware both that an attempt at reinforcement was probable and that *Star* had sailed. Fort Moultrie and the battery on Morris Island were alerted to prepare to stop any expedition. In addition, the governor directed that a steamer loaded with armed men proceed to the bar with instructions to intercept any incoming vessel.[4]

At daylight *Star* crossed the bar and started up the ship channel, with the Stars and Stripes having been raised. With all troops ensconced below, she had the appearance of the merchant vessel she actually was. Still, when abreast of Morris Island, the shore battery roared. Thereupon, the long-range cannon in Fort Moultrie, almost straight ahead, went into action. A few rounds found their mark, though none inflicted serious damage. Without guns to answer, *Star* could not have returned fire even if her officers had so desired. The ship withdrew.

From Fort Sumter, Anderson and his garrison witnessed the encounter. No official word had come from the War Department that succor was en route. A message had been sent on the fifth, which had not reached him. Anderson did hear unofficially, from a newspaper account, that *Star* was headed toward him. He gave no credence to it, however, for he believed that any troops sent to him would arrive in a naval warship, not in a commercial steamer. No matter, when the state artillery opened on *Star*, Anderson and his officers could hear and see. Uncertain about his own duty and response, Anderson hesitated. After a short time it was decided that Sumter's guns probably could not hit the target on Morris Island, but could certainly bombard Fort Moultrie. Before any order to do so was given, however, *Star* turned away. "Hold on; do not fire," Anderson directed. "I will wait."[5]

At this point battle was not joined. Civil war was averted. Anderson's superiors praised him. Applauding Anderson's judgment in holding his fire, Secretary of War Holt, writing on the sixteenth, specified that the president concurred in that view. Holt also indicated relief that Anderson had expressed confidence in his own security. The secretary reiterated that administration policy remained unchanged: Anderson should continue a defensive posture. Holt went on to tell his commander that for the successful defense of Fort Sumter should he need additional supplies or troops, he should immediately inform Washington. At that time, an effort would be undertaken to forward the requisite men and matériel.[6]

Tension still riveted Charleston harbor, however. On the very day of the *Star of the West* incident, Major Anderson by special messenger informed Governor Pickens of his distress and intentions. That batteries fired on "an unarmed vessel bearing the flag of my government" appalled Anderson. He knew of no declaration of war by South Carolina against the United States. Thus, he could only believe that Pickens had not sanctioned what Anderson termed "this hostile act." Anderson then requested the governor to disavow the action. If not, Anderson said, he "must regard it as an act of war." In response, he would not "permit any vessel to pass within range of the guns in my fort." Closing, he hoped for a quick answer.[7]

Pickens wasted no time. He told Anderson that because South Carolina had seceded the state considered any change at the forts a belligerent act. That message seemed to signal imminent hostilities. Responding, Anderson urged Pickens to allow him to refer the matter to Washington. He did not want the shedding of blood to begin, certainly not solely on his own authority. Pickens agreed, but he also sent an official delegation out to Fort Sumter imploring Anderson to deliver the fort and all other "public property" under his authority to South Carolina. Politely, Anderson declined. He replied to Pickens that he could not do so without instructions from his government. In addition, he suggested that one of his officers accompany the governor's emissary to Washington. Pickens agreed.

In his delicate and precarious position Anderson never wavered from his two deep convictions: he desperately hoped to avoid war, and he fervently held to his sense of duty as a soldier serving his government. Every communication with Governor Pickens and discussion with his envoys emphasized these two points. To friends, with expression of great emotion, he evinced the same goals. To his fellow Kentuckian John J. Crittenden he declared, "I am doing, and shall continue to do, all that honor will permit to keep the peace." While he admitted his sympathies were with the South, he had lost "all sympathy with the people who govern [South Carolina]." He thought them "resolved to cement their secession with blood." Even so, he affirmed, "I shall do all I can with honor to prevent the occurrence of so sad an event—but," he continued with a heavy heart, "fear that all will be of no avail." In his terrible dilemma, he could only cry, "God save our poor Union from fratricidal strife."[8]

As the year 1861 opened, only South Carolina had seceded, but from all appearances she would not be alone for very long. Elections for delegates to secession conventions had occurred in three states in December (Alabama on the twenty-fourth, Florida on the twenty-second, and Mississippi on the twentieth) with three more scheduled for January (Georgia on the second, Louisiana on the seventh, and Texas on the eighth). In all these states excitement prevailed. In the southern tradition campaigns heralded by impassioned speeches, blazing newspaper editorials, and barbecues pervaded the region. Everyone spoke of the ever-increasing enthusiasm, even passion. Some areas saw the formation of local vigilance committees to guard against alleged schemes to foment slave unrest while others witnessed the raising of militia companies. Young men paraded, preparing for war; young women sewed flags.[9]

The electoral contests were not organized along party lines. In most instances no kind of partisan brand tagged the contestants for convention seats. Candidates overwhelmingly identified themselves as immediatists or cooperationists. Yet the precise meaning of these terms is not clear. A basic problem derived from almost everybody's believing in the right of secession. The sole difference among both voters and contenders focused on whether secession should take place, and if so, when. The immediatist position was clear; they advocated immediate secession by each individual state.

The cooperationists were not so unified, however. "Cooperation" had multiple meanings. For some, it meant no secession until at least one other state had gone out. Others advocated waiting until several states had opted to leave the Union. Then, there were those who wanted a convention of slave states that would present an ultimatum spelling out southern demands to Congress or to the Republican party, or both. Only upon rejection of that final statement would secession be justified. Wherever they stood within this range, cooperationists hoped postponement would give the North time, in the words of one, "to do justice."[10]

In any political contest the immediatists had a sharp advantage, for they had a clarion message. And, borrowing from today's political vocabulary, they had no problem staying on message. In contrast, cooperationists had great difficulty finding a unified message, much less holding to it. Thus, they found themselves on the defensive, without a ringing call for anything. The South was clamoring for action, for protection, and they could only offer delay.

With Congress hobbled and no recourse from the feared Republicans in sight, clinging to "wait" risked one's being branded as a submissionist to the Republicans. In southern culture few epithets were so loaded, for only slaves submitted. Independent, honorable men would never submit. An Alabama congressman made the point emphatically, writing that he would "rather die a freeman than live a slave to Black Republicans." To stress his conviction, he added, "I would be an equal, or a corpse." This politician expressed disdain for submission no more fervently than the wife of a Georgia slaveowner. As much as she hated the prospect of war, she told her son, "even that, *if it must come,* would be preferable to submission to Black Republicans, involving as it would all that is horrible, degrading, and ruinous." A major cooperationist newspaper made clear its priorities, warning the North, "It may prove a fatal, an unretrievably fatal error," should the cooperationist stance "be misconstrued into *submission,* or a delay designed eventually to lead to submission."[11]

To overcome their inherent disabilities, cooperationists needed a vigorous effort from their leaders. But leadership formed a critical weakness. Few entrenched politicians of real stature had aligned themselves with the cooperationists. And practically none had statewide followings, much less reputations that stretched across the region or into the North. Most major leaders had either gone over to the immediatists or waited upon evidence of Republican intentions to make clear their position. In the Deep South in December only two truly preeminent political leaders had made public their anti-immediatist stance, Governor Sam Houston of Texas, who was an outright Unionist, and Alexander Stephens of Georgia. By the beginning of 1861, Houston was obviously out of touch with the overwhelming majority of Texans. In addition, the Texas election of delegates to its convention would not take place until January 8, after all the states to the east had voted.[12]

Stephens's situation was different, however. Georgia would vote for its delegates on January 2; at that time only South Carolina had seceded. Moreover, back in mid-November, Stephens had spoken forthrightly, even eloquently, against immediate secession. Asserting that he could fathom no reason for haste, he urged Georgians to slow down, to wait and find out whether a Republican administration really intended something terrible. At that point, but only then, he declared, Georgia should act, with him in the vanguard. But in the following campaign to elect delegates to the state convention, Stephens fell silent. He never mounted the hustings to plead for his cause. Even in his home county, he made but a simple, brief, uninspiring effort. Calls for him to go on the political offensive went unheeded. He did not rise up as the champion of cooperation.[13]

Stephens's personality possibly explains his apathy. His leading biographer suggests that he may have withdrawn because his advice had been ignored by his fellow Georgians. Yet no one knew the outcome of the voting that would occur on January 2. Stephens was a professional politician who had campaigned successfully in his state for the previous decade and a half. He had fought and won against powerful opponents, both individual and ideological. It seems more likely that he could sense no enthusiasm among his fellow cooperationists. Moaning, "We have fallen on sad times," he refused to take up the political cudgels. It is as if his own had disappeared. He only saw a forlorn cause. Perhaps in the depth of his being he thought the immediatists correct. Perceiving only a hopeless cause, he backed away, grouching, "I am inclined to let those who sowed the wind reap the whirlwind, or control it if they can." His conclusion: "It does seem to me that we are going to destruction as fast as we can." And that rush he would make little effort to block.[14]

While Stephens's grim assessment shuttered his activity, the reaction of others who viewed affairs as equally dismal presents a sharp contrast. Their vision of blackness had a different origin, however—failure of any congressional compromise and the seemingly indisputable evidence that Republicans did not intend to assuage southern fears with any concrete measures. A close friend of Stephens made that point emphatically, avowing conservatism but now feeling that "developments" left "*no hope*" but secession. Jefferson Davis, giving a speech in the Senate on January 10, left no doubt about his position. In remarks articulating what many in his section felt, he said that from the moment Congress convened, southerners had hoped for Republicans to show their respect for southern rights. "We have waited long," Davis announced, but to no avail. With no hand reaching out, he declared, "we have come to the conclusion that you mean to do nothing." The time had come for the South to secure her own safety. Inaction by the Republicans, Davis concluded, necessitated southern action.[15]

In Washington, Davis and his congressional colleagues prepared for the fact of secession and what would follow. From the beginning of the year solons from the Deep South were convinced their states were rapidly heading out of the Union. As a result, they began to plan for a southern government. A call for southern states to gather in Montgomery, Alabama, had originated in South Carolina in late December. A formal proposal was made on January 3 to hold such a meeting in early February. The Carolinians wanted haste, for they desired "to hold [the states] together while they are hot." The senators, especially, and the representatives who had spoken for the South in Congress surely expected to occupy leadership roles in the new southern republic.[16]

In addition to planning for a new government, the southern leadership in Washington was deeply involved in two other crucial activities. First, with Davis in the lead they strove to restrain South Carolina. When Governor Pickens asked Davis for advice on Fort Sumter, the senator in frequent messages implored him not to act, maintaining that a premature strike would only hurt the southern cause. He reminded Pickens, "The little garrison in its present positi[on] presses on nothing but a point of pride, & to you I need not say that war is made up of real eleme[nts]." Moreover, Davis assured him, "we shall soon have a Southern Confederacy that shall be ready to do all which interest or even pride demands."[17]

Then the southern senators corralled Pickens's emissary to President Buchanan. Following his agreement with Major Anderson, Pickens had sent an envoy to Washington with an ultimatum for the president about Fort Sumter. The governor offered in the name of South Carolina to buy the fort, but said that if his bid was refused, he would seize it. Aware that the president's certain refusal could very easily spark gunfire in Charleston harbor, the senators prevailed upon Pickens's representative to hold off presenting the incendiary demand.[18]

The senators also wrestled with their proper role in Congress. They discussed whether they should remain in their seats until March 4 and the adjournment of Congress or withdraw when their states seceded. They initially feared their absence could enable the Republicans "to enact every species of legislation which hate of the South and lust of power and plunder may suggest." At the same time a number believed they would have no legitimate place in the Congress after their states had left the Union. They never had to choose between these options, however. They became convinced that the combination of northern Democrats and members from slave states still in the Union would have the ability to stymie any nefarious Republican initiatives, and therefore they left with their states.[19]

At the same time the senators joined with the governors of their states in an unprecedented and provocative action. Federal fortifications in the Deep South were like Fort Sumter; almost all of them lacked garrisons. Only at Pensacola, Florida, did a small detachment of U.S. Army troops guard federal property. In the aftermath of President Buchanan's adamant refusal to withdraw Anderson from Fort Sumter, the rebuffed and angry Carolinians assumed that a new reinforcing expedition would soon follow. They knew they would use force to halt it, meaning war would probably result. They informed the governor of Georgia to that effect.[20]

With that news, Governor Joseph Brown took radical steps that resulted in nothing less than a revolutionary plot. With his state still in the Union, on January 2 he ordered Georgia volunteers to seize the unoccupied Fort Pulaski at the mouth of the Savannah River. Almost simultaneously he confidentially wired his fellow chief executives in Alabama, Florida, Louisiana, and Mississippi informing them that because the federal government intended a "coercive policy," he had ordered the occupation of Fort Pulaski. Moreover, he "hope[d]" that they would similarly take the forts in their states.[21]

The four men telegraphed that they would indeed cooperate with Brown. On January 4, Alabama forces moved into forts Gaines and Morgan, which covered the entrance to Mobile Bay, as well as the Mount Vernon Arsenal north of Mobile. Before Louisiana seceded, the state seized Fort Pike at the entrance to Lake Pontchartrain as well as forts Jackson and St. Philip, down the Mississippi River from New Orleans. Additionally, the arsenal at Baton Rouge came into state hands. On January 20 Mississippi militia occupied Ship Island with its Fort Massachusetts, just off the Gulf Coast. All went smoothly—no shots fired, no casualties.

In Florida events were a bit more complicated. On the order of Governor Madison Perry, on January 7 the Florida flag flew over Fort Marion at St. Augustine on the Atlantic coast. Five days later at Pensacola, on the Gulf Coast, state troops overwhelmed several U.S. institutions, including the naval yard, but the giant prize escaped them. When the militia initially approached the garrisoned Fort Barrancas on the mainland, the army officer in charge fired a few warning shots, then transferred his fewer than one hundred men across Pensacola Bay to Fort Pickens, on Santa Rosa Island.

Like Sumter, Pickens provided a formidable defensive position; it sat on an island, though natural, not man-made like Sumter's. A land-based force could not reach the position without crossing a substantial body of water. Moreover, its southern face bordered the Gulf of Mexico, from whence the U.S. Navy could protect and secure it, if directed to do so. Ironically Fort Pickens, which along with Fort Sumter became a critical spot in the ongoing crisis, took its name from a hero of the American Revolution, General Andrew Pickens of South Carolina, who was also the grandfather of Governor Francis W. Pickens.

Without any doubt the occupations of U.S. forts and arsenals by states still in the Union constituted treason. These acts came as a result of plotting by the governors of five states. One of them, Andrew Moore of Alabama, tried to justify his motives, and by extension his colleagues'. Writing to President Buchanan on January 4, he asserted his conviction that the U.S. government intended to use force, and shed blood if necessary, to prevent the secession of Alabama. To preclude any bloodletting and to maintain the peace while his state exercised its right of secession, which he saw as inevitable, he acted unilaterally. Any presence of federal force, he informed Buchanan, would have "provoke[d] hostilities between the State and Federal Government." He did what he did because "there is no object save the honor and independence of my State, which is by me so ardently desired as the preservation of amicable relations between this State and the Government of the United States."[22]

While this missive by no means absolved Moore and his fort-seizing comrades of their traitorous conduct, it expressed in a fundamental sense the president's view: neither did he want any armed conflict. To that end, after the *Star of the West* fiasco he rejected advice to make a second effort to reinforce Fort Sumter. He knew, just as the Carolinians did, that it would mean war. He would only move upon Anderson's request. Likewise, he had no intention of sending soldiers to any of the vacant federal fortifications between the Savannah and Mississippi rivers. Convinced that he could not influence political events in Congress, his great goal in the two months remaining in his term became to avoid war. Force would be a last and unwanted resort. As he had made clear in a message to Congress on

January 8, "It was my determined purpose not to commence [civil war] nor even to furnish an excuse for it by an act of this Government." He made clear he would only use force to defend federal officers resisted in carrying out their duties. Although he also mentioned his duty "to protect the public property," he clearly had no intention of risking war if only buildings and geography were at stake. His action would require violence against U.S. forces.[23]

The southern leaders in Washington understood the president perfectly well. In that same message, he referred directly to assurances from "distinguished and upright gentlemen of South Carolina" that the state would not attack. Thus he openly defined the modus vivendi governing his relations with South Carolina. The South Carolinians closest to the president knew that while steadfastly on the defensive, Buchanan would employ force if any U.S. personnel came under attack. William Trescot informed Howell Cobb in Georgia that the president would hold that ground "to the last extremity." When the southern leadership in Washington learned that the Federals in Pensacola had settled in at Fort Pickens, they made unequivocally clear they wanted no operation mounted by Florida forces against the fort. On January 18 seven senators wired Governor Perry: "We think no assault should be made. The possession of the fort is not worth one drop of blood to us." Their message concluded, "Bloodshed now may be fatal to our cause." Underscoring the imperative of holding back, two days later both Florida senators signed a telegram to Governor Perry repeating the admonition "that the fort is not worth one drop of blood at this time." Each message indicated that delay might be temporary, however. "Measures pending" united the seven in their advice while the two Floridians instructed, "First get the Southern Government in operation."[24]

The establishment of a southern government depended upon the success of the secession movement beyond South Carolina. The decision of whether or not to secede was made in elections and conventions held from late December 1860 until the beginning of February 1861. These did not occur in a political vacuum, however. Events taking place beyond polling places and meeting halls fundamentally affected the choices made in them.

The elections, which began in Mississippi on December 20, the day South Carolina seceded, and ended in Texas three weeks later, revealed that unanimity for breaking up the Union did not extend west of the Savannah River. Mississippi had the densest slave population after South Carolina;

in 1860 for the first time slaves exceeded 50 percent of the total population. Even with the slave system spreading through most of the state, immediatists took only 41 percent of the vote, with approximately 30 percent each for professed cooperationists and candidates whose positions were not clearly stated. Two days later in Florida immediatists won the day with around 60 percent of the vote. On the twenty-fourth Alabamians gave the immediatists 36,500 votes, but awarded cooperationists 28,100.[25]

Two states with elections in January showed even closer margins. In both Georgia and Louisiana, which voted on January 2 and 7 respectively, the cooperationists came very close to winning. Georgia voters preferred immediatists by only 44,152 to 41,632 while in Louisiana immediatists polled 20,214 to the cooperationists' 18,451. In both states, in order to advance their cause, pro-secession governors refused to make public just how close the election had been.[26]

In Texas the entire process was irregular because Governor Sam Houston refused to convene the legislature so that it could call a special election. Thereupon, in early December, a gathering of secessionist leaders in the state capital, Austin, announced an election for delegates to a secession convention. January 8 was the date set, but some counties voted earlier. In light voting the immediatists handily carried their state. At that point Governor Houston did bring the legislature into special session, urging it to deny recognition to the convention. The legislators spurned their governor by validating the convention, though they did mandate that it subject its resolutions to a popular vote.

Interpreting the outcome and meaning of the elections in these six states is not simple. One glaring fact does stand out, however. The number going to the polls dropped immensely between the presidential election in November and the contests for delegates to secession conventions. For example, fewer than half as many Georgians voted in the election of convention delegates; almost thirty thousand fewer cast ballots in both Alabama and Mississippi, and some eleven thousand fewer in Louisiana. Explaining that decline is considerably more difficult, however, than showing it. Perhaps the short lead time between the notification of elections and the elections themselves depressed turnout. Possibly many potential voters could find no easily discernible distinctions among the various candidates. The absence of any notable figures campaigning vigorously for cooperation could have affected the response of citizens. It is even conceivable that an undetermined number had become convinced that their states would secede. More likely, a combination of these factors was responsible. The one conclusion that can safely be drawn is that voters in these states did not rush to make their views known. As a result, a smaller electorate than usual participated in these critical elections.

It is also clear that the "black-belt counties," those with the heaviest slave populations, formed the strongholds of the immediatists. Conversely, the "white counties," those with few or no slaves, comprised the bastion of cooperationist strength. Northeastern Alabama and northern Georgia provide perfect examples. Those areas, mostly upper piedmont or even mountainous, the southern end of the Appalachian chain, contributed massively to cooperationist vote totals in both states.

Although black-belt counties housed large numbers of slaves, that circumstance did not mean all whites residing in them were planters, large slaveowners, or even slaveowners at all. Planters were a minority, with most whites owning few slaves or none. Yet residence in these locales with dense slave populations and wealthy planters influenced all whites' outlook and their politics. A slaveless white in a plantation county was much more likely to be affected by issues and concerns touching slavery directly, as well as by the planters' views of such matters, than his counterpart in a county with few planters and slaves. No matter the racial and socioeconomic makeup of a county, the majority of the voters were men who had few or no slaves. Thus, even in black-belt counties success for immediate secession required support of those men who possessed few or no slaves.

Yet, what at first glance appears to be a clear-cut correlation becomes more complex upon closer examination. In Louisiana and Mississippi wealthy plantation counties diverged sharply from this pattern. In the cotton areas of Mississippi bordering the great river and in the sugar bowl of south Louisiana, heavily slave counties were stalwart for cooperation. Both had been Whig citadels during the Democrat-Whig rivalry. In them rich, conservative planters acted in an unsurprising manner—wary of revolutionary rhetoric and rash action. Even so, their stance does not gainsay the force of immediatism in slave domains.

Despite the drop in voting and that non-slaveowners outnumbered slaveowners, the immediatists won. They had significant margins only in Florida and Texas, and even in the former the cooperationists probably gained 40 percent of the vote. In most places the immediatists succeeded by a narrow margin. A more exacting look raises additional questions. Most important, no one really knows the depth of commitment of most successful contestants. As an experienced Georgian politician wrote Alexander Stephens, it was difficult to "decide from the returns what is the complexion of the Convention." Because their public identity was not always obvious, there was no certainty about how they would vote on crucial questions. Those elected would not have much time to ponder their positions, for the severely compressed schedule had conventions set for only a week or two after the elections.[27]

It is also essential to recognize that these elections had occurred before three critical events that would surely influence public opinion and how delegates viewed the national scene had taken place or become widely known. These occurrences would impact how delegates responded to the crucial issue of separate state or immediate secession. The failure of the Committee of Thirteen as well as hope for the Crittenden Compromise or some other acceptable plan had not happened before the vote in Alabama, Florida, or Mississippi and not in time to be widely known in Georgia. Likewise, all took place either before the *Star of the West* episode or before its news could spread, and also before or during the states' takeover of federal military installations from Georgia to Louisiana.

All the conventions met after these developments. Thus, the delegates would have known about them by then, even if they had not had time to digest their implications. As a result, the divisions apparent in the elections did not always hold in the conventions. A shift was readily apparent in Mississippi, whose conclave assembled on January 9. Whereas immediatists had gained only 41 percent of the vote back on December 20, in the convention fully 75 percent of delegates overpowered all cooperationist attempts to slow secession. And in the final vote on the secession ordinance, 85 percent cast ballots to sever the Union.

Yet, in three other states the sharp disagreements evident in the selection of delegates did not immediately disappear. In Alabama, the balance between the two sides remained remarkably stable. The immediatists turned back proposals for delay, 55–45. Then, on January 11, the delegates decided by 61–39, to leave the Union immediately. Although the two sides had been almost even in Georgia, those deciding the state's fate did not end up with that same balance. Cooperationists tried to block the dash to disunion with a proposal for a southern convention and a territorial ultimatum. They failed, 164–133. Finally, these men had to face the reality that a convention majority was determined on immediate action. When the ultimate test came on January 19, a significant number capitulated. The immediatists triumphed by 208–89. In Florida, on preliminary measures roughly 40 percent of delegates tried to halt the disunion express. Like their comrades in Alabama and Georgia, they could not. On January 10, the convention adopted an ordinance of secession by the lopsided margin of 62–9. Overwhelmingly the cooperationist minority became part of the majority. Once again, state loyalty conquered.

The two westernmost of the Deep South states, Louisiana and Texas, acted after their eastern sisters had taken their giant steps out of the Union, providing a powerful impetus for the immediatists in the last two. Even though Louisiana cooperationists had garnered almost half the vote in the contest for delegates, their strength almost dissolved in the convention, which commenced on January 23. They mounted but feeble opposition to immediate secession; three days later the convention decided by the massive margin of 113–1 to leave the Union. On February 1, Texas delegates did likewise, 166–8. Three weeks later, in the only popular referendum on secession, Texas voters ratified disunion by more than three to one, 44,317 to 13,020.

The final vote in these six conventions indisputably demonstrated a powerful allegiance to individual states. When their various stratagems to impose delay by derailing immediate secession failed, cooperationists formed no last-ditch opposition to what was taking place. In some states before the final vote they moved almost en masse into the immediatist column. Even where they did not, they did not return to their home counties bent on trying to undo secession. Rather, they joined their fellow citizens in expressing the depth of their loyalty to their states.

Many delegates to these conventions as well as an untold number of their constituents came only with great reluctance. An Alabamian wrote that his "every feeling of patriotism" along with his "every sense of good judgment" decreed that "I must share the state's destiny." A Mississippian announced to President Buchanan that southerners only wanted "redress & protection" but instead found themselves "threatened." In an almost audible lament, he concluded, "I again ask you in the name of God & my country what shall we do & what would you have us do under all these facts."[28]

From Georgia, former congressman Nathaniel G. Foster told his ex-colleague in the House of Representatives, John Sherman, that he deeply regretted his state's secession. At the same time he believed it "a vital necessity." He emphasized to Sherman that the "back bone men" of Georgia would match their loyalty to the country beside any man's. Pointing out that he was named for General Nathanael Greene of Revolutionary War fame, under whom his father had fought, he asked, How could it be otherwise? He so wished the feelings that had animated their fathers could energize them, but he did not see it happening. Yes, he and Sherman could communicate, but he and so many like him perceived nothing but animosity toward them in Sherman's party. To him and them a fanaticism as much "in earnest" as the Biblical Saul of Tarsus drove a partisan and irrational hatred of the South. And he could not see that Sherman could check such zealots. In sum, southerners did as they must.[29]

With seven separate acts between December 20 and early February, seven states solemnly declared themselves out of the Union. Yet, all looked to the future and their unification in a single southern government. That unifying would take place in Montgomery, the capital of Alabama, where a gathering of representatives from seceding states would come together on February 4. These men would have the charge and responsibility to create a formal southern confederacy.

As the Cotton States left the Union, the president-elect of the country they were departing watched from his home in Illinois. The year 1861 began with Abraham Lincoln the unchallenged leader of his party. His dealings back in mid-December with Thurlow Weed and William Henry Seward and their responses to his stance removed any doubt about who headed the Republican party. With his primacy in the party settled, Lincoln did not have to worry about serious opposition in his ranks.

Just as important for him, with Seward firmly on his side, he could rest assured that congressional Republicans would back no measure of which he disapproved. Convinced of Seward's loyalty, he made no efforts to direct the movement of Republican solons. Nor did he make any serious attempt to initiate congressional action on the crisis.

His assurance about Seward and Congress did not mean, however, that Republican politics were less central for him. On the contrary, he continued to wrestle with management of his party. His focus became the cabinet; its composition and whom to appoint to specific ministries had been on his mind since the election. But with inauguration now only two short months away, he still had critical decisions to make. At that point he had filled only two posts, Seward as secretary of state and Edward Bates of Missouri as attorney general. On January 3, he wrote Seward that it would be advantageous for Seward to know the identity of his colleagues, especially in the War and Navy departments, but their names were not yet known.[30]

The official family remained unsettled for several reasons, but none had more importance than the question of whether a southerner or southerners would have a place. That by definition meant a non-Republican, for Bates lived in a slave state. But he was a good Republican, who had been put forward for the party's presidential nomination that went to Lincoln. Seward and Weed had argued for southerners, as did the vice president–elect, Hannibal Hamlin, and others, including old Whigs from the Border states. They mostly focused on men who had supported John Bell. At the same time hard-line Republicans wanted no southerners or non-Republicans to get the coveted cabinet slots. "We are the victors ours are the spoils," cried one in Lincoln's hometown.[31]

Despite that kind of Republican opposition, Lincoln had decided to take the southern route. In fact, just after his election he had confided to his law partner William Herndon that he wanted to give the South a place "by way of placation." He stated that "if not interfered with," he would do so in a manner "as would satisfy all persons interested."[32]

Still, he had legitimate concerns. He worried about the reaction of those Republicans who wanted only solid party members tapped for the official family. He also realized that naming a southerner could have another, equally vexing, dimension. He wondered if any of the men suggested would agree to join his cabinet, if asked. But there was even more—"And if yea, on what terms" he asked. "Do they come to me? or I go to them? Or are we to lead off in open hostility to each other?" Although he could not give a complete answer to his interrogatories, he did know that he was not going to them.[33]

Finally, he decided to offer a post to John Gilmer. He went through Seward, who remained the North Carolinian's champion. He chose Gilmer because the congressman had "a *living* position in the South" and because he was from farther South than anyone else Lincoln seriously considered. Because Gilmer was away in his home state when Lincoln's letter reached Washington, it took some time to get his reply. Lincoln had even invited him to Springfield to discuss his appointment and policy. Gilmer did think seriously about saying yes, but in the end he declined. He decided accepting would do neither him nor Lincoln any good, nor could it advance his cherished cause, sectional compromise.[34]

After Gilmer turned him down, Lincoln dropped the idea of a southerner in his cabinet. His thoughts dealing with the southern slot illustrate his fundamental lack of awareness about the South or southern politics. Explaining to Seward his preference for Gilmer, the president-elect indicated that only Gilmer's southerly residence placed him ahead of Henry Winter Davis of Maryland. Yet, a great deal more than distance separated these two men. Gilmer was in fact a southerner. Yes, he opposed secession and strove for compromise, but in his letters to Lincoln and Thurlow Weed he made plain his conviction that southerners had legitimate grievances that Republicans should heed. Davis, in contrast, had little interest in particularly southern matters. A former Know-Nothing looking for a new political home, Davis would soon begin his rapid journey into Republican ranks, where he would become a stalwart figure.[35]

The Gilmer case was by no means Lincoln's only vexing decision concerning his cabinet. He still had party loyalists pushing for their favorites. Of these favorites none gave Lincoln more trouble than Simon Cameron of Pennsylvania. In fact, Lincoln said that handling Cameron was his most troublesome task in forming his cabinet. A former Democrat, Cameron in 1860 was a Republican United States senator. In Pennsylvania, a vital state for Republicans, Cameron was the key member of the party. He had a legion of supporters, but as many detractors. Cameron had a reputation not unlike that of Thurlow Weed, as a crafty manipulator with few scruples. A number of his opponents thought him plainly dishonest. But, Cameron was a political force. Acknowledging that reality, Seward told Lincoln, "I should dread exceedingly the army of Cameron's friends in hostility."[36]

Reluctantly, on New Year's Eve, the president-elect informed Cameron that he would have either the Treasury Department or the War Department. But only three days later Lincoln withdrew that invitation. A Cameron enemy had arrived in Springfield bearing documentation spelling out Cameron's venality. Rebuffing his rebuff, Cameron and his allies struck back. Lincoln retreated, a bit. The Cameron appointment remained in flux, with haggling and recrimination from friend and foe bombarding

Lincoln. Not until March 1 did he decide to hand the War Department to the controversial Pennsylvanian.

While Lincoln was consumed with cabinet making, he was aware that secession was ongoing. As state after state severed its ties with the Union, Lincoln held to his pledge of public silence. Not even the dismemberment of the country he was poised to lead could move him to make any statement to his countrymen. Yet, he was clearly concerned. Noting the "gloomy" national situation, Lincoln's adviser David Davis described him as "care worn and anxious." He still had to contend with a multitude of visitors; so many eager politicians descended upon Springfield that a number had to spend nights in train cars. Still, on January 12, the president-elect abandoned his daily receptions and restricted the visitors to his home.[37]

Although Lincoln said nothing for public distribution, privately he was not reticent. Speaking with a friend, Lincoln said he wished he could take the oath of office immediately. He saw "every hour add[ing] to the difficulties I am called to meet"; yet the Buchanan administration was doing "nothing to check the tendency toward dissolution." He was willing to face "this awful responsibility" coming to him. He felt "secession [was] being fastened rather than repressed." Moreover, the possibility of secession by the Border states distressed him mightily. That would be a terrible blow to the government.[38]

Repressing secession to Lincoln evidently meant using some kind of force, though he did not specify what. At the same time, he repeatedly made unequivocally clear his disdain for compromise. In his judgment compromise had two unacceptable dimensions. First, he professed that agreeing to any measure such as the Crittenden Compromise would only whet the secessionists' demands, which in his view, would never cease because he defined compromise as giving in or submitting. The insistence on territorial division today will mean tomorrow "we shall have to take Cuba as a condition upon which they will stay in the Union." He informed a Pennsylvania congressman that the "one compromise which would really settle the slavery question . . . would be a prohibition against acquiring any more territory." That apparent belief never, however, became central in what he wrote or said, even privately.[39]

His second reason for rejecting compromise was based on his conviction that it meant Republicans' surrendering their electoral victory. "We have just carried an election on principles fairly stated to the people," he wrote. "Now we are told in advance the government shall be broken up, unless we surrender to those we have beaten before we take office." Never, he shouted. With deep feeling he exclaimed, "I will suffer death before I will consent or will advise my friends to consent to any concession or compromise which looks like buying the privilege of taking possession of this government to which we have a constitutional right." That opinion seemingly entailed any provision not sanctioned by the Chicago platform. Lincoln had come to this outlook by mid-December, if not earlier. Nothing that had happened since then had caused him to alter his outlook.[40]

With Lincoln still in Springfield, Seward set out to prove himself the president-elect's man in Washington. Seward had accepted his subordinate role in his party. For a man as inscrutable as Seward ("Delphic," a fellow senator described him), it is difficult to know how onerous he found that adjustment. The young but perceptive Henry Adams, who saw him often, commented, he "puzzles one more and more." Besides that characteristic Seward also had an amazing self-confidence, writing his wife that only "posterity" could adequately judge him.[41]

In one sense he had time to prepare for his new role. More than a half year had passed since his failure to gain his party's presidential nomination. At the same time, it could not have been easy for this veteran to have to make his political salute to a man most considered a newcomer. No matter the emotional and psychological obstacles, Seward was determined to remain influential in his party and have a substantive voice in national politics.

By the end of December, he was clearly building his relationship with the president-elect by keeping him informed on the Washington scene. His letters concentrated on three subjects. Congressional affairs and the political outlook were central. In addition, he apprised Lincoln that he had an entrée to Buchanan's inner council. And, finally, he commented on rumors circling about schemes to block the accession to power of the first Republican president. Besides writing to Lincoln, he conversed with Lincoln's confidential adviser Leonard Swett, who was visiting Washington. As Seward doubtless expected, Swett relayed Seward's opinion and information back to Springfield.

Seward wrote about "a fervent excitement" occasioned by Lincoln's actually becoming president. That excitement had spawned all kinds of rumors, he reported. One even spoke of "a plot" to seize Washington on or before March 4, or to gain control of the railroad and the telegraph between the capital and Baltimore with the goal of preventing the inauguration. Although Seward expressed his doubts about all the chatter and tattle, he noted their existence, and that some Republicans credited them. At the same time, his outlook was generally positive. He did, however, urge Lincoln to come to Washington earlier than president-elects generally did. In his judgment Lincoln's presence in the capital "would probably be reassuring and soothing."[42]

While alerting Lincoln to the swirling gossip in the capital, Seward also dealt with hard information. He declared to Lincoln that he had managed to attain "a very effective communication" with Buchanan's administration. His source provided information on confidential discussions within Buchanan's inner circle. To Lincoln he relayed the president's struggle in deciding what to do about Fort Sumter and Major Anderson. Initially Seward worried about the administration's intentions. But after Buchanan had determined to maintain Anderson and Fort Sumter, he informed the president-elect that policy was headed in the right direction, although, Seward admitted, "much less firmly or rapidly" than he wished. Still, he did not foresee any imminent change in Charleston harbor unless the Carolinians actually assaulted Fort Sumter. Thus, the status quo would hold. Seward never divulged to Lincoln the name of his conduit, Attorney General Edwin Stanton, who did not honor his chief's trust.[43]

Seward additionally provided details on his own views on Congress and the course of secession. He recounted deliberations in the Committee of Thirteen, telling Lincoln that it would not report any plan of settlement to the Senate. Relating the collapse of the committee to secession, he simply stated that South Carolina was gone. He added that Georgia, Alabama, Mississippi, and Louisiana stood on the brink, but this information from "persons" acting for these states indicated that reviving the Missouri line might halt their secession. Seward, however, discounted such news; at this point he thought nothing would stop them.

The territorial issue was also critical for the Upper South and Border. Seward admitted that he was "uncertain" about what these states would do. Only something like the Crittenden Compromise would guarantee their rejection of secession. He had urged them to wait to see Republican moderation—but was unsure they would. At the same time, a strong

Unionist sentiment abounded in them. He would not predict the outcome. "Time and accident would determine what they do," he concluded. Even with that admission he still hoped the emotion propelling secession would dissipate.

After that realistic assessment, Seward told Lincoln what the president-elect had assuredly discerned on his own—that the first Republican president would preside over a broken country. Just how broken no one could know that January. The only hope for mending the country, in Seward's mind, required a "conciliatory forbearing and fraternal" attitude and policy by Republicans. He thought Lincoln's inaugural should address that matter, with the goal of helping guide the seceded states back into the Union.

Underscoring the hostility Lincoln would face, Seward put a choice to him. As president, Lincoln would have to "reduce" animosity either by "force or conciliation." Force, Seward argued, would be denounced throughout the North, even though, he admitted, a number of Republicans "are anxious for a fray." He considered those "reckless." They either believed no war possible or believed that it would "be less disastrous than I think it will be." No matter what these Republicans thought, the New York senator asserted, the North would not "consent to a long civil war." Thus, conciliation must mark Lincoln's policy.[44]

While striving to demonstrate his loyalty to Lincoln and his reliability as the congressional agent of the president-elect, Seward operated on two other fronts. As had been his goal since the convening of Congress, he worked to keep his fellow Republicans on his definition of a moderate course. He also expended a great effort in courting the Upper South and Border men, attempting to assuage their fears about Republican intentions. Meeting with members of Congress and visitors to Washington alike, he labored to keep them from turning to secession. That endeavor would not cease.

By early January, with his tasks in view, Seward was ready to make his first major public statement. On the twelfth he stood before his colleagues in the Senate. Not only did the senators fill their desks, but because of his stature, and that only enhanced by the knowledge that he would occupy the first chair, secretary of state, in the Lincoln cabinet, visitors crowded in. Charles Francis Adams noted that he had never seen the galleries, lobbies, and outlying rooms so jammed.[45]

Seward began by affirming the glory of the Union: "The American citi-

Major Robert Anderson

James Buchanan

Charles Francis Adams

Howell Cobb

John J. Crittenden

John J. Crittenden House, Frankfort, Kentucky, present day

Jefferson Davis

Stephen A. Douglas

House of Representatives Chamber

Senate Chamber

Inauguration of Abraham Lincoln

A beardless Abraham Lincoln,
at the time he was elected president

President Abraham Lincoln

William Henry Seward

Alexander H. Stephens

Thurlow Weed

General Winfield Scott

zen has been accustomed to believe the Union immortal." Throughout his lengthy remarks he repeatedly referred to its splendor. It must stand, he preached. Dissolution could come "only by the voluntary consent of the people of the United States," not from secession. Only the Union protected the people and the states from foreign aggression and influence.

Without the Union, he predicted, the country would break down into several confederacies. These weakened entities would be no match for foreign predators. Even worse, he now envisioned them engaged in perpetual civil wars. For him nothing could be worse. "I dread, as in my innermost soul I abhor, civil war."

In Seward's rendering the primacy of the Union did not, however, negate the constitutional rights and authority of the states. In their sphere they remained paramount. The variety in the states "quickens and amplifies manufacture and commerce." For Seward, even "the different forms of labor" did not have "to constitute an element of strife in the Confederacy." If only "slavery were not perverted to the purposes of political ambition," he declared, the institution need not contribute to national disharmony.

Distancing himself from his party's radicals and narrow sectionalism, he stated unequivocally that he stood not only behind the constitutional protection of slavery, but also that he supported measures southerners thought essential for their safety and prosperity. In his reading the Constitution left slavery "exclusively to the care, management, and disposition" of the states. Moreover, he averred, "If it were in my power, I would not alter the Constitution in that respect." He made clear that the Constitution required the return of fugitive slaves; as a result states should repeal all contravening laws. He also held himself ready as he had always been to vote for laws designed "to prevent mutual invasions of citizens of other States, and punish those who shall aid and abet them." He would support the construction of two transcontinental railroads, one connecting with the mouth of the Mississippi and the other with the Missouri River and the Great Lakes.

With the inestimable value of the Union indisputable and constitutionalists like himself in place, Seward asked the obvious and crucial question—"What is the cause of this sudden and eternal sacrifice of so much safety, greatness, happiness, and freedom?" The crisis, he asserted, did not derive from foreign intrigue nor from a tyrannical federal government. The country enjoyed peace with the nations of the world, and "the Federal Government smiles more benignantly, and works today more beneficently than ever." The crisis had come because of Abraham Lincoln's election to the presidency. But he could find no legitimate reason for such an exaggerated reaction as the threat to dismember the Union. No one had questioned the legality of Lincoln's victory, nor was a presidential election unusual. Men had no reason to fear that the new president would "usurp dictatorial powers." Describing Lincoln as a conservative man with no such intentions, Seward went on to note that Lincoln could not do so even if he wanted. The Congress controlled by his political enemies would block him. Without congressional assent, "he cannot . . . appoint a minister or even a police agent, negotiate a treaty, or procure the passage of a law, and can hardly draw a musket from the public arsenal to defend his own person."

"What, then, is the ground of discontent?" Answering his own question, Seward was succinct. The disunionists simply disagreed with the policies Republicans advocated in the canvass. That disagreement, he found normal. And in the American constitutional system a remedy was at hand—the next election. The new Republican administration had never held power; thus it had never "perverted power to the purposes of oppression." And, as he plainly stated, it could not.

Still, the crisis had enveloped the country. That meant, said Seward, a solution must be found. In his search for a way out, he noted and rejected several common prescriptions. Neither paeans to the Union, though worthwhile, nor "mutual crimination" between sections would do any good. Constitutional arguments about the legality of secession and slavery in the territories provided no salve because opinions had become "dogmatical." He even discounted Congress, the traditional forum for settling great national disputes, for he found absent "a prepondering mass of citizens, so far neutral on the issue which separates parties, that they can intervene, strike down clashing weapons, and compel an accommodation." He also thought that compromises which "sacrifice honestly held principles" less apt "to avert imminent evils" than "to produce ultimately even greater danger." After that pronouncement he pointed out that legislation in 1850 and 1854 had not brought any permanent settlement.

At this point he did refer to one specific measure that aimed at compromise. He indicated that if the admission of Kansas to the Union were accomplished, he could vote to authorize and admit two new states encompassing all remaining territory, provided current laws in them were repealed, and reserving the right to create additional states from them when appropriate. This was a proposal quite similar to Senator Rice's, which had been rejected in the Committee of Thirteen, and which Seward had voted against. In Seward's view, the repeal requirement would, of course, eliminate the provisions possibly permitting slavery in New Mexico and Utah territories. But even with that caveat he hastened to add that he did not believe "such reservations" to be constitutional. In fact, he was only making a circumlocution of orthodox Republicanism doctrine—no territorial compromise.

Seward did propose a solution, however. The people, and only the people, he asserted, could satisfactorily handle this matter. Furthermore, the Constitution mapped the road to harmony, a constitutional convention. Yet, he held that this conclave could not be immediate. First, he said, "the eccentric movements of secession and disunion" would have to end. Calm would then ensue, in two or three years. At that time, he maintained, the people could come together and finally settle the matter.

Seward concluded where he began, with the grandeur and inevitability of the Union. Everything, all parties and sections, must subordinate themselves to it. All "ought to disappear in the presence of the great question of the Union." "Dissolution would not only arrest," he intoned, "but extinguish the greatness of our country. Thus, it cannot happen." With his customary aplomb and public confidence, Seward proclaimed, "I feel sure that the hour has not come for this great nation to fall."

Seward had multiple goals for his address. By emphasizing his love for the Union and the Constitution, he wanted to convey an essential moderation, even conservatism. In doing so he aimed to temper anti-Republican and secessionist emotion in the Upper South and the Border. He also hoped to impress northern Democrats with Republican prudence. At the same time, he had no intention of departing from Republican orthodoxy on sectional matters or moving beyond Lincoln's stipulated policy, especially on territorial compromise.

On the whole he succeeded. Most important for him, Lincoln found no fault with his discourse, writing Seward, "Your recent speech is well received here; and, I think, is doing good all over the country." Some hard-liners castigated him for even mentioning compromise. His senatorial colleague from Maine William Pitt Fessenden mauled him as "a poor creature—utterly selfish, false and mean. I am getting fairly to detest him." More wished he had been tougher, but most were pleased that he had "really yielded so little." While Seward generally satisfied his party, he also received praise from northern Democrats as well as from the Border for his focus on the joys and benefits of the Union.[46]

Yet, northerners and men on the Border most committed to compromise—the Constitutional Unionists of 1860—realized that Seward did not end up where they wanted him. They liked what he did say, but were distressed that he offered no specific plans or ideas to settle the crisis. To them he exhibited too much partisanship. As the Boston attorney Robert C. Winthrop commented, they wanted a Henry Clay performance, specifying concrete proposals, which they did not get. They saw Seward moving quite close to Crittenden, but unwilling or unable to take that final critical act and raise the banner of compromise.[47]

Those not within his influence or grasping for hope wherever they could find it responded differently, however. *The New York Herald* termed the speech "silky" but with the "door of reconciliation closed." Delaware's Democratic senator James A. Bayard saw Seward trying to unite the North, but offering the South nothing. He characterized the speech "as the most artful & detestable he has ever made." A conservative New Yorker condemned Seward for outright duplicity: "He is a demagogue in the fullest sense of the word and, as far as thundering patriotism or statesmanship is concerned, nothing also." The trumpet of the fire-eaters, the *Charleston Mercury*, bugled, "Seward is the Belial of the Black Republicans, the smooth spoken wily orator, who employs the most copious language when he could say nothing."[48]

Perhaps the most telling assessments of the speech came from one good Republican and one southern Conservative. Reporting on reaction in Massachusetts, a correspondent of Congressman Adams thought it on the mark: the Constitutional Unionists "are delighted with it because it is so conciliatory and the Republicans because it is so uncompromising." United States Senator Thomas Bragg of North Carolina, who had been in the audience, termed the New Yorker's remarks conciliatory "in manner." But Bragg went on to add his general opinion of Seward: "He has a wonderful faculty of appearing to say a great deal, while saying very little." Both men realized that Seward the politician had made a political speech that basically hit its political target.[49]

Despite reservations from some and dismissals from others, Seward had made good use of his Senate pulpit. Because of his speech, Republicans were able to maintain a generous, judicious visage. Keeping partisanship in harness did not drive away northern Democrats, and Seward's conscious embrace of the Constitution, specifically its adherence to slavery and the rights of the states, encouraged the Border to hold on.[50]

Seward's major effort strove to block any possibility that his party could be legitimately charged with radicalism on slavery or race. He constantly drummed the Union and the Constitution, with protection of slavery where it existed and the rights of the states guaranteed. He did speak for the great center of his party, but on slavery and race not all Republicans stood in the same place.

Although the Republican party was clearly antislavery, that statement requires two explanatory qualifications. First, "Republicans" and "abolitionists" were not synonymous. Abolitionists demanded the immediate, uncompensated emancipation of slaves everywhere in the country, including in the fifteen states that sanctioned the institution. Abolitionists had never made up more than a tiny minority of Americans. Even in 1860 they operated on the fringe of American society and politics. At the same time, those articulate, committed moralists pounded incessantly the message that slavery was un-Christian, un-American, and a blemish on the body politic. While a few on the far left of the Republican party, like Charles Sumner, were basically abolitionists, neither abolitionists nor their doctrine ever captured the prewar party.

Overwhelmingly, Republicans valued freedom far above slavery, but they also viewed slavery as protected by the Constitution in the states where it existed. An Ohio Republican probably overstated a bit when he declared, "The *great mass* of Republican voters are imbued with an intense hostility to slavery." Yet, his generalization has meaning when applied to the future of slavery. Republicans hoped for a country that barricaded slavery within its 1860 borders. Horace Greeley's *New York Tribune* spoke for the party when it defined the election of Lincoln as ending discussion about the constitutional rights of slavery. Beyond the states that authorized it, slavery had no rights under the Constitution. Thus, the Constitution provided no authority for slavery to expand anywhere in the national domain. Propounding this view, the party rejected the Supreme Court's ruling in the *Dred Scott* case that slaveowners had the constitutional right to take their slave property into any territory owned by the United States.[51]

While Republicans were united on the necessity to restrict slavery, not all agreed on assigning the relative moral primacy of the institution. For the left, those closest to abolitionism, there was no issue. For them nothing else could match the moral grandeur of antislavery assaulting the grotesque horror of slavery. Conservative Republicans did not, however, concur. While agreeing that slavery could never match freedom morally, they attached primary moral importance to the Union. The Union outweighed slavery.

The great middle of the party never wanted to have to decide between slavery and the Union. They saw slavery as an institution and the slave South as fundamentally unprogressive and even, in the mid-nineteenth century, as un-American. In their judgment, bottling it up would solve the problem. Convinced in their view of an antiquated and backward South with its outdated slave institution that would be overpowered by freedom and progress, by the North—they had no doubt about the certainty of their virtue and eventual triumph. Facing a massive crisis with the Union at stake, this majority of Republicans would confront a terrible decision—give on slavery's extension or endanger the Union.

In this exigency Lincoln as president-elect would have an essential role. No doubt can exist about either his abhorrence of slavery or his rejection of abolitionism. From the birth of the Republican party he had held to its orthodox position on slavery in the nation. In fact, he helped create it. Because of the Constitution, Lincoln believed slavery in the states inviolable. Beyond those states, however, constitutional guarantees did not reach. Everywhere else the Constitution and America stood for freedom and liberty. For him, liberty mandated the eventual destruction of slavery.[52]

Lincoln always kept the moral dimensions of slavery in the forefront of his rhetoric and his sense of Republican policy. His cherished Union must be an antislave Union, as he interpreted antislave. In that Union slavery could not have an unlimited future—thus the necessity for territorial restriction. The adjective "unlimited" is crucial, for Lincoln did not expect slavery to end soon, perhaps not for another century. That happy event could only occur when the states decided to abolish it. This long view made him willing to guarantee slavery in the states, but never to permit, even to contemplate, its advance.

While differences did denote Republicans' outlook on slavery, disunity did not mark their attitude on race. In the middle of the nineteenth century almost all white Americans as well as Western Europeans agreed on the supremacy of the white race. Republicans did not differ, except on their extreme left, where men like Senator Sumner joined most abolitionists in viewing whites and blacks as fundamentally equal. The vast majority of Republicans, including the hard-liners, had no interest in what we call racial equality or in the promotion of any modern definition of civil rights. They were men of their time. Before 1860 almost every decision regarding such rights resided in the individual states, where blacks were generally excluded from them. Few Republicans led fights to give blacks the vote, to permit them to serve on juries, or to allow them to join militias or participate in any other possible civic duty. Anything approaching social equality was anathema to most. Interracial marriage was especially condemned. Most Republicans did believe, however, that African-Americans were entitled to a basic freedom, the right not to be enslaved.

Republicans differed from their northern Democratic opponents in a key aspect, however. While both parties believed in the superiority of the white race, Republicans did not make race a major campaign issue. In contrast, Democrats often attacked Republicans for advocating political and social rights for African-Americans and even for favoring racial equality. They regularly employed the term "Black Republicans." The Democrats strove to turn Republican antisouthern rhetoric and opposition to slavery's expansion into a program aimed at putting both races on the same plane. To borrow from the contemporary political lexicon, Democrats regularly played the race card. Although this assault grossly exaggerated Republican intentions and goals, it forced Republicans constantly to deny any such objectives and to proclaim that they, too, rejected any thought of wanting to make African-Americans and whites equals.

Most Republicans were far from eager to have African-Americans in their midst. The great majority wanted blacks to remain in the South. When the demise of slavery eventually came, they thought, the freed slaves should stay put or possibly be transported to designated areas of the national territories or out of country. Even the ardent antislavery governor of the most antislavery state in the Union, Governor John A. Andrew of Massachusetts, declared that he did not accept the idea that blacks and whites could live together with both having access to the rights of citizenship. He spoke of shipping blacks to Haiti or a special territory in the West. War did not change his view. In the fall of 1862, when presented with a proposal to resettle in Massachusetts slaves who had come into Union lines in Virginia, Andrew refused. He applauded Lincoln's emancipation plan, but announced almost simultaneously that former slaves would receive no welcome in his state.[53]

Regarding race, Lincoln stood where most of his fellow Republicans did. Growing up, living, and politically active in a world where white superiority was a given, a man with political ambition could stand nowhere else. Moreover, Lincoln's Illinois was one of the most negrophobic states in the Union, having a draconian exclusion law that practically forbade African-Americans from entering the state. On a personal level, Lincoln accepted white supremacy. Yet, he did believe that the promises of the Declaration of Independence applied to blacks as well as whites. Precisely what that meant for him is murky, except he clearly believed that a man should receive compensation for his labor. He never advocated any kind of social equality.

Although Lincoln rejected racial equality, he never embraced racist ideology, either. He did not think it possible for blacks to prosper in a world dominated by whites, for white prejudice was too powerful. In his judgment, and here he followed his political hero, Henry Clay, Lincoln felt colonization in some fashion was probably the best solution for America's racial situation. He, too, mentioned Haiti. But he never fully developed his thoughts on colonization, what it would entail and mean. As the historian Eric Foner has so aptly observed, "Race is our obsession, not Lincoln's."[54]

Lincoln did not anticipate any swift change in the racial world he knew. With slavery still so politically powerful, neither did he expect any quick end to the institution. Moreover, with racial attitudes, with which he had little disagreement, so thoroughly ingrained and omnipresent, he could not foresee a country with notably different race relations emerging any time soon.

Of course, the coming of war in April 1861 eventually brought momentous change. But, in the winter of 1860–1861, that war had not come. Wherever Lincoln stood on race and black-white relations in 1865, still a vexed question in Lincoln scholarship, he was not there before Fort Sumter.

While the Republican party and its leaders positioned themselves to take power, major congressional forces for compromise kept up their efforts to find a solution to the Republican-southern conundrum. Despite the demise of the Committee of Thirteen, Senator Crittenden did not give up, though he admitted to a Kentucky friend that prospects looked bleak. "Every thing here looks gloomy & foreboding," he wrote at the end of 1860. "*Washington is in black!* God help us!" Yet he remained undeterred: "I mean still to struggle for *peace* & *union*." To a group of Georgia citizens, he urged, "Don't give up the ship. Don't despair of the Republic." He retained hopes for his basic plan, even if particulars were altered. Senator Douglas, noting that he and Crittenden acted "in concert," also pushed ahead, searching for some way around the impasse.[55]

Even before the committee disbanded, Douglas tried to win support for his version of compromise. Concluding that Republican obduracy doomed any hope of getting any measure akin to extending the Missouri line through the committee, he hoped his own proposition just might. He brought forward a version of his traditional popular-sovereignty idea: Congress would affirm the existing status in all territories, with a provision that upon reaching a white population of fifty thousand a territory could automatically apply for statehood. Douglas realized that "it does not q[uite] suit any body, but may possibly be taken by both parties as a compromise." According to Douglas, it would accomplish his chief purpose—"banish[ing] *the slavery question from Congress* and plac[ing] it beyond the reach of Federal Legislation." In trying to sell his plan to the South, he told Alexander Stephens that by retaining Mexican peonage in New Mexico, the South would get "all the South can wish." Stephens disagreed, however. No matter, for Douglas's project never went anywhere; after the committee rejected it, he basically abandoned it.[56]

He gave his wholehearted support, however, to Crittenden's continuing efforts. After the collapse of the Committee of Thirteen, Crittenden tacked promptly to another course. On January 3 he put before the Senate a resolution that would take his compromise directly to the people; he wanted Senate approval for a plebiscite. Its results would only be advisory, with Congress retaining the power of decision. From Douglas he added two items to his package: one prohibited voting by blacks in territories, the other dealt with colonizing free blacks. Recognizing his proposed procedure lacked precedent, he argued that the grave crisis confronting the country demanded it. In this moment the people's direct voice should be heard, he declared. After all, Crittenden reminded his audience, all power of the government derived from them. He certainly had no fear of their verdict. Whatever it might be, he would accept it, "more surely and more firmly . . . strengthened with their strength, and honored with their advice." In his view the people might break the spell paralyzing Congress caused by "party politics, and in opinions which they have generated and fastened . . . upon us against our will."[57]

After Crittenden's appeal, Douglas pledged his support. Although Douglas did not think Lincoln intended to harm slavery in the South, he said southerners entertained such fears, in part because of the emphasis Republicans had put on Lincoln's "House Divided" speech during the presidential campaign. To the Republican assertion that back in November the people had spoken, Douglas stated simply that in November they did not face a broken Union and the prospect of civil war.[58]

Despite repeated examples of Republican intransigence, Crittenden had reason to think that this time he had a decent chance of success. He wanted the Senate to pass a resolution, which required only a simple majority, not the two-thirds necessary for a potential constitutional amendment. Moreover, he could point to the huge outpouring of support from northern citizens. Letters poured in to him from across the region. Business leaders, notable politicos, wealthy as well as average men all expressed enthusiasm for his plan. "The disposition to do right is increasing," declared a New Englander. Of course, these epistles were private and came mostly from non-Republicans.[59]

But there was more. More meetings took place throughout the free states. The New Jersey legislature resolved to back Crittenden's plan. A veritable cascade of petitions chorusing approval flooded Congress. They came from Maine all the way to the upper Mississippi Valley and from the Border. Seward presented one from New York containing forty thousand names. This was the second petition he presented; the first had twenty-five thousand. The deluge engulfing Congress even included a torrent from Massachusetts. Crittenden offered petitions from 182 towns and cities containing more than twenty-two thousand signatures. All of these asked that Congress say yes to Crittenden's compromise or something similar.[60]

This public outpouring of acclaim for Crittenden's or some other serious compromise presented Republican senators with a dilemma. There is no way, of course, to know with certainty the outcome of a popular referendum in early 1861—whether it would have boosted or blasted Crittenden's hopes. Yet, the chances were extremely good for a positive outcome for the Kentuckian. In the free states opponents of compromise might have prevailed, if all Lincoln voters sided with the opposition. But, available evidence points to the conservatives among them lining up for compromise. Thus, voters in the North could have divided fairly evenly, or the compromise could have won by a narrow margin. No doubt can exist, however, about the result in the eight slave states of the Upper South and the Border. In them pro-compromise sentiment was overwhelming. In a plebiscite with the issue sharply presented—compromise like Crittenden's or none—the popular vote would most likely have given the pro-compromise position a solid triumph.

In January 1861 experienced politicians of all persuasions would surely have perceived that probable outcome. Republican leaders did not view such an occurrence favorably; it would either undermine or ridicule their unyielding opposition to territorial settlement. At the same time, voting against Crittenden's resolution would be denounced for preventing the people from speaking. From their perspective, Republican senators had but one safe option, blocking any direct vote by the Senate. Once more they would follow the pattern that had been followed by congressional Republicans since the commencement of the session—obstruction through parliamentary maneuvering directed at postponement and procrastination.

On January 9, Crittenden attempted to get action. At that moment Daniel Clark, Republican of New Hampshire, moved a substitute, with the straightforward declaration that nothing besides the Constitution as written was needed to preserve the Union. Enforcing the laws, Clark's proposal stated, rather than any new amendments or concessions, would eliminate any danger to the country. Thereupon, his colleague Henry Wilson of Massachusetts successfully got debate postponed. Wilson's move signaled Republican tactics. Constantly they strove for delay or pushed to take up other bills. A disgusted Douglas thundered, "I am aware, if the majority are determined that we shall not have a vote, they can call for another special order, or they can postpone this subject. They have the power to give it the go-by." Without success, he pressed for Republicans to agree to a vote.

Finally, on January 16, it appeared that a vote would take place. Crittenden and his allies beat back Republican efforts to stall with the Pacific railroad bill and the admission of Kansas. But at the critical moment, Senator Clark put forth his earlier proposal, the substitute for Crittenden's resolution. The question was called, and the Senate by 25–23 agreed to it. When the tally was made, Douglas was momentarily absent from the chamber. Upon his return, the Republicans denied his request to have his vote counted in the negative column. All twenty-five yes votes came from Republicans, and not a single nay. Throughout the process the Republicans had voted in unison to block any ballot on Crittenden's resolution.

A second key to Clark's triumph rested, however, with southerners. Six senators from Deep South states that had not yet actually seceded were present, but did not participate in the poll. If they had voted, Clark's substitute would have been defeated, and Crittenden's original then passed. In fact, their votes plus Douglas's would have given Crittenden a 30 to 25 margin. Then it would have gone to the House, where it would have faced an uncertain future. Still, passage by the Senate would have given it a major boost. In their refusal to take part, the southerners followed the policy Jefferson Davis had set for the Committee of Thirteen. A victory in the face of unanimous Republican opposition was no victory at all. These senators, with their states on the brink of secession, required some indication of Republican willingness to compromise on the central territorial issue. Without that signal, they considered any congressional action meaningless.[61]

The Republicans in the House were especially successful in diverting roll calls on serious territorial compromise. Responding to an Illinois Democrat begging for a vote on his resolution in favor of the Crittenden Compromise, a hard-liner from Pennsylvania retorted, "The Republican side of the House will vote when it pleases them." It never did.[62]

Yet, the House differed in one notable respect from the Senate. While the Committee of Thirteen was defunct, the Committee of Thirty-three still met. In its deliberations from early December until mid-January, Republicans, like their counterparts in the Senate, managed to block or sidetrack all proposals dealing with the territories. Even so, the committee debated other matters, including the legitimacy of the presidential election of 1860, slavery in the District of Columbia, the constitutionality of slavery, and fugitive slaves. Through these discussions the Republicans did not all find themselves on the same side. Although a division between hard-liners and moderates was evident, they did not form two distinct lineups on every issue.[63]

After much jockeying, the Committee of Thirty-three held final votes on these key issues. Republicans divided in favor of admitting New Mexico as a state by 14 to 9; Republicans cast all nine nays, but five were ayes along with two not voting. On that same day the proposed Thirteenth Amendment, which would make abolishing slavery practically impossible for the foreseeable future, prevailed overwhelmingly, by 20 to 5. Republicans cast the nays, but eight said yes and three failed to vote. Three days later a new version of fugitive slave legislation barely survived, by 12 to 11, with Republicans numbering ten of the nays while three voted yes and three did not vote.[64]

These divisions remained stark when the committee attempted to prepare a report for the full House. It could not come to any agreement on what specific measures should receive the committee's stamp of approval. In the end, it decided by the narrow margin of 16 to 13, with Republicans split 10 to 6 between majority and minority, that Chairman Corwin should present several propositions discussed in the committee, the journal of the committee, and "such views as he may think proper to submit." Corwin did as directed but, in a move that underscores the sharp split among his colleagues, seven separate minority reports accompanied his majority statement.[65]

Although Corwin did report to the House, specifying ideas his committee had backed, privately he could find little reason for optimism. To President-elect Lincoln he confided that if the disharmony exhibited in the committee accurately reflected public opinion, "a long and bloody civil war *must* follow." He lamented "the madness of the time," which he confessed he could not understand. He had no patience with the hard-liners in his own party. The "extreme northern men," he told Lincoln, "are practical fools," who are "mad." Describing "this horrid picture," he concluded, "God alone can help us."[66]

In his accounting, Corwin recommended the adoption of three major items. First, he urged the House to admit New Mexico as a state, with or without slavery as its citizens desired. This New Mexico would include all of the Mexican Cession below the old Missouri line, southern California excluded. All recognized that New Mexico would most probably come in as a slave state. The Compromise of 1850 had permitted slavery within its borders, and in 1860 there were reportedly a few in the territory, though the census of 1860 listed none.

The idea of the immediate admission of New Mexico as a state originated with the ambitions of Henry Winter Davis of Maryland, a member of the Committee of Thirty-three. An adherent of the American or Know-Nothing party, Davis had been gravitating toward the Republicans, voting with them in the committee against taking up a resolution to extend the Missouri line, the only non-Republican to do so. Davis pressed Charles Francis Adams to sign on for New Mexico as a way to show southern Unionists that Republicans had good intentions toward the South. A political dividend could result for Republicans if with New Mexico they could isolate the Deep South from the other slave states.

Adams agreed, calling Davis's idea "a cannon shot through the line." With New Mexico, Adams wanted "to convince" the Border states that Republicans "are not animated with the ferocious temper that is attributed to them for the sake of forcing these too into revolution." He thought New Mexico could fulfill that hope because the Deep South as well as other southerners wanted the area under the extension of the Missouri line, not as a state. Not only did Adams concur with Davis, a caucus of Republicans on the Committee of Thirty-three expressed its willingness to go along. Chairman Corwin wanted Adams, with his impeccable antislavery credentials, to place New Mexican statehood before the committee. Adams accepted the task, and on December 29, he cast his ballot with the majority when by 13 to 11 the committee initially approved the design. Southerners voting did divide, but Adams did not get his phalanx of Border men embracing New Mexico.

In taking this step, Adams realized the political danger he could incur. By his own definition he did receive a mountain of mail criticizing his New Mexico stance; most of his correspondents rejected any compromise on sectional or slavery matters. Resigning himself, Adams confided to his diary, "But all public life is made of great hazards on trying occasions." When the hard-liner Senator Preston King of New York queried him on the tenacity of his upholding New Mexico statehood, Adams responded that he would not be "tenacious," as was his wont. He saw it as good policy, but would not press the issue if it divided the party. He made the same declaration to Senator Seward. And, in fact, when the committee took its final vote on New Mexico, it carried by a wider margin than originally. Adams, however, had shifted to the losing side.[67]

Along with the bill for New Mexican statehood, Corwin advanced the proposed Thirteenth Amendment to the Constitution. If passed by Congress and ratified by the states, this would become the first amendment since 1804. It affirmed what almost all white Americans in 1860 believed, including a substantial majority of Republicans—that the Constitution protected slavery in the states that sanctioned it. The proposed amendment stated: "No amendment to the Constitution aimed to interfere with slavery in the states where it now exists shall originate with any current free state, or be valid without the consent of every state in the Union."

Corwin's third submission addressed the contentious Fugitive Slave Act of 1850. While it reaffirmed federal responsibility for apprehending alleged fugitives, it also mandated procedural rules that required substantial involvement by the federal judiciary. Moreover, it stipulated two changes aimed at pacifying northern opposition. The first set the fees of federal agents arresting fugitives at the same level, whether the person was found to be a slave or set free. The second declared that "no citizen of any state shall be compelled to aid in the capture of a fugitive."[68]

None of Corwin's three recommendations, however, dealt with the most vexing issue, slavery in the territories. Still, with Republican disunity on them and Deep South congressmen rapidly exiting through the disunion door, even they faced a most uncertain future in the House. Nothing like the Crittenden Compromise had made any headway in the committee. That approach had had no more likelihood of success there than in the Committee of Thirteen or in either house of Congress. With Lincoln's position firmly set and his leadership of the party indisputable, the possibility of anything similar was slim indeed.

Despite Congress's continued inaction, the Upper South and Border forces still clamored for serious compromise, including on the territories. Refusing to believe that obduracy and intransigence could prevail, John P. Kennedy prophesied, "I am convinced that we are soon to have a clearing up." To each other these men lamented what they saw as Republican devotion to partisanship. "They shall look to the masses," Governor Hicks of Maryland wrote, "& not believe themselves to be the entire country." Capturing their sense of a world gone awry, a correspondent of the Virginian William C. Rives drew upon an old folk saying: "Up with Folly, down with wisdom is the order of the day."[69]

The Upper South and Border men also pled directly to Republicans to break the political logjam. A North Carolinian wanted Weed to get Seward to make a strong conciliation speech. If he did so, "it would make him the greatest man on earth." Republicans were asked why they refused to assist those attempting to withstand secession. Lincoln heard from a "dear friend" in Washington that Border men "implore[d] in tears, for something upon which to stand, else they are crushed beneath the wheels of a Jaugernaut car." From Nashville, Lincoln received an appeal "to speak out manly" to save the Union. "Let no party put a padlock on your mouth," this Tennessean beseeched the president-elect.[70]

In Congress neither did the Border men give up. While futilely trying to get his compromise through the Senate, Senator Crittenden became intimately involved with another initiative, which seemed to have promise. He chaired an ad hoc gathering of fourteen congressmen from the Border states, on both the northern and southern sides of the Mason-Dixon Line and the Ohio River. Disturbed that nothing seemed forthcoming from official committees, this self-selected group strove to give an impetus to serious compromise.

The group met initially on December 28, with Crittenden presiding. But the upheaval and disagreement caused by news of Major Anderson's move to Fort Sumter caused a temporary disbanding. After a week of informal recess, the body came together once more. Some southern Unionists, including John Gilmer, were in their number. At least five Republicans attended, from New Jersey, Pennsylvania, Ohio, Indiana, and Iowa. All concurred generally on three matters—a constitutional amendment forbidding congressional interference with slavery in the states; enforcement of the Fugitive Slave Act; and extending the Missouri line in some fashion. Crittenden agreed to substitute this plan, called the Border State Plan for his own. Republican Congressman Samuel Curtis of Iowa recorded in his journal, "It would seem to me a matter we ought to arrange."

The territorial provision was introduced by James Hale, Republican from Pennsylvania. He and his colleagues wanted to alter the Crittenden Compromise to delete the points most onerous to Republicans. Instead of decreeing that slavery be protected south of the Missouri line, they simply stipulated no federal interference with the institution in that area. Additionally, they chopped Crittenden's reference to all territory "hereafter acquired." Then they altered Crittenden's architecture, specifying the amendment process only for certifying protection of slavery in the states. All else would be handled with congressional legislation. That would mean a simple majority vote on all measures, not the two-thirds required for constitutional amendments, except for the one that had widespread support, guaranteeing no federal move against slavery in the states. With the committee's agreement, Senator Crittenden went to the White House and informed the president.[71]

Behind the scenes the deft Thurlow Weed utilized his lobbying skills on behalf of the compromisers. He came to Washington for several reasons, including conferring with John Gilmer about the cabinet position. In addition, he worked quietly for the Border State Plan. He even helped get Lincoln's close adviser Leonard Swett, also in Washington, to write positively to the president-elect about the proposed settlement. Given their intimate relationship, it is impossible to believe that Seward did not know about Weed's activity.[72]

When House Republicans learned about the handiwork of the Border group, they dodged the issue. To a caucus of his fellows, Congressman Hale on January 4 reported on the Border state gathering. Adjourning without any decision, the caucus met again on the fifth to take action. Hard-liners pelted Hale and his plan. Castigating secession and compromise, Owen Lovejoy of Illinois struck their chord: "There never was a more causeless revolt since Lucifer led his cohort of apostate angels against the throne of God, but I never heard that the Almighty proposed to compromise by allowing the rebels to kindle the fire of hell south of the celestial meridian of thirty-six thirty." Lovejoy and his comrades declared they would never acquiesce in any compromise. Although they did not get the caucus to come up to their hard line, the majority decided to do nothing. Instead, they agreed to take up the business of the country in the House; it evidently did not include the crisis of the Union. Without taking any vote on the Border State Plan, the caucus adjourned *sine die*. In his diary, Charles Francis Adams noted "the extreme of vehemence and rigidity."[73]

On January 7, Congressman Emerson Etheridge, a Tennessee Unionist, attempted to get his version of the Border State Plan before the full House. He combined Hale's territorial measure with restrictions on acquiring new territory that had originated with John Sherman of Ohio. They would require a two-thirds vote of both House and Senate to bring in any new territory. To get his proposal debated, Etheridge required a suspension of the rules which necessitated a two-thirds majority. With Republicans overwhelmingly against him, Etheridge could manage but a narrow majority, 83–78. Republicans torpedoed the hopes of the Border state men. Yet, they willingly supported suspension of the rules for a resolution applauding Major Anderson's move to Fort Sumter and President Buchanan's backing of him.[74]

At the same time the Border State Plan encountered congressional rough seas, Republicans on both sides of that effort reached out to the president-elect. Congressman Hale wanted Lincoln to stand with the "true and loyal men" of the South in their battle "against demagogues and traitors." But the hard-liners also appealed to the man in Springfield. A political friend, Congressman Elihu Washburne, also from Illinois, alerted Lincoln to consternation in Republican ranks "in regard to a *compromise* that is supposed to be hatching by the Weed-Seward dynasty." Noting Weed's presence in the capital, Washburne warned that Weed had even influenced Leonard Swett on compromise. Although he did say he was not worried about Lincoln's stance, he left no doubt about his view of the stakes. "If you waver, *our party is gone*." Lincoln acted as Washburne wanted and as he had been doing all along. To Hale, Lincoln penned a strong remonstrance. Marking his letter "confidential," Lincoln condemned all plans for compromise as "surrender to those we have beaten." He asserted that any Republican concession would destroy both the party and the government. Republicans must reject all such initiatives.[75]

Later in the month Senator Seward provided Lincoln his perspective on affairs. He told the president-elect that the appeals from the Border Union men were "very powerful" because they say without some deal, they cannot withstand the secessionists. My argument, Seward wrote, has been telling them "to wait." He advocated "a truce on slavery" and after emotions had subsided, then remedies could be found for constitutional questions. Simultaneously he assured Lincoln that pro-Union sentiment was "rising in the popular mind." His contacts indicated that Unionists dominated in Maryland and were gaining strength in Virginia.

Then Seward warned Lincoln that a hostile Confederacy—the Deep South—would greet him when he took the oath of office. Confronting it, Lincoln would have a choice: "You must reduce it by force or conciliation," Seward advised. He warned that many in the North would denounce force; moreover, in his opinion, the North would not "consent to a long civil war." And in his view war, if it came, would be "disastrous." He thought Lincoln's proper policy should entail collecting the revenue, retaining the forts in the Gulf of Mexico, and maintaining the administration in Washington. Overall, he advocated a policy that would permit time for a Union party to rise in the South and guide the seceding states back into the Union. He saw addressing that matter as appropriate for Lincoln's inaugural. Seward's agenda for the first Republican president had an overriding theme, "conciliatory forbearing and fraternal."[76]

Seward's watchwords certainly described President Buchanan's hopes and the goals of his policy. Following the truce in Charleston harbor agreed to by Governor Pickens and Major Anderson, deputies of each traveled to Washington. Isaac Hayne, the attorney general of South Carolina, representing the governor, carried a letter from Pickens to the president demanding that the United States turn Fort Sumter over to the state. As far as Pickens was concerned, the fort now lay within the borders of independent South Carolina; he was willing, however, to pay for the property. Anderson sent an officer to obtain guidance from his superiors. Both sides had agreed that the informal arrangement between governor and major would hold until Hayne returned with Buchanan's response.[77]

On January 14, Hayne called on Buchanan at the White House. The president informed him that all communications had to be in writing. He would engage in no oral discussion about Fort Sumter. Only when Hayne presented proposals in written form would he respond. All involved, from South Carolinians to the Deep South politicians remaining in Washington to Republicans, knew, or thought they knew, how the president would react. In a message to Congress on January 8, Buchanan had stated clearly that the "right and duty to use military force . . . against those who assail the property of the federal government is clear and undeniable."[78]

The president also declared that his position and that of his troops in their beleaguered bastion was purely defensive. He would initiate no action against South Carolina unless the state assaulted federal property. Closely observing events in South Carolina and Hayne's mission, leading politicians from the states in the process of seceding who were still in Washington wanted no change in the status quo. If hostilities broke out in Charleston harbor, then their states would surely become involved. That eventuality they opposed, at least at the moment. They were focusing on a new southern confederacy, but it had not moved beyond the planning stage.

To ensure that armed conflict did not occur, these politicians worked on three fronts. First, on January 16, they sent Senator Clay of Alabama to visit Buchanan, to plead once more for him to withdraw Major Anderson. In this private conversation the president said that "it was quite out of the question" for him to have discussions about Fort Sumter. He also stated that he "would not under any circumstances withdraw the troops from Fort Sumter." Clay proposed a plan that his group thought would mean no bloodshed. The South Carolina authorities would guarantee the government free access to Anderson as well as permitting Anderson to purchase all needed supplies. In turn, the president would pledge not to send reinforcements. Buchanan replied that he would require a written communication that he would take before his cabinet prior to making a decision.[79]

On the second front, the southerners sent a letter signed by ten senators from seceding states to Hayne requesting that he postpone delivering the letter he carried from Governor Pickens to the president. They knew Buchanan's response, and felt that negative would force Pickens's hand. His letter was an ultimatum: Fort Sumter must be given up. Its rejection would mean that Pickens would have to order an attack on the fort or lose all credibility in his state. From Hayne, the senators asked for time for their efforts to solve the situation and for the realization of a southern confederacy. To this entreaty Hayne agreed.[80]

The third battlefront was for the southern politicians, recognizing that South Carolina was a tinderbox, to remonstrate directly with Governor Pickens. In Charleston, Pickens had to deal with radicals who demanded immediate action against Fort Sumter. The senators decided Jefferson Davis should go to Charleston, consult with Pickens, and get him to hold off. Illness prevented Davis's trip, but he did write Pickens, imploring him not to act and maintaining that a premature strike would only hurt the southern cause. He reminded Pickens, "The little garrison in its present positi[on] presses on nothing but a point of pride, & to you I need not say that war is made up of real eleme[nts]." Moreover, Davis assured the governor that "we shall soon have a Southern Confederacy that shall be ready to do all which interest or even pride demands."[81]

Buchanan had an equal stake in preserving the status quo in Charleston harbor. He turned down advice, chiefly from Black, to reinforce Major Anderson, reiterating that he would only do so if Anderson said he needed it. For his part, Anderson in regular reports to the War Department affirmed his well-being. He indicated that he had ample basic supplies for three months. He also mentioned that state authorities permitted his purchase of meat and vegetables. At the same time he noted the building of works against him while he spelled out his improvements in Fort Sumter. He had also taken the precaution of sending all women and children to the North. Yet, at the end of the month he made a clear statement of his views: "I do hope that no attempt will be made by our friends to throw supplies in; their doing so would do more harm than good." Anderson's superiors let him know that they intended to heed his counsel; no aid would be forthcoming unless he requested it. They also signaled their approval of his course.[82]

On January 19 the southern senators made still another appeal to the president, this time in writing. They wanted a commitment from Buchanan that he would not dispatch additional troops to Fort Sumter; in turn, South Carolina would keep in place the arrangements that allowed Anderson access to the mainland. With their letter they included one from Hayne to them stating that "so far as his authority extend[ed]" he agreed. Replying for the president, Secretary of War Holt repeated what the president had said so many times. His policy was defensive and would remain so unless South Carolina took the offensive. But no promise would be forthcoming not to reinforce Major Anderson. At present there was no intention to do so "because he makes no such request, and feels quite secure in his position." But, should he feel reinforcements essential, "every effort will be made to supply them." The president, Holt asserted, could give no assurance about hostilities toward South Carolina because only Congress had the power to declare war. Concluding, Holt pointed out that "Major Anderson is not menacing Charleston" and then went to the heart of his and his chief's hopes: "I am convinced that the happiest result which can be obtained is, that both he and the authorities of South Carolina shall remain in their present amicable footing, neither party being bound by any obligations whatever, except the high Christian and moral duty to keep the peace, and to avoid all causes of mutual irritation."[83]

At month's end no change had taken place. Hayne finally left for Charleston, stating that his lengthy stay in Washington had given South Carolina more time to prepare. Hayne, Pickens, and Holt, writing for the president, exchanged wordy missives going over the same ground all had previously covered thoroughly, with no one giving on any central question.[84]

Even with the standoff between South Carolina and Buchanan, collision had been avoided. Neither side had fired any guns at the other. President Buchanan's great objective was to have none fired prior to March 4 and the end of his term. Yet, he had made unequivocal declarations that the flag would remain flying over Fort Sumter. Additionally, he had instructed his secretary of war to develop a plan to reinforce Anderson, if "practicable, with the means in our power." Still, he, like Seward, could continue to hope that somehow in some way reasonable, patriotic men would fashion a good ending.[85]

CHAPTER FIVE

"You Can Still This Storm"

DESPITE THE CONTINUING impasse in Congress and the ongoing tension in Charleston, Conservatives in the Upper South and along the Border kept up their hopes for finding a path to settlement. As they had done from the beginning of the crisis, they bombarded Republican leaders with pleas for some movement to aid them in their struggle against disunionists. Writers hailed from the Chesapeake Bay in the east to beyond the Mississippi River in the west. They appealed directly to Lincoln and addressed others like Charles Francis Adams and Simon Cameron, but mostly they came to Seward, correctly perceiving him as the best chance for a positive Republican reaction.[1]

In the letters to Seward, two themes predominated. First, they pressed for conciliation, claiming that with a conciliatory policy forthcoming from the Republicans they could not only hold on, they could prevail. James Barbour of Virginia told Seward his side could triumph only by offering "tolerable evidence that there was a hope of obtaining by rational appeals to the Northern People constitutional guarantees of our slave property rights." Second, they saw that their prevailing would lead to what Seward so wished for, a Union party opposed to Democrats in general as well as disunionists in particular. On that point, a Tennessean was direct, telling Seward that in his state they could build "a strong party of friends," but only "if we are met with a spirit of moderation on the part of the North." He meant, of course, from the Republican party. These Conservatives envisioned their Union party moving easily, as Barbour wrote, into "a national conservative Party which will dominate over all other Party organizations

North & South for many years to come." They also foresaw Seward's reaping the leadership rewards in this new political kingdom.[2]

The aspirations expressed by Seward's correspondents derived chiefly from his posture toward them. Yes, they clung to Crittenden's and Douglas's assertions that rapprochement remained possible, but Seward was an eminent, card-carrying member of the enemy Republican party. Moreover, he spoke in moderate tones and in individual encounters treated them with respect. Although in his major Senate speech back on January 12 he did not travel the distance they desired, he did not shut every door to reconciliation. Additionally, in private conversation he generally communicated optimism about something positive getting done. Perhaps "optimism" is too strong a word, but Seward never said some kind of satisfactory deal was impossible. And he knew that for the Upper South and Border men a satisfactory deal had to at least touch upon the territorial issue. Even so, he never took an implacable stance. In his own words, he was battling to head off "mad men North and mad men South," who aimed to destroy the Union "by civil war."[3]

At private social events attended by capital notables, Seward also evinced sanguineness about the probability of a satisfactory settlement. His demeanor and his words at such affairs went beyond parlor and dining room. Men utterly committed to serious compromise, like Crittenden and Douglas, witnessed Seward on these occasions. At one dinner party Seward made a toast in which he declared that devotion to the Union must trump allegiance to party; Crittenden, so gripped with emotion, "shattered his glass when he replaced it on the table." In the Senate on January 31, Douglas announced, "I have reason satisfactory to myself upon which to predicate that firm hope that the Union will be preserved." He told his fellow senators that he saw "indications every day of a disposition to meet this question new and consider what is necessary to save the Union."[4]

With his outreach to these men, Seward was engaged in a bold high-wire act. He knew two critical things that they did not know. He understood Lincoln's unbending hard line on the territories. If he had any doubt, Lincoln disabused him of it in a letter of February 1 marked "*Private & Confidential.*" "I am inflexible," the president-elect pronounced. "I am for no compromise which *assists* or *permits* the extension of the institution [slavery] on soil owned by the nation. And any tricks by which the nation is to acquire territory," he continued, "and then allow some local authority to spread slavery over it, is as obnoxious as any other." Aside from his knowledge of Lincoln's granitelike stance on the territories, Seward was well aware that he had become Lincoln's subordinate, though he pushed his independence as far as he thought possible while he tried to inch his chief toward his own view. He often agitated the hard-liners in Congress, who yearned for the Republican congressional caucus to denounce the New York senator and keep him out of Lincoln's cabinet.[5]

Nimbly, Seward kept himself upright because he never deviated too far from Lincoln's commandment. He also kept Lincoln informed about his contacts with the Border and Upper South men. Doing so, he praised their loyalty and their worthiness, always insisting that they merited all the assistance the Republicans could afford. His strategy kept their claims, which he deemed legitimate, before the president-elect.[6]

Perceptive fellow Republicans noted Seward's gymnastics. In his diary, Charles Francis Adams commented on Seward's talking about his efforts to retain Lincoln's approval. The Republican loyalist George Templeton Strong in New York City got word of Seward's declaration that he "pledged his honor as a man and his capacity as a politician that all this agitation should be ended within sixty days." Reflecting on that vow, Strong decided, "If Seward said so, he is either the greatest of fools, the most astute of politicians, or the boldest of political liars—perhaps with good intent." Based on my understanding of Seward and the desperate mission he had taken on for himself, Strong was probably on the mark in the final two depictions, with perhaps a tincture of the first added. Their sum total went a long way toward indentifying the artful and shrewd senior senator from New York.[7]

Seward was not the only suitor wooing the Upper South and the Border. The seceding Deep South states also focused attention on their dallying sister slave states. By February the seven states from South Carolina west to Texas had severed their ties to the Union. Yet, political leaders in these states fully understood that eight slave states remained in the Union. Even more disturbing to these men, the Upper South and Border did not seem to share with their more southerly brothers the conviction that the Republican triumph heralded impending doom for the South, especially its slave institution. Above the Deep South there was certainly no rush to leave the Union and join the new enterprise.

To spur their reluctant fellow southerners, the majority of Deep South states dispatched emissaries to the Upper South and Border. These agents, known as commissioners, became missionaries for the gospel of secession. The vast majority came from Alabama, Georgia, Mississippi, and South Carolina. From December 1860 to the spring of 1861 they traveled widely, even to other Deep South states. Not every state sent a commissioner to every other slave state, but revivalists made it everywhere in the Upper South and Border.[8]

These ambassadors delivered a passionate, emotional message. Republican victory, cried one, meant the federal government "will be perverted into an engine for the destruction of our domestic institution and the subjugation of our people." They pronounced their dire warnings in formal addresses to legislatures and in speeches to crowds in the streets. Their baleful alarms made absolutely clear why they believed secession essential. Their sermons announced that Republican dominance meant annihilation of slavery. In vivid colors they painted the horror of an abolitionized South. Republicans, they asserted, really aimed at racial equality. Moreover, the spectre of race war loomed with the terrifying prospect of racial amalgamation. After describing such a frightening future, the commissioners provided an escape, secession. For the preservation of the society and the economy, even of the white race, secession was not a choice, but a requirement.

Despite their sincerity and fervor, the commissioners made few converts in the Upper South and Border. Courtesy and respect they found, but no commitments to secede. The majority of citizens in this region simply did not share the ghastly vision of what lay ahead propounded by their inflamed visitors. With a smaller percentage of slaves within their borders and more direct contact with northerners, they required overt acts against the South and slavery before embracing the radical solution of secession. Apprehension alone would not move them.

Not only did the Upper South and Border generally shun the commissioners' message, many in the region viewed with considerable dislike the Deep South's rush to secession. A Nashville editor complained that "the ultra South is treating us badly and hence [I] have but little sympathy with them." Maryland's John Pendleton Kennedy blasted the fire-eaters for their "abominable, unprincipled treason." Decrying hasty secession, in Tennessee former governor William B. Campbell stated that he was not "yet satisfied that the evils that are complained of are sufficient to justify a dissolution of the Union & civil war."[9]

South Carolina came in for special disgust. A North Carolinian denounced the arrogance of his southern neighbor, declaring that his state would postpone as long as possible any alignment with the initiator of secession. A Maryland supporter of President Buchanan described a strong antipathy generated by "the untoward and hasty conduct of South Carolina in seeming to disregard her obligation to you or her sister states." John Pendleton Kennedy lacerated the action of the Palmetto State: "It is the mock-heroic of men who do not comprehend their own incapacity, who mistake passion for a just sense of honor, and who cannot perceive the desperate extremes of their own folly."[10]

Although the Deep South wanted the entire Upper South and Border to join with it in leaving the Union, the key was Virginia. Most in the Deep South had a deep affection for "the mother of the South." Virginia had been a primary force in the American Revolution, whose legacy secessionists cherished and embraced. Two of the titans of that epoch, George Washington and Thomas Jefferson, were Virginians. For most of the founding generation of the United States as a nation the Virginia dynasty guided its fortunes. Even though Virginia's importance in the nation had diminished since the 1830s, southerners still saw it as special. Any southern movement without Virginia would be incomplete.

At first glance Virginia appeared a likely prospect for secession. The states'-rights doctrine so central in southern political thinking traced its origins back to Thomas Jefferson and James Madison, especially their Virginia and Kentucky Resolutions of the late 1790s. In addition, the state's two most influential men in Congress, senators Robert M. T. Hunter and James M. Mason, usually lined up with the Deep South. Virginia also had an able, vigorous coterie of fire-eaters. Although unable to control the direction of the state, they exercised considerable influence. And they were using Republican intransigence to try to motivate Virginians toward secession. Finally, Virginia had a larger slave population than any other slave state.[11]

Yet advocates for secession encountered serious obstacles. Virginia's slaves were not evenly distributed within the state. The two great mountain chains that bisected the state from north to south divided it into three principal regions. East of the Blue Ridge the oldest, the Tidewater and the Piedmont, remained the heart of Virginia slavery, along with the Southside, the area below the James River, extending down to North Carolina.

West of the Alleghenies there were few slaves. This portion of the Old Dominion, which would become West Virginia during the Civil War, stretched all the way to the Ohio River. And much of its commerce and society were closer in character to its near neighbors Ohio and Pennsylvania than to the rest of Virginia to the east. Between the two ranges, the Alleghenies and the Blue Ridge, ran the great Valley of Virginia. Settled chiefly by Scots-Irish and Germans, the valley provided fertile land for farmers, some who owned slaves and some who did not. Many ironworks dotted the region, and again, some utilized slave labor, others not. In the valley, moderate politics held sway; sectional radicals found it uncongenial.

Lincoln's election did worry many Virginians, and Republican refusal to entertain serious compromise only increased that anxiety. When the legislature met in January, it recognized the tumult gripping the country. While Congress foundered, Deep South states were leaving the Union. In Richmond, Virginia secessionists prodded legislators to place their state in that parade. "We have been almost under a reign of terror," wrote a Conservative from the valley. "The disunionists are assembled in full force . . . , & we who are conservative & union-loving are denounced without stint. . . . " Still, this stalwart announced, "I am gratified to find that our friends have the courage to stand up firmly to their duty."[12]

With Conservatives holding their ground, the legislature responded to the crisis, as its counterparts in the Deep South had, by calling for a state convention to set Virginia's course. Elections for delegates were set for February 4, with the convention to meet in Richmond on the thirteenth. In addition, the voters were asked to specify whether they had to be consulted again should the convention desire to take Virginia out of the Union.

The Virginia legislators thought about the nation as well as their state. Recognizing that Congress seemed unable to advance compromise and lacking sanguinity about its prospects for doing so, they called for a convention of states to meet in Washington to try to save a country in peril. The thinking went that, coming fresh from the people, delegates to this conclave might get past the raw partisanship that had gridlocked Congress. This gathering was to convene the same day as the Virginia election. Perhaps the Old Dominion could once again guide the nation.

Upper South and Border Conservatives closely watched the Virginia election. Many feared that the defeat of their cause there would mean the end of the Union. If Virginia opted for secession, then Maryland might very well follow. Moreover, with Virginia out, North Carolina would find herself in a most uncomfortable position, sandwiched between Virginia to the north and South Carolina to the south—a twin pressure that probably could not long be withstood. With those states gone or tottering, the Union position west of the mountains would be jeopardized. As a Tennessee congressman recognized, "it will increase terribly our perils."[13]

The results of the balloting on February 4 did not turn out as expected. Most observers and participants anticipated a close contest between the secessionists and those not ready to give up on the Union. The outcome, however, was a rout, with the Conservatives or Unionists trouncing the disunionists. Of the 152 delegates chosen for the convention, no more than one-third were committed secessionists. The Conservatives had prevailed by a two-to-one margin. This result was not, however, simply the result of antisecessionist non-slaveowners outpolling secessionist slaveowners. Voters from both groups lined up on both sides; there were non-slaveowners voting for secession and slaveowners voting against. Yet, it is absolutely clear that the transmontane region with few slaves overwhelmingly supported the Conservatives while the older eastern sections with the bulk of the slave population provided the chief backing for secessionists. Additionally, by an identical tally, voters mandated that the convention submit to them for ratification any declaration for secession.

To those trying to slow the disunion express, the Virginia outcome was a tonic. John Pendleton Kennedy noted "a most happy change" brought about by the Conservative victory. With Virginia unwilling to get aboard, it appeared that the fire-eaters could not move their train beyond the border of the Deep South. That would give more time for those pursuing an effective formula to settle the crisis. Even while savoring their triumph, the victorious Virginians made clear to Republican leaders that they needed a deal. With one, a Virginian professed to Seward, his state and region would be "all true as steel to the Union."[14]

Outside Virginia, the Upper South states generally showed even less support for disunion. North Carolina, Tennessee, and Arkansas all held mid-February contests for the people to decide whether or not to call state conventions to deliberate and decide on secession. In each of them voters rejected secession. In North Carolina and Tennessee, they turned down the convention itself—in the former narrowly, 50.3 percent to 49.7 percent, in the latter by the much wider margin of 59 percent to 41 percent.

Only in Arkansas was a convention approved, to meet on March 4, the day the new president would be inaugurated. But the delegate selection placed secessionists in a distinct minority; they garnered only 43 percent of the popular vote.[15]

Along the Border the secessionists suffered even more severe setbacks. In Delaware, Maryland, and Kentucky, referendums for conventions were never held. Indeed, Governor Hicks of Maryland steadfastly refused to call the legislature into special session so that it could consider calling a convention. In contrast, Kentucky's governor, Beriah Magoffin, who was sympathetic to the secessionist cause, did summon his legislature to a special session. It summarily dismissed any idea of having a convention. In Delaware and Missouri, legislatures meeting in regular sessions differed. The former acted as Kentucky had. In the latter, legislators did call for an election for a convention set for mid-March. At the polls the secessionists received a drubbing, however.[16]

Thus, in none of the eight Upper South and Border states did disunionists make notable headway. These decisions and elections delighted the Conservatives and disheartened the secessionists. Commenting from Washington on "the consternation & dismay of the conspirators [secessionists] here," Congressman Hatton noted that the news from his state, Tennessee, generated "universal observation & remark." Yet, knowledgeable men recognized that in many of these states, especially in the Upper South, Unionism prevailed in no small part because of Seward's efforts. His constant striving to soothe feelings and sustain hope had an enormous impact. His efforts coupled with assurances from Crittenden and Douglas that compromise remained within reach calmed many troubled southerners while giving Unionist leaders a positive message they could convey to voters. As James Barbour from the Virginia Piedmont informed Seward, "If we had not been able to hold out tolerable evidence that there was a hope of obtaining by rational appeals to the Northern People constitutional guarantees of slave property rights," his side would have lost. If such a prominent Republican as Seward maintained the real possibility of an adjustment of the fundamental issue, then region-wide secession was not inevitable.[17]

There was even talk of reconstruction. The term "Reconstruction" is usually applied to the period after the Civil War when Republicans attempted a fundamental alteration of southern society. In the winter and spring of 1861, it referred to the return to the Union of the seceded states.

Senator Hunter of Virginia entertained the proposition that Virginia could secede, then use her separation from the Union as a lever to obtain the serious compromise southerners sought. Fire-eaters, too, worried about the possibility of reconstruction. "I am oppressed by the apprehension that we are in great danger from reconstruction," warned an Alabama radical. From Washington and Richmond, friends counseled Howell Cobb that seceders had to squelch publicly any possibility of reconstruction, for talk about its occurring is having "a deleterious influence on deciding the course of the border slave states." In this opinion, by clutching to the prospect of reconstruction, they could cling to the Union.[18]

But even in the midst of these happy legislative decisions and election results, southern Conservatives tempered their optimism with a critical caveat. The ultimate outcome in Virginia and in many of the other slave states still in the Union depended on no coercion by the federal government. Throughout the crisis the word "coercion" meant the use of force by the federal government against any seceded state. Most Conservatives in the Upper South as well as a considerable number along the Border believed that a state had a constitutional right to secede. Asserting that at the moment sufficient cause did not exist, they insisted secession should await some blatantly unconstitutional or anti-South act by Lincoln's administration. These men were not absolute Unionists, placing the Union above all else. A Tennessee Unionist declared that to ensure that his state stood with the Union he and his fellow Tennesseans required something like the Crittenden Compromise as well as forbearance by the federal government. Not mincing words, James Barbour underscored that point to Seward: "I tell you this as no menace but *as a fact*. You can make your calculations accordingly." These cries resounded through the Upper South and the Border. The federal government must embrace patience, not armed might; the truce in Charleston must hold.[19]

While southern Unionists pled for forbearance, they directed their hopes on a conclave of states slated to convene in Washington on February 4. When the Virginia legislature set elections for a secession convention, it also adopted resolutions calling for this meeting of states. This gathering would be extralegal, for it had no authorization in law, not even in precedent. Since 1789 and the beginning of the republic under the Constitution, no coming together of states from across the country had occurred outside of Congress and national nominating conventions. But in this instance the convention's inaugurators perceived Congress wallowing in indecision powered by partisanship. Articulating that outlook, the well-known Virginian William C. Rives, former United States senator and diplomat, announced that because Congress had not and seemingly would not act, the lovers of the Union had to go "behind and above" the failing national legislature to the states and the people. Only that reaching out, in Rives's estimation, could overcome partisanship and prevent the dissolution of "the noblest fabric of political wisdom."[20]

Even before the convention, which became known as the Peace Convention, met, Virginia's senior statesman, former president John Tyler, had been appointed by the legislature to carry its message to President Buchanan. For this assignment the seventy-one-year-old ex–chief executive left his retirement on the family plantation in the Tidewater. Just before the legislature acted, Tyler himself had issued a public letter appealing to the Border states, both slave and free, to join together to save the Union. In it he cried, "I will not despair of the good sense of my countrymen." He only thought in terms of the Border states, those slave and free that abutted each other, or almost did, but the legislature broadened the call.[21]

Upon reaching Washington, Tyler received a cordial welcome from his successor in the White House. Buchanan embraced Virginia's idea. Convinced that Congress would not hold the Union together, he desperately reached out for any alternative that seemed even remotely plausible. After assuring Tyler of his support, he sent to Congress the resolutions the Virginian brought with him, averring, "I hail this movement on the part of Virginia with great satisfaction."

In his conversations with Buchanan, Tyler also brought directly to the president's attention Virginians' fixation on coercion. He was especially concerned about rumors that the *Brooklyn* with troops aboard had sailed for Charleston and that the guns at Fort Monroe, which guarded Hampton Roads where the James River emptied into Chesapeake Bay, had been turned landward. Buchanan responded that the *Brooklyn* had no belligerent intent; in fact, it was headed toward Pensacola, not Charleston. As for Fort Monroe, he assured Tyler that he had issued no such orders and would make sure no one else had, and if so, reverse them.

But on one key point Buchanan would not give Tyler what he and his state wanted. Pending the results of the Peace Convention, they asked the president to pledge that he would avoid "any and all acts calculated to produce a collision of arms between the States and the Government of the United States." Buchanan told Tyler and repeated in his message to Congress that he possessed no power to make such a commitment. According to him, only Congress, under its power to declare war, could give such a guarantee. For his part, he would take no aggressive action, but remain on the defensive. If, he declared, no state attacked federal property, "the danger so much deprecated will no longer exist." Still, he left no doubt about his most fervent desire: "I cherish the belief that the American people will perpetuate the Union of the States on some terms just and honorable for all sections of the country." He prayed that "the mediation of Virginia may be the destined means, under Providence, of accomplishing this inestimable benefit."[22]

With the presidential blessing, though by this time it was practically weightless, the delegates to the Peace Convention came together in Washington on the designated date. But only twenty-one of the thirty-four states were represented. The seven seceded states did not participate, nor did Arkansas. The Pacific coast states of California and Oregon appointed no delegates; neither did the uppermost states of the old Northwest: Michigan, Wisconsin, and Minnesota. Even so, seven slave states and fourteen free states had representatives present, many of them with considerable political experience, including several sitting members of Congress. They met in the spacious Willard Hall adjacent to the Willard Hotel. Attempting to limit distractions and encourage honest discussion, they determined to conduct their proceedings in secrecy. No reporter would be admitted to their deliberations, and they were to refrain from speaking about them except to other members. For their presiding officer, the delegates turned to their most distinguished member, Tyler. Views of the septuagenarian Virginian depended in part upon the perspective of the viewer. North Carolina senator Thomas Bragg thought Tyler looked "very old." When he first saw Tyler and his young wife, Julia, thirty years younger than her husband, he took them for an old man and his daughter. In contrast, Julia Tyler described him as "quite bright, bearing up wonderfully and *looking* remarkably well." No matter whose description was more on the mark, Tyler's role in the chair would be largely honorific.[23]

As it organized, the Peace Convention faced the fact that the two chief antagonists in the crisis had no more use for its success than they had in a settlement in Congress. Neither the fire-eaters nor the hard-line Republicans wanted a successful compromise. When the convention met, the fire-eaters had propelled seven states in the Deep South out of the Union. At this moment they were preoccupied with their own convention. When the Peace Convention began, delegates from the seven seceded states were coming together in Montgomery, Alabama, to form a new southern government.[24]

Hard-line Republicans displayed adamant opposition to the Peace Convention. They denounced it as a trick to cheat the North in order to gain time for spreading secession. Having blocked settlement in Congress, they wanted, in Carl Schurz's phrase, to explode "the 'compromise' air-castle." Without question their major concern was their party. Determined that they "would not accede to anything which might show a weakness on the part of the Republican party," they castigated what Horace Greeley's *Tribune* derisively termed "the Concession Convention."[25]

Many of the hard-liners were wary of even sending delegates. Initially, the caucus of Republican legislators in New York rejected by an overwhelming margin that possibility. Governor John Andrew of Massachusetts only slowly, and after hearing from the congressional delegation, decided to appoint representatives. In the western heartland of the party, governors and other leaders seemed to be waiting on each other. Most who contemplated taking part thought like Oliver Morton, governor of Indiana, that participation would "prevent positive evil"—that is, the adoption of some compromise proposal. Although Illinois Republicans evinced little enthusiasm for the project, they looked to President-elect Lincoln for guidance. He advised that the state do nothing, asserting "he would rather be hung by the neck till he was dead on the steps of the Capitol, before he would beg or buy a peaceful inauguration." Taking this position, he remained unyielding; any serious compromise, meaning the inclusion of the territories, was intolerable. In the words of an Illinois legislator, Lincoln was as "firm as the base of the Rocky Mountains."[26]

Eventually, however, key governors concluded that sending delegates was the lesser evil. The presence of those Governor Morton defined as "good men and true" could thwart the impulse of weaker Republicans who might "compromise the integrity and future of the Republican party." These leaders envisioned a Republican country, meaning the fifteen slave states had to accept whatever the Republican party was willing to give them. These governors kept their delegations secure, appointing not only Republicans, but solely hard-line Republicans. To no avail, the leading Democratic journal in the Illinois capital bitterly complained that in a national crisis the hundred sixty thousand voting Democrats in the state had a right to have a voice, not just the hundred seventy thousand Republican voters. According to this paper that commitment to keen partisanship animated both Lincoln and his party.[27]

Not all Republicans stood with their chieftain and his inflexible supporters, though. The moderate Republican reaction to the convention underscored the existing division in the party. Some of these men advocated a Republican presence in the convention simply because they could see no harm from it. Others genuinely desired an agreement that would ensure the Upper South and Border slave states' remaining in the Union. These Republicans felt compelled to aid southern Unionists who were begging for something from Republicans to help them blunt the secessionist advance. The election results in Virginia, especially, and in Tennessee gave credence to their loyalty to the United States. Moreover, congressional speeches pleading for Republican assistance reached a receptive audience among moderates. Even Congressman Williamson Cobb of Alabama, in his final, heavyhearted remarks before leaving Washington for his home state, now out of the Union, joined that chorus: "And now gentlemen of the Republican party, let me say that you have this question in your own hands, and that you can still this storm before the sun shall set to-day."[28]

On January 28, in the House of Representatives, John Gilmer had made a particularly powerful and emotional appeal. Like Cobb, he maintained that Republicans had it in their power to destroy secession. He asked for fairness in the territories. That given, "you will see a set of men [secessionists] die off quicker than you ever saw a set of men die off before. You will send them home to hide their heads, mourning and disappointed." Republicans now had power, he pointed out; they would control appointments. No national policy could be adopted without their concurrence. He beseeched his Republican colleagues to back the Crittenden Compromise, the Border State Plan, or the Committee of Thirty-three's propositions, any of them modified, if necessary.

As for the fractious territorial question specifically, he thought for the present the matter should be "substantially settled. . . . " Slavery would not exist, he declared, where climate and geography rendered it unprofitable. But "ultra partisans have magnified and misrepresented it for the purpose of inflaming the public mind North and South."

Gilmer admitted that Republicans claimed they intended no harm to the South, but southerners, he stressed, were bombarded by pronouncements from fire-eaters that Republicans intended to subjugate the South, in time abolishing slavery. Gilmer insisted that Republicans had to recognize that truth and alter southerners' perception with visible measures.

Foreseeing a "day of butchery and destruction" that would follow dissolution of the Union and civil war, Gilmer wondered about the reaction of the man who "if he had yielded a matter of no practical importance to him, or his constituents, all trouble could have been avoided." To forgo such an outcome, he cried, "let us all go together, every man who loves this country and this Union, for something that will give peace to our distracted and distressed countrymen of all sections."[29]

Gilmer's address as well as implorations from his allies had an impact on the moderates. *The New York Times* described one speech as "one of the noblest and boldest proclamations of devotion to the Union ever pronounced." Other Republican newspapers also applauded such efforts, noting that even some Republican congressmen congratulated these southern speakers. Additionally, they reported that moderate Republicans said they wanted to do something to assist men like Gilmer. Still attempting to influence Lincoln, Seward emphasized the emotional dimension of the southern Unionist entreaties: "The appeals of the Union men in the border States are very painful, since they say that without it [Republican assistance] their States must all go with the tide."[30]

With Republicans still debating their response to it, the Peace Convention got under way on February 4. To hasten their efforts, the delegates without dissent set up a resolutions committee to draft a report for the full convention to consider. One representative from each state in attendance would comprise this group. To chair the unit, the assembly named James Guthrie, who had proposed it. A Kentucky Democrat, Guthrie was currently a railroad president, but also an experienced political hand on the national level; he had served in President Franklin Pierce's cabinet.[31]

Three days after the initial gavel fell, the delegates paid a courtesy call on President Buchanan. The men trooped together the short distance from Willard Hall to the White House. One of them recalled that their march displayed "the solemnity of a funeral procession." Consumed with "apprehension and anxiety," the president eagerly received his visitors, grasping them as practically his last hope for staving off disaster. He embraced many of them, pleading all to do whatever necessary, yielding whatever was required to avoid his greatest fear, a "bloody, fratricidal war." A delegate described him as "advanced in years, shaken in body, and uncertain in mind." A bit earlier another observer saw "a pityable object, haggard and worn—his cheeks fallen in, his color bloodless." The crisis had beaten him down. He had been defeated by his own vision of his power, his uncertainty about his course, the disaffection of his former allies, and the recalcitrance of the Republican party.[32]

By the time of the meeting at the White House, the convention, including its resolutions committee, had begun its work. Northern states outnumbered southern, and in northern delegations Republicans commanded a majority, often a 100-percent majority. Yet, when face-to-face with earnest southern Unionists, even stalwart Republicans could waver on the no-compromise pedestal. This possibility distressed hard-liners in Congress as well as in the convention, who feared that their less intransigent comrades might bend before pro-compromise and pro-Union pressure. Viewing the scene, Massachusetts delegates spoke of "surrender." These men were especially troubled by Republicans from Rhode Island, New York, New Jersey, Pennsylvania, Ohio, and Indiana. To close off the possibility of compromise, they called on the governors of the upper states of the old Northwest, Republicans all, to send promptly hard-line delegations.[33]

Telegraphing that some states were "caving in," Senator Zachariah Chandler of Michigan begged his governor "for God's sake, to come to [our] rescue and *save the republican party from rupture*." He left no doubt about whom he wanted; send "stiff-backed men or none," he instructed. In a postscript, Chandler added his opinion, shared by only the bitterest of hard-liners: "Without a little blood-letting this Union would not be worth a rush." When his message was leaked, this apparent bloodlust caused an outcry among many, including moderate Republicans.[34]

The moderates and their leader, Senator Seward, did hope the convention would lead somewhere. For Congress, Seward had adopted a holding pattern. He still labored feverishly to persuade southern Unionists that a Republican administration did not endanger them. With that assurance he urged them to continue resisting secessionists. At the same time, to preserve both party unity and his position with Lincoln, he warranted no congressional movement on compromise. Spurning any overt initiative, he looked to the Peace Convention as the only option for direct action. In conversation, Seward impressed a hard-liner from Massachusetts as resembling an attorney striving to bring a client "safely out of his perils." Although no specific client was mentioned, this person surely meant the Union. On that point he was correct, but in reality Seward had two clients, the Republican party with its new chief as well as the Union. Shepherding both through the crisis unscathed was his great challenge. He did not turn from it.[35]

All the while, the Guthrie committee struggled to find agreement on a serious compromise plan that it could report to the full convention. Almost daily optimism and pessimism seesawed back and forth. In regular letters to his wife, North Carolina delegate Daniel Barringer charted the fluctuations. As a moderate Unionist, Barringer's qualitative judgments would not apply to everyone, but his gauge registered the oscillation. On February 4 he reported, "Things look very gloomy here." Two days later he could see little progress. By the eighth, he brightened: "I have some hope that good may yet grow out of our actions." The next day brought more positive news. But on the thirteenth, he found nothing encouraging.[36]

After receiving two extensions of its deadline from the convention, the committee submitted its effort on February 15. Having rejected both southern secessionist demands for the Crittenden Compromise and the hard-line Republican insistence on no action, the committee majority settled on a proposal that tracked the Border State Plan. On the most vexing matter, the territories, it extended the Missouri line, prohibiting slavery north of it and allowing slavery to the south. But in permitting slavery, it excluded Crittenden's guarantee for federal protection. Rather, it stated that neither Congress nor territorial legislatures could meddle with it. On the "hereafter acquired" component that offended Republicans, the committee exceeded the Border State Plan by requiring a four-fifths vote in the Senate to acquire any new territory. The remaining elements covered familiar and largely undisputed ground. The federal government could not interfere with slavery either in the District of Columbia or a slave state; any amendment to constitutional provisions regarding slavery would necessitate the support of all states; the foreign slave trade would never be permitted; the Fugitive Slave Law would be enforced, with slaveowners compensated for fugitives lost because of violence. Procedurally—and here the committee adopted Crittenden instead of the Border State Plan—all provisions were placed in one recommended constitutional amendment.

On the eve of the committee's report, several highlights in Washington's social world offered a momentary respite from serious business for delegates, members of Congress, and other capital luminaries. These affairs provided counterpoint to the serious, albeit frustrating and futile, conversations taking place in the Capitol and Willard Hall. On the evening of February 12, a White House levee attracted a multitude. A reporter termed it "very brilliant," and recorded, "Everybody seemed to be merry, the outgoing as well as the incoming." The band serenaded North and South, playing both "Yankee Doodle" and "Away Down in Dixie." The next evening Mrs. Stephen A. Douglas gave a ball that drew a throng. Julia Tyler thought it grand. She interpreted praise for "the Peace Commissioners" as people "catching at straws as a relief to their pressing anxieties." Also attending, the cocky, young Henry Adams, who saw no triumph in compromise, provided a counterpoint. Speaking about John Tyler and John J. Crittenden specifically, he put his acerbic wit on display: "Ye Gods, what are we, when mortals no bigger—no, damn it, not so big as—ourselves are looked up to as though their thunder spoke from the real original Olympus."[37]

Back in Willard Hall, the delegates began grappling with the Guthrie group's results. In addition to the majority report, two minority ones were on the table, one from the secession-minded southerners and one from the hard-line Republicans. The latter called for a national convention to consider the crisis, nothing more; the former demanded more specific guarantees of southern rights and power, including a southern veto on legislative as well as executive appointments. The convention quickly dispatched each, with neither generating much support. Then the delegates turned their attention to the majority report.

The ensuing debate fundamentally replicated what had been taking place in Congress for two and a half months. The pro-secession southerners and the hard-line Republicans brandished their sharpened rhetorical weapons while moderates on both sides held up the glories of the Union and the need for compromise. Giving voice to the extreme southern position, James A. Seddon of Virginia, eventually to become the longest-serving Confederate secretary of war, insisted on clearer constitutional protection of slavery and southern power. Furthermore, he defined slave property as being "as rightful and honorable as any property to be found in the broad expanse between ocean and ocean." Then he condemned the North for venerating those like "John Brown and his ruffian invaders of our soil" who assailed the South. Responding in like manner, George Boutwell of Massachusetts asserted that the North hated slavery. As for secession, "The North will never consent to the separation of the States. . . . " With eerie prescience, he predicted that if the South persisted in secession, the resulting war would end only with southern armies reaching the Great Lakes or northern forces marching to the Gulf of Mexico.[38]

With such heated words flung about, emotions were at times on edge. When Seddon announced, "Virginia *will not permit coercion*," Lot Morrill of Maine accused him of comforting "those who trample upon the laws and defy the government." Thereupon, New Jersey's Robert Stockton remonstrated and charged Morrill "with violent and angry gesticulations." Approximately two dozen Republicans gathered around Morrill; one bellowed, "Back to your seat, you bully!" Likewise, southerners "rushed" to Stockton. Fisticuffs appeared imminent. Responding quickly, President Tyler shouted, "Order," continuing, "Shame upon the delegate who would dishonor this conference with violence." All retreated to words.[39]

Trying to calm the oratorical storm, proponents of settlement appealed for conciliation. The businessman William Dodge of New York urged the delegates to agree and prevent "the destruction of the Government." In his judgment Americans would approve their fair agreement, "and their approval will give us *peace*." North Carolina's Thomas Ruffin implored all to act like brothers. From his presiding chair, John Tyler took the floor. Defining his own mission, he told the convention, "I aspired to the glory of aiding to settle the controversy."[40]

Settling it, as Tyler learned to his great disappointment, proved almost impossible. The portion of the majority report that received the most attention unsurprisingly involved territorial provisions. The full convention altered the committee's proposal in two ways. First, it specified that the territorial language read to apply solely to territory already possessed by the United States. Second, it changed the congressional approval requirement for acquiring new territory to half the senators from both slave and free states. The remaining sections survived basically intact.

Even with the changes, adoption was not a foregone conclusion. On February 26, three weeks after it opened, the convention made its decision. Voting would be by state, each state with a single vote. The key ballot came on the amended territorial segment. It went down 11 to 8. The defeat was occasioned in large part by the negative response of three slave states—Virginia, North Carolina, and Missouri. In each, by a three-to-one margin the stronger southern-rights advocates bested the moderates. They insisted on terms, in Daniel Barringer's words, that would "satisfy the seceded states"—in other words the Crittenden provisions, or something very close. These men joined the hard-line Republicans to vanquish the key element of the proposed deal. The result devastated the southern Conservatives; "some of them wept like children," said George Boutwell.[41]

In the aftermath, moderates from North and South successfully moved for adjournment in order to reconsider. During the recess both sides pressed and lobbied, with nondelegates also avidly participating. A group of Republican hard-liners exhorted "*strongly* the necessity of an *uncompromising* policy." It was reported that Senator Douglas urged Lincoln to get involved and that the governor of Maryland said he would turn to secession if the convention failed.[42]

Reconvening on the twenty-seventh, the convention reconsidered. Change did occur. Because of divided delegations, decisions to abstain, and reversals, the 11-to-8 defeat became a 9-to-8 victory. Five free states (Rhode Island, New Jersey, Pennsylvania, Ohio, Illinois) and four slave (Delaware, Maryland, Tennessee, Kentucky) made up the majority. The secondary provisions encountered little difficulty.

The convention had reached agreement, which it promptly dispatched to Congress in the form of an amendment to the Constitution. The chances for congressional approval were almost nonexistent, however. The session of Congress had but a week before its legally mandated adjournment. Its failure to act on its own for the past three months provided little reason for optimism in this instance. Additionally, the deep divisions in the convention along with the extremely narrow margin by which its key proposal passed dulled its impact. Even before the compromise had been delivered to Congress, Charles Francis Adams, who had little use for the convention's work, had noted that because the delegates were not "harmonious," what they produced "will therefore have little force in the House." He could have easily included the Senate. Put simply, the Peace Convention had not found a formula that satisfied many. Although a gloomy outlook clouded congressional reception, the final act had not yet been staged.[43]

In mid-winter the adherents of the Peace Convention were not the only Americans endeavoring to find a formula to end the crisis. Along with *The Philadelphia Inquirer*, they maintained that over time, only compromise had preserved the Union. As a result, those who rejected further compromise rejected the basis of the Union. The *Inquirer* found the territorial issue an absurd reason to wreck the Union because, it insisted, climate controlled slavery. As a result, slavery was most unlikely to expand below the Missouri line.[44]

One initiative that some of these promoters of settlement found attractive involved the four living former presidents of the country. They wanted to bring the hoped-for prestige of these ex–chief executives to the side of serious sectional compromise. Writing Franklin Pierce on January 27, the conservative Massachusetts industrialist Amos A. Lawrence explained the motive and timing of his letter and invitation. He told Pierce that leading men in Congress (he specified Crittenden, Douglas, and Seward) "all express their inability to operate on parties & they desire all the outside influence that can be obtained." But, Lawrence opined, the gathering in the capital of all the living who had held the nation's highest office might just nudge partisanship aside. He pointed out that at the moment Tyler was already in Washington. He also had word that Martin Van Buren had agreed to come and that Millard Fillmore had been invited. Lawrence closed with the tribute that Pierce's presence would have a positive influence.[45]

This wished-for reunion never occurred. And even if it had, it would probably have resulted in no more than a momentary spasm of hope. It would have had no more than a remote possibility of accomplishing the goals desired by initiators like Lawrence. None of the four who had lived in the White House had any influence with Republican politicians, a substantial regiment of whom would have to sign on for any meaningful movement toward settlement to take place. Still, the scheme does highlight the creativity or, more accurately, the desperation, of the fervently active proponents of compromise.

Another effort did take place, and for a time it offered more likelihood of success. From the onset of the crisis, business and financial circles along the eastern seaboard, especially in New York City, took an active role in pushing for a settlement. They had written letters, signed petitions, and held meetings, all aiming at what the New York merchant A. T. Stewart termed "the reestablishment of fraternal relations between the North and South." After the new year, these men also decided to take more direct action. They would go to the capital themselves.[46]

During the last week of January, businessmen descended on Washington. Railroad presidents, bankers, industrialists, and merchants comprised this band of lobbyists. They did not all join together behind any particular compromise plan. Some preferred Crittenden's; others thought the Border State Plan offered the surest route to approval. All, however, wanted a serious settlement that would ensure peace between the sections and for the country. Moreover, they yearned for prompt action.[47]

The largest city and the most important commercial center provided the most notable delegation. This New York City group even traveled to the capital by special train, bringing along a memorial carrying the signatures of almost forty thousand businessmen. It had a central message: "The perpetuity of the Union of these United States as one nation, is of vastly more importance than the establishment or rejection of this or that subject of controversy."

Early during the first week in February these men of commerce secured a meeting with congressional Republicans. To it they invited colleagues from Boston and Philadelphia. The New Yorkers told the politicians they had the mission of taking home "some substantial encouragement in reference to a speedy settlement of the pending difficulties." And they hoped their particular gathering would further their cause.

William E. Dodge, who also belonged to the New York delegation to the Peace Convention, made a major statement. He admitted that many of his fellows had begun to think their task "hopeless," but he would make every possible exertion to secure a settlement. Making his case for action, he likened secession to a burning building. States had already left the Union, with more possibly going, even all fifteen slave states. Yet, with the structure of the Union being consumed, firemen only watched. They did not bring water "to stay the conflagration." The roof has fallen in, Dodge continued, "story after story burns, and the danger is that not even a beam or timber may remain to indicate the spot where the noble edifice stood." Concluding, he focused directly on Republicans' intransigence. He asked whether they intended to continue standing on a platform constructed for a different time and circumstance. Or would they "be willing to make any advance, and yield some fair concession, without any sacrifice of principle?"

The assembled Republicans—a dozen or so—did respond. Most claimed they were indeed ready for meaningful compromise. Their number included individuals from eight states, from New Jersey westward to Iowa. Some of these men even professed that Republicans "had not done all that the country had a right to expect of them." Yet transferring such declamations to policy did not come easily. Hard-liners wanted none of it. One, Galusha Grow of Pennsylvania, made clear he would never vote to alter "the great, free, organic instrument [the Constitution] bequeathed by the wisest founders of the Republic." Others agreed with Michigan's Zachariah Chandler that "the great mercantile centers" had no commitment to any principle other than financial gain. Still, as this gathering disbanded, the Peace Convention was convening and Congress remained in session.

While the Peace Convention organized and businessmen lobbied, representatives from the seceded states gathered to form a new government. In fact, only six of the seven states that had left the Union were present, for the delegation from Texas, which did not secede until February 1, reached Montgomery only after the Confederate States of America had been set up. Plans for the Montgomery meeting had been initiated in Washington in January. There leading members of Congress from the Deep South met and discussed the shaping and manning of the new republic.[48]

On February 4, the men designated to give life to a southern government came together in Montgomery, the capital of Alabama. A quiet port on the Alabama River, Montgomery had a population of around nine thousand, half black and half white. The thirty-seven delegates recognized that they were involved in an unprecedented enterprise. Since the American Revolution, the United States had remained whole; now the country had splintered. Alexander Stephens, a member of the Georgia delegation, captured the moment: "We are now in the midst of a revolution. That may be acted upon as a fixed, irrevocable fact."[49]

The delegates were generally men of substance and experience. Politically they ranged from fire-eaters like Robert Barnwell Rhett, Sr., the dean of that fervent band, to Alexander Stephens, who on the first ballot taken in the Georgia convention had voted against secession. Although influential in their states and familiar with politics, these founders could not be called a distinguished group, except for three men from the same state. In the 1850s, Howell Cobb, Alexander Stephens, and Robert Toombs had dominated Georgia and became notable on the national stage. The delegates named Cobb president of the convention.

The men composing the Montgomery convention engaged in a remarkable series of activities, performing tasks matched by no other single group in American history. Initially, they organized as a constitutional convention in which they drafted and adopted the document that would provide the foundation for their new republic. Then, they constituted themselves as an electoral college to select a provisional president and vice president, who would hold office temporarily, until elections in November 1861 when the voters of the Confederate States would choose their executive officers. Finally, they designated themselves a unicameral Provisional Congress to enact statutes that would add flesh to the skeleton of their fledgling country.

Their organic law illustrated their commitment to the Constitution of the United States. After all, they had consistently professed reverence for the Constitution of the Founding Fathers, which, they asserted, the Republicans had subverted. In fact, some wanted simply to replicate the document they had cherished. But they made alterations to clarify points that most southerners claimed were at least implicit in the federal Constitution. The Confederate Constitution specifically protected slavery in states and territories. Moreover, it said Congress could never abolish the institution. Yet, provision was made for the admission of free states. Additionally, states' rights was raised to a first principle, though on secession, or its possibility, silence reigned. It also prohibited a protective tariff.

In addition, the Confederate framers made structural changes intended to address what they saw as the corruption of the system they had left behind. The delegates provided for a single six-year term for the president. With no possibility of reelection, politicking would not be the hallmark of a Confederate president's administration. Satisfied that they had depoliticized their chief executive, these constitution-writers then set out to rein in the rapacity of legislators. In an effort to prevent logrolling and pork-barrel projects, the president received a line-item veto on appropriation bills. Furthermore, a two-thirds vote in both houses of Congress was required for any appropriation not requested by the president. In their handiwork they underscored that their president "should not be a party leader but instead should stand as a patriot rallying the people to the cause of Southern independence."

The delegates agreed on their Constitution in a matter of days. During the debates differences of opinion did exist. Some fire-eaters wanted to reinstate the international slave trade; some also wanted to ban the possible admission of free states. On both they failed. But despite these disagreements the Confederate founders were determined to stand together and not permit conflict to disrupt their proceedings. Harmony became their watchword. The convention president, Howell Cobb, explained that a determination to remain harmonious pervaded all deliberations. And on February 8, the delegates, voting by state, unanimously adopted their Constitution. They wanted all watching—the slave states still in the Union, the free states, and Europe—to see a committed, unified assemblage.

With the preparation of a Constitution behind them, the delegates became electors to select the provisional president and vice president. In their electoral college each state would have one vote; thus, four votes would be needed to win. Although many ambitious politicians were in Montgomery, intense politicking did not characterize the selection process. These self-appointed electors wanted the man they perceived as best for their Confederate States of America.[50]

There were several potential contenders. Everyone recognized that because of its size, location, and the prominent men in its delegation, Georgia would have an influential vote in the selection. No other state sent men with the reputations of Cobb, Stephens, and Toombs. If Georgia backed one of these notables, he would immediately become a formidable candidate, probably the favorite. Yet each had his liabilities. Cobb did not want the position and refused to let his name be put forward. Stephens was too conservative, having opposed secession on the first ballot in the Georgia convention. Toombs relished the prospect of becoming president, but he had his own problem. In Montgomery, his penchant for excessive imbibing was quite visible, generating serious doubts about his fitness for the office. Robert Barnwell Rhett, Sr., would have welcomed the call, and may have even believed it his due, yet even a majority of his fellow Carolinians considered him too radical.[51]

In Montgomery, and even before, one name always came up: Jefferson Davis. Among political leaders in the Deep South, no one else could match his combination of political, military, and administrative experience. A graduate of West Point, he had spent seven years on active duty in the regular army and during the Mexican War became a war hero while commanding a regiment of volunteers. Then he had been secretary of war during Franklin Pierce's administration. Finally, he had served in both House and Senate; in the latter he had become highly respected and quite influential. Fundamentally a conservative, he had never been a fire-eater and was not viewed as a fomenter of secession. That conservatism appealed to many, for the delegates in Montgomery were acutely aware that eight slave states remained in the Union. To attract the Upper South and the Border states, the new government would have to exhibit judiciousness. In sum, Davis's name appeared on everyone's short list.

In the end, the balloting held little surprise. With the Georgians out of the contest, no one seriously challenged Davis. Howell Cobb thought Davis would get the nod. The evidence makes clear that Mississippi, Louisiana, and Florida preferred him. He also had a majority in South Carolina. Alabama came to him, influenced by commissioners sent by the state to Virginia, who reported that leading men in Virginia wanted Davis. When on February 9 the delegates elected a president, only Davis's name was placed in nomination. No one else received a vote. Then, with the same unanimity, Alexander Stephens was chosen vice president. The entire process took only half an hour.[52]

The tandem of Davis and Stephens sent a clear signal to all in the United States. Moderates and conservatives would mark the Confederate government. The radicals would not control the new enterprise. Observers noted the Confederate leadership seemed "in earnest." Even *The New York Herald* commented on "the statesmanship and diplomatic foresight of those who have guided [Confederate] counsels."[53]

The man chosen to lead the Confederacy responded promptly. When news of his election reached him at his Mississippi home, Davis took only a day before departing for Montgomery. After a train trip of five days he arrived in the Confederate capital on February 16. Along the way he spoke several times, always emphasizing independence as the southern destiny and goal. He said that he wanted only peace with the United States, but would not shy away from war if necessary for independence. Upon reaching Montgomery, he did not change. He did, however, underscore his sense of the moment. "Fellow Citizens and Brethren of the Confederate

States of America—for now we are brethren, not in name, merely, but in fact—men of one flesh, one bone, one interest, one purpose, and of identity of domestic institutions."[54]

Two days later, on February 18, Davis gave his inaugural address as provisional president of the Confederate States. Speaking in front of the state Capitol, which had become the Confederate Capitol, he urgently and forcefully defined the Confederate cause. He began by proclaiming that the Confederacy "illustrates the American idea that governments rest upon the consent of the governed, and that it is the right of the people to alter or abolish governments whenever they become destructive of the ends for which they were established." Fusing the southern past to the southern present, he said the southern people had "merely asserted a right which the Declaration of 1776 had defined to be inalienable." Because the Union of the Fathers had been "perverted from the purposes for which it was ordained, and had ceased to answer the ends for which it was established," southerners in "a peaceful appeal to the ballot-box declared that so far as they were concerned, the government created by that compact should cease to exist." Confederates would emulate their ancestors: "Doubly justified by the absence of wrong on our part, and by wanton aggression on the part of others, there can be no cause to doubt that the courage and patriotism of the people of the Confederate States will be found equal to any measures of defense which honor and security may require."

Davis sounded no call to war, however. He congratulated the new nation on its peaceful gestation and birth. There had been neither "aggression upon others" nor "domestic convulsion." He found both the agricultural and industrial sectors of the economy functioning "as heretofore." Yet, Confederates feared not. If anyone "desire[d] to inflict injury upon us," the result would be "the suffering of millions," which would "bear testimony to the folly and wickedness of our aggressors." He concluded by calling on "the God of our fathers" to continue "His favor" upon the Confederates in their effort to carry forth the principles which He had permitted their fathers "to establish and transmit."[55]

Even before his inauguration, Davis addressed one issue directly and emphatically. Immediately upon detraining in Montgomery he announced, "Our separation from the old Union is complete. NO COMPROMISE; NO RECONSTRUCTION CAN NOW BE ENTERTAINED." Reconstruction—fears of it and hope for it stirred many. By reconstruction all meant a rapid reunion with the United States. Fire-eaters worried that moderates wanted to engineer such a move. A rumor in Montgomery was that an agent of Senator Stephen A. Douglas was maneuvering to that end. Some in the non-seceding slave states yearned for it.

But the founders in Montgomery would not have it. They chorused Davis's pronouncement, making clear their opposition to any such reconstruction. In fact, even the notion only helped to solidify the delegates in their nation building. They shared the view of a former South Carolina congressman that southern "pride" required showing the North that the South could build a nation. The men in Montgomery did not view the secession of their states as a mere diplomatic ploy designed to gain concessions from the North. They had a different motive. In Washington, Senator Thomas Bragg of North Carolina understood their determination to forge "a permanent separate Government."[56]

Beyond the Confederate States, reaction to the actions in Montgomery varied. The staunch Unionist congressman from Tennessee Robert Hatton denounced the Confederacy as "a cotton Republic—in which *cotton* is to be King—a few nabobs the ruling power, & our rights & honor treated with sovereign contempt." In contrast, the conservative *New York Herald* praised "the statesmanship" of those who created the Confederate government. Republicans united in condemning the new polity, though not all did so with the same vehemence. Thurlow Weed's *Albany Evening Journal* asserted that although the Confederacy began as despotism, Union-loving southerners would soon reassert themselves and undo it. Commenting on Davis's inaugural, a Republican editor proclaimed that the Confederate president preached "that it is the chief end of man to cut his neighbor's throat." According to Republicans, when Davis linked the Confederate founders to the Founding Fathers of the United States, "he either willfully falsifie[d] history, or [was] made insane by a rotten conceit."[57]

No matter the opinion beyond his borders, President Jefferson Davis set about constructing a government. Comprehending the monumental task he confronted, he commented, "We are without machinery without means and threatened by powerful opposition, but I do not despond and will not shrink from the task imposed on me." Literally, he had to build a government from nothing. The seven states in the Confederacy had governments, of course, but in them no central governmental apparatus had ever existed. Davis turned first to appointing a cabinet. The official family in the Confederacy would replicate that in the old Union, with one exception. The newest federal ministry, the Department of the Interior, would be excluded, in large part because to Confederates it symbolized a too powerful central government. Although Davis had no personal debts to pay and no party factions to satisfy, he did have geographic considerations. He awarded a post to each state, save his own Mississippi. While not particularly distinguished, his cabinet matched in experience and prestige most of those that had been chosen in the old Union. He certainly picked seasoned politicians, with four recent members of the United States Congress, three senators and one congressman. Notably, he shunned leading fire-eaters.[58]

Choosing a cabinet did not end Davis's involvement with appointments and patronage. Like the man from Illinois who would soon become the president of the United States, Davis found himself immersed in questions of whom and where. Speaking only of his home state, Howell Cobb claimed that half of all Georgians were in Montgomery looking for office while the other half remained at home writing letters on the same topic. Every day the lines of people waiting to see Davis seemed unending. At least fifty men came every day with plans, suggestions, or pleas.[59]

In setting up departments, Davis followed advice to embrace the old federal bureaucracy and its rules, at least initially. Thus, United States postmasters became Confederate States postmasters, and officers of the United States courts became officers of the Confederate States courts. This process was materially assisted by former civil servants in Washington who volunteered their services and experiences in Montgomery. Some even appeared with copies of regulations and procedures that could be promptly distributed and implemented.

The possibility of armed conflict with the United States was never out of Davis's mind. He had long believed that secession would result in war, unless all the slave states left the Union. His new country contained less than half of them. Because he wanted an army prepared for a lengthy, difficult war, he urged Congress to provide for enlistments of three years or the duration of the conflict. He failed. Most congressmen, like most of their constituents in the states, were convinced either that no fighting would occur or that, if it did, the struggle would be brief and successful. As a result, most of them advocated only six months of service. President and Congress compromised on one year. Davis also courted officers in the U.S. Army, many of whom he knew from his tour as secretary of war. Although most officers resigned upon the secession of their home states, Davis's overtures ensured that a majority offered their services to the Confederacy.

President Davis recognized the centrality of the forts within Confederate borders still held by the United States. During the course of secession, most of these had come under control of individual states. They could easily be transferred to the new government, which they were when the Confederate Congress on February 22 passed a resolution charging the Confederate government to take them over. Yet, the Stars and Stripes still flew over four—two far away in the Florida Keys; Fort Pickens at Pensacola, Florida; and the most visible, Fort Sumter. Davis wanted the garrisons withdrawn from Pickens and Sumter.

From the moment Major Robert Anderson occupied Fort Sumter, it had been a potential flashpoint—initially between the United States and South Carolina, now between the United States and the Confederate States. While still a senator in Washington, Davis had assiduously endeavored to prevent the outbreak of hostilities. As president of the Confederacy, he wanted to make sure that his government, not South Carolina, managed potential military action in Charleston harbor. Governor Pickens of South Carolina concurred, communicating often. Thus, when Davis wrote Pickens, "I hope you will be able to prevent the issue of peace or war for the Confederate States from being decided by any other than the authorities constituted to conduct our international relations," the governor agreed. Davis took control on March 1, when he dispatched a Confederate general to assume command of all forces in the Charleston area. Brigadier General Pierre G. T. Beauregard only two months earlier had been a major in the United States Army on duty as superintendent of the United States Military Academy at West Point.[60]

Davis wanted to make sure that any decision on using force in Charleston harbor was made in Montgomery, not in Charleston, but, most important, he wanted an agreement with the United States that would result in his government taking over Pickens and Sumter. Davis was prepared to offer compensation for them as well as for all the other federal property that had already come under Confederate authority. To convey his position and carry out negotiations, on February 27 he appointed a special mission to Washington. Forthwith it headed north.

While Jefferson Davis and his compatriots were occupied with organizing the Confederate States, Republicans in Washington were nervously awaiting their assumption of power. Rumors and more rumors of secessionist plots to take over the city reverberated through their ranks. One scheme had volunteers from Virginia and Maryland led by a Texan attacking the federal district. Another posited twenty-five thousand "minute men" with a former governor of Virginia at their head marching on the capital. Even Attorney General Edwin Stanton, by now secretly conveying the inner workings of the Buchanan administration to leading Republicans, contributed to the chatter and prattle racing through the city. Stanton helped persuade Seward that danger lurked from menacing cabals. General Scott also for a time feared serious trouble. Capturing the mood, Henry Adams observed, "The terror here among the inhabitants is something wonderful to witness." He caught the fright: "At least half of them believe that Washington is to be destroyed by fire and sword."[61]

This dread did not last, however, mainly because of a lack of substance to the rumors. No serious design to subvert the government or stage any kind of coup d'état ever existed. Moreover, General Scott promised that he would safeguard the capital, though he would have to do so with fewer troops than he wanted. Fearing the reaction in Maryland and Virginia to the movement of large numbers of soldiers, President Buchanan forbade any provocative action. The House of Representatives formed a committee to look into possible conspiracies; it found none. But even before the conclusion of that investigation, Seward had become convinced that no credible threats menaced the government or the city. Lincoln was informed that Washington was safe.[62]

With reassurances about conditions in the nation's capital, President-elect Lincoln began his journey from Illinois to Washington. Unlike Jefferson Davis, he did not travel directly or with haste. When he left Springfield, on February 11, three weeks remained before his inauguration. His brief remarks at the train station as he departed his hometown certainly indicated that he had a sense of the vexed situation he would confront. "With a task before me greater than that which rested upon [George] Washington," Lincoln noted his success would require "the assistance of that Divine Being who ever attended him." "With that assistance," he continued, "I cannot fail." His conclusion was hopeful: "Trusting in Him, who can go with me, and remain with you, and be every where for good, let us confidently hope that all will yet be well." He surely evinced "a sense of an appointment with destiny."[63]

To that appointment Lincoln took a circuitous route, traveling east through Indiana, Ohio, Pennsylvania, and New York State to New York City. Then he turned south with stops in New Jersey and again in Pennsylvania. He would not reach Washington until February 23. All along his route from beginning to end enthusiastic crowds turned out to see the president-elect, a reception that pleased him and his supporters.[64]

Along this road he made several significant speeches from Indianapolis in Indiana to Philadelphia and Harrisburg in Pennsylvania, addresses widely covered in the press. In them several themes predominated. He emphasized the superiority of the Union over individual states, employing humor to ridicule states'-rights zealots. "In their view," Lincoln asserted, "the Union, or a family relation, would not be anything like a regular marriage at all, but only as a sort of free-love arrangement, to be maintained on what that sect calls passionate attraction." That metaphor brought forth laughter from the audience.[65]

He also underscored that the Constitution emphasized majority rule. If the majority did not, then, Lincoln said, the minority must. He followed that declaration with a rhetorical question, asking if that would be right. He gave his own answer: "Assuredly not!" But the majority can be wrong, he admitted. If so, in four years the people could correct their mistake. In the meantime, he and his party could do "no great harm." At almost every stop Lincoln asserted that crowds gathered to see him as president-elect, not as Abraham Lincoln the man. He then went on to affirm that they would also have turned out if one of his opponents had been the victor. In his words, Americans honored the office of president and would respect any man elected to it.[66]

In Indianapolis Lincoln called himself "an accidental instrument" of what he termed "a great cause." In Newark, New Jersey, he harked back to his farewell remarks in Springfield, stating that "without the sustenance of Divine Providence" he could not succeed. Later that same day in Trenton, he identified himself as a "humble instrument in the hands of the Almighty." Always his mission remained unchanged: "That this Union, the Constitution, and the liberties of the people shall be perpetuated in accordance with the original idea for which that struggle [the Revolution] was made."[67]

In Independence Hall in Philadelphia he left no doubt about his view of that "original idea." The Declaration of Independence, "giving liberty, not alone to the people of this country, but hope to the world for all future time," formed the keystone of his vision of America. The Declaration "gave promise that in due time the weights would be lifted from the shoulders of all men, and that *all* should have an equal chance." Having given his understanding of the Declaration, he asked, "Can this country be saved upon that basis?" If so, he would be delighted "if I can help save it." Failure to save it "upon that principle" would be "truly awful." But Lincoln did not hedge. "If this country cannot be saved without giving up that principle—I was about to say I would rather be assassinated on the spot then to surrender it."[68]

On several occasions Lincoln did address directly the crisis consuming the country and its manifestations, though disjointedly. In one speech he described the crisis as "an *artificial* one," declaring "*there is no crisis*, excepting such a one as may be gotten up at any time by designing politicians." If Americans will only "keep cool," he said, the trouble would pass. But in another place he spoke of doing all in his "power to promote a peaceful settlement to all our difficulties." The suggestion that the settlement might not be peaceful does not correlate with a contrived problem. Lincoln surely knew that a monumental problem existed, but he gave no indication of how he intended to address it, short of employing armed might. While avowing, "the man does not live who is more devoted to peace than I am," he made clear his willingness to adopt a different policy: "But it may be necessary to put the foot down firmly." Still, he did not want to use force, "to shed fraternal blood." Should that eventuality occur, however, as he informed the Pennsylvania legislature, the responsibility would not be his. "I promise," he averred, "that (in so far as I may have wisdom to direct,) if so painful a result shall in any wise be brought about, it shall be through no fault of mine."[69]

He did talk about the South, chiefly in Cincinnati, the closest he came to a slave state until his hurried journey through Maryland on his final approach to Washington. There he looked across the Ohio River to the state of his birth, Kentucky. In his remarks he iterated what he had said in the same city back in 1856. He focused on the decency of southerners and his intention "to treat you, as near as we possibly can, as Washington, Jefferson, and Madison treated you." Addressing the former point, Lincoln declared, "We mean to recognize, and bear in mind always, that you have good hearts in your bosoms as other people, or as we claim to have, and treat you accordingly." He even stated unequivocally that he intended "in no way to interfere with your institution"—slavery.

Soothing words, undoubtedly, but he never touched on why southerners feared Republicans. His pledge "that you are as good as we" contradicted the Republican assaults on the South as un-American. Yet he neither acknowledged nor explained that sharp discrepancy. When he announced that "the examples of those noble fathers—Washington, Jefferson, and Madison" would guide him, he overlooked or disregarded that each of these presidents was not only a slaveowner but also oversaw the opening of new territory to slavery or the admission of new slave states, or both. As in his Cooper Union speech, Lincoln either misread history or, more likely, saw in the past what he wanted to see. Whatever the logical problems inherent in his Cincinnati speech, he nowhere else on his road to Washington dealt with this subject.[70]

Many Republicans cheered Lincoln's performance on his preinaugural tour. His first public pronouncements since his election certainly caused no distress among hard-liners. They heard nothing about compromise or backing away from the Chicago platform. But more conservative Republicans, especially Seward and his allies, were alarmed. Meeting with Lincoln in New York City, Weed even tried to get the president-elect to moderate his tone. To no avail, however, for Weed told Seward that he had no reason to think that Lincoln "listened with profit."[71]

The Upper South and Border state Conservatives were really upset. They saw no "generous spirit" in the reports of Lincoln's speeches. Convinced that they had sacrificed much to stand firm against the secessionists, they saw nothing reciprocal coming from the Republicans. Lincoln's addresses caused them "vast harm," as a Virginian put it. They saw a growing distrust of Republicans in their ranks—a mistrust that could only benefit the secessionists. They desperately wanted a sign that Lincoln would moderate his party's hard line, and they told Seward so. Without that they feared for their cause. Even the usually upbeat Seward fought despondency.[72]

Yet, Seward would soon be in a face-to-face situation with his chief. When Lincoln reached Philadelphia, a credible plot of a planned assassination was uncovered. The attempt would be made as he passed through Baltimore, where he had to travel between train stations. He was urged to cancel his appearance in Harrisburg and proceed promptly to Washington. He refused.

But in Harrisburg, he did alter his plans. Senator Seward sent his son with a message to Lincoln that both the senator and General Scott felt it imperative that the president-elect avoid unnecessary risk. Lincoln finally agreed. Secrecy governed. On the evening of February 22 he slipped out of Harrisburg and traveled incognito through the night via Philadelphia and Baltimore, reaching Washington at sunrise on February 23. He was clandestinely whisked away to the Willard Hotel, where he would stay until his inauguration.[73]

Finally in Washington, Lincoln had just over a week before that day. On his first morning he breakfasted with Seward and toured the city with the secretary-of-state designate. Then he went to the White House, where he met President Buchanan and his cabinet. Back at the Willard, Lincoln met with various groups, including Senator Douglas and the Illinois congressional delegation.

Although he had a full social calendar, he still had critical decisions to make regarding his cabinet. Before reaching Washington, he had firmly decided on only two positions, Edward Bates as attorney general and Seward; he had named both back in 1860. His chief difficulty involved whether to award the second cabinet post, secretary of the treasury, to Salmon Chase or Simon Cameron. Both were United States senators, and both had powerful support. The Ohioan Chase, fervently freesoil, came from the hard-line wing of the party. He vehemently opposed any compromise on the territorial question. Just as vigorously Seward and his allies opposed Chase's appointment. Cameron, from Pennsylvania, was quite different. He was more flexible and friendly to the Sewardites, but he had a reputation as an unprincipled political fixer. The hard-liners detested him. Still, Republicans in the key state of Pennsylvania pushed him. In order to help him choose, Lincoln polled Republican senators. That they preferred Chase did not surprise him; in fact, their vote gave him cover to do what he probably wanted to. He handed the Treasury Department to Chase. He did not spurn Cameron altogether, however, offering him either the War Department or the Interior Department. Cameron selected the former.

At this point Lincoln still intended to place a southerner in his official family. He had come down to two finalists, John Gilmer of North Carolina and Montgomery Blair of Maryland. His equating those men as representing the South underscores his misunderstanding of the South and southern politics. The Upper South Conservative Gilmer had worked diligently for serious compromise, even pleading with Lincoln to support such an initiative. On the eve of Lincoln's arrival in the capital, Gilmer had penned a desperate plea: "Pardon me when I again beg & entreat you to do what I have so anxiously urged on you—I pray you to do this, & fully all I have suggested—Nothing below—" The president-elect made no known response. Blair, on the other hand, stood among the hard-line Republicans. He and his father, Frank Blair, Sr., were adamant against any settlement. That Seward lobbied for Gilmer and opposed Blair highlighted the political differences between the two men. Lincoln decided to give the nod to Gilmer. Although he wanted to accept, the North Carolinian in the end declined the offer. Senator Bragg, also of North Carolina, opined that Gilmer wanted the job, but was concerned about political reaction in the state. Gilmer also worried because he saw nothing forthcoming from Lincoln to meet even moderate southern demands on the territories. Despite three months of corresponding with Lincoln and Seward and conferring with the latter, he concluded that the Republicans would not provide a satisfactory territorial settlement. His refusal meant a seat for Montgomery Blair, strengthening the Republican hard-liners.

Lincoln completed his cabinet with two noncontroversial men, Gideon Welles of Connecticut for the Navy Department and Caleb Smith of Indiana for Interior. Now his official family was set. In shaping it he did not choose between moderates and hard-liners—he had both, even the leaders of the two groups, Seward and Chase. Yet giving Chase pride of place over Cameron and including Blair signaled a hard edge on his official family. It was not a group that pleased Seward. When on the last day of February Charles Francis Adams asked the New Yorker if all was right at headquarters, he answered immediately, "No they were not wrong, but scarcely quite right."[74]

In addition to settling on his cabinet, Lincoln held two important meetings outside his Republican family. As soon as he appeared in the capital, the pro-compromise forces in the still-sitting Peace Convention hoped for his aid. If they had had access to Senator Seward's mail, however, they would have found little reason for optimism. Thurlow Weed, who supported the goal of the convention but found congressional Republicans reluctant to do so, visited with Lincoln in both Albany and New York City during the latter's journey to Washington. Although Weed informed Seward that he would not put on paper "things which should not be left to any chance of exposure," he left no doubt about the results of his discussions. He confided to his close friend that the two men kept their conversation of February 20 focused on "a single point." Weed then confessed that he did not think he had persuaded Lincoln to come to his way of thinking.[75]

With Lincoln not only in the capital, but also staying at the Willard, the convention voted unanimously to request an audience with him. The president-elect promptly assented. At nine that evening the delegates called upon him. After introductions and pleasantries, Lincoln made some general remarks. Thereupon, Virginia's William C. Rives spoke, saying, "Everything depends upon you." Disagreeing, Lincoln observed that everyone should obey the Constitution. William Dodge brought up commercial concerns: "It is for you, sir, to say whether grass should grow in the streets of our commercial cities." Lincoln responded, "If it depends on me, the grass will not grow anywhere except in the fields and meadows." Dodge wanted to know whether that reply meant the president-elect "[would] not go to war on account of slavery." Lincoln would not be boxed. He made clear that his oath of office would require him to see that the Constitution be "respected, obeyed, enforced, and defended, let the grass grow where it may."[76]

The meeting provided nothing concrete that the pro-compromise men could use to their advantage. Strong Republican opposition remained to any territorial settlement. There is no evidence that Lincoln directly influenced the stance of the convention, or even tried to do so. It is most unlikely that he did do so. His inflexibility on the territories was abiding. Speaking specifically about the Peace Convention, he declared, "the Union could not be saved by nationalizing and extending slavery as they proposed to do."[77]

Lincoln's response to the Peace Convention as well as his final cabinet lineup certainly held to his firm line on the sectional question. He continued to shun compromise and to resist reaching out to the South as he had on the trip between Springfield and Washington. Yet, his reactions on three other occasions suggested a tempering of his attitude.

After a few days in the capital, he met informally, probably on February 26, with several Unionist leaders from the Border and Upper South, a number of whom had participated in the Peace Convention. This group included John Bell; most probably Senator Douglas was also there. The meeting was arranged by Charles Morehead, a former governor of Kentucky, a delegate to the Peace Convention, and an acquaintance of the president-elect.

The interview began predictably. Lincoln told the men that neither he nor his party harbored any ill will toward the South. He pledged to uphold the constitutional rights of the South and professed that the southern antipathy toward him puzzled him. But he went on to reaffirm his territorial stance, defining it as personal and political. Writing soon afterward, a congressman from western Virginia said the president-elect's words confirmed his view that Lincoln was really an abolitionist and, worse, "a cross between a sandhill crane and an Andalusian jackass." In the meeting itself southerners answered Lincoln with predictions of a terrible civil war if a territorial compromise could not be reached. They also said that coercion by the federal government, using force in any way against a seceded state, would drive their states out.

Into this conversation, William C. Rives intruded himself. Almost sixty-eight years old, the veteran Virginian statesman launched an emotional entreaty for the Union. He said to Lincoln "that he was then a very old man; that there had never been a throb in his heart that was not in favour of the perpetuation of the Union." He had come to the Peace Convention to try to preserve it. Then, "with a trembling voice," he added that he agreed a horrible war was in the offing, and if Lincoln did choose coercion, Virginia would leave the Union. "Nay, sir," came his conclusion, "old as I am, and dearly as I have loved this Union, in that event I go, with all my heart and soul."

According to Morehead, Lincoln "jumped up from his chair" and walked toward Rives. He said to Rives that if Virginia would stay in the Union, he would take the troops out of Fort Sumter. Rives replied that he had no authority to speak for his state, but if Lincoln would guarantee that act, he would use all his influence to promote the Union. That exchange ended the conversation.[78]

Lincoln's motive in this instance is unclear. Perhaps it was the spontaneous reaction of a man moved by an eloquent plea. Perhaps he was testing Rives and his colleagues, striving to discover what kind of commitments he could get. Or perhaps he saw the possibility of a deal he could accept. Referring to this meeting he asserted, "A state for a fort is no bad business." Whatever precisely motivated Lincoln, he revealed that under the right circumstances he could be less inflexible than he had previously shown.[79]

In another matter Lincoln also evidently exercised a moderating influence. In late February, House Republicans brought forth a so-called Force Bill that would empower the president to place state militias in federal service to put down a rebellion against the federal government. Additionally, it would permit certain volunteers to enter federal service. At that time, according to the attorney general, the president did not possess such power. The prospect of this measure becoming law terrified the Upper South and Border Unionists. They saw it as practically a declaration of war. The Virginians were particularly alarmed, for they feared it might spur the Virginia Convention to embrace secession. The bill advanced slowly, but a key vote was scheduled for March 1, a vote that would most probably result in its passage because most Republicans would vote aye.

Virginia Congressman Alexander Boteler was so distraught that he took it upon himself to go to the president-elect, whom he did not know. On the afternoon of March 1, Boteler went to the Willard, where he obtained a session with Lincoln. After explaining the purpose of his visit—the Force Bill and its dangers—he asked if Lincoln could intervene to block it. Following a brief silence, the president-elect smiled and said, "Well, I'll see what can be done about the bill you speak of. I think it can be stopped, and that I promise you it will be." He then told Boteler to keep that commitment confidential.

Boteler did not find a hard-liner. He described Lincoln as "kind-hearted man," who "was, at that time, willing to allow the moderate men of the South a fair opportunity to make further efforts for a settlement of our intestine and internecine difficulties. . . . " He saw Lincoln as refusing "to yield to the clamorous demand of those bloody-minded extremists, who were then so very keen to cry 'havoc!' and 'let slip the dogs of war.' "

The record does not reveal Lincoln's precise involvement in what happened in the House, though the outcome strongly indicates that he did exactly what he promised. When the proposed legislation came up for consideration on the evening of the first, it got sidetracked. Motions to adjourn, with Republicans participating, including Lincoln's confidant Elihu Washburne, prevailed before any vote could be taken. Because of Congress's imminent adjournment, the Force Bill was effectively dead.[80]

Lincoln also revealed this more thoughtful and moderate face in two public statements. On February 27, he replied to the welcome extended by the mayor of the city, and on the next day he responded to the U.S. Marine band and a crowd that gathered outside the Willard. On both occasions he admitted that a serious problem did exist between North and South, one he hoped to help resolve.

He was direct: "I think very much of the ill feeling that has existed and still exists between the people of the section whence I came and the people here is owing to a misunderstanding between each other which unhappily prevails." He then assured his listeners that he had "as kindly feelings toward [southerners] as to the people of my own section." "With great confidence," he was sure that when "we shall become better acquainted . . . , we shall like each other the more."

When he spoke to the group in front of the Willard, he again brought up "misunderstanding." He went on to say that he hoped "I may be enabled to convince you [southerners] and the people of your section of the country, that we regard you as in all things being our equals—in all things entitled to the same respect and to the same treatment that we claim for ourselves." He concluded with a reaffirmation: "I hope that by thus dealing with you we will become better acquainted and be better friends."[81]

As in Cincinnati, Lincoln did not ever attempt to explain the disconnection between what he said on this occasion and Republican rhetoric. Southerners certainly saw no equality. But, if Lincoln had begun making this kind of declaration much earlier, and then expanded upon it in a fashion that at least alleviated the sting of the Republican assault on the South, and assuaged southern fears of Republican intentions, secessionists would have had a much more difficult task. Lincoln seemed to be realizing, or at least voicing for the first time, that settling the crisis would require moderating his stance. But at this point it was not clear whether he either could or would. Even with the president-elect apparently sidling toward less intransigence, tension still gripped the country. America knew not what the future held. Congress was in its last week with little to show but furious rhetoric and omnipresent obstruction. The Confederate States of America was a fact, yet the majority of slave states remained in the Union, if somewhat tenuously. The unofficial truce in Charleston harbor was holding, though the volatile ingredients on the ground there remained in place.

CHAPTER SIX

"Fraternity Is the Element of Union"

AMERICANS DID NOT all greet the arrival of March 1861 in the same spirit. Some eagerly anticipated Lincoln's inauguration, four days away. Others dreaded it. Still others remained ambivalent. Hopes, stretching back to December, that Congress would resolve the national crisis, had been dashed. But Congress had yet to adjourn, and there was still a chance for it to assert itself before Inauguration Day, while the president-elect was in the city.

But neither they nor he seemed to know what could possibly be done to end the impasse. Results of the Peace Convention and reports from the Committee of Thirty-three faced obstructionist interference. New Mexican statehood was front and center, and fit squarely into the North-South dispute. A proposed Thirteenth Amendment, guaranteeing the continuation of slavery where it existed, would have a final hearing. John J. Crittenden and William H. Seward, two men of different political stripes but a common interest in seeking compromise, would each have a last chance to be heard.

While the Peace Convention deliberated and the president-elect made his way to the capital, Congress was still in session but remained stalled. For most of February mind-numbing motions and speeches on the reports from the Committee of Thirty-three consumed the House of Representatives. Unending obstruction on both sides of the Capitol blasted wishes for any substantive action. At the end of the month, with the measures from the Committee of Thirty-three languishing, the Peace Convention report reached Congress.

It did not receive a hearty welcome. Because of the lateness of the congressional hour and a full calendar, taking up the report in the House would necessitate suspending the rules, which required a two-thirds vote. Signaling general Republican unwillingness even to discuss its contents, Speaker Pennington, who received it on February 27, did not try to bring it before the House for two days, not until March 1. A few Republicans thought the House should permit its consideration. Because the report advocated peace and came from respectable men, Charles Francis Adams believed suspension of the rules appropriate. Even a hard-liner member of the convention concurred with Adams, though both men said they opposed the report.

But, on March 1 the attempt to get the report before the House failed, 93–67, far short of the needed two-thirds, with but few Republicans like Adams and Corwin in the majority. The bulk of House Republicans ensured its defeat. They concurred with Owen Lovejoy of Illinois, who declaimed there was "no peace congress at all. There is no such body known to this House." He asserted that ten thousand matters should go ahead, anything but serious compromise measures.[1]

In the Senate, the procedure differed, but not the outcome. When the Peace Convention report reached the upper chamber, Senator Crittenden got it referred to a select committee of five, two Democrats, two Republicans, and himself. By a 3-to-2 margin this committee backed the report and urged its adoption. The two Republicans, Seward and Trumbull, cast the negative ballots. For both of them, harking back to his January speech, Seward proposed a resolution calling for a national constitutional convention.

On this matter Republican senators followed their established pattern. They opposed bringing up the report; they obfuscated; they wanted delays. Through the lengthy debates from the report's delivery to the Senate on February 27 until the final vote five days later only one, Edward Baker of Oregon, ever spoke in favor of allowing the states, or the people, to vote on the suggested amendments. The report finally died ingloriously in the early hours of March 4. Only seven senators cast aye ballots.[2]

Almost simultaneously with the demise of the Peace Convention Plan, the last vestiges of the Committee of Thirty-three's work finally came up for a vote in the House. For six weeks debate and delay had prevented any decision. With the backing of both Thomas Corwin and Charles Francis Adams, both Republican moderates and Upper South and Border Conservatives saw passage of New Mexican statehood as well as the authorization of the proposed Thirteenth Amendment as signals that Republicans did intend to conciliate the South. Hopes were especially high for New Mexico, for admission of a state required only a majority vote. Moreover, Lincoln had indicated that he did not oppose bringing in New Mexico as a state, even though in all probability a slave state.[3]

New Mexican statehood failed, however. When the bill came up on March 1, the House tabled it by a 115–71 tally. Republican hard-liners wanted no part of it. By a three-to-one margin, the party stood firm in opposition. Southern congressmen divided almost evenly. Many saw no territorial benefit. If in fact the southerners had united behind it, a sufficient number of Republicans would have come over to pass it. But, as on other occasions, southerners wanted to see significant Republican support for measures designed to address southern concerns. It was not forthcoming.[4]

Although the House said no to New Mexico, it did sign off on the Thirteenth Amendment, though not easily. On February 26 and 27, Congressman Corwin pushed it. On the twenty-seventh, the House finally voted. The proposed addition to the Constitution did carry, 123–71, short of the required two-thirds. Republicans were in opposition by almost two to one, 68–37. The next day, however, reconsideration took place. The initial failure had distressed moderates like Adams, who denounced his colleagues' performance: "I can scarcely imagine a more remarkable exhibition of folly." To him and others the failure of this amendment told southerners that Republicans might very well move against slavery in the states at some future moment.[5]

Preparing for a new vote, Adams and his friends obviously lobbied successfully, for on the twenty-eighth the amendment garnered the necessary two-thirds, 132–65. A majority of Republicans still opposed, but seven more said yes, while six fewer said no. In this instance, Lincoln's role, if any, remains unclear. Yet, he told the group of Upper South and Border men that "he was willing to give a constitutional guarantee that slavery should not be molested in any way directly or indirectly in the states." Additionally, in his inaugural address four days later, he specifically stated that he had "no objection" to it.[6]

Even though the proposed amendment made it through the House, the Senate did not eagerly embrace it. In the upper chamber, Senator Douglas took the lead. He was met with what had become the standard Republican tactic—delay in whatever form best served Republican interests.

The Illinois senator also faced procedural obstacles from the vehemently pro-southern James Mason of Virginia, who thought it useless, and, surprisingly, from the equally ardent pro-compromise George Pugh, Democrat of Ohio, who wanted the language edited to make it more grammatical. Douglas feared that doing so would doom the amendment because any alteration would require its return to the House. There a new vote would probably kill it. Furthermore, with the session literally in its last hours, time might very well run out. After more wrangling, Douglas finally prevailed. In the predawn hours of March 4, the Senate voted. This Thirteenth Amendment passed by the requisite constitutional majority, 24–12, without a vote to spare. Every negative vote was Republican, though eight cast aye ballots. This proposed amendment, which would make slavery in the states untouchable, was on its way to the states for ratification.[7]

While congressional Republicans obstructed and stymied every single measure designed to deal with the crisis of the Union, the Thirteenth Amendment excepted, they moved apace on bills dear to them. In its platform of 1860, the Republican party had called for a higher tariff. Since 1846 tariff policy had been controlled by Democrats; with southerners paramount, they had kept duties down. With their northern orientation and a vigorous protectionist constituency, Republicans wanted them increased. Some Republicans wanted rates raised more than others, but all supported their going up. In the spring of 1860, they got an increased tariff bill through the House only to see it blocked by the Senate, where Democrats and southerners reigned. When southerners began leaving Congress in January 1861, the Republicans did not hesitate. The Morrill Act, named for the man who first introduced it, Representative Justin Morrill of Vermont, traveled easily through the Senate as well as the House. President Buchanan signed it into law.[8]

On the most vexing issue of all, the territories, the Republicans acted in an unexpected manner. As southerners rapidly exited Congress in February, the Republican majority created three new territories—Colorado, Dakota, and Nevada. What made the legislation establishing them notable was the absence of any mention of slavery. None of the bills contained the Wilmot Proviso or similar wording prohibiting slavery. Initially, the language of popular sovereignty was included, but it eventually came out because, as Senator Wade admitted on the Senate floor, Republicans and Democrats could not agree on its meaning. Even without specifying popular sovereignty, these measures left the decision regarding slavery to the people in the territories.[9]

In an amazing irony the first Republican territorial legislation fundamentally incorporated Stephen A. Douglas's doctrine, though silently. After years of pounding him and southerners with the club of no slavery in any territory, the Republicans evidently felt no need to make their creed law. Even Abraham Lincoln, who made no extension holy writ, said nothing. Of course, no one thought slavery would ever exist in these three territories, but that fact had also been the case elsewhere. Douglas did not let this Republican silence escape unnoticed. On March 2, he pointed out "that the Republican party, in both houses of Congress, by a unanimous vote, have backed down from their platform and abandoned the doctrine of congressional prohibition." The Wilmot Proviso, he noticed, had disappeared.[10]

Even though some of their own, as well as Douglas, recognized that they had jettisoned the Wilmot Proviso, Republicans did not slow down. They now had Congress, with the presidency very soon also theirs. The political force and power of the Proviso, of overt reference to free soil, they no longer needed. Unthinkingly, and again ironically, congressional Republicans and even the silent Lincoln acknowledged the accuracy of Thurlow Weed's declaration that with Lincoln's victory the territorial issue had served its political purpose for the party.[11]

The Senate Republicans did, however, take a swipe at the one branch of the federal government beyond their immediate control. They amended the bills removing the right to appeal any property issues from territorial courts to the Supreme Court. As a result, no judicial review could protect property rights, including those of slaveholders. Senator Douglas challenged them, remarking on the politics involved: "Suppose, four years from now, there should be a southern President; then are we to be called upon to change the law again, to give the right of appeal from the territorial judges to the Supreme Court of the United States? Are we to change the law and the territorial system according as the politics of the President may be changed?" For Republicans, their legislation gave their answer: yes. Of course, the sitting Supreme Court might very well have ruled that provision unconstitutional, if the issue had ever come before it. Events ensured that it never would.[12]

On a specific matter they considered political the Republicans held firm, however. In the evening of March 3, literally in the concluding hours of the session, Senator Crittenden made his last eloquent plea for conciliation, a plea he knew would be futile. At that point, his compromise, initially submitted back in December, had never come to a vote in either chamber. Republicans had seen to that. Before dawn on March 4, Crittenden moved to substitute the Peace Convention Plan. It was defeated. Then, finally, the Crittenden Compromise came up. It went down 19–20. No Republican voted for it; all twenty negative votes came from Republicans. Several moderates, headed by Seward and Cameron, were in the chamber, but did not cast a ballot. At seven o'clock in the morning the Senate recessed. The House had already adjourned.[13]

The Second Session of the 36th Congress had come to its end. It was March 4; the new president would be inaugurated at noon. For three months this Congress had had the fate of the Union in its hands. During that time both House and Senate set up special committees to search for a resolution to the crisis of the Union. To no avail—the Senate committee failed utterly; the House committee did make some proposals, only one of which made it through Congress. Neither committee could come up with a plan for the most contentious issue, slavery in the territories. After witnessing the secession of seven states, leaving the Union broken, this Congress could not find the will or the way to take positive action. In its last days it received a report from the convention held in Washington, to which twenty-one states had sent delegates, putting forth a blueprint to address the crisis. The majority Republicans buried it. This record of futility or impotence could only please those who advocated disunion and those with priorities that took precedence over keeping the Union whole. The great American political tradition of compromise stemming from the Constitutional Convention of 1787 had foundered.

On the morning the 36th Congress bumbled to its end, Abraham Lincoln prepared to take the oath of office as the sixteenth president, and with his inaugural address give the country a sense of what course he would pursue as chief executive. He had the speech with him when he arrived in Washington, having had it "blocked out" since early February. In a practice he did not usually follow, he allowed a few friends and political associates to read it or listen to his reading of it.[14]

Lincoln's initial draft took a hard line. He began by declaring that he was elected on the Chicago platform and there he would stand. He also announced that he would "reclaim" the federal property already taken over by the states as well as defend property still possessed by the government. Secession he defined as treason.[15]

In Springfield he let David Davis read the draft, and behind a locked door he read it to Carl Schurz. Davis, who liked it, made no suggestions for change. Neither did the hard-liner Schurz, who was impressed. Upon completing his reading, Lincoln informed Schurz, "Now you know better than any man in the country how I stand, and you may be sure that I shall never betray my principles and my friends." When the interview had concluded, Schurz wrote his wife that the president-elect's words and determination delighted him.[16]

A week later in Indianapolis during his preinaugural journey, Lincoln gave a copy to his friend Orville Browning, who had traveled from Springfield with him. He asked Browning to read and comment on it. Like Schurz, Browning was pleased, telling Lincoln that he thought it "able, well considered, and appropriate." All in all Browning found it "a very admirable document." Browning did have one suggestion, however; he advised the elimination of any reference to reclaiming federal property. In his opinion retaining what the government still held would serve Lincoln's purpose, for eventually the states would probably attack those posts, allowing Lincoln to respond from a defensive position. Lincoln permitted Browning to keep that copy, provided he showed it to no one but his wife.[17]

When Lincoln reached the national capital, the speech was basically unaltered. He did, however, take seriously Browning's recommendation regarding his intention to reclaim. On his first day in Washington he showed it to Seward and later he read it to the hard-liner Francis Blair, Sr. Blair, who was adamant against compromise, as was his son Montgomery, liked it very much. Seward, on the other hand, was appalled.[18]

Seward had spent the winter trying to keep the Upper South and the Border states from seceding. And he had succeeded, operating chiefly in two ways. First, he worked to prevent Republican excess in Congress. Although at times hard-liners spouted harsh language, Seward had managed to keep his radical colleagues basically in check. They did obstruct, but did not push hard on measures that would offend Seward's southern audience.

Although Seward's failure to support substantive compromise distressed some southern Conservatives, they were pleased that the congressional Republicans had not enacted any enforcement or coercive legislation. Second, Seward kept talking to these southerners, both in and out of Congress. He kept all lines of communication open. His message was simple: neither his party nor the new president intended any harm to them or their institution of slavery. Conciliation, he insisted, would be Lincoln's policy, just as it was his. There would be no vehement anti-South rhetoric from the new administration, much less any use of force. He even confessed to William C. Rives that his "irrepressible conflict" speeches "were intended for effect at home, and not designed for the ears of the South." Many Conservatives in the Upper South and Border accepted his assurances. He was evidently sincere. Furthermore, these southerners desperately wanted to believe him. They did not want to leave the Union, and Seward offered a future Union that guarded their rights. The alternative, secession and possible civil war, they did not want to contemplate.[19]

Seward believed that Lincoln's address, in its present form, would explode the tenuous accommodation he had striven to arrange. He envisioned the Upper South and Border marching straight into the Confederate States, leaving a Union too ruptured to be restored. He had good reason to worry. A day after Lincoln had given him a copy of the address, one of his contacts reported from the Virginia Convention that Virginia would surely go out if Lincoln proclaimed no to settlement or backed coercion. Thereupon, Seward undertook a risky project. He wrote a lengthy critique of the speech in which he implored Lincoln to make significant changes. In this missive he did not hold back.[20]

Seward began by spelling out his credentials for taking exception to Lincoln's draft. He had already tried to demonstrate conclusively his loyalty to the new party chief. Additionally, once Lincoln arrived in Washington, Seward was constantly at his side. Now came his defense of himself. He maintained that most hard-liners "know nothing of the real peril of the crisis." But he understood it. He informed Lincoln that he had "devoted [himself] singly to the study of the case," keeping contact "with all parties of all sections." He was not bashful about what he thought he had accomplished: "Only the soothing words which I have spoken have saved us and carried us along this far."

Seward admitted that his advice would not sit well with all Republicans, but they were not his chief concern. That an inaugural of moderation would distress hard-liners did not bother him. "I do not fear their displeasure," he stated to Lincoln; "they will be loyal whatever is said." Lincoln's pledging loyalty to the Chicago platform, however, would drive Virginia and Maryland out of the Union. Seward even envisioned that the occurrence would within two months cause the Lincoln administration to have to fight for Washington against a united South with "a divided North for our reliance."

He also wanted other changes. Any references to treason should be dropped because the southerners he wanted to soothe did not consider themselves potential traitors. Branding them with that opprobrium would violate the conciliatory promises that Seward had been making. He also desired nothing in the speech about either reclaiming federal property or a terse rejection of compromise.

Finally, Seward advised a shift of emphasis in the final paragraph. In the version he saw, Lincoln closed by telling southerners that only they could initiate conflict. They had, he declared, "no oath registered in Heaven to destroy the government, while *I* shall have the most solemn one to 'preserve, protect, and defend' it." Southerners did not have to assault federal property, he said, but he could "*not* shrink from the *defense* of it." His last statement took the form of an interrogatory: "With *you;* and not with *me,* is the solemn question of 'Shall it be peace, or a sword?' " Seward, in contrast, advocated an ultimate paragraph that emphasized a common national experience and heritage. Harking back to Thomas Jefferson's inaugural in 1801, Seward asked for a call for unity akin to Jefferson's famous pronouncement, "We are all Federalists, all Republicans."

In writing so boldly, Seward took a considerable risk. Although he had been with the president-elect from the moment of his arrival in Washington, the secretary-of-state designate did not know how Lincoln would react to such forthright criticism. Seward took that chance because he saw so much at stake. He feared the secession of at least some, if not all, of the Upper South and Border states, making restoration of the Union all but impossible.

Seward had a second concern. The final forming of the cabinet did not please him at all. Not only had Lincoln not filled it with former Whigs, he had named two vigorously anti-Seward and vehemently anti-compromise former Democrats, Salmon Chase and Montgomery Blair. Both of these men Seward had tried to keep out. Moreover, they would hold the two most important positions for dispensing patronage, secretary of the treasury and postmaster general. In addition, Gideon Welles, in the Navy Department, who shared their political background and approach to the crisis, would line up in their column. The conservative ex-Democrat Simon Cameron, as secretary of war, Seward could count on as an ally, along with the former Whigs Edward Bates as attorney general and Caleb Smith as secretary of the interior. This was not the cabinet that Seward had exerted himself for.

At this juncture Seward took a radical step. While the official family was not to his liking, his chief worry focused on what he perceived as the probable rejection of Upper South and Border Conservatives to Lincoln's stern inaugural. By March 2, only two days prior to the inauguration, he had received no reply concerning his suggested revisions to Lincoln's tough speech. Thereupon, he sent the president-elect a brief message. "Circumstances" since he had agreed to become secretary of state, he wrote, "seem to me to render it my duty to ask leave to withdraw my consent." He did not spell out the "circumstances," but he clearly meant what he discerned as a hard-line administration and policy.[21]

Lincoln's immediate response to Seward's note is unknown. He did spend much of March 3 and the morning of the fourth revising his address. Also, he had accepted Browning's suggestion on removing the reference to reclaiming federal property, and he had made his offer to the group of Upper South and Border men to withdraw from Fort Sumter in turn for Virginia's pledge of loyalty to the Union. Thus, he seemed to be inclining toward a less hard-line position. Yet Seward did not have that knowledge. He had heard nothing from Lincoln about either his proposed revisions or his request to leave the cabinet.

At noon on March 4, Abraham Lincoln stood on the east front of the Capitol facing a huge throng. The venerable Chief Justice Roger Taney, author of the *Dred Scott* decision, administered the oath of office. Thereupon, Lincoln made his first statement as president of the United States. In his audience, Charles Francis Adams recorded that the new chief executive spoke in a "clear, distinct" voice that all could hear.[22]

Lincoln's words indicated that he had heeded Seward's advice in part, but that he also clung to his deeply held verities. Gone was any reference to the Chicago platform. He no longer used the word "treason." There was no blunt declaration against compromise. Moreover, he specifically stated his support for the constitutional amendment approved by Congress earlier that morning, the Thirteenth, guaranteeing slavery in the states where it existed. Additionally, he noted that some Americans desired further amendments to the Constitution. Because they had that right, he did not object, though he had none to offer.[23]

At the same time, Lincoln reiterated his views on slavery and the Union. While he affirmed his determination to uphold every constitutional protection given to slavery, he recognized a sharp difference of opinion about the institution. "One section of our country believes slavery is *right* and ought to be extended, while the other believes it is *wrong*, and ought not to be extended." With these words he made himself and the entire North into one; and he conflated the South's insistence on its constitutional right with its desire, both problematical propositions.

He underscored his conviction, "the Union of these States is perpetual." That definition meant secession had no legitimacy. Thus, no state "upon its mere motion, can lawfully get out of the Union,—that *resolves* and *ordinances* to that effect are legally void." Secession as an act against "the authority of the United States" becomes "insurrectionary or revolutionary, according to the circumstances." Yet he acknowledged that some states considered themselves outside the Union. Against them he avowed "no invasion—no using force against, or among the people anywhere." Simultaneously, he announced his intention to hold federal property still in the government's possession and to collect customs duties.

If his profession of conciliation coupled with his definition of his stance vis-à-vis secession created any doubt about his bedrock position, the penultimate paragraph seemingly dispelled it. It had steel, repeating basically the wording from his initial draft where it had concluded the speech. "In *your* hands, my dissatisfied fellow countrymen, and not in *mine*, is the momentous issue of civil war," he averred. Then, he asserted that no conflict could result "without being yourselves the aggressors." They had no "oath registered in Heaven" to attack the government, but he had "the most solemn one" to defend it. With this avowal, Lincoln was apparently saying that no action of his could in any way lead to conflict. Full responsibility for such an outcome he placed on his "dissatisfied fellow countrymen."

He did not close there, however. Turning away from talk of any clash, his last paragraph showed the impact of Seward's advice. In eloquent, almost poetic, language Lincoln accented the unity of Americans. "I am loath to close," he said. Insisting "we are not enemies, but friends," he pronounced, "we must not be enemies." In his words the "passion" that caused so much antagonism "must not break the bonds of affection." Then came the magnificent final sentence: "The mystic chords of memory, stretching from every battle-field, and patriot grave, to every living heart and hearthstone, all over this broad land will yet swell the chorus of the Union, when again touched, as they surely will be, by the better angels of our nature."

Partisans reacted to the speech predictably. Republicans united in praise. Setting the example for the rival wings of the party, both Horace Greeley and Thurlow Weed cheered. Greeley's *Tribune* described the entire event as passing off "brilliantly"; Weed's *Evening Journal* praised the inaugural as "equally firm and conciliatory." In general the Republican press chorused these sentiments. Party editorialists applauded Lincoln for fulfilling all expectations, for leaving no doubt about his policy. "It is clear as a mountain brook," asserted the *Detroit Daily Tribune*. They lauded Lincoln's declaration about the sanctity of the Union and what they defined as his conciliatory tone. Many were also delighted that they saw no sign of compromise. Some hard-liners took the next step, contemplating the possibility of armed conflict without flinching. "Blood built [the Union]," proclaimed the Springfield *Daily Illinois State Journal*, "and blood alone will destroy it or make it stronger."[24]

In contrast, northern Democrats expressed disappointment or distress. *The New York Herald* found no clarity, rather a "paraphrase of vague generalities," with "craft and cunning" at its core. Most newspapers, including those who had backed the Constitutional Unionists, decried what they saw as the inaugural's murkiness. Lincoln spoke of desiring peace, they noted, but seemed to embrace a coercive policy. Furthermore, they did not think he dealt with the reality of secession. Moreover, his equating his party with the North and claiming for it majority status upset some; they pointed out that in the country Lincoln received only 40 percent of the popular vote. Although most of these editors did not go so far as Jeremiah Black, who termed the speech "beastly," they did concur with Edwin Stanton that it would "do no good towards settling the difficulties." The Democrats worried that Lincoln intended harm.[25]

Harm heading toward them is what Lincoln's most "dissatisfied countrymen" perceived. Denouncing the content of the address, The *Charleston Mercury* located Lincoln still astride the Chicago platform just as he had been all along. According to the *Mercury*, the result could be "summed up in three words—ignorance, fanaticism, brute force." In Montgomery,

Howell Cobb read Lincoln's words as "indeed a declaration of war against the seceded states." Thomas Bragg, senator from North Carolina, regarded the speech as presaging "the storm."[26]

With a critical audience the reaction was mixed. A major North Carolina newspaper was emphatic: "It is not a war message." Likewise, William A. Graham characterized it as "quite as pacific as Mr. Buchanan's annual message," but he also realized that many moderate newspapers in his state deemed it "portending *horrida bella.*" Virginians reluctant to secede were deeply concerned. To them the inaugural was a mystery, unclear about Lincoln's real intentions. They worried that his remarks aimed at coercion, the use of federal force in some fashion, against the seceded states. Such a step would destroy them politically and hand the state to the disunionists. They feared that Lincoln had jettisoned them. Still, they planned to hold on, to remain on the defensive until the new president made clear his stance toward the South, both the states that had already seceded and those that had not.[27]

Obviously, Lincoln's inaugural could be understood in different ways. The thoughtful historian of Lincoln's speeches Ronald White defines the address as an exercise in "political persuasion," in which Lincoln had two goals: "assuage" the South and "strengthen the resolve" of the North. Those embodied contradictory purposes, however. With conciliation of one section a key aim, resolve of the other seems out of place, and vice versa. Additionally, while Lincoln addressed the nation, he also spoke directly to his own party. There he had undoubted success, witness the approval of both Greeley and Weed. After listening to Lincoln, Charles Francis Adams immediately recognized that the speech would please both wings of the party, bringing "all to stand upon a common ground."[28]

On March 4, Abraham Lincoln clearly did not know how events would unfold. Still, he was seemingly certain about his determination not to compromise the territorial issue and to hold the forts and collect the tariff revenue. The former could not help the Upper South and Border Conservatives, and the latter could result in armed hostilities. Despite the elevated closing of his speech, the America he would support and defend was America as he defined it. Perhaps the most astute reading of Lincoln's address came from a Republican attorney and civic leader in New York City, George Templeton Strong, who noted that a number of his conservative acquaintances called it "pacific" and likely to prevent conflict. "Maybe so," Strong recorded in his diary, "but I think there's a clank of metal in it."[29]

Abraham Lincoln now occupied the Executive Mansion. He would make decisions on the ongoing, vexing matter of federal property in the seceded states. His inaugural adopted a defensive posture, specifying that his duty involved protecting that property still controlled by the federal government. He had dropped his initial language which spoke of reclaiming posts the states had occupied. Even though he had been aware of the problem posed by the forts, especially Fort Sumter, since December, he had not revealed his intended policy. Privately, he had been in touch with General Scott and General John E. Wool, commander of the army's Department of the East, stating his gratitude for their patriotism as well as his reliance on their advice on military affairs. Furthermore, he had exploded at the possibility of Buchanan's giving up Fort Sumter.[30]

The historical record does not permit precise knowledge of what Lincoln thought when he took the oath of office. Yet, it appears most probable that he planned to maintain his predecessor's policy—the informal truce arranged by Buchanan and southerners. That entailed holding on to forts Sumter and Pickens without any effort to strengthen their garrisons. The great hope, of course, was that some kind of general settlement would be reached before hostilities could break out. Continuing this modus vivendi would mean that he could go about the business of organizing his administration without having to worry unduly about his southern policy.

President Lincoln had much to learn. Fundamentally a stranger in Washington, he had to discover the ways of the capital. Moreover, he had to find out what it meant to be president. Never having held any prior executive office, he had no experience in ensuring that subordinates carried out his directives and policies. He was at the same time a student and his own teacher.

He expected one task to assume primary importance: patronage, the lifeblood of professional politicians. Deciding about positions, who got which, had engulfed him back in Springfield. In Washington, the torrent did not recede. After he made his final cabinet choices, days before his inauguration, multitudes of lesser places awaited his attention. As in Springfield, he immersed himself in this central role of political leaders, handing jobs to party loyalists. Lincoln went all the way down to making decisions about local postmasters. Senator Charles Sumner was critical: "The Prest. makes the great mistake of trying to deal with all possible cases, this fritters away his valuable time." Within a month of his inauguration, Lincoln himself confessed that "the office-seekers demanded all his time." And he rarely denied them, robbing himself of the ability to focus on other matters, including the southern question. "I am," he said, "like a man so busy in letting rooms out one end of his house, that he can't stop to put out the fire that is burning the other."[31]

His chief patronage complication concerned his designated secretary of state, who two days prior to the inauguration had asked to withdraw his name. Lincoln had no intention of dropping Seward from his official family, however. He needed the New Yorker, the most influential former Whig in the party aside from Lincoln himself, a force with Congress, and the avenue to Conservatives in the Upper South and Border.

Seward sent the note for two reasons. First, Lincoln's final cabinet choices alarmed him, both because they signaled hard-line and diminished influence for Seward. Second, and more important, he feared the hard-line cabinet coupled with what he saw as an intransigent inaugural would drive the Upper South and the Border into the Confederacy. To him that would presage the complete destruction of the Union. Thus, he wanted to push Lincoln toward moderation. At the same time, however, his request was part bluff. To influence the president and his administration, Seward had to be in it. That political reality had as much relevancy in early March as back in December when he initially accepted Lincoln's offer.

In sum, each man needed the other. Seward's message clearly had an impact on the content and tenor of the inaugural, though Lincoln probably already had in mind tempering at least part of it. But on the cabinet he stood firm, not allowing Seward to play kingmaker. Pondering how to respond to the withdrawal, Lincoln uttered his famous line, "I can't afford to let Seward take the first trick." While the inauguration procession was forming, Lincoln, at the Willard, wrote Seward that he must "countermand the withdrawal." "The public interest, I think, demands that you should," Lincoln penned, "and my personal feelings are deeply enlisted in the same direction."[32]

Yet, upon close examination, neither Lincoln nor Seward bested the other. Each got something he termed consequential. After the inaugural, when the public reception had ended, Seward visited Lincoln at the White

House, where they engaged in "a long and confidential talk." Although we cannot know exactly what they discussed, the result is not in doubt. The next morning Seward withdrew his withdrawal. He would become secretary of state. But exactly how he and the president would work together was not yet clear.[33]

Even before Lincoln could think about settling in as president, events robbed him of the opportunity for a quiet season of learning. As had so often been the case since December, unsettling tidings originated in Charleston harbor. On the morning of March 4, a dispatch from Major Anderson arrived at the War Department. Dated February 28, it informed his superiors that because his supplies were becoming exhausted, the garrison could be maintained for no more than an additional six weeks. This news shocked Secretary of War Holt, for Major Anderson had given no previous indication that he faced any serious difficulty.[34]

Anderson's report contained even more dire information, however. Because such imposing batteries and fortifications had been erected around him, he asserted that it would require a force of twenty thousand to thirty thousand well-armed men to force their way into the harbor and relieve him. Of course, naval cooperation would be a necessity. Anderson buttressed his judgments with independent assessments he had required from each of his officers. Although these eight men did not all agree on precise numbers, they did concur on the scale of an operation needed for the successful relief of Fort Sumter.[35]

Secretary Holt brought word of this stunning development to the final cabinet meeting of the Buchanan administration. With no more than an hour remaining before Buchanan departed the White House for the inauguration, Holt advised the president and his official advisers of the contents of the documents. It was obviously too late for Buchanan to make any more decisions about Fort Sumter. He simply delegated Holt, who requested the assignment, to convey this intelligence to Lincoln.[36]

That evening Holt prepared a lengthy covering letter to accompany the Anderson papers. Without doubt he wanted to remove any possibility that the new president would think that his predecessor had intentionally conspired to pass this bombshell to him. Holt began by underscoring the "unexpected" nature of Anderson's information. Drawing on the substantial correspondence between Anderson and the War Department, Holt highlighted Anderson's repeated assurances of his satisfaction with his position. Holt also made clear that the Buchanan administration stood ready to reinforce Anderson, should he make such a request. In fact, Holt pointed out, an expedition was at the ready, but its numbers were nowhere close to those Anderson estimated it would take for a successful relief mission.[37]

On his very first morning as president, Lincoln received this utterly astonishing news. It shocked him—so much so that just a few months later he remembered getting it just after the inauguration, not on the next day when he actually did get it. Immediately he sent the material to General Scott for his appraisal.

Scott replied promptly, his response going through Seward. He informed the new president that he had consistently urged Buchanan to reinforce Fort Sumter, but that the president had refused to do so. In Scott's opinion such an operation could have succeeded at any time from late December until early February. But now the situation in Charleston harbor had changed. He agreed with Anderson that the works arrayed against Fort Sumter had grown too powerful for the kind of relief undertaking the military could mount. He told Lincoln what Anderson also knew, that it would take months to put together such an operation. In fact, that force, using Anderson's numbers, would exceed the total existing strength of the United States Army. Considering all the factors, Scott concluded, "Evacuation seems inevitable," a judgment he noted that the army's chief engineer shared. Having made that bleak determination, the general still worried that within the week attackers would overwhelm "the worn out garrison."[38]

The day before, Lincoln had also heard from General Scott, albeit indirectly. In his campaign to bring Lincoln closer to his own moderate position, Seward had forwarded to the new chief executive on his inaugural date a letter that Scott had written him on March 3. In all probability Seward had influenced Scott, perhaps even coached him. The two men had long known each other and had been in touch during the winter. In this epistle, which Seward clearly intended to send to Lincoln, Scott expanded upon the crisis and the options he saw available to the new administration.[39]

General Scott outlined four. His first was what Seward had envisioned since shortly after Lincoln's electoral triumph. The Republican party could embrace the Crittenden Compromise or the Peace Convention proposals and become the great Union party. Doing so, in Scott's opinion, again echoing Seward, would halt the secession process and prompt the return of some seceded states. If, however, the Republicans rejected this course, Scott saw the remaining slave states soon making their way to the Confederate States of America, leaving Washington literally besieged. Second, the government could collect customs duties on the high seas, or by act of Congress close the ports in the seceded states and blockade them. Third, the United States could wage war against the seceded states, a conflict Scott said would last two to three years and require an army of three hundred thousand men. It would result in horrendous casualties and cost hundreds of millions of dollars. The Union could prevail, Scott believed, but in addition to the cost in blood and treasure, victory would leave an angry, devastated part of the country, which would necessitate an expensive occupying garrison for decades. No one in his right mind, Scott left unsaid, would choose to travel such a ruinous road. Finally, the general said, to tell the seceded states, "*Wayward sisters, depart in peace!*" In this letter, General Scott never made an explicit recommendation, but neither did he hide his opinion. The first option was clearly his choice, as it was surely Seward's.

Just as Abraham Lincoln was confronting his own dilemma with Fort Sumter, the Confederate commissioners began arriving in Washington. Among his first acts as president of the Confederate States, Jefferson Davis had appointed a delegation to go to Washington "for the purpose of establishing friendly relations between the Confederate States and the United States." He charged the delegation, or the commissioners, to confer with any "persons duly authorized by the Government of the United States" who possessed similar powers. The commissioners could enter into negotiations on "all matters and subjects interesting to both nations" as well as sign treaties.[40]

Immediately paramount, however, were the military posts within Confederate territory still garrisoned by the United States Army. Davis wanted a settlement that covered all former federal property, the installations that had been taken over by the states, and the forts still occupied by federal troops. The latter numbered four: Fort Sumter in Charleston; Fort Pickens in Pensacola; and two far away in the Florida keys, Fort Taylor at Key West and Fort Jefferson on the Dry Tortugas. Although the Confederates asserted that all were within their borders, the former two commanded prompt attention, especially Fort Sumter.

The Confederate States' new secretary of state, Robert Toombs, instructed his diplomats to press upon their counterparts that the Confederacy wanted peace. Hostilities would commence only if the United States employed military force within Confederate territory. While the Confederate government hoped for an early agreement, it authorized the commissioners to accept delay, provided the president of the United States stated that he needed time to consult with the Senate or until Congress convened again. Meanwhile, though, Lincoln would be asked to pledge that he would make no attempt to enforce federal authority within the Confederate frontier. At the same time, Secretary Toombs cautioned his agents to watch for delays designed to cover surprise military action. They should do their utmost to obtain reliable information on the intentions of the Lincoln administration.[41]

For this critical mission, Davis chose three well-known men who had wide experience in public affairs. Martin Crawford of Georgia, who had been a member of the House of Representatives since the mid-1850s, headed the group. His colleague the Alabamian John Forsyth, editor of *The Mobile Register*, had served as minister to Mexico under both Franklin Pierce and James Buchanan. The third commissioner, André Roman, was a former governor of Louisiana and influential in his state.

Crawford reached Washington first, arriving on March 3; Forsyth followed on the fifth, with Roman joining them a few days later. Crawford had hoped to see Buchanan before the Pennsylvanian left office, but there was no chance. Soon thereafter Seward learned that Crawford had arrived in the capital, with instructions to obtain an official or unofficial interview with the president. The rejection of that initiative could result in what Seward wanted most to avoid—a belligerent stance on both sides that might mean war.[42]

To make his initial overture to the Lincoln administration, Crawford enlisted the pro-southern Democratic senator from California, William Gwin. Gwin met with Seward on March 5. In the meantime, Seward had been reliably informed by a mutual friend of his and Gwin's who had participated in a discussion with Gwin and other southerners, including a recent visitor to Montgomery, that Jefferson Davis wanted peace, but his government could not wait indefinitely for the Lincoln administration to decide on its policy. To that end, should Crawford and his colleagues leave Washington unacknowledged, even offended, public opinion in the Confederacy might force Davis to attack the forts. With this information, the Confederate commissioners clearly hoped to press Lincoln to adopt a conciliatory position that would result in his turning the forts over to the Confederacy.[43]

When Gwin brought this same intelligence from the same sources as well as from Crawford, Seward took his first steps down a peril-fraught diplomatic path. According to Gwin, Seward said that he had "built up the Republican party" and "brought it to power." But massive difficulties accompanied its assuming that power. Still, he was determined to "save the party and the government in its hands." Doing so, Seward asserted, necessitated avoiding war as well as dropping both "the negro question" and the "irrepressible conflict." Those accomplished, he would put together a Union party that embraced the Upper South and the Border. He told Gwin he had made a good start by keeping Virginia in the Union, and he would eventually best Davis and his fellow Confederates. His conclusion: "Saving the Border states to the Union by moderation and justice, the people of the cotton states, unwillingly led into secession, will rebel against their leaders and reconstruction will follow."[44]

For events to unfold as Seward wanted, he needed time. He knew that any immediate Confederate ultimatum regarding recognition of the forts would wreck his goals and hopes. Lincoln would never agree to acknowledge the Confederacy as an independent nation. Seward required an interval of calm to bring the president to his conciliatory position. Moreover, the news from Fort Sumter had the administration in turmoil. Although he gave assurances that he and his chief wanted peace, there were certain things he could not do at that moment.[45]

Seward's intentions, relayed to Crawford by Gwin, did not perturb the Confederate commissioners. They also wanted time, time to strengthen the Confederate military in general and the works in Charleston and Pensacola in particular. Should conflict come, their government wanted to be as prepared as possible. Furthermore, they had no worries about a desire for reconstruction in the Confederate States. At this early date an enthusiastic embrace of independence dominated the new country. Thus, the commissioners prepared to cooperate with Seward.

The next step came when the commissioners insisted on a pledge that the federal government would not alter the military situation within Confederate borders. They would present the secretary of state with a written statement spelling out their requirements for postponing a demand for immediate recognition. Seward had evidently consented to sign such a document. To the commissioners that act would signify almost a "virtual recognition" of their government. On March 8, Gwin delivered the paper to the State Department. In it, the commissioners stipulated that they would put their mission on hold for twenty days upon a pledge from the Lincoln administration to refrain from changing its military status in the Confederacy. Upon Gwin's arrival at the department, he received the news that Seward was at home, ill. Initially, the Confederates were concerned that he had deceived them, but upon investigation they were convinced that he was sick, which he was.[46]

They saw delay, not deterrence. Thus, they would submit their memorandum a second time. On this occasion Senator Robert M. T. Hunter of Virginia became their liaison with Seward, Gwin having departed Washington. On March 11, the senator met with the secretary at the State Department. Because Hunter was a senator from a state still in the Union, Seward could not very well refuse to meet with him. In addition to handing Seward the document, Hunter requested that the secretary grant an interview to the commissioners.

Senator Hunter found Seward "perceptibly embarrassed and uneasy." Seward stood on unsteady ground, and he knew it. He did not have Lincoln's agreement to confer with the Confederates. As a result, he told Hunter that he would have first to consult the president. The next day he informed Hunter in writing that he could not see the Confederate commissioners.[47]

Now the commissioners perceived obstruction, or even a rebuff, not delay. Accordingly, they prepared a statement addressed to Seward, avowing the peaceful intentions of their government. They also declared themselves accredited commissioners from the Confederate States of America and asked the secretary "to appoint a day as early as possible, in order that they may present the credentials which they bear and the objects of the mission with which they are charged." Dated March 12, their formal note was delivered to the State Department on the thirteenth. On the next day, when an emissary of the commissioners called at the department for a reply, he was told that because the secretary had been very busy, a response had not yet been prepared, but would very soon be forthcoming.[48]

Acting for the administration, Seward found himself in a delicate spot. Yet he had been in the same place since mid-December. His great goal remained no armed clash. To achieve it, he had to keep the Confederate commissioners from feeling rebuffed. He did not want these men reporting to Montgomery that they and their government had been insulted. Such a reaction could spur the Confederates to start shooting. At the same time, he did not yet know where his chief would end up. Seward was surely pushing for conciliation and moderation, as he had been for three months, yet he had always been careful not to get too far in front of Lincoln.

Now, in addition to the Confederate initiative, he had to confront the new, unsettling situation at Fort Sumter. On handling that problem, he had a key ally, General Scott. The new president's chief civilian and military advisers provided the same advice, withdrawal of the garrison. But Seward did not know whether he, even with Scott, could persuade Lincoln to do so.

While Seward and the Confederate commissioners warily eyed each other in their diplomatic dance, a conclave had gathered a hundred miles to the south, in Richmond, Virginia, that was central to both, as well as to President Lincoln. Of all the Upper South and Border states, only in Virginia did a secession convention continue sitting throughout March. Back on February 13, the delegates had commenced their work of deciding what Virginia should do during the crisis. The United States and the Confederate States considered the decisions made in Richmond critical. Many in each believed that Virginia's course would influence the entire Upper South and Border.

In the month of March two other gatherings took place in the northwestern corner of the slave states. The only secession convention in a Border state convened in St. Louis on March 4, Inauguration Day. As the drubbing disunionist candidates had received during the election for delegates predicted, immediate secession never had a chance in Missouri. On March 19, by the overwhelming margin of 89 to 1, the assembly adopted a resolution stating that no legitimate reason existed for breaking up the Union. Three days later the convention adjourned until December, not to meet earlier unless called by a special standing committee.[49]

Also on March 4, the Arkansas Convention met. Soon thereafter, by the close vote of 39 to 35, it turned down a proposal to submit to voters in May the question of whether or not Arkansas should secede. That rejection spurred ardent secessionists to threaten that the pro-secession southeastern part of the state, the most heavily slave, would break away and join the Confederacy. Thereupon, the immediate secessionists agreed on a compromise with the cooperationists and the few outright Unionists, postponing the popular referendum until August. With that agreement, the convention disbanded with no set date to reconvene, but the president could call it back in the case of exigency.[50]

Although the Virginia Convention did not break up as its counterparts to the west did, neither did it set a final course for the state to take. The delegates divided into three major groups: immediate secessionists, unconditional Unionists, and Conservative Unionists. The first, concentrated in the heavier slave areas of eastern Virginia, wanted to take their state out immediately. The second, hailing mostly from the trans-Allegheny region that would become West Virginia during the Civil War, was determined to cling to the Union. Neither of those two could rally the convention around its standard. Their inability to move their colleagues in the face of what they defined as grave danger frustrated the immediatists. Addressing their opponents, they charged, "You close your eyes . . . " to the mortal threat. They disparaged those who disagreed: "The men who belong wholly to the past are unfit for the duties before us."[51]

The great middle, the Conservative Unionists, dominated in Richmond. Observers as well as participants understood who had the numbers to decide the action of the convention. Senator Hunter, strongly pro-southern, reported to Howell Cobb in Montgomery that the Conservatives controlled the convention, precluding the passage of any secession ordinance unless coercion occurred. The Conservatives themselves, along with the unconditional Unionists, recognized the location of real power among the delegates. This intelligence reached Republican heavyweights in Washington, especially Seward, who had established cordial relations with several of the Conservatives.[52]

While the Conservatives had an indisputable majority, they were not united behind a particular positive program. Some pushed for the eight Upper South and Border slave states to convene and make recommendations for settling the crisis. Others wanted the Virginia Convention itself to offer a plan for settlement. Then there were those who just wanted to hold on, praying that somehow a solution would be found. All were unified, however, in opposition to immediate secession and to coercion, identifying each as equal evils. Secession they termed radical and without just cause, at least at the moment. Coercion they equated with tyranny. It would not be tolerated. The federal government must pursue a peaceful policy; "Everything depends upon it," one informed a Washington editor.[53]

The major work of the convention took place in the Committee on Federal Relations, though the unending and often lengthy speeches seemed to crowd out all else. Yet, the committee worked unceasingly. A stalwart Conservative member, Robert Conrad, detailed to his wife the laborious effort involved. He described fourteen-hour days that seemed like "the English factory system." He spent much time "in allaying discontents and overcoming difficulties" within Conservative ranks. Striving for solid backing for its report, the committee also anxiously awaited the results of outside events like the Peace Convention and Lincoln's inaugural.[54]

Finally, on March 9, the committee delivered its report to the full convention. It contained no surprises; in fact, it went over old ground. It recommended that the convention devise constitutional amendments and send them out to the states for comment. Although they had not been finalized when war struck, they would have been basically a reprise of the Crittenden Compromise. The report also called for the eight slave states still in the Union to convene at Frankfort, Kentucky, in late May in order to formulate a resolution to the national distress. If the convention and the Kentucky meeting produced differing designs, they could surely be reconciled. These Virginians obviously did not foresee any quick end to the crisis.

While the committee clearly wished somehow to find conciliation, it underscored its conviction that a state had the right to secede because American government rested on "the consent of the governed." As a result, Virginia would never acquiesce in the use of federal force against the citizens of any seceded state. Coercion would mean civil war.[55]

Throughout the Upper South and the Border, Conservatives chorused that cry. "*Forbearance* . . . is the *word*," a Kentuckian stressed to Seward. Just after repudiating immediate secession, the Missouri Convention by the lopsided count of 89 to 6 denounced coercion. These men understood that armed conflict would undermine their political strength. They would immediately decline from formidable to weak. They feared that the Union cause in their states would "receive a blow from which it [might] never recover." Many Conservatives concurred with the Virginian who said that, should the Lincoln administration start down a coercive road, "resistance by a united South must immediately follow."[56]

In the national capital the competition between conciliation and coercion took place around the forts, especially Fort Sumter. Working hard to assure all southern men in contact with him that the administration intended to follow a peaceful policy, Seward had an ally in Senator Douglas, who, though a partisan rival, wanted the same thing. As chief of the northern Democrats, Douglas found himself in a difficult position. His efforts to fashion a compromise during the congressional session had failed. Now, with a Republican in the presidential office, he would lead the loyal opposition. For his party to return to power, the sectional rupture that had spurred the Democratic downfall had to be repaired. For that mending to occur the Upper South and Border had to stay in the Union; then a major effort would have to take place to accomplish the return of the seceded states.

Douglas made clear that he would support Lincoln as the president of the country, all the while pressing him to back conciliation. To that end, on March 6 and 7, he took the floor during a special session of the Senate, sitting mainly to act on new presidential appointments, to praise Lincoln's inaugural as pacific. He made it out to be more pacific than it actually was, but by doing so he gave himself the option, if the president ultimately took a hard line, of charging that the chief executive had failed to live up to his inaugural pledge. In addition, Douglas brought up Fort Sumter, telling his fellow senators that he had learned about the altered situation there. Douglas concluded that Lincoln must eventually order the evacuation of the post because he had neither the men nor the money to do otherwise. To obtain either he would have to call a special session of Congress. Although Douglas asserted that the facts about Fort Sumter were generally known, they were not. When Douglas spoke, Lincoln had not even informed his entire cabinet. In all probability Douglas's information came from Seward, who desired all the assistance he could obtain in his ongoing campaign to prevent armed conflict.[57]

While the sudden emerging status of Fort Sumter was not common knowledge, word about Anderson's news was slowly becoming public. Lincoln did not bring this intelligence to his first cabinet meeting on March 6, though on that day at his direction Joseph Holt, General Scott, and other senior officers briefed Secretary of State Seward, Secretary of War Cameron, and Secretary of the Navy Welles. Why Lincoln waited is unclear, but most probably he wanted to collect his own thoughts about this unexpected and shocking development. Like other Republicans, he had assumed that he would have ample time to formulate his approach to the forts, Sumter included. After all, since the *Star of the West* incident in early January, the informal truce in Charleston harbor had held. When Lincoln took the oath of office, he had no reason to think it could not continue for weeks, or even months. He finally informed his cabinet on March 9; the group was stunned. Attorney General Bates capsulated the stunning news in his diary: he and his colleagues were "astonished to be informed that Fort Sumter *must* be evacuated."[58]

With Major Anderson's report, Lincoln confronted circumstances quite different from anything his predecessor James Buchanan had encountered. Buchanan had upheld his commitment on the unofficial arrangement in Charleston harbor, but he always maintained that he would resupply or reinforce Fort Sumter whenever his commander requested men or matériel. Before March 4, Anderson never did; on the contrary, he assured his superiors he needed neither.

Although Anderson's message of February 28 did inform the War Department about his dwindling supplies, he did not ask for their restocking. Instead, he said that any attempt to succor his command would be impractical. In his view the Confederate works in and around the harbor had become so strong that it would take an armada and thousands of men to mount a successful reinforcing mission. Buchanan never had to decide how to proceed given this situation.

Lincoln not only had Anderson's assessment of the military lineup in Charleston harbor, he also had the concurring opinion of Winfield Scott, the commanding general of the U.S. Army and the most prestigious military figure in the country. Still, to reassure himself about Scott's views, on March 9 Lincoln requested from the general answers to three specific questions: How long could Anderson hold out "without fresh supplies or reinforcement?" Could Scott carry out reinforcement with existing resources? If not, what would he require to reinforce and resupply Anderson within the time specified in his answer to the first query?[59]

Scott answered two days later. In his opinion Anderson had bread, flour, and rice for about twenty-six days, but precisely how long the major could maintain himself the general could not say. As for number two, he could not. Finally, Scott told the president he would need a fleet of war vessels and transports plus five thousand additional regular troops along with twenty thousand volunteers. Assembling such a force, the general stated, would require new legislation from Congress and take six to eight months. Lincoln could not have been pleased with that detailed response.

Still, the opinion of Scott and the seconding one from the army's chief engineer, General Joseph Totten, in addition to Anderson's, seemingly carried the day. The generals even convinced senior naval officers, who had initially claimed their service could get through Confederate defenses to Fort Sumter. At the cabinet meeting on the ninth, Lincoln's official family heard the dire news from the military men. All but one agreed that there was but a single option, the withdrawal of Anderson. Only Postmaster General Montgomery Blair dissented, asserting he would resign if the administration took that course.[60]

Word spread through the city and beyond that the evacuation of Fort Sumter was imminent. By March 11 the northern press began reporting the story, emphasizing that military necessity required the retreat. On the twelfth General Scott wrote orders for Anderson, telling him that no relief expedition would be forthcoming and directing him to inform the governor of South Carolina of his instructions to withdraw. He further charged Anderson to arrange appropriate transport by sea and take his entire command to New York City. Scott sent this directive to the War Department for approval and transmittal.[61]

Upon getting the news, one prominent Republican rushed to the White House in a rage. On March 12, Frank Blair, Sr., Montgomery's father, vented his wrath in a face-to-face meeting with Lincoln, who listened patiently. A former close adviser of Andrew Jackson, Blair viewed these events as he was sure his patron and hero, Jackson, would have. Smash all enemies! He relished what he remembered as the unsheathed sword Jackson had pointed at South Carolina during the Nullification Crisis of a generation earlier. Blair's recollection of Jackson's conduct at that time was one-dimensional, however. President Jackson had had a more complex response to Nullification than Blair professed to recall. To Lincoln, Blair thundered that surrendering Sumter meant giving up the Union. He even accused the president of abetting treason.

Blair's explosive visit just added to the enormous pressure being exerted on the new chief executive. When Blair erupted, he had no knowledge of Scott's advice to withdraw from Fort Sumter for purely military reasons. Learning that fact, on the next day he wrote to Montgomery, asking his son "to contrive some apology for me." Yet, he still urged that Lincoln issue a ringing proclamation affirming federal supremacy akin to Jackson's of 1832 denouncing nullification.[62]

Blair's backpedaling to a more accepting position matched where many Republicans ended up. Although not happy that the flag over Fort Sumter would come down, they acceded to what they saw as military reality. And they had a great political out. The *New York Tribune* said it could stand the embarrassment because the blame rested with the "evil" Buchanan administration. A Maine hard-liner expressed both resignation and satisfaction to Lincoln. While he did not like it, he wrote that Republicans understood withdrawal as "a legacy of humiliation from the last administration." Even that hardest of hard-liners Charles Sumner told his fellow Republican senators that Fort Sumter was a military matter that should not concern them. Secretary of the Navy Welles, who did not prefer evacuation, captured how loyal Republicans handled their disappointment. "An impression has gone abroad that Sumter is to be evacuated and the shock caused by the announcement has done its work," he noted in his diary. Then, he went on to say that as soon as the public understood that the cause rested with the previous administration, not the current one, any anger would dissipate. On March 15, Welles informed the president directly that "the shock" occasioned by the news about Sumter "has done its work." Furthermore, he was confident that public opinion "will become fully reconciled to it" upon the realization that evacuation could be "attributable to no act of those who now administer the government." Put bluntly, the Lincoln presidency would not suffer political damage.[63]

Despite the assumption of General Scott, the cabinet, and the public, Lincoln had made no final decision on Fort Sumter. He did not authorize the forwarding of Scott's order to Anderson, though earlier, on the fifth, he had instructed the general to ensure that the government held on to Fort Pickens as well as the two installations in the Florida Keys. In a dinner at Charles Francis Adams's house a week later, Seward observed that "violent remonstrations" against withdrawal by some Republicans had had an effect on the president. Although his chief military adviser and his commander on the scene told him that relieving the fort was impossible, Lincoln clearly did not want to accept their judgment. Even Seward's adding his political weight to the soldiers' advice did not move the president. Later, Lincoln told his friend Joshua Speed that he had been "firm about [Fort Sumter's] defence."[64]

He was searching and hoping for some alternative to withdrawal. On March 13, he met with Montgomery Blair, who had never accepted even the possibility of evacuation, and his brother-in-law Gustavus V. Fox. Aware that Fox had devised a plan to relieve Fort Sumter, which he had presented to the Buchanan administration, Blair had him come to Washington. Fox had spent a decade and a half as a naval officer before entering the textile business in Massachusetts in the mid-1850s. A fervent proponent of his scheme, he avowed his plan would work.

Fox's approach envisioned a combined naval-civilian sortie to Charleston. He would dispatch a steamship loaded with supplies, some troops, and two tugboats escorted by two warships. Upon reaching Charleston, the warships would sink or scatter any opposing Confederate gunboats, with Major Anderson's guns joining in. Then the steamship would off-load its cargo, men and matériel, onto the two tugs. Under the cover of darkness they would cross the bar and easily reach Sumter. Fox did not put much credence in the possibility that the Confederates might sink his little fleet. His study of recent conflicts, especially the Crimean War, convinced him that swift ships could successfully run by land-based artillery. Two senior naval officers who also listened to Fox were less persuaded, however. They did not think his plans would succeed.[65]

Fox intrigued Lincoln sufficiently for the president to invite him to the cabinet meeting on the fifteenth. Fox informed his wife that "Uncle Abe Lincoln has taken a high esteem for me." General Scott and other high-ranking officers also attended. All spoke. Afterward the president requested each cabinet minister to provide written responses to a single question: "Assuming it to be possible to now provision Fort Sumter, under all the circumstances, is it wise to attempt it?" With this question, Lincoln turned what had been considered by almost everybody essentially a military matter into a political problem.[66]

Seward submitted a lengthy missive, numbering twenty-nine pages. In it he made the most detailed, systematic argument for his position that he had ever put in writing. He began by asserting that if it were possible to provision Fort Sumter peacefully, "it would be both unwise and inhuman not to attempt it." But, he went on, it was clear that force would be employed, which would mean civil war, the wrong choice.

In the rest of his epistle he developed his case for why it would be the wrong choice. He maintained that no legitimate basis existed for secession. The disunion movement resulted from apprehension about what the administration might do, not from anything it had done. Of course, he pointed out, the administration had no intention of taking action that would validate the secessionists' fears. Even if it did, Congress, controlled by the administration's political opponents, would block any such move.

As a professional politician and Republican loyalist, and aware that the president shared both identities, Seward acknowledged the political dimensions of any administration decision. Recognizing that the administration had to retain the confidence of the Republican party, he insisted that only the unnecessary or unauthorized "sacrifice of its essential principles" could "demoralize" the party. Yet, he asserted, if "pacification is necessary to prevent dismemberment of the Union or civil war, or either of them, no patriot and lover of humanity could hesitate to surrender party for the higher interests and humanity."

Seward spent time discussing what had consumed so much of his energy since January, the Upper South and the Border. He told Lincoln that citizens in those states had a divided loyalty, to the Union and to the seceded states. He insisted they were wrong in this division, for they had no reason for their weakened allegiance to the Union. Yet, he asserted, the administration had to deal with the reality that this disjunction existed. Seward expressed confidence that these states' fidelity to the Union would prevail provided it had time to reassert itself. Time was critical. He wrote that the previous administration "partly by design, partly by chance" had restricted the spread of secession. In his view, Lincoln had to continue that policy of taking no provocative steps. He must do nothing that would increase the excitement in an already aroused Upper South and Border.

Seward defined the Union as "inestimable and even indispensable to the welfare and happiness of the whole country, and to the best interests of mankind." He did not hesitate to say that the federal government must maintain it "peacefully if it can, forcibly if it must, to the last extremity." As soon as Seward had made that declaration, he rushed to say, "Next to Disunion itself, I regard civil war as the most disastrous and deplorable of national calamities, and as the most uncertain and fearful of all remedies for political disorders." As a result, he had concentrated all his "study and labor" on how "to save the Union from dismemberment by peaceful policy and without civil war."

After making his general case for moderation and nonintervention,

Seward turned his attention specifically to Fort Sumter. He would hold it as long as doing so did not involve "some danger or evil greater than the advantage of continued possession." In his judgment that moment had now arrived. Continuing, he noted that the military authorities had stated that even attempting to resupply Sumter would require considerable force. Even if successful, and two hundred and fifty to four hundred additional men were placed in Fort Sumter, he wanted to know what purpose they would serve. As he saw it, the same mission would have to be repeated in a few months, unless the government intended to subjugate Charleston or South Carolina. And he knew there was no plan of conquest. He went on to point out that news of the expedition would become known, with the mail and the telegraph promptly transmitting the information to Charleston. Thereupon, he could envision two possibilities: either the Confederates would overwhelm the small garrison in Sumter before help arrived or Confederate guns would sink at least some of the federal ships and kill some of the men. His conclusion: whether the action succeeded or failed, it would start a civil war. Seward declared that outcome would destroy the administration and, even more important, postpone reunion indefinitely.

Finally, the secretary of state underscored that in his opinion the administration must reject force. Instead, it should adhere to the legacy of our forebears. "Fraternity is the element of Union. War the very element of disunion." He made a dire prediction. If "[we] take up the sword," then "an opposition party [would] offer the olive branch," restore the Union, and defeat the Republicans. Seward ended by asking and answering the question of whether in any case he would employ force. He would not begin a war "to regain a useless and unnecessary position on the soil of a seceded state. I would not provoke war in any way *now*," he emphasized. He would, however, use armed might to collect the revenue because that collection was both essential and legitimate. But he would do so only offshore with naval vessels. On land he would do nothing until "we hold the defence." Then, he stated we would have the country behind us.

He closed with a powerful appeal. We must have "the courage to practice prudence and moderation at the cost of temporary misapprehension." He turned to a historical analogy to buttress his advice to the president. "If this counsel seems to be impassive and even unpatriotic, I console myself by the reflection that it is such as Chatham"—the great British statesman

William Pitt the elder—"gave to his country under circumstances not widely different."[67]

Not surprisingly, Montgomery Blair urged direct action. Like his father and other hard-liners Blair averred that any other course would only encourage the secessionists. If the administration stood firm, he informed Lincoln, a revival of patriotic fervor in the South would cause Union men to rise up and overpower the disunionists. Blair claimed that even Buchanan could have accomplished that goal; surely, he insisted, this administration must.

Blair realized that dispatching a relief mission to Fort Sumter could result in casualties but saw that eventuality as "indicat[ing] the hardy courage of the North and the determination of the people and their President to maintain the authority of the Government. . . . " Southerners did not believe the North had such fortitude, he said. Demonstrating it, he projected, would destroy secession and restore the supremacy of the federal government. As his father had, he evoked the memory of the Blairs' sainted Andrew Jackson. He wanted Lincoln to act exactly as Jackson had during the Nullification Crisis. Yet, again like the elder Blair, Montgomery failed to mention that Jackson gave time for Congress to find a compromise, which he supported and signed into law.[68]

Among the remaining cabinet members, Seward's outlook prevailed. Bates, Cameron, Smith, and Welles all advised withdrawal. Of the seven men in the official family, only Chase tried to answer both yes and no, though with qualifications. While he began his letter supporting aid for Sumter, he tempered that opinion by saying that if doing so would initiate a civil war, he could not advise it. Yet, he thought war could be averted if, while sending aid, Lincoln issued a proclamation "setting forth a liberal & generous yet firm policy toward the disaffected States." With the chance of war thus eliminated, Chase said, he would respond to the question affirmatively.[69]

President Lincoln now had his cabinet on record. Still, he would have to provide the crucial answer to his own question. Thus far he had not decided which way to go. Even so, it had become obvious that he was reluctant to give the order for withdrawal.

While Lincoln collected the opinions of his cabinet members and pondered his own decision, his secretary of state continued his sensitive, though unofficial, dealings with the Confederate commissioners. On the same day that he penned his lengthy reply to the president's question, his relationship with the commissioners took a new turn when two justices of the U.S. Supreme Court called on him at the State Department. Justice Samuel Nelson of New York and Justice John Campbell of Alabama came together on what they saw as an errand of peace.[70]

The two judges inserted themselves into the Seward-commissioners story, with neither the commissioners nor the secretary initially inviting their services. On his own Justice Nelson had undertaken a study of whether or not the federal government had the legal right to coerce a seceded state. Concluding from his investigation of the statutes that it did not, he took his findings to three members of the cabinet, Bates, Chase, and Seward. Seward welcomed Nelson's views, for they coincided with his goal of avoiding armed conflict. He informed Nelson that peace was his preoccupation.

After leaving Seward's office, Justice Nelson encountered his judicial colleague Justice Campbell, who had opposed the secession of his native Alabama and remained in Washington. Nelson relayed to Campbell his conversation with the secretary of state, including the news that the commissioners had sent him a letter asking that they be received and negotiations opened. But because the administration opposed the reception of the commissioners, Seward told Nelson that he could not accede to their request. At the same time, he worried that refusing the commissioners could cause them to leave the city and ultimately could lead to war.

Their discussion led the two justices to decide they should go jointly on that very day, March 15, to see Seward. To the secretary, they would argue that the cause of peace would be best advanced by his meeting with the Confederates and permitting them to explain fully their demands. In their opinion this interview would not have to entail any formal recognition of them as accredited officials of an independent government.

After listening to the judges with what Campbell termed "courtesy and attention," Seward replied. He basically said he could never meet with the commissioners, as the cabinet would not agree to it. "If Jefferson Davis had known the state of things here, he would never have sent those commissioners." He explained: "It is enough to deal with one thing at a time. The surrender of Sumter is enough to deal with." Quoting from a letter from Thurlow Weed, Seward emphasized that withdrawing from Sumter would be "a bitter pill" for the administration and the Republican party. Seward's two visitors had not previously known about Fort Sumter.[71]

The justices concurred with Seward that the fort and reception were two different matters, which could be handled separately. Campbell told Seward that he would carry the information about Fort Sumter to the commissioners and obtain their agreement to delay their insistence on a response to their note. Seward accepted Campbell's offer, insisting, however, that Campbell not divulge his source and that he get the commissioners' reaction back to Seward that same day. Seward declared that their response might mean the difference between war and peace.

Campbell also said he would write directly to Jefferson Davis on the subject, asking Seward what he should say. Seward was direct: "You may say to him that before that letter reaches him, the telegraph will have informed him that Sumter will have been evacuated." Seward added that Campbell could also include a statement to the effect that the government "contemplate[d] no action" regarding the forts in the Gulf of Mexico.[72]

When Campbell went to see the commissioners, he found Martin Crawford. At first, Crawford objected to any delay, specifying that he and his compatriots had an assignment to fulfill. If they failed, they would return promptly to the Confederacy. Campbell urged him to wait at least until he got a reply from his letter to President Davis. Finally, Crawford consented to delay, provided Campbell gave assurances about Sumter's evacuation in five days and revealed the authority for his intelligence. Although the judge refused to do so, he told the commissioner that he took responsibility for what he said, and he disclosed the involvement of Justice Nelson, who would attest to all that he had related. Crawford logically assumed, however, that Seward was Campbell's source. He also required Campbell to put in writing the contents of their conversation. Campbell did so. Then he posted Seward on what had transpired; the secretary of state no longer had to worry about an immediate response to the commissioners' letter of the twelfth.[73]

The commissioners informed the Confederate government via telegraph about Campbell's message. They communicated that by pressing they could get a quick answer to their official note, but they believed it would be negative. In the meantime they had been promised that within five days the garrison at Fort Sumter would be withdrawn. Furthermore, they expressed certainty "that no steps will be taken to change the military status." Then they asked for guidance. Replying, Secretary of State Toombs authorized them to "wait a reasonable time and then ask for instructions."[74]

The five days passed with no word either from Seward or from the government. On the twentieth the commissioners wired Toombs that he had heard nothing from them "because there is no change." They retained confidence, however. "If there is faith in man we may rely on the assurances we have as to the status." They urged no precipitate action. "We are all agreed," they closed.[75]

On that same day they telegraphed General Beauregard in Charleston, wanting to know whether he saw any signs of evacuation at Fort Sumter. Beauregard sent a terse reply: "Sumter not evacuated; no indication whatever of it. Anderson still working on its defenses."[76]

At this point, the Confederate commissioner, Martin Crawford, went to Campbell to find out why Major Anderson remained at Fort Sumter. On the twenty-first Campbell took Nelson with him to see Seward. In an abbreviated meeting Seward reassured the two justices that policy had not been altered. He also made an appointment for a longer visit with them the next day. Once more, Campbell informed the commissioners that nothing had changed.[77]

On the morning of the twenty-second Campbell recorded that a "buoyant and sanguine" Seward greeted the two men. In what Campbell described as "a free conversation," the secretary spoke positively about keeping the peace. He did not know why a delay had occurred at Fort Sumter, but he had no doubt that withdrawal would soon take place. He begged for no action from the Confederates, telling Campbell and Nelson that he would surely know if the government had changed its purpose. Furthermore, Seward said no modification was planned for Fort Pickens.[78]

After this session Campbell prepared a memorandum for the commissioners which he cleared with Seward. "As the result of my interviewing of to-day," he wrote, "I have to say that I still have unabated confidence that Fort Sumter will be evacuated, and that no delay that has occurred excites in me any apprehension or distrust, and that the state of things existing at Fort Pickens will not be altered prejudicially to the Confederate States." Closing, he counseled "inactivity" in making any demands on the Lincoln administration. He reminded them that he would learn about any intended change.[79]

The commissioners apprised their government of Campbell's most recent discussion with Seward. Basing their outlook on his judgment, they spoke optimistically about the situation with the forts. Moreover, a reasonable delay gave the Confederacy more time to get ready for whatever might be forthcoming. They also realized that the peace advocates in the administration had no interest in aiding the Confederate States, but hoped that avoiding an armed clash would eventually lead in the seceded states to a resurgence of pro-Union sentiment.[80]

Despite the positive bulletins from Washington, the Confederate government never became totally convinced that Lincoln would hand over Fort Sumter. The leadership in Montgomery realized that its commissioners really did not know what was actually going on within the Lincoln administration. They did have access to a senior and allegedly influential member, but they had only his word. They had to assume he spoke for the president. Campbell surely assumed this. Yet, the authorities in Montgomery were not so sure. In mid-month the Confederate secretary of war cautioned General Beauregard to stay alert for the arrival of a possible relief expedition. On the fifteenth he explicitly warned his general, "Give but little credit to the rumors of an amicable adjustment." Beauregard should "not slacken for a moment [his] energies."[81]

President Davis had never been optimistic about peaceable secession, unless all fifteen slave states exited the Union. He did not foresee his commissioners completing their mission successfully. On March 18, he shared his thoughts with Governor Pickens. After general remarks on defending the coast between Charleston and Savannah, he came to the immediate crisis. "I have not been of those who felt sanguine hope that the enemy would retire peacefully from your harbor," he wrote. Ultimately, Davis declared, the garrison would leave, either by its own decision or by force. The Confederacy did have an influence on that eventuality, however. "His [the enemy's] story," Davis declared, "must soon be measured by our forbearance." For many reasons he hoped for a peaceful withdrawal, including the Confederacy's gaining "Fort Sumter uninjured." Yet, Davis's skepticism informs his letter.[82]

Whatever the Confederates thought, Seward had placed himself in a precarious spot. He made promises to Campbell about Fort Sumter knowing that Lincoln had not yet made a final decision. As it turned out, Lincoln had already ordered the reinforcement of Fort Pickens. Seward had permitted his all-consuming drive to prevent armed conflict to make a huge commitment that he lacked the authority to see through. Throughout his activities during the winter, he had never gone beyond boundaries Lincoln had clearly set. In this instance he did know that the majority of the cabinet lined up with him; he also knew the military leadership argued against relief. Most probably at this point he was convinced that Lincoln would act as Seward wanted and informed Campbell of this. Seward had never lacked confidence in himself nor doubted his ability to influence events. As he shared with his wife, "these cares fall chiefly on me."[83]

Although Seward's motive is clear, little else is. Did he intentionally deceive Campbell and through him the Confederacy? Through March 22, Campbell did not think so. He saw Seward as a sincere advocate of peace. In that judgment Campbell did not err, but Seward had exhibited a willingness to take extraordinary chances to achieve his goal. During the previous three months he had placed himself on political precipices. Now, however, he found himself on an even steeper one. There is also the question of how much Lincoln knew about Seward's dealing with the Confederate commissioners. With the evidence sketchy at best, no conclusive answer can be given. The president surely knew of the commissioners' presence, and it is almost as sure that he was aware of Seward's unofficial contact with them. But that determination does not mean that he had knowledge of precisely what Seward told them. At the same time, he and Seward saw each other regularly. In the end, the historical record is frustratingly unrevealing.[84]

Seward represented Lincoln as having made a firm decision, when the president had made none. He could not wait much longer, however. By March 22, approximately half of the six weeks that Anderson said he could hold out had passed. Although Lincoln had not yet decided on his exact course, he had begun moving toward holding Fort Sumter.

CHAPTER SEVEN

"The Quicksands That Environ Our Ship of State"

DETERMINED TO OBTAIN intelligence about Charleston and Fort Sumter from his own sources, Lincoln dispatched three emissaries southward. They had two different missions, one military, the other political. To Fort Sumter he sent Gustavus Fox, the designer of a plan to relieve the fort, a proposal that intrigued the president. The man he selected for Charleston, Stephen Hurlbut, was a native South Carolinian who had settled in Illinois. Hurlbut would have a traveling companion, Ward Lamon, another southerner transplanted to Illinois. Both men were avowed Lincoln loyalists.

On the evening of March 19, Fox left Washington by train, arriving in Charleston on the morning of the twenty-first. He promptly called upon Governor Pickens and requested permission to go to Sumter. Pickens wanted to know the nature of Fox's assignment. Fox replied that he had no written orders; he simply wanted to discover the conditions of Major Anderson's command and the status of his provisions. Concluding that Fox had only peaceful intentions, the governor said yes, though he had one of his officers, whom Fox had known when both served in the U.S. Navy, accompany the northerner.

Fox made a short visit to the fort. This was his first opportunity to observe the harbor, its defenses, and Fort Sumter's place in it. While there he met privately with Major Anderson. Although Fox did not share his specific ideas with his host, he did point out what he considered an appropriate landing spot at the fort for vessels the government might forward. Anderson also knew that his visitor had proposed a relief expedition. To Fox, the major iterated his opinion that no relieving force could successfully enter the harbor and reach him. He also expressed his conviction that any attempt at reinforcement would result in the catastrophe of civil war. Fox did not inform Anderson of the government's intentions, for he had no such information—at that date Lincoln had not yet come to a final decision.

Thereupon, Fox was given a list of the garrison's provisions. He and Anderson were in accord that unless new supplies arrived, Anderson could not hold out beyond April 15, and to then only provided that he place his troops on short rations. But, before taking that step, Anderson indicated, he would await orders to do so. After little more than one hour actually in the fort, Fox returned to the city and entrained for Washington.

To the president he reported that his personal reconnaissance of Fort Sumter and the harbor only confirmed his certainty that his plan would work. He also brought news about Anderson's supplies and the two men's agreement that the garrison could maintain itself until April 15. Major Anderson did not allow Fox to have the only word, however. On the morning after he had seen Fox, he sent a message to the War Department spelling out why in his judgment any ship fortunate enough to make it to the landing spot envisaged by Fox would confront grave danger. The old artilleryman and the former naval officer had radically different views on the probability of success for the mission Fox contemplated. Finally, Anderson said his superiors would have to make the ultimate decision. Thus, President Lincoln had two different opinions from two experienced men who had studied the site of possible conflict.[1]

The day following Fox's trip to Fort Sumter, Hurlbut and Lamon departed the capital for Charleston, also by rail. According to Hurlbut, Lincoln told him that Seward kept saying that a strong Union party existed in the South, even in South Carolina. The president wanted him to find out if this was true. Hurlbut had no official status; he traveled as a private citizen with no visible connection to the administration. That camouflage posed no problem, for Hurlbut intended to stay with his sister, who still lived in Charleston. Moreover, he had many friends in the city, including the state's most prominent Unionist, James L. Petigru, a distinguished attorney with whom Hurlbut as a young man had read law. In contrast, Lamon would have an official capacity. He was purportedly charged with settling postal accounts with the local postmaster and would so identify himself to Governor Pickens.

Hurlbut reached Charleston on Sunday, March 24, and spent that day and the next visiting with as many of his friends and acquaintances as possible, Petigru among them. He also saw Governor Pickens, who turned down his appeal to go to the islands surrounding the harbor. The unity of the Carolinians struck him. Even men who had been keen on the Union side during the Nullification Crisis now professed their loyalty to South Carolina. Hurlbut found no one, other than Petigru, who still retained a primary commitment to the United States. He uncovered no Unionist feeling to which the government could appeal. In his judgment "the Sentiment of the National Patriotism always feeble in Carolina, has been extinguished and overridden by the State." He also recommended the immediate evacuation of Fort Sumter. "At present the garrison can be withdrawn without insult to them or their flag," he told the president. In no more than a week, he added, that might not be possible.

Lamon concurred with Hurlbut's conclusions. Lamon had also visited Governor Pickens, who permitted him to go to Fort Sumter. Without any authorization, Lamon told the governor and Anderson that the garrison would be withdrawn. Though pleased with that news, Pickens stated bluntly that if Lincoln refused to accept the fact of secession, South Carolina was willing to fight. Both Hurlbut and Lamon believed that the harbor's defenders would forcibly resist any effort to resupply Fort Sumter.[2]

That these three men could travel by rail unhindered to and from South Carolina, be civilly received by the governor of the state, and mingle freely with the population illustrates the fluidity of the situation. Furthermore, Governor Pickens's permitting Fox to go to Fort Sumter shows that civilian and military authorities in Charleston still hoped for a peaceful outcome and probably assumed the evacuation of the fort was at hand. Of course, neither Fox nor Hurlbut had been entirely open and honest about his purpose. With their return, Lincoln had the eyewitness reports from men he trusted.

With Anderson's deadline looming and his agents routed to Charleston, Lincoln directed his chief attention toward Fort Sumter. At the same time, however, he had to consider Fort Pickens. The Buchanan administration had sent the *Brooklyn*, with reinforcements aboard, to Pensacola. Yet, because of the unofficial truce between the government and Florida, the vessel stood offshore, with troops still aboard. On March 5, the very day he learned about Anderson's letter, the president orally directed General Scott to reinforce Fort Pickens. A few days later he followed up with a written

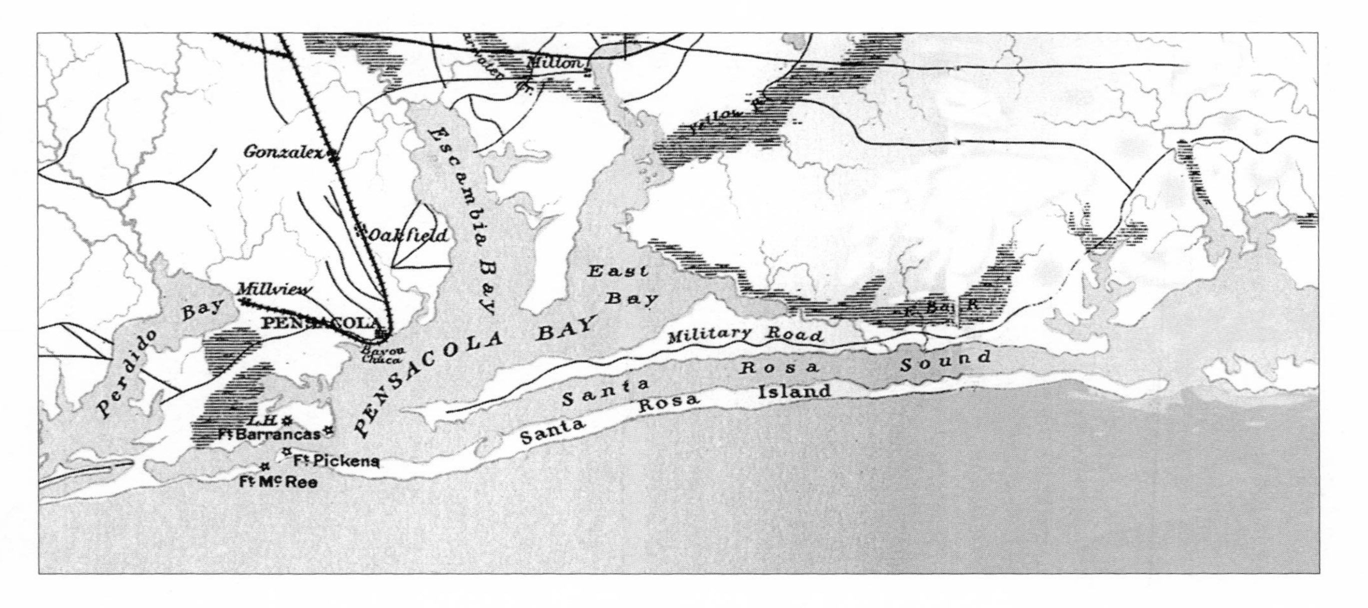

Fort Pickens and Pensacola Harbor

directive. On March 12 Scott issued the order that instructed the soldiers to disembark and hold the fort. For this directive he did not trust the mail or a messenger, either of which would have to go through the Confederate States to reach Pensacola safely. Thus, his order went by sea, ensuring that it would take considerable time to get to the *Brooklyn*.[3]

While Lincoln pondered what to do about Fort Sumter, his secretary of state was busy telling the Conservatives in Virginia exactly what he had relayed to the Confederate commissioners—the government intended to withdraw from Fort Sumter. This news delighted the Virginians. A Conservative leader, George Summers, caught their spirit. "The removal from Sumter acted like a charm," he rejoiced in a letter to a confidant in Washington. He voiced his confidence that he and his Conservative colleagues were "masters of our position here, and can maintain it if left alone." To the convention itself Summers announced that the administration had "wisely determined" on "a pacific policy" that would soon have the troops out of Fort Sumter. The convention kept working on a plan to bring before the Border-state gathering set for May.[4]

Newspapers spread the tidings of Sumter's imminent evacuation. In the rest of the Upper South that news had an equally positive impact. Pro-Union Tennessee senator Andrew Johnson was sure the abandonment of Fort Sumter would demolish the secessionists. Congressman Robert Hatton echoed, "Secession is making no headway. Can't for a moment." A North Carolinian wrote Senator Douglas that only armed conflict could rescue the disunion cause in his state. Describing the mood in his region at the time, the senior statesman William A. Graham a month later recollected that "the public mind in all the eight slave holding States that had not yet seceded, was settling down in the conviction that the forts were to be evacuated and repose was to be allowed, so favorable to conciliation and harmony."[5]

At this moment, from mid-March to early April, leaders like Graham and Summers envisioned a new political age dawning. Conservatives and Union-loving men in both the free and slave states and from disparate partisan backgrounds were coming together. In Tennessee even the arch-antagonists from the old Democratic-Whig rivalry, John Bell and Andrew Johnson, seemed headed toward rapprochement. Such conciliation heralded the formation of the nucleus of a national party that would emblazon Conservatism and Union on its banner. These people overwhelmingly identified Seward, on whose promises they had anchored their political hopes and fortunes, as the man responsible. A Virginia contact did not hold back: "I rely upon yourself to save the Union." A Tennessean wrote even more extravagantly: "You ought to have been President are now the Government." His praise knew no bounds, assuring Seward that if peace triumphed, the New Yorker would be rewarded with "a higher historic name in the Temple of fame, than did Washington or Jackson [have]."[6]

Even though the prospect of withdrawing the garrison from Fort Sumter buoyed these Conservatives, they realized that danger still lurked. The correspondent who informed Seward that his fame would exceed all others cautioned that using force would wreck everything. George Summers warned that if collision occurred anywhere, "we can't answer for the result." A Seward connection in Virginia reminded the secretary of state "of all the quicksands that environ our ship of state."[7]

But as days, then a week, and even longer, passed with Major Anderson still ensconced in Fort Sumter, doubt and fear began to erode the spirit and vision of the Unionists. Pointing to the delay, George Summers wanted to know, "Is there any truth in the suggestion that the thing is not to be after all?" The prospect horrified him: "This will ruin us." A fellow conservative in Richmond recognized that the wrong signal from the government would overpower the Conservatives in the Virginia Convention. A correspondent begged Seward to make it possible for the Conservatives "to state, *authoritatively*, that the policy of the administration is to be pacific."[8]

Even though his directions on the forts preoccupied Lincoln, wrenching squabbles over patronage and the hard reality of Republican factionalism confronted him almost daily. From the time of his election through his first weeks as president, the clamor for political jobs and the need to placate various Republican notables consumed an enormous amount of Lincoln's time. The White House seemed like Springfield East, with unending lines of callers, pushing either themselves or their friends forward for public positions. Lincoln himself complained that "the office-seekers demanded all his time." With the Senate sitting to confirm the numerous presidential appointments, he also had to deal with pressure from Republican senators and the need to get people chosen so that the Senate could act on them.[9]

Even some of his fellow Illinois Republicans, including Senator Trumbull, became disenchanted when patronage decisions went against them.

"I see very little of Mr. L.," Trumbull complained. At the White House, the senator grumbled, the president "is constantly beset by a crowd, & it is difficult to get to see him at all, & when you do, it is only for a hurried interview."[10]

Trumbull also acted for hard-liners in the Senate with a resolution he introduced on March 28. Its language articulated the views the Blairs had already expounded to Lincoln. The resolution stated: "That, in the opinion of the Senate, the true way to preserve the Union is to enforce the laws of the Union; that resistance to their enforcement, whether under the name of anti-coercion or any other name, is encouragement to disunion; and that it is the duty of the President to use all the means in his power to hold and protect the public property of the United States, and enforce the laws thereof, as well in the States of South Carolina, Georgia, Florida, Mississippi, Alabama, Louisiana, and Texas, as within the other States of the Union." Because the Senate went into executive session just after Trumbull put forward his pronouncement and then adjourned *sine die* later that same day, a vote was never taken on it. Yet, the wording carried an unmistakable tenor and thrust—no toleration for any deviation from the policy laid down by the hard-liners.[11]

In addition to the forts and party unity, Lincoln had another vexing worry. He had to make a decision about collecting revenues, which meant the tariff. The question of the tariff and its collection had two components. The first had to do with the potential loss of federal revenue from the customs duties normally generated by the states that had seceded. The Confederacy now controlled the customhouses in each of them. The possibility existed, however, that the federal government could collect money offshore as merchant ships from abroad approached ports from South Carolina to Texas.

The president clearly had this option in mind. The entire cabinet, Seward included, judged this activity as legitimate and one the government should undertake. Lincoln asked Chase on March 18 whether he thought this project could be successful and how many ships controlled by the Treasury Department could take part. On the same date, he also wanted to know from Welles what naval force he could put at the disposal of the Treasury both immediately and in the future. Chase responded that he did think offshore vessels could collect the revenue, but all eleven currently in service would have to be rearmed, some would have to be replaced, and naval protection would be required. Replying, Welles said he could provide twelve ships promptly, but his future ability would depend on the legally authorized strength of the navy, though in the next few months he could add three ships currently on duty in foreign waters. There were also fifteen not in commission. Although Lincoln did not settle on a revenue-collecting strategy before the outbreak of hostilities, he clearly intended to act.[12]

The second factor regarding the tariff had a political as well as an economic dimension. When the Morrill Tariff enacted by the Republicans went into effect, on April 1, its rates would almost double those in the tariff law of the Confederate States. This differential could mean the potential shift of foreign trade from northern ports to southern. With rates so much lower in New Orleans than at New York City, a significant portion of the commerce from the Northwest now moving east might very well turn south.

Northeastern mercantile and financial interests quickly became aware of the possible negative consequences for them. At the end of March a committee of New York merchants came to the White House to press the president on the government's policy. To a reporter they revealed their distress: "The present uncertainty as to the new tariff is destroying trade and legitimate speculation." This tariff conflict and its possible financial repercussions caused a shift in business opinion. Before it had been almost monolithic against coercion, but now it was turning to form up behind Lincoln's inaugural pledge to collect revenue and hold the forts. As one merchant asked, "Can New York afford not only to lose its trade with the South, now amounting to more than 200 million a year, but hazard the loss of the trade of the eight millions of inhabitants of the Northwestern states?" The conservative New York financier August Belmont, at once a Democrat and ardently pro-compromise, answered, "It is now a question of national existence and commercial prosperity and the choice cannot be doubtful."[13]

Although Lincoln had never thought pleasing northeastern commercial interests of primary importance, their coming toward him could only strengthen him. However these businessmen calculated, Lincoln knew that the government needed the revenue from the imports currently bound for southern ports. The possibility that in the future that volume could vastly increase only magnified the problem. Yet, southerners, including Upper South and Border Conservatives, maintained that even collecting duties offshore could lead to conflict.

Collecting the revenue, no matter its undeniable importance, did not have the immediacy as an issue as did the incendiary problem of the forts. On the evening of March 28, just before the president's first state dinner, Scott handed him a document that gave him a jolt. It advised not only withdrawal from Sumter, which had been the general's advice since Anderson's notice about dwindling provisions, but also that Pickens be given up. Scott had never before said anything about abandoning Pickens. Yet even more troubling to the president, his chief military adviser based that recommendation on political considerations. Because leaving Sumter was looked upon as a necessity, it would not necessarily hold the Border and Upper South in the Union. Scott claimed that information from there indicated that the government must also relinquish Pickens.[14]

No evidence makes Seward's involvement indisputably clear, yet little doubt can exist. He had had Scott's confidence since the winter, before Buchanan left office. He and the general had become closer, though Gideon Welles surely exaggerated in calling Scott no more than Seward's pawn. The secretary of state and the general had given Lincoln identical advice on Fort Sumter since the outset of the crisis. But Scott had never before mentioned politics in suggestions he had given his commander in chief. Seward knew firsthand, however, that his Conservative Unionists wanted federal authority gone from Pickens as well as Sumter. If Seward and Scott had hoped with this double-barreled counsel to bring the president closer to them, they grossly miscalculated.[15]

Lincoln exploded. Prior to this occasion he had listened respectfully to Scott's opinions because he considered them based solely on military judgment. Although he did not necessarily like what Scott told him about Fort Sumter, he felt compelled to take seriously what the general said. But now Scott had raised a political standard alongside his military one. Before going to dinner, coping with the "cold shock" of Scott's statement, the president upbraided the general for "want of consistency" regarding Fort Pickens. He even accused Major Anderson of purposefully misleading him. A disillusioned and embittered Lincoln cried out in frustration "that his administration would be broken up unless a more decided policy was adopted." He made clear to a chastened Scott that if the general had difficulty carrying out presidential instructions, others surely would not.[16]

Following the dinner, which Scott did not attend, the president apologizing for him, Lincoln kept his cabinet to inform the members about Scott's message. Not unexpectedly, Montgomery Blair blew up. The staunchest hard-liner in the official family lambasted the general for acting like a politician, not a military man. Of course, the president had already noticed this new uniform on Scott. Then, he set a reassembly for the next day.[17]

On March 29, Lincoln and the cabinet met to go over this new development. After initial discussion that seemed inconclusive, Attorney General Bates suggested that right there each man put in writing his view and read it to the others. Lincoln said yes. On the matter of Fort Pickens all agreed that reinforcement should take place. In addition, all concurred that strengthening of the navy offshore from southern ports should occur. But regarding Fort Sumter, disagreement prevailed. Once again Blair and Seward staked out their ground. South Carolina, Blair exclaimed, must be brought to heel; the federal government must immediately use force to exert its power and authority. In contrast, Seward declared that any effort to send supplies would inaugurate civil war, which he wanted to avoid. Moreover, he continued, if hostilities did break out, the Union could not hold the fort. Thus, the order to evacuate should be issued.

This time Seward did not have a majority of the cabinet on his side, as he had two weeks earlier. Only Secretary of the Interior Smith backed him. Bates simply said the time had come to make a decision on Sumter, a place Lincoln had not yet reached. Secretary of the Navy Welles, who on the previous occasion had sided with Seward, and Secretary of the Treasury Chase advocated reprovisioning the fort, but not by throwing the mailed punch of Blair. They did not want a secret mission, however, instead a publicly announced expedition to reprovision the garrison. Welles expected it would meet opposition, at which point the government from a defensive posture would employ force. Chase chorused Welles's argument. He noted that war would result from any attempt to succor either fort; thus, war seemed inevitable, for the government had no intention of giving up Pickens. Summing up his case, he emphasized a critical point: "I perceive no reason why it may not be best begun in consequence of military resistance to the efforts of the administration to sustain troops of the Union stationed, under the authority of the Government in a Fort of the Union, in the ordinary course of service." Chase and Welles wanted to order events so that the administration could never be cast in the role of aggressor.[18]

Thus the cabinet remained divided, though not so sharply as it had been after the March 15 meeting. At that time only Blair had unequivocally advocated standing by Fort Sumter. Now, Chase and Welles urged the same policy, though not in such belligerent fashion. Seward was left almost alone. Possibly Secretary of War Cameron would have been his ally, but that official was absent.[19]

Even after his formal advisers had announced their positions, Lincoln did not share his. Concerning Fort Pickens, he had already sent reinforcements, though he still had not heard whether the mission had been successful. He did take an additional step, however. That same day he forwarded Fox's requirements for the Fort Sumter foray to the secretary of war, instructing him to cooperate with the secretary of the navy. The purpose: "I desire that an expedition, to move by sea, be got ready to sail as early as the 6th of April next."[20]

The deliberations in the cabinet meeting on the twenty-ninth stimulated Seward to rapid action. Although the president did not state unequivocally that he intended to hold Fort Sumter, the thrust of the discussion and his instructions to the secretaries of war and the navy pointed in that direction. To Seward, maintaining Fort Sumter in such fashion would destroy all he had labored for since December. It would mean war. That determination did not rest solely with William Henry Seward. Discussion in the cabinet made clear that his colleagues in the official family agreed, though the prospect did not trouble everyone.

For Seward, armed conflict would be disastrous. He firmly believed that preserving the Union with the Upper South and Border slave states remaining loyal and with any hope of the seceded states returning required peace. Guns blazing would jeopardize all—he was convinced that such an occurrence would cause some or all of the Upper South and Border to join the Confederacy. Moreover, no one knew how a military contest would develop. Even if the Union prevailed and brought the errant states back within the fold, bitterness and hatred generated by war could leave an embittered minority that would poison national harmony for decades.

To prevent this catastrophe Seward could perceive only a single alternative. Secure Fort Pickens speedily. Then persuade the president that flying the flag over Pickens would demonstrate the determination of the administration to uphold its claim of an unbroken Union. Yes, orders had already been sent to reinforce the fort, but Washington did not yet know if they had been carried out. Eventually, of course, Fort Pickens could pose the same dilemma the government confronted at Sumter—withdraw or fight—but not at the moment. Besides, all agreed Pickens would be much easier to defend. If, Seward thought, he could divert attention from Sumter to Pickens, he could gain what he most needed, time.

To achieve his ambitious goal, Seward reached far beyond the bureaucratic boundary of his State Department. He assumed for himself the role of minister without portfolio, or even minister plenipotentiary. On the morning of Sunday, March 31, he corralled two army officers, Captain Montgomery Meigs, who had impressed him and Lincoln, and Lieutenant Colonel Erasmus Keyes, General Scott's military secretary. He told the two men to prepare "a project for relieving and holding Fort Pickens." Upon completion of the task they were to consult with General Scott, then by 4:00 p.m. present their plan to the president. According to Meigs and Keyes, they reported to the president before four o'clock, not having had an opportunity to see General Scott. Seward was also present. After listening to their proposal, Lincoln sent them to the general with instructions that the president "wished this thing done and not to let it fail." At Scott's house, Seward appeared, and "the matter was talked over and resolved upon."[21]

The next day at the Executive Mansion the president signed the necessary orders. They included sending the same powerful warship to Pensacola that Welles intended to assign Fox. Seward had held nothing back in his attempt to derail the Sumter mission. When later Welles learned of this move, he told the president something had gone awry. Lincoln admitted he had not read all the papers carefully; he was affixing his signature to so many documents that when Seward handed him just another batch he signed. Upon Welles's remonstrance, Lincoln reversed his order, but the Pickens expedition had already departed.[22]

These transactions took place in secrecy, without the knowledge of either the secretary of war or the secretary of the navy. Seward, who with Lincoln's authorization had procured ten thousand dollars from the Secret Service budget for this enterprise, wanted Meigs promoted so that he could assume command of the mission. Even though General Scott said the law would not permit it, Seward wanted Meigs to go anyway. The captain assented. Seward even told him that "fame would come from Pickens." Meigs and Keyes, along with Seward's other handpicked officers, headed for New York City. Their departure date was set for April 6.[23]

With his design for Fort Pickens in motion, Seward engaged in a vastly more brazen tactic. On April 1 he sent to Lincoln his famous paper titled "Some Thoughts for the President's Consideration." Abruptly, he told his chief that the administration had neither a domestic nor a foreign policy. After criticizing Lincoln for spending too much time on patronage, he harked back to Weed's argument of December. The issue, he insisted, must be framed in terms of "*Union or Disunion*," not of sectionalism or slavery. Because Sumter had become a partisan question, Seward asserted that the government should jettison it. At the same time, buttressing the Gulf forts would emphasize the Union. On the foreign front he would "demand explanations from *Spain* and France, categorically, at once," and also from Great Britain and Russia. In addition, he proposed sending agents into Canada, Mexico, and Central America to instigate unrest against "European intervention." In sum, he seemed to suggest fomenting war. Concluding, he wrote that either the president must take charge or "Devolve" authority on a cabinet member. Never bashful, he offered himself: "I neither seek to evade nor assume responsibility."[24]

Scholars have generally interpreted this missive as an almost bizarre overreaching by Seward. And the text of the document certainly lends itself to that interpretation. Yet Seward's son writing long after the event argued that it was no ultimatum. Rather, his father intended only to raise points for discussion during his next meeting with the president. Frederick Seward stated that he carried many such messages from his father to Lincoln. Furthermore, he maintained that the administration adopted many of the suggestions, notably to emphasize the Union, not slavery, and to dispatch agents to Canada and Mexico. As for any private political agenda, Frederick declared that had ended in Chicago when Lincoln won the Republican nomination for president. Perhaps he really understood his father's intentions, but the language of the memorandum is considerably more dramatic than one would expect in the normal transmission of thoughts from a cabinet member to his president.[25]

The record does not reveal Lincoln's private reaction. His written response differed sharply in tone from Seward's, however. On the same day he responded that Seward had advised the quiet and waiting policy he had followed. He said that while he welcomed the advice of his cabinet, he had the final word. He used a single declarative sentence: "*I* must do it." Nothing had changed in the dealings between the two men since December when Lincoln asserted his authority. Yet, most probably Lincoln never sent this reply, retaining the only known copy in his files. For a number of reasons, including Seward's influence with Upper South and Border Conservatives and his own credibility, Lincoln could not easily dismiss Seward. He would not have failed, however, to let his secretary of state know that he was president.[26]

Like his Republican counterpart grasping for a peaceful way out of an escalating crisis, Stephen A. Douglas turned to a desperate scheme. If Seward found it increasingly difficult to influence the administration of which he was a key part, the Democrat Douglas had no hope of doing so. Even in his forte, the Senate, he had failed to advance any serious compromise measure. Now, he brought up the possibility of a North American customs union. He worried about a possible trade war between the Confederate States and the United States which would inevitably involve Illinois and the rest of the Northwest in nasty disputes. Shooting was even a possibility. He advocated a union of "the north and south for commercial purposes as a condition for political separation." He thought the United States would have to lower its new tariff schedule to compete with the Confederate States. In that competition he felt the Confederacy would eventually lose to the wealthier Union. When that happened, reunion could likely take place. But this suggestion went nowhere in either the Confederate States or the United States. Douglas could only look on helplessly as armed conflict appeared more and more likely.[27]

Although Douglas operated in a considerably more restricted space than Seward, the latter's room for maneuver was being severely curtailed. Yet, even with the Fort Pickens initiative and his, at the least, remarkable memorandum for Lincoln, Seward confronted still another complicated circumstance, the Confederate commissioners.

For a week after seeing Justice Campbell on March 22, Seward had no contact with him or anyone else representing the commissioners. He did, however, cancel a scheduled conversation with André Roman. When talking with Baron Eduard de Stoeckl, the Russian minister to the United States, Seward requested that the Russian arrange a rendezvous with Roman. De Stoeckl planned to invite the two men to tea and then have himself called away on business, leaving Seward and Roman alone. But on the morning of March 26, the date set, Seward sent de Stoeckl a note saying that upon reflection he had to decline seeing Roman, for the meeting might get to the newspapers.[28]

Seward's obvious turnabout upset the commissioners. They were becoming weary of what they correctly perceived as Seward's lack of forthrightness in dealing with them. Wiring Secretary of State Toombs on the day Seward canceled, they wanted to know "whether we shall dally longer with a Government hesitating & doubting as to its own course," or whether they should demand an immediate answer to their note of March 12. In the same message, they repeated that they still thought the garrison at Sumter would be withdrawn. They added that they did not believe Lincoln would risk starting a war over Fort Pickens. In closing, however, they informed Toombs that they had been assured they would receive notification should Lincoln adopt a different policy. That final piece of information underscored their basic ignorance of what was transpiring inside the administration. They had no knowledge that two weeks earlier Scott had sent Lincoln's order for the reinforcement of Pickens.[29]

Governor Pickens prompted the commissioners' next move with a telegram on Saturday, March 30, asking why Ward Lamon had not returned to Charleston to remove the troops from Sumter as he had promised. The commissioners contacted Justice Campbell, who went to Seward on that very day. Seward said he could not reply until Monday, April 1.

When Campbell returned to the State Department on Monday, jolting news greeted him. Seward informed him that Pickens's communication had distressed the president, for Lamon had no authority to make any statements regarding Fort Sumter. The secretary of state went on to say that Lamon would confirm that fact in person, if necessary. After delivering those shocking tidings, Seward penned a note for Campbell to transmit to the commissioners. Its thrust pointed in a different direction from all of his previous statements to Campbell. He wrote that "the President may desire to supply Fort Sumter, but will not undertake to do so without first giving notice to Governor Pickens."

This declaration took Campbell aback. Previously, Seward had always assured him that Sumter would be evacuated. According to Campbell, he asked Seward directly whether Lincoln intended to resupply the fort. Seward answered negatively. He then expanded. "It is a very irksome thing to him to evacuate it. His ears are opened to everyone, and they fill his head for schemes for its supply." Even so, Seward reassured Campbell, "I do not think that he will adopt any of them. There is no design to reinforce it."

Campbell told Seward that it would be perilous to tell the commissioners that Lincoln might send additional provisions. They might translate possibility into an intention, which could spark an assault on the fort. At this point in Campbell's account he says that Seward stated he would have to talk with the president. He left to do so. Upon his return he prepared a new reply for Governor Pickens: "I am satisfied the Government will not undertake to supply Fort Sumter without giving notice to Governor Pickens." This second version jettisoned any mention of Lincoln's desiring to supply the fort. This change of wording along with Seward's comments satisfied Campbell, who left the secretary of state persuaded that the assurances of the previous weeks still held. Seward obviously gave a masterly, if less than candid, performance, and Campbell clearly heard what he wanted to hear.[30]

Campbell's conviction informed a report he sent to President Davis on April 3 detailing his dealings with Seward. He went over his meetings with the secretary of state and his accounting of them to the commissioners. He told Davis that he had "every reason to suppose" that Lincoln was aware of what transpired between him and Seward. After commenting on his perception that Lincoln's "reluctance to abandon the forts is undisguised," he still wrote, "I do not doubt that Sumter will be evacuated shortly, without any effort to resupply it." But he was less certain about the future of Pickens. In his judgment, the Lincoln administration at "present desire[d] to let things remain as they are without action of any kind." He made clear to Davis, however, that he made "these assurances on *my own responsibility*." He obviously still had complete trust in Seward. "I have no expectation that there will be bad faith in the dealings with me," he professed.[31]

The day before Campbell wrote, Secretary Toombs responded to the commissioners' query about whether they should "dally." He instructed them to stay in place. Delay in decision-making by the Lincoln administration allowed the Confederacy more time to build its military defenses and organize its government.[32]

At the same time, Confederate authorities took precautions. In early April the commissioners regularly informed Montgomery on activity in the War and Navy Departments and other military and naval movements and preparations. Less sanguine than Campbell, the commissioners warned Toombs to "be ever on guard," for they had "no confidence in the administration." On April 2, the Confederate secretary of war, LeroyWalker, informed General Beauregard that the Confederate government placed no faith in assurances coming from Washington that Fort Sumter would be yielded. In fact, at any moment, he added, the mission of the commissioners might fail. He instructed his commander to conduct himself "precisely as if you were in the presence of an enemy contemplating to surprise you."[33]

While the wary Confederates awaited developments in Washington, Lincoln moved toward his crucial decisions. The enormous pressure bearing down on him took its toll. His wife, Mary, said that he "keeled over" with a migraine headache; she put him in bed. That collapse, however, neither curtailed his activity nor deterred him. After Scott's memorandum on the forts, the president no longer relied on the general. Without Scott's direct participation, Lincoln ordered the new expedition to Fort Pickens to go forward, and he directed Fox to make ready his mission to Fort Sumter. In addition, he instructed Scott to report daily in writing the activities of the general and those in his department.[34]

With new plans for Pickens and Sumter in motion, Lincoln seemingly had control of events. He had closed off no military options, though he had not decided precisely what to do about Sumter. He did not head an inactive administration, as Seward charged, but what he had done was basically invisible beyond his cabinet and the military officers involved. By the beginning of April rumors of what was being done and not being done abounded. Yet, for many Republicans in particular and northerners in general, inactivity and indecisiveness described the administration.

Unhappy Republicans made their feelings known. On April 4, several Republican governors descended upon Washington to confer with the president. They told him their states stood behind a hard-line policy, even to the use of force. Republicans also attributed party setbacks in recent local and state elections in Connecticut, New Hampshire, and Rhode Island to the administration's vacillation. An irate Ohioan fumed to the president that in his hometown, Cincinnati, the party faced annihilation. The city government would go to "the Democratic, Union party," he exploded, "and we are compelled to lay the fault at your door." Republican editors blasted away: "WHAT WILL BE DONE?" "COME TO THE POINT!" Even *The New York Times,* long a supporter of Seward and his conciliatory policy, editorialized on April 3 "Wanted—A Policy." The writer declared, "We trust this period of indecision, of inaction, of fatal indifference, will have a speedy end." Otherwise, he feared there could be no hope "of saving the Union from destruction and the country from anarchy."[35]

With his party pushing for decisiveness, Lincoln had to cope with new information on Fort Sumter. A message from Major Anderson, dated the first, reported that his supplies would last barely more than a week. Furthermore, the major asked why the order for his withdrawal, which he had expected since Lamon's visit, had not yet arrived. Anticipating his evacuation and receiving no instructions to place his men on half rations, he had not done so.[36]

Military and political influences were now converging and pointing toward keeping the flag flying over both Pickens and Sumter. Even facing this stern truth, Seward was still trying to head off the disaster of armed conflict. On April 1, with the president's concurrence, he telegraphed the Virginia Conservative leader George Summers in Richmond stating that the president wanted to see the Virginian as soon as possible. Summers declined; with the Virginia Convention set to vote on a secession ordinance, he felt he needed to be present. At that juncture Lincoln dispatched an agent to Richmond to tell Summers that he must come immediately, or send a trusted friend. After consulting with a few colleagues, Summers chose John B. Baldwin. Baldwin and Lincoln's emissary departed promptly. On the morning of April 4, they were in Seward's office at the State Department. He took Baldwin to the White House.[37]

Around eleven the president met privately with Baldwin. The president opened the conversation: "Mr. Baldwin, I am afraid you have come too late." He wished the Virginian had arrived a few days earlier. A baffled Baldwin asked too late for what? Without really answering, Lincoln turned to a question. He wanted to know why the Virginia Unionists or Conservatives did not adjourn the state convention *sine die*. Perturbed, Baldwin set out to apprise Lincoln of the situation in Virginia. The Unionists needed this convention to keep the disunionists in check. Adjourning it without securing a settlement of the crisis, in Baldwin's judgment, would undoubtedly undermine his own credibility and that of his friends. He urged the president to hold to "a conservative, conciliatory, national course."[38]

Lincoln listened and then wanted Baldwin to spell out exactly what he meant. Baldwin did not hesitate, saying, "If I had control of your thumb and forefinger five minutes I could settle the whole question." He then got specific. Lincoln should issue a proclamation announcing that his administration would pursue peace while upholding national authority. To that end, he should abandon both Pickens and Sumter. When the president responded that his fellow Republicans would not favor that policy, Baldwin replied that Lincoln would obtain ten new supporters for every one he lost. In sum, Baldwin described the new Union party that Seward, John Gilmer, and others had contemplated and advocated. Lincoln showed no more interest at this moment than he ever had. He never considered altering the makeup of the Republican party that elected him. Maintaining the party in that form had been and continued to be a cardinal goal. Only the prosecution of a bloody, difficult war changed his mind.

Lincoln did, however, bring up the possibility of withdrawing from Fort Sumter as a military necessity. Baldwin wanted evacuation of both forts as a gesture of peace, not because of military requirements. Finally, Lincoln mentioned the prospect of simply reprovisioning Fort Sumter, not sending in men or munitions. Rejecting this tactic, Baldwin responded that Confederates would allow no vessels to reach Sumter. He underscored his critical point, telling the president, "If there is a gun fired at Sumter—I do not care on which side it is fired—the thing is gone." He went on, "Virginia herself, strong as the Union majority in the Convention is now, will be out in forty-eight hours." A startled Lincoln responded, "That is impossible." Baldwin's emphasizing that hostilities would drive the Upper South out of the Union should not have surprised the president. For weeks he had been told the same thing by Seward and others. To Lincoln's cry of "impossible," Baldwin said simply that he knew of the temper of his state while the chief executive did not.

Accounts of this meeting, which left both men dissatisfied, have had a vexed history. In its aftermath, Lincoln claimed that he had offered to trade withdrawal from Fort Sumter for the adjournment of the Virginia Convention only to have his proposition rejected. Possibly Lincoln thought about making Baldwin the same offer he had made to William C. Rives back on February 26. But the evidence indicates that he did not do so on April 4. In fact, he never again did so after the meeting Rives attended. When Baldwin reported back to Summers and his other allies in Richmond, he made no mention of any such overture. It is inconceivable that he would have withheld from them such momentous news, which would have fulfilled their deepest wishes while securing their political supremacy in their state. Lincoln's motives for spreading the story are not entirely clear, but it seems reasonable to conclude that he wanted others, including Virginians, to think that he had done all possible to make an accommodation with the state.[39]

Later that same day Lincoln made his final turn from accommodation. He and Gustavus Fox went over concluding arrangements for Fox's mission to Fort Sumter. Moreover, a message was sent to Major Anderson by courier informing him that he should look for an attempt to resupply him in seven or eight days. With his orders to Cameron and Welles on March 29, Lincoln had taken the first crucial step. Now, he was ready to put them into action.[40]

On that very day, the Virginia Convention acted on secession. Tired of continuous waiting and delay, the secessionists pressed the convention to take up a resolution that would carry the state out of the Union. The disunionists lost by the resounding vote of 88 to 45. By a two-to-one margin the Conservatives demonstrated that they still had the upper hand. This balloting occurred, of course, before Baldwin's return to Richmond and before the convention was aware of all Lincoln's decisions.[41]

Yet, newspaper reports of military preparations and possible coercion created alarm among a number of delegates. On April 6, a group led by William B. Preston, a former Whig congressman and secretary of the navy, proposed that the convention send a three-man delegation to Washington to meet with the president. It would find out directly from him what he intended to do. Not until Monday, the eighth, did the convention adopt Preston's proposal. It then named him, another Conservative, and a secessionist to travel to the national capital. Weather delayed their trip, however. Heavy rain disrupted rail service, and they had to go by boat from Norfolk. They did not get to Washington until the twelfth and not to the White House until the next day. By then events had bypassed them.[42]

Even as the Virginia Convention determined it needed a formal interview with the president, Lincoln made his fateful decision. On April 4 he had directed Fox to make every preparation to get under way, and he had sent word to Anderson that assistance was forthcoming. But he had not informed South Carolina authorities of his intent. Two days later he did just that.

On April 6, the day Captain Meigs's squadron departed for Florida, news arrived that Fort Pickens had not yet been reinforced. A classic bureaucratic imbroglio had aborted Lincoln's directive of March 12. Signed by General Scott, that order had reached Union commanders off Pensacola on March 31. The naval officer in charge refused, however, to obey an army general because he was acting under instructions from the secretary of the navy, albeit the one from the Buchanan administration. To resolve this tangle a messenger was promptly dispatched to Washington. Even though he traveled by rail through much of the Confederacy, he did not reach the capital until April 6. New orders were immediately prepared and carried by a naval lieutenant along the same route back to Pensacola. He made it to his destination and even aboard a Union ship on April 12. That the two men could make this lengthy journey without undergoing careful scrutiny illustrates the lack of any serious effort by Confederates at this early date to notice who traversed their territory.[43]

In the meantime, President Lincoln decided to follow through on Fort Sumter. On the sixth he sent Robert S. Chew, a clerk in the State Department, to Charleston with a letter for Governor Pickens. Lincoln had no intention of communicating with any Confederate official, civilian or military. For him the Confederate States of America did not exist as a legal government. But the governor of a state was different, for in his view no state could constitutionally leave the Union. His message to Pickens was short and direct. On April 8, as instructed, Chew read the words Lincoln had written: "I am directed by the President of the United States to notify you to expect an attempt will be made to supply Fort Sumter with provisions only; and that, if such attempt be not resisted, no effort to throw in men, arms, or ammunition, will be made, without further notice, or in case of an attack on the Fort."[44]

Although the Confederate commissioners did not know that Chew had left for Charleston, the accounts of military activity, especially the outfitting of expeditions, alarmed them. On Sunday, April 7, they approached Justice Campbell, wanting him once more to contact Seward. Wasting no time, the justice wrote the secretary of state noting the commissioners' anxiety while recounting the assurances he had relayed to them regarding prior notice before any move against Pickens or Sumter. If, he concluded, he had conveyed more than he had been authorized to say, "I pray you will advise me." On the next day at his lodgings Campbell received an undated, unsigned paper: "Faith as to Sumter fully kept; wait and see." Campbell relayed this message to the commissioners, stating he still thought Governor Pickens would get word before any action toward Fort Sumter, but was unsure about Fort Pickens.[45]

Now both Campbell and the commissioners decided that hostilities were imminent. On the evening of the seventh, even before the justice got his answer from Seward, the commissioners telegraphed Secretary of State Toombs, "We believe that a hostile movement is on foot and part of it sailed against the Confederate States." They also informed Toombs that they intended to demand an answer to their note of March 12. If unsatisfactory, "we shall consider the gauntlet of war thrown down and close our mission." On the eighth, they got exactly what they expected. When the commissioners' secretary called at the State Department, he was given an unsigned memorandum which Seward had filed back on March 15 declaring that he would neither recognize the Confederacy as independent nor deal in any way with the commissioners. That very night Martin Crawford received a telegram from General Beauregard informing him of Chew's announcement to Governor Pickens. The commissioners' unrestrained access to the telegraph matches the ease with which the Union couriers traveled between Washington and Pensacola. At this moment the Union was just as lax in taking precautions against a potential enemy.[46]

Lincoln decided to deviate from Fox's proposal. Fox had conceived of an unannounced assault on Charleston harbor that would result in the successful landing of men and matériel at Fort Sumter. Lincoln altered this scheme in two critical ways. First, he would have no surreptitious approach; instead, he would make the governor of South Carolina aware of what he was going to do. Second, and more important, he eliminated the reinforcing component of Fox's plan. Soldiers and war matériel would not be in the ships coming toward Fort Sumter, only provisions. Precisely when Lincoln came to this design is unclear, but it was most probably around the first of April. He did, however, inform his friend Orville Browning that "he himself conceived the idea and proposed sending supplies without an attempt to reinforce, giving notice to Governor Pickens of South Carolina." The president wanted his move to be seen as a mission of mercy, not a belligerent maneuver. From Lincoln's perspective his two alterations meshed perfectly—an open effort to resupply brave men. It was a brilliant insight.[47]

In coming to this determination, Lincoln was supremely conscious of the need for unity in the North behind his administration. A divided northern public opinion would not provide the support essential for him and the Union to prevail in an armed conflict, whether that conflict turned out to mean one battle, as many assumed, or a more protracted campaign. To achieve this solid backing he could not be perceived as a bringer of civil war.

The northern public must perceive his strategy as purely defensive and humanitarian. Seward and Weed had long talked about the need for a unified North should war ever occur. In the cabinet meeting on March 29, Chase and Welles based their recommendations on a defensive posture that would make the Confederates the aggressors. By the time Lincoln made his decisions on April 4 and 6, Seward was undoubtedly on board with them. With all his striving to avoid a probable clash of arms having failed, he wanted to stay with his chief. After all, he had never placed himself too far in front of Lincoln. With his keen political sensitivity he understood that the way a mission to Sumter was conducted would have an impact on northern public opinion.

Although Lincoln couched his strategy as defensive, he knew the Confederate States would not view it that way. Based on his southern contacts, Seward had for weeks told the president that southerners would define any overt federal military action as coercion. And that would cause guns to fire. Moreover, Lincoln himself had been given the same information, most recently on April 4 from John Baldwin. Of course, Confederates could always surprise him, but he must have anticipated they would act as they said they would. Thus, he had to assume that the Fox mission would fail in its ostensible purpose of reprovisioning Fort Sumter. Giving Governor Pickens advance notice made it highly unlikely that Fox's ships would ever reach the fort. In fact, the Confederates might choose to reduce it before Fox could even get to Charleston. Either way, Anderson would never greet Fox.

Politically, the outcome would be a different matter, however. Two weeks after the beginning of the war, Lincoln reassured Fox, telling him not to let the failure of his mission annoy him. The president still thought highly of him. "You and I both anticipated," Lincoln wrote, "that the cause of the country would be advanced by making the attempt to provision Fort Sumter, even if it should fail." He concluded, "It is no small consolation now to feel that an anticipation is justified by the result." Somewhat later he made the same point in conversation with Orville Browning, accenting that the plan succeeded. "They attacked Sumter," he noted. "It fell," he summarized, "and thus did more service than it otherwise could."[48]

From Lincoln's perspective, he had no choice but to order Fox forward. For him, keeping the flag flying at Pickens and Sumter, or at least one of them, was mandatory for his sense of keeping the Union and the forts. In addition, he thought he had been forbearing. He surely agreed with his secretary of the navy, who, with Fox's fleet under way, expressed to his wife Lincoln's sentiment as well as his own: "The time has arrived when the government must maintain its existence, involving the welfare of all within its limits, or abandon all to anarchy and confusion, even if our course results in calamaties."[49]

To hold to his vision of the Union, Lincoln would surely risk war in Charleston harbor, even if it meant taking the chance he would lose the Upper South and maybe even the Border. Although the loss of either would leave him with a truncated Union, he obviously had confidence that even in that situation he could prevail on the battlefield. At the same time, of course, he could expect to weld the Republican party behind him, and also hope to coalesce northern public opinion in the cause of his Union.

In his message to the special session of Congress he called together on July 4, 1861, Lincoln said that he made his final decision on Fort Sumter only after he knew for certain that Fort Pickens had not been reinforced. Yet, the evidence provides at best only shaky support for that conclusion. Lincoln had never said in cabinet meetings or elsewhere he would give up one for the other. He wanted both. And from the beginning, as he informed his close friend Joshua Speed, his "mind was fixed on this matter [Fort Sumter]." He intended to defend it. When, on March 12, he issued his written order to reinforce Fort Pickens, he had no reason to think it would not be carried out.[50]

Moreover, he had taken crucial steps toward relieving Sumter before he learned on April 6 that his directive regarding Pickens had been thwarted, at least temporarily. Additionally, on that same day, April 6, two enterprises aimed at Pickens got under way. Meigs's squadron sailed from New York City, and new orders for the naval commander off Pensacola left Washington. One of these, or even both, might have been implemented before Anderson would be forced to capitulate. For Lincoln to hope for that outcome would be taking a chance, but with his operation at Fort Sumter, he also took a risk. Yet, that risk, with its most probable consequence, he understood, or thought he did.[51]

The Confederate government in Montgomery had no way of knowing the direction of Lincoln's thinking. The regular communications from its delegation in Washington during the final two weeks of March evinced optimism, relaying the positive intelligence obtained from its source within the Lincoln administration. Although the commissioners never claimed that they knew definitely that their information came directly from Lincoln, they believed Campbell, who trusted Seward. To the best of their knowledge the Confederacy would get the evacuation of Fort Sumter and no action toward Fort Pickens.

Yet, Jefferson Davis and his advisers never placed complete faith in the positive news coming from their agents. Also, by April 1, reports of escalating Union military activity made them increasingly wary. President Davis himself was never convinced that peaceable secession would be possible unless all fifteen slave states went out, and on the first of April more than half of them still remained in the Union. Despite the optimistic word from Washington, Secretary of War Walker reminded General Beauregard to keep alert for a surprise attempt at Fort Sumter. Upon learning that the federal government had broken off negotiations with the commissioners, Walker wired the governor of every Confederate state that the Confederate government expected force to be used against it. Secretary of State Toombs wrote Vice President Alexander Stephens on April 6 that signs during "the last few days indicate a hostile purpose."[52]

The Confederate leadership had a particular concern in addition to Fort Sumter. Although Charleston harbor held everyone's attention, and without question it was the most inflammable point, the Davis administration never forgot Fort Pickens. The guidance given the Confederate commissioners specified that the Confederate States must control Pickens as well as Sumter. For the Confederates, Fort Pickens was both a military target and a diplomatic goal.

Fort Pickens presented a tough military objective for Confederates. To reach the fort, which sat on narrow Santa Rosa Island, any attacking force would have to cross a mile and a half of Pensacola Bay. Then, if the attackers made it to the island, they would come under fire from the warships just offshore in the Gulf of Mexico. The fort's location also made reinforcement easy. Federal soldiers could be put ashore on the Gulf side, beyond the range of Confederate cannon. The Confederate commander in the Pensacola area, Brigadier General Braxton Bragg, kept his superiors informed about the status of his command. He told them he lacked the manpower and the firepower to take the fort, even before any reinforcement of the post might occur.

On April 3, President Davis instructed Bragg to consider Pickens a military problem. Bragg should design a plan to capture it. To enable his general to do so, Davis promised the men and weapons needed. The president spent much of his letter describing possible methods Bragg could employ. Bragg never got to try, however. As Gustavus Fox's ships approached Charleston, Union reinforcements moved into Pickens. By April 12, the bastion was too strong for Bragg even to contemplate an attack. The fort would stay in Union hands for the duration of the forthcoming conflict.[53]

While Davis spent time thinking about Fort Pickens, his decisive decision, like Lincoln's, would concern Fort Sumter. As soon as Robert Chew read Lincoln's announcement to Governor Pickens on April 8, its content flashed to Montgomery. Now Jefferson Davis would have to decide whether to permit the reprovisioning to take place. If no, then he had to resolve how to prevent it. He could direct the shore batteries to fire on the ships and keep them from getting to Fort Sumter, or he could order the reduction of the fort before the vessels reached Charleston.[54]

Even before learning about Lincoln's dictum to Governor Pickens, Davis was moving toward a course he preferred not to follow. He had long feared that partial secession of the slave states would end in a war, a prospect he hated. He had spoken of its costing "thousands of lives and millions of treasure." Even with his foreboding, though, he could not see the scale of the destruction that lay ahead. Circumstances seemed to be pointing toward an increased probability of armed conflict. Furthermore, Davis worried that Seward had misled John Campbell. Campbell, who became the Confederacy's assistant secretary of war, would conclude that Seward had deceived him.[55]

Still, on April 6, Davis wrote that he eagerly desired "peace between those who though separated have many reasons to feel toward each other more than the friendship common among other nations." Yet, he could not dismiss the centrality of the forts. "We have waited hopefully for the withdrawal of garrisons which irritate the people of these states and threaten the respective localities, and which can serve no purpose to the United

States unless it be to injure us." He emphasized that his government had not moved against them and did not want to use force. Now, however, he observed, "The idea of evacuation has been abandoned."[56]

In Davis's view, Lincoln controlled the future of the forts. Any attempt to relieve Sumter, whatever the term employed, Davis would interpret as an assault on the Confederacy. At that point the Federal presence would touch upon more than the matter of pride he had mentioned to Governor Pickens back in January. Instead, it would become a powerful threat to the vital interests of his country. To a visitor he was blunt: "They mean to compel us into a political servitude we disown and spurn."[57]

Before coming to his final decision, Davis huddled with his cabinet. Potent arguments supported the president's judgment that the Confederacy could not allow the relief of Fort Sumter. First, the Federal occupation of the post mocked Confederate independence. To permit it to continue indefinitely meant the Confederacy would tolerate a foreign country keeping an uninvited military force within its borders. That status would imperil the standing of the Confederate States as an independent nation. Second, despite the Confederate command structure in Charleston, Davis and his advisers justifiably feared that if they held back, hotheads in South Carolina might hit Fort Sumter on their own. Such a move would undermine the authority of the Confederate government and commit it to a road it had not chosen. The Confederate leadership also recognized that a clash of arms would mobilize citizens behind their new country and, even more important, push the Upper South, especially Virginia, and possibly even the Border into the Confederacy.[58]

At the same time, Davis knew that firing first entailed danger. Secretary of State Toombs reportedly cautioned that doing so would probably alienate potential northern friends of the Confederacy. That caveat did not deter Davis and his counselors, however. They uniformly supported action, agreeing with Vice President Stephens, who insisted that the decision to use force "was not resorted to until every effort at a peaceful adjustment of all matters of controversy with the United States had failed." In President Davis's opinion Lincoln had taken the initial step toward war by dispatching a relief mission to Fort Sumter. Although Davis recognized the benefit of keeping his guns quiet, he informed General Bragg "to relieve our territory and jurisdiction of the presence of foreign garrisons that advantage is overbalanced by other considerations." Like Lincoln, Davis concluded that the integrity and legitimacy of his government demanded that he act. Each man knew he embraced great hazard.[59]

His decision made, Davis had to settle on method. The option of halting the ships sailing toward Fort Sumter with shore batteries had serious liabilities. Firing on those vessels would not repeat the *Star of the West* encounter. The warships in the Federal flotilla would return fire, and Major Anderson would surely use his weapons to aid the relieving force. The possibility also existed that some ships might come through the bombardment and make it to Fort Sumter. In sum, the fort might end up stronger than before.

Reducing the fort prior to the arrival of the Federal expedition offered the surest tactic for success. Accordingly, on April 10, the War Department ordered General Beauregard to demand the surrender of Fort Sumter. If Major Anderson refused, Beauregard was instructed to take it. The next day the general sent officers to the fort with the ultimatum. Presented with the alternative of surrendering or facing an attack, Anderson said he would fight, but he added that unless he received new supplies in a few days, he would have to evacuate. Aware that peace or war now rested in the balance, Beauregard reported Anderson's response to his superiors. A new directive did not alter the Confederate government's fundamental position, though it did give the general some latitude. If Anderson would stipulate a specific date for his withdrawal, Beauregard was not to open fire. Late on the night of April 11, his messengers returned to Fort Sumter with their new ultimatum. After considering his situation and his options, Major Anderson announced that he would depart at noon on the fifteenth, unless before then he received either additional supplies or further instructions from his government. Because the Confederates knew that supplies and possibly reinforcements were en route, Anderson's qualifications made his response unsatisfactory. In fact, Fox's ships were arriving off Charleston that very night. Beauregard's delegation informed Anderson that Confederate guns would begin firing in one hour.[60]

On April 12 at 4:30 a.m., a signal shot burst over Fort Sumter. Immediately, general cannonading commenced.

EPILOGUE

"Both Marching to the Field of Blood"

For the next thirty-one hours guns roared in Charleston harbor. From all directions Confederate batteries hurled shot and shell into Fort Sumter, crumbling the masonry walls and setting fires. From inside the beleaguered bastion Federal cannon blasted away at the attackers. But it was not an equal contest; the result was never in doubt. Because of dispersement of his ships and rough seas, Fox did not participate.

By midday on Saturday, the thirteenth, the fight was over. With food gone, ammunition almost depleted, and flames blazing in the fort, Major Anderson surrendered. At 11:30 a.m. he raised a white flag. Amazingly, even withstanding such a fusillade, no man in his command lost his life. Anderson agreed to leave the post, with evacuation set for Sunday at noon.

At the onset of what would become a terrible, bloody war, the victor had no interest in humiliating the vanquished. General Beauregard permitted Anderson's troops to retain individual weapons and company property. The garrison could march out with colors flying and drums beating. Even more, the Confederate commander allowed Anderson what he most wanted, to salute his flag. On the morning of the fourteenth, Anderson intended to fire a hundred rounds, but on number forty-six a freak accident with a prematurely bursting shell killed one soldier and mortally wounded another. They became the first two battle deaths; tens of thousands would follow. The mishap caused delay. Not until 4 p.m. on that Sunday did Anderson and his men quit the fort, board Fox's ships, and depart Charleston for New York City.[1]

With such minimal casualties at Fort Sumter, a policy of containment might have been possible. Lincoln could have chosen to say that the practically bloodless explosion in Charleston harbor provided a last opportunity, even a requirement, for Americans on both sides to turn from employing arms to searching for a peaceful solution. Given his expectation for Fox's mission, there is no reason, however, to think that he ever contemplated such a course. No evidence suggests that he did.

President Lincoln's response to the assault on Fort Sumter was immediate and forceful. When William Preston and his two colleagues from the Virginia Convention met with him on the thirteenth, the president made his intentions indisputably clear. If the reports about an attack on Fort Sumter were confirmed, he informed the Virginians, he would "repel force by force." For him, Fort Sumter meant "the commencement of actual war."[2]

With confirmation in hand, on April 15 Lincoln issued a proclamation calling the militias of the states promptly into Federal service and Congress into special session on July 4. He wanted seventy-five thousand troops to put down what he termed "combinations too powerful to be suppressed by the ordinary course of judicial proceedings, or by the powers vested in the Marshals by law." Throughout the document Lincoln focused his summons on the Union, the necessity to protect it. He declared at stake "the honor, the integrity, and the existence of our National Union." He never mentioned slavery or anything referring to sectional politics.[3]

The Confederate government certainly expected Lincoln's action. To Jefferson Davis and his advisers, Lincoln's decision to reprovision Fort Sumter and reinforce Fort Pickens signaled that the president of the United States had decided on war. Davis assumed that when he ordered the reduction of Fort Sumter, armed hostilities would take place. One cannot know how he would have responded had Lincoln called for restraint and negotiation. It is safe to conclude, though, that after the experience of the Confederate commissioners, Davis would have demanded concrete guarantees. Moreover, at this moment nothing would have brought the seven seceded states back into the Union. Their independence they would have, at least for the short term.

In the North, the clash at Fort Sumter brought forth an outpouring of support for the Union and for President Lincoln. Republicans rejoiced. The hard-liners were exuberant. One reacted to the news of Fort Sumter: "In the name of God,—Amen!" The moderates embraced the cause of the Union. They saw "a war of democracy against oligarchy, God defend the right and confound all traitors."[4]

Because backing the Union cause also required standing with the Republican Lincoln, many northern Democrats had misgivings. As a party they had fought vigorously for settlement and against Republican intransigence, constantly warning that obstinacy would result in war. Still, realizing, that, as a member of Buchanan's cabinet wrote, "we have the War upon us," most rallied behind the Union, though not all. The majority that did took their cue from their foremost leader, Senator Douglas. "There are only two sides to the question," he announced. "Every man must be for the United States or against it." At the same time, he insisted he would still oppose Lincoln and the Republicans on political questions, but not on the preservation of the Union.[5]

In contrast, anguish gripped the Upper South and the Border. From the beginning of the crisis, back in November, no Americans had striven more for settlement than the Conservatives in these states. In large part because of Seward's massive, untiring efforts Conservatives in all eight of them had resisted the pleas and pressures of the disunionists. Fort Sumter shocked and dismayed them. They had persuaded themselves that Seward could follow through on his assurances that Lincoln would maintain a policy of no coercion. Fort Sumter revealed that they had been clinging to an unraveling rope. Furthermore, now even their paladin, Seward, had aligned himself with his president in adopting coercion. Even facing these bleak circumstances, a number believed they could hold on if only Lincoln would show restraint.

Lincoln's proclamation exploded all hope. It made plain that he intended to invade the Confederate States. Such military action meant coercion in its baldest form. The Upper South began racing toward secession. Almost overnight in Virginia, North Carolina, Tennessee, and Arkansas top-heavy Conservative-Unionist majorities turned into lopsided secessionist majorities. In these four states conventions, legislatures, and popular referenda all testified to the powerful shift in public opinion. By early June, all had joined the Confederate States.[6]

The Border was more complicated. Deeper political divisions, stalwart Unionist sentiment, and Federal military action stymied disunion efforts in Maryland, Kentucky, and Missouri. Secession never really threatened in Delaware.[7]

In all of these states, those that went with the Confederacy and those that did not, the Conservatives finally understood that war had overtaken them.

Their options had run out. Their unofficial leader, John J. Crittenden, still preached that if given the opportunity the people of America would save the Union because of the powerful ties binding Americans together. He was sure partisanship had prevented that possibility. He declared that control by party had hobbled Congress and even blocked taking a possible settlement to American citizens.

Even though the shooting war had begun, Crittenden could not imagine participating on either side. He would hold fast to the Union, but never agree to sending armed soldiers into the Confederate States. Losing touch with reality, he urged his own Kentucky to adopt neutrality and sit out the conflict. As it did to so many others, the war tore apart Crittenden's family, bringing him a distinction he never wanted. No other father in America had a son attain the rank of major general in each army, one in a gray uniform, the other in blue.[8]

For one of Crittenden's most fervent allies, John Gilmer, who would follow his state, Lincoln's proclamation was a dirge. All that he and his colleagues in the free and slave states had done to stave off war ended in cannon smoke. Writing Seward, in whom he had placed such faith, he lamented a united South and a united North "both marching to the field of blood."[9]

NOTES

ABBREVIATIONS USED IN NOTES

AEJ — *Albany Evening Journal*
AHR — *American Historical Review*
AHS — Alexander H. Stephens
AL — Abraham Lincoln
ALPL — Abraham Lincoln Presidential Library, Springfield, IL
CFA — Charles Francis Adams
CG — *Congressional Globe*
CM — *Charleston Mercury*
CWH — *Civil War History*
CWL — Roy P. Basler et al., eds., *The Collected Works of Abraham Lincoln* (8 vols.; New Brunswick, NJ, 1953–55)
DAB — Allen Johnson and Dumas Malone, eds., *Dictionary of American Biography* (20 vols.; New York, 1928–36)
DU — Rare Books, Manuscripts and Special Collections Library, Duke University, Durham, NC
Genesis — Samuel W. Crawford, *The Genesis of the Civil War: The Story of Sumter, 1860–1861* (New York, 1887)
HAL — J. C. Levenson et al., eds., *The Letters of Henry Adams* (6 vols.; Cambridge, MA, 1982–88)
HSP — Historical Society of Pennsylvania, Philadelphia, PA
JB — James Buchanan
JD — Jefferson Davis
JDA — William J. Cooper, *Jefferson Davis, American* (New York, 2000)
JDC — Dunbar Rowland, ed., *Jefferson Davis, Constitutionalist: His Letters, Papers and Speeches* (10 vols.; Jackson, MS, 1923)
JDE — William J. Cooper, ed., *Jefferson Davis: The Essential Writings* (New York, 2003)

JJC John J. Crittenden

JPK John Pendleton Kennedy

JSH *Journal of Southern History*

LC Division of Manuscripts, Library of Congress, Washington, D.C.

MHS Massachusetts Historical Society, Boston, MA

M & P James D. Richardson, comp., *A Compilation of the Messages and Papers of the Presidents* (10 vols.; Washington, D.C., 1896–99)

M & PC James D. Richardson, comp., *A Compilation of the Messages and Papers of the Confederacy* . . . (2 vols.; Nashville, TN, 1906)

MVHR *Mississippi Valley Historical Review*

NEDS Howard Perkins, ed., *Northern Editorials on Secession* (2 vols.; New York, 1942)

NYH *New York Herald*

NYPL New York Public Library

NYT *New York Times*

NYTR *New York Tribune*

OR *War of the Rebellion: A Compilation of the Official Records of the Union and the Confederate Armies* (70 vols. in 128; Washington, D.C., 1880–1901)

ORN *Official Records of the Union and Confederate Navies in the War of the Rebellion* (30 vols.; Washington, D.C., 1894–1922)

PJD Lynda L. Crist et al., eds., *The Papers of Jefferson Davis* (13 vols.; Baton Rouge, LA, 1971–)

Pratt Enoch Pratt Free Library, Baltimore, MD

SD Stephen A. Douglas

SEDS Dwight Lowell Dumond, ed., *Southern Editorials on Secession* (1931; Gloucester, MA, 1964)

Seward Frederick W. Seward, *William H. Seward* (3 vols.; New York, 1891)

TSC Ulrich Bonnell Phillips, ed., *The Correspondence of Robert Toombs, Alexander H. Stephens, and Howell Cobb* (Washington, D.C., 1913)

TW Thurlow Weed

UC Special Collections, Joseph Regenstein Library, University of Chicago, Chicago, IL

UGA Hargrett Rare Book and Manuscript Library, University of Georgia, Athens, GA

UNC Southern Historical Collection, Wilson Library, University of North Carolina, Chapel Hill, NC

UR Rush Rhees Library, University of Rochester, Rochester, NY

VHS Virginia Historical Society, Richmond, VA

Weed Harriet A. Weed and Thurlow Weed Banner, eds., *Life of Thurlow Weed Including His Autobiography and a Memoir* (2 vols.; Boston, MA, 1883–84)

WHS William Henry Seward

Words Don E. Fehrenbacher and Virginia Fehrenbacher, comps. and eds., *Recollected Words of Abraham Lincoln* (Stanford, CA, 1996)

PREFACE

1. David M. Potter, *The South and the Sectional Conflict* (Baton Rouge, LA, 1968), 246. The number 750,000, which is considerably larger than the generally accepted 620,000, comes from the most recent and sophisticated, as well as persuasive, analysis: J. David Hacker, "A Census-Based Count of the Civil War Dead," *CWH*, 57 (December 2011), 307–48. In our time, because of a population ten times greater than during the Civil War, the figure would explode to 7.5 million dead.

   My title, *We Have the War Upon Us*, is a quotation taken from a letter Edwin Stanton wrote to JB, April 12, 1861, JB Papers, HSP (all other citations in this book are to this collection unless otherwise noted). In this book I have not differentiated in my citations from manuscripts in archives that I visited and manuscripts that I utilized in microform and electronic formats. Still, I always cite the location of the original document.
2. William W. Freehling, *The Road to Disunion*, vol. 2: *Secessionists Triumphant, 1854–1861* (New York, 2007) and Russell McClintock, *Lincoln and the Decision for War: The Northern Response to Secession* (Chapel Hill, NC, 2008).

PROLOGUE: "IS THIS NOT A REMARKABLE SPECTABLE?"

1. *NYH*, March 4, 1861; *NYT*, March 5, 1861; *NYTR*, March 4, 1861; *Washington Evening Star*, March 4, 1861. For JJC consult Albert D. Kirwan's excellent biography, *John J. Crittenden and the Struggle for the Union* (Lexington, KY, 1962); a good description is on p. 323.
2. The most recent treatment of Clay is David S. Heidler and Jeanne T. Heidler, *Henry Clay: The Essential American* (New York, 2010), but Robert V. Remini's *Henry Clay: Statesman for the Union* (New York, 1991), remains the best biography.
3. *NYH*, December 4, 8, 1860.
4. Private letter from Washington, January 16, 1861, in *Memoirs of John Adams Dix*, comp. by His Son (2 vols.; New York, 1883), 1:364.
5. For JJC's speech see *CG*, 36th Congress, 2d Session, 1375–80 (all future references in this book are to this session of this Congress unless otherwise noted) and Mrs. Chapman Coleman, ed., *The Life of John J. Crittenden, with Selections from His Correspondence and Speeches* (2 vols.; Philadelphia, 1871), 2:270–90. These two versions are basically identical, except for the very beginning of the speech; I have used Coleman.

CHAPTER ONE: "THE FUTURE IS . . . SHROUDED IN THE VERY BLACKNESS OF DARKNESS"

1. Horace B. Sargent to WHS, November 7, 1860, WHS Papers, UR (all other citations in this book are from this collection unless otherwise noted).

2. On the Republican party, William E. Gienapp, *The Origins of the Republican Party, 1852–1856* (New York, 1987), is essential; also see Eric Foner, *Free Soil, Free Labor, Free Men: The Ideology of the Republican Party before the Civil War* (New York, 1970) on ideology and Michael F. Holt, *The Political Crisis of the 1850's* (New York, 1978) and *The Rise and Fall of the American Whig Party: Jacksonian Politics and the Onset of the Civil War* (New York, 1999) particularly on changes in the 1850s. My account follows them.
3. Gienapp, *Republican Party,* 360, n. 52.
4. *Historical Statistics of the United States: Earliest Times to the Present* (5 vols.; New York, 2006), 1:37, 175, 5:161 (for apportionment).
5. Elizabeth R. Varon, *Disunion! The Coming of the American Civil War, 1789–1859* (Chapel Hill, NC, 2008), 317.
6. Kirk H. Porter and Donald Bruce Johnson, comps., *National Party Platforms, 1840–1964* (Urbana, IL, 1966), 27–28, 31–33.
7. On Republicans in 1860 major Lincoln biographies provide ample coverage; see especially Michael Burlingame, *Abraham Lincoln: A Life* (2 vols.; Baltimore, 2008) and David Hebert Donald, *Lincoln* (New York, 1995). Also note Douglas R. Egerton, *Year of Meteors: Stephen Douglas, Abraham Lincoln, and the Election that Brought On the Civil War* (New York, 2010).
8. W. Dean Burnham, *Presidential Ballots, 1836–1892* (Baltimore, 1955), 246, 888.
9. On Lincoln in the 1850s see the biographies cited above in note 7. Also, Allen C. Guelzo, *Lincoln and Douglas: The Debates that Defined America* (New York, 2008) covers the Douglas contest in detail.
10. Harold Holzer, *Lincoln at Cooper Union: The Speech that Made Abraham Lincoln President* (New York, 2004); the speech is printed on 252–84.
11. *NYH,* November 25, 1860, has projected congressional lineups; I have also made projections. The two have no significant differences.
12. Roy F. Nichols, *The Disruption of American Democracy* (New York, 1948), remains unsurpassed on Democrats in the late 1850s. The best general coverage is David M. Potter, *The Impending Crisis, 1848–1861,* comp. and ed. Don E. Fehrenbacher (New York, 1976).
13. Burnham, *Presidential Ballots,* 246, 888.
14. Albany *Atlas and Argus,* November 10, 1860, in *NEDS,* 1:87.
15. William P. Miles to Christopher Memminger, January 10, 1860, Christopher Memminger Papers, UNC. No thorough study of the fire-eaters exists; see, however, Eric Walther's suggestive *The Fire-Eaters* (Baton Rouge, LA, 1992) and also William Freehling's *The Road to Disunion,* vol. 2, *Secessionists Triumphant, 1854–1861* (New York, 2007), the best study of secession. I did not find Shearer Davis Bowman, *At the Precipice: Americans North and South During the Secession Crisis* (Chapel Hill, NC, 2010) very helpful.
16. William J. Cooper, *Liberty and Slavery: Southern Politics to 1860* (New York, 1983).

17. James L. Huston cites these figures in his *Calculating the Value of the Union: Slavery, Property Rights, and the Economic Origins of the Civil War* (Chapel Hill, NC, 2003), 28.
18. William J. Cooper and Thomas E. Terrill, *The American South: A History* (2 vols.; 4th ed.; Lanham, MD, 2009), 1:435–50, has a bibliographical essay with full citations for pertinent titles; chaps. 8–10 provide a good overview.
19. *CM,* July 10, 1860.
20. William Scarborough, ed. *The Diary of Edmund Ruffin* (3 vols.; Baton Rouge, LA, 1972–89), 1:473; on John Brown, consult Potter, *Impending Crisis,* chap. 14.
21. Both of these pamphlets came from the pen of a superb polemicist, the South Carolina planter John Townsend: *The Doom of Slavery in the Union: Its Safety Out of It* (Charleston, 1860) and *The South Alone, Should Govern the South, And African Slavery Should Be Controlled by Those Only Who Are Friendly to It* (Charleston, 1860). For a valuable collection of these pamphlets consult Jon L. Wakelyn, ed., *Southern Pamphlets on Secession, November 1860–April 1861* (Chapel Hill, NC, 1996).
22. *CM,* November 3, 1860.
23. Ibid., December 3, 1860.
24. Thomas Ruffin to "my dearest Anne," December 8, 1860, Thomas Ruffin Papers, UNC; Jere Clemens to JJC, November 24, 1860, JJC Papers, LC (quotation). I use upper case for Conservative to clarify its reference to a particular political position. I also use Conservative and Unionist interchangably, though the Unionists divided between the majority who would follow their states out of the Union and the minority who would not.
25. Jere Clemens to JJC, November 24, 1860, JJC papers, LC. For the full range of secessionists' views consult Freehling, *Secessionists Triumphant.*
26. Alfred Huger to Joseph Holt, November 12, 1860. Joseph Holt Papers, LC.
27. The Rhett quotation is in William C. Davis, *Robert Barnwell Rhett: The Life and Times of a Fire-Eater* (Columbia, SC, 2001), 331. Walter Edgar, *South Carolina: A History* (Columbia, SC, 1998), chap. 15, has a solid overview of the state from Nullification to the early 1850s. For detailed treatment consult Richard E. Ellis, *The Union at Risk: Jacksonian Democracy, States' Rights, and the Nullification Crisis* (New York, 1987); William Freehling, *Prelude to Civil War: The Nullification Controversy in South Carolina, 1816–1836* (New York, 1966) on Nullification; and John Barnwell, *Love of Order: South Carolina's First Secession Crisis* (Chapel Hill, NC, 1982), on the state's initial flirtation with disunion.
28. John G. Nicolay and John Hay, *Abraham Lincoln: A History* (10 vols.; New York, 1909), 2:306–14, has the Gist correspondence.
29. JD to Rhett, Jr., November 10, 1860, in *JDE,* 182–84; on the Rhetts' activities, see Freehling, *Secessionists Triumphant,* 388, 394.
30. JD to Rhett, Jr., November 10, 1860, in *JDE,* 182–84.
31. *Daily Pittsburgh Gazette,* November 14, 1860, in *NEDS,* 1:91 (1st quotation); Howard K.

Beale, ed., *The Diary of Edward Bates, 1859–1866* (Washington, 1933), 157 (2d quotation); *AEJ,* November 10, 1860 (3d quotation); *NYH,* November 20, 1860 (4th quotation); *NYTR,* November 9, 1860 (5th quotation).

32. Frank Sawyer to John Sherman, December 23, 1860, John Sherman Papers, LC (1st quotation); Edw. Winslow to CFA, December 22, 1860, and Adams Diary, November12, 1860, Adams Family Papers, MHS (2d quotation); (all other citations in this book are to this collection unless otherwise noted); Sumner to Duchess of Argyll, December 14, 1860, in Beverly W. Palmer, ed., *The Selected Letters of Charles Sumner* (2 vols.; Boston, 1990), 2:38.

33. *Indianapolis Daily Journal,* December 22, 1860, in *NEDS,* 1:331 (1st quotation); Augusta *Kennebec Journal,* January 25, 1861, in *NEDS,* 1:304 (2d quotation); Chandler to Lyman Trumbull, November 15, 1860, Lyman Trumbull Papers, ALPL (3d quotation).

34. William Hodge to WHS, November 17, 1860, WHS Papers (1st quotation); *New York Evening Post,* November 12, 1860, in *NEDS,* 1:159 (2d quotation); Henry Adams to C. F. Adams, Jr., January 2, 1861, in *HAL,* 1:217–18 (3d quotation); Truman Smith to AL, November 8, 1860, AL Papers, LC (all other citations in this book are from this collection unless otherwise noted).

35. Hobart Berrian to WHS, November 18, 1860, WHS Papers (1st quotation); Lyman Trumbull to Benjamin Wade, November 9, 1860, Benjamin Wade Papers, LC (2d quotation); see also *Boston Daily Atlas and Bee,* November 12, 1860, in *NEDS,* 1:88–91.

36. *AEJ,* November 3, 1860 (quotation). On WHS the best biography is still Glyndon Van Deusen, *William Henry Seward* (New York, 1967); a new study of this critically important figure is sorely needed.

37. S. S. Southworth to WHS, November 18, 1860 (quotation); J. K. Morehead to WHS, November 21, 1860; J. M. Palmer to WHS, November 21, 1860; CFA to WHS, November 11, 1860, WHS Papers; CFA Diary, November 10, 17, 1860, Adams Family Papers.

38. WHS to Simon Cameron, November 15, 1860, Simon Cameron Papers, LC (quotation); Leonard Swett to TW, November 26, 1860, in *Weed,* 2:301; Simon Cameron to TW, November 13, 1860, TW Papers, UR (all other citations in this book are from this collection unless otherwise noted).

39. CFA to WHS, November 11, 1860, and Simon Cameron to WHS, November 13, 1860, WHS Papers. For insightful treatment of Seward early in the crisis see Michael Robinson, "William Henry Seward and the Onset of the Secession Crisis," forthcoming in *CWH.*

40. M.T.E. Chandler to WHS, November 13, 1860, and WHS to James McQueen, November 13, 1860, WHS papers.

41. WHS to TW, November 18, 1860, TW Papers. No other major political figure of this period cries out more for current biographical treatment, except Seward, than Weed.

Amazingly, nothing has replaced Glyndon Van Deusen, *Thurlow Weed: Wizard of the Lobby* (Boston, 1947).

42. For AL in Springfield consult Ronald C. White, Jr., *A. Lincoln: A Biography* (New York, 2009), chap. 16, and especially Harold Holzer, *Lincoln President-Elect: Abraham Lincoln and the Great Secession Winter, 1860–1861* (New York, 2008), which treats the topic in great detail. On descriptions see the marvelous Philip B. Kunhardt III et al., *Lincoln, Life-Size* (New York, 2009), 66–68, 72–73.
43. Clifton A. Moore to AL, November 14, 1860 (1st quotation); Samuel Haycroft to AL, November 9, 1860 (2d quotation); Joshua Speed to AL, November 14, 1860 (3d quotation), all in AL Papers; AL to Speed, November 19, 1860, in *CWL*, 4:141.
44. St. Louis *Daily Democrat*, November 7, 1860, in Holzer, *Lincoln, President-Elect*, 62 (1st quotation); Gideon Welles, *Lincoln and Seward: Remarks Upon the Memorial Address of Chas. Francis Adams* (New York, 1874), 38 (2d quotation).
45. *Words*, 438 (1st quotation); B. F. Smith to Lyman Trumbull, December 3, 1860, Lyman Trumbull Papers, LC (2d quotation).
46. *NYH*, November 12, 1860.
47. *Words*, 438 (1st and 3d quotations); AL to Samuel Haycroft, November 13, 1860, in *CWL*, 4:139 (2d quotation).
48. Smith to AL, November 7, 1860, AL Papers; Lincoln to Smith, November 10, 1860, in *CWL*, 4:138.
49. Cobb to "Dr. Col.," November 16, 1860, Howell Cobb Papers, UGA. Philip Shriver Klein provides sympathetic, full biographical treatment in *President James Buchanan: A Biography* (1962; Newtown, CT, 1995); more recently Jean H. Baker has written a brief, slashingly critical study, *James Buchanan* (New York, 2004). Nichols, *Disruption*, remains the best on his administration; also consult Potter, *Impending Crisis*, and Elbert B. Smith, *The Presidency of James Buchanan* (Lawrence, KN, 1975). My treatment leans heavily on Nichols, Klein, and Potter.
50. J. Henley Smith to AHS, November 24, 1860, AHS Papers, LC.
51. Scott to Floyd, October 29, 1860 (copy), JB Papers; Scott to JJC, (copy), November 12, 1860, JJC Papers, LC; Elihu B. Washburne to AL, December 17, 1860, AL Papers.
52. Quotation in Nichols, *Disruption*, 381.
53. Quotation in Klein, *Buchanan*, 358.
54. Black to Geo. W. Woodward, November 24, 1860 (copy), Jeremiah Black Papers, LC.
55. Susan Sparks to "Mother," December 22, 1859, Lawrence Keitt Papers, DU; Nichols, *Disruption*, 75–76.
56. Black to JB, November 17, 1860, JB Papers.
57. Black to JB, [November 20, 1860], JB Papers.
58. *M & P*, 5:626–53, especially 626–39. For a more direct comparison of JB with Andrew Jackson see text pp. 119–20.

59. CFA Diary, December 4, 1860, Adams Family Papers.
60. Cobb to "Dear Col.," December 1, 1860, Cobb Papers, UGA; *CM,* December 6, 1860; C. Eames to Samuel Tilden, November 20, 1860, Samuel Tilden Papers, NYPL.
61. Henry W. Philips to JB, December 4, 1860 (1st three quotations); William B. Reed to JB, December 4 (4th quotation), 6 (5th quotation), JB Papers; Journal, December 4, 1860, JPK Papers, Pratt.
62. Nelson Poe (Maryland) to TW, December 19, 1860, TW Papers.
63. Journal, December 3, 1860, JPK Papers, Pratt (1st quotation); George Kinkead (Kentucky) to N. W. Edwards, December 1, 1860, AL Papers (2d, 4th, 5th quotations); Kenneth Rayner (North Carolina) to Caleb Cushing, December 9, 1860, Caleb Cushing Papers, LC (3d quotation).
64. Journal, December 5, 1860, and JPK to Philip Pendleton, December 26, 1860, JPK Papers, Pratt; Rayner to Cushing, December 9, 1860, Cushing Papers, LC; Washington Hunt (New York) to Millard Fillmore, November 19, 1860, Millard Fillmore Papers, Buffalo Historical Society.

CHAPTER TWO: "WE NEED A STATESMAN OF NERVE TO MEET THE TERRIBLE CRISIS"

1. *NYTR,* December 1, 1860 (1st quotation); CFA Diary, December 3, 1860, CFA Papers (2d quotation); Samuel Curtis Journal, December 5, 1860, Samuel Curtis Papers, ALPL (3d quotation); Preston King to Gideon Welles, December 15, 1860, Gideon Welles Papers, LC (4th quotation); WHS to Home, December 1, 1860, in *Seward,* 2:478 (5th quotation).
2. John Sherman to "My Dear Brother," November 11, 1860, in Rachel Sherman Thorndike, ed., *The Sherman Letters: Correspondence Between General and Senator Sherman from 1837 to 1891* (1894; New York, 1971), 87 (1st quotation); Chase to George G. Fogg, December 1[5], 1860, in John Niven, ed., *The Salmon P. Chase Papers* (5 vols; Kent, OH, 1993–98), 3:41; Fessenden to Hamilton Fish, December 15, 1860, Hamilton Fish Papers, LC (2d quotation); Colfax to Uriah Reavis, December 10, 1860, Uriah Reavis Papers, Chicago History Museum (3d quotation) and Curtis Journal, December 11–12, Curtis Papers, ALPL; James Dixon to Leonard Bacon, December 2, 1860, in Charles Royster, *The Destructive War: William Tecumseh Sherman, Stonewall Jackson and the Americans* (New York, 1991), 293 (4th quotation).
3. CFA Diary, December 3, 1860, Adams Family Papers (1st quotation); WHS to Home, December 1, 7, 1860, in *Seward,* 2:478, 480 (2d quotation); WHS to TW, December 3, 1860, TW Papers (3d quotation).
4. WHS to TW, December 2–3, 1860, TW Papers.
5. WHS to TW, December 3, 1860, ibid. (1st quotation); *CG,* 9–10 (2d quotation).
6. CFA Diary, December 2, 1860, Adams Family Papers (1st quotation); WHS to Home, December 8, 10, 1860, in *Seward,* 2:480 (4th quotation), 481 (2d quotation); WHS to TW, December 2, 1860, TW Papers (3d quotation).

7. Belmont to SD, November 2, SD Papers, UC (all other citations in this book are from this collection unless otherwise noted); John A. McClernand to Charles Lanphier, December 3, 1860, Charles Lanphier Papers, ALPL.
8. J. Henly Smith to AHS, December 2, 1860, AHS Papers, LC; *NYH,* December 3, 1860; *CG,* 28 (quotation); SD to Belmont, December 25, 1860, in Robert W. Johannsen, ed., *The Letters of Stephen A. Douglas* (Urbana, IL, 1961), 505. The SD Papers are full of such letters.
9. *CG,* 28.
10. HA to CFA, Jr., February 13, 1861, in *HAL,* 1:231.
11. *CG,* 52–53, 56–58.
12. Belmont to John Forsyth, November 22, 1860 (1st quotation), to Herschel Johnson, November 22, 1860 (2d quotation), to Julius Pringle, November 26, 1860, to William Marten, November 30, 1860, in August Belmont, *Letters, Speeches, and Addresses of August Belmont* (np, 1890), 23–25, 26, 27, 29, and Belmont to Johnson, December 11, 1860, Herschel Johnson Papers, DU.
13. Belmont to Johnson, December 11, 1860, Johnson Papers, DU (1st quotation), to Johnson, November 22, 1860, in *Belmont Letters,* 26 (3d quotation); *NEDS,* 1:88 (2d quotation).
14. *NYH,* December 14, 1860.
15. Belmont to Herschel Johnson, November 22, 1860, in *Belmont Letters,* 26 (1st quotation); *NEDS,* 1:151 (2d quotation), 159 (3d quotation); John R. Dickinson, ed., *Speeches, Correspondence, Etc., of the Late Daniel S. Dickinson of New York . . .* (New York, 1867), 695–702 (final quotations 697, 702).
16. McClernand to Charles Lanphier, February 4, 1861, Lanphier Papers, ALPL (1st quotation); R. Hamilton to SD, December 4, 1860, SD Papers; Webster to Caleb Cushing, November 11, 1860, Caleb Cushing Papers, LC (2d quotation).
17. *New Orleans Daily Crescent,* December 11, 1860, in *SEDS* (1st quotation); Herschel Johnson to AHS, November 30, 1860, Johnson Papers, Duke (2d quotation); M. J. Crawford to AHS, December 8, 1860, AHS Papers, LC; *NYH,* December 9, 1860.
18. J. Henley Smith to AHS, December 9, 1860, AHS Papers, LC (1st quotation); John A. Gilmer to William A. Graham, December 5, 1860, in Max R. Williams and J. G. de Roulhac Hamilton, eds., *The Papers of William Alexander Graham* (8 vols.; Raleigh, NC, 1957–92), 5:200 (2d quotation); *CG,* 11 (4th quotation), 13 (3d quotation).
19. Hunter to Robert M. T. Hunter, Jr., November 22, 1860, Robert M. T. Hunter Papers, Albert and Shirley Small Special Collections Library, University of Virginia, Charlottesville, VA.
20. *JDA,* 332, 339–40; JD to Rhett, November 10, 1860, in *JDE,* 182–84.
21. Howell Cobb cries out for a good biography; the best treatment remains an unpublished dissertation: Randy Reid, "Howell Cobb of Georgia: A Biography" (Ph.D. diss., Louisiana State University, 1995).
22. Cobb to "Dr. Col.," November 16, 1860, Howell Cobb Papers, UGA (1st, 2d, 5th quotations); Toombs et al. to Cobb, November 12, 1860, ibid. (3d and 4th quota-

tions); Cobb to JB, December 8, 1860, in *TSC,* 517 (final quotation). Also see Cobb to his wife, December 6, 1860, and to Buchanan, March 26, 1861, in *TSC* 516–17, 555.

23. *TSC,* 505–14.
24. Weldon Edwards to G. A. Barksdale, December 21, 1860, Weldon Edwards Papers, VHS (1st quotation); Tho. Hicks to JJC, December 13, 1860, JJC Papers, LC (2d quotation); JPK Journal, JPK Papers, Pratt (final quotation).
25. Bell to William A. Graham, September 6, 1860, in Williams and Hamilton, eds., *Papers of William Graham,* 5:172.
26. Hicks to JJC, December 13, 1860, JJC Papers, LC; *CG,* 5.
27. *CG,* 6.
28. Martin Crawford (congressman) to AHS, December 8, 1860, AHS Papers, LC (1st and 2d quotations); *NYTR,* December 10, 1860; *CG,* 37 (3d quotation).
29. *CG,* 6; J. L. Giddings to CFA, December 10, 1860, and CFA Diary, December 4, 1860, Adams Family Papers.
30. Corwin to AL, December 10, 1860, AL Papers.
31. *House Reports,* 36th Cong., 2d Sess., No. 31 (Serial 1104), 1–2 (cited hereafter as *House Committee Journal*); CFA Diary, December 5, 1860, Adams Family Papers.
32. John McClernand to Charles Lanphier, December 10, 1860, Lanphier Papers, ALPL (quotation); *NYH,* December 7, 1860; *CG,* 36.
33. *House Committee Journal,* 7–8.
34. Reuben Davis, *Recollections of Mississippi and Mississippians* (Boston, 1891), 399; CFA to CFA, Jr., December 7, 1860, Adams Family Papers.
35. *CG,* 19 (quotation), 117; on obstruction note pp. 19–117 passim.
36. William Kelley to AL, November 29, 1860 (1st quotation), William Lewis to AL, December 11, 1860 (2d quotation), AL Papers; Phillip S. Foner, *Business & Slavery: The New York Merchants and the Irrepressible Conflict* (Chapel Hill, NC, 1941), 208 (3d quotation).
37. Benjamin Field to AL, December 10, 1860, AL Papers; Foner, *Business & Slavery,* 226–34.
38. *NYH,* December 16, 1860; *Memoirs of John Adams Dix,* comp. by His Son (2 vols.; New York, 1883), 1:347–49; Foner, *Business & Slavery,* 226–34; Augustus Schell to Millard Fillmore, December 8, 1860, Millard Fillmore Papers, Oswego State University, Oswego, NY.
39. W. S. Gelman to Trumbull, December 11, 1860, Lyman Trumbull Papers, LC.
40. Donn Piatt, *Memories of the Men Who Saved the Union* (New York and Chicago, 1887), 132 (1st quotation); Peter Sweeney to John T. Hoffman, January 11, 1883, John T. Hoffman Papers, NYPL (remaining quotations).
41. *Weed,* 1:306 (1st quotation); TW to Lyman Trumbull, November 21, [1860], Trumbull Papers, LC (2d quotation); *AEJ,* November 24, 1860.
42. *AEJ,* November 30, 1860.
43. *NYT,* November 26, December 7, 1860; New York *Courier and Enquirer,* December 2, 1860, in Russell McClintock, *Lincoln, and the Decision for War: The Northern Response*

to Secession (Chapel Hill, NC, 2008), 76; TW Papers, November-December 1860, passim (quotation R. P. Marion to TW, December 5, 1860). The number of letters from Republicans in the TW Papers expressing sympathy for his views surprised me. McClintock and Patrick Sowle, "The Conciliatory Republicans During the Winter of Secession" (Ph.D. diss., Duke University, 1963), have more detailed accounts of pro-compromise Republicans.

44. James T. Sherman to TW, December 8, 1860, TW Papers, LC (1st quotation); Webb to AL, December 1, 1860, AL Papers (2d quotation); William Dwight to TW, December 19, 1860, TW Papers (3d quotation); Moses Grinnell to WHS, December 4, 1860, WHS Papers; M. H. Simpson to CFA, December 7, 1860, Adams Family Papers.
45. *AEJ*, December 24 (quotation), 27, 1860. Also see W. S. Gelman to Lyman Trumbull, December 11, 1860, Trumbull Papers, LC; [signature missing] to Simon Cameron, December 12, 1860, Simon Cameron Papers, LC; A. M. Mitchell to TW, December 14, 1860, and Thos. J. Patterson to TW, December 29, 1860, TW Papers.
46. Geo. Morgan to TW, December 8, 1860, Wm. Chase to TW, December 8, 1860 (quotation), Geo. Harrington to TW, December 10, 1860, TW Papers.
47. TW to Preston King, December 10, 1860, in *Weed*, 2:309 (1st and final quotation); John Defrees to TW, December 19 (2d quotation), Geo. Morgan to TW, December 8, 1860 (3d quotation), T. Patterson to TW, December 21, 1860, TW Papers.
48. Allen Munroe to TW, December 10, 1860 (1st quotation), Fish to TW, December 15, 1860 (2d quotation), John Defrees to TW, December 19, 1860 (3d quotation), TW Papers.
49. John Defrees to TW, December 19, 1860, TW Papers (3d quotation); W. H. Winder to Cameron, December 20, 1860 (2d quotation), [signature missing] to Cameron, December 12, 1860, (1st quotation), Cameron Papers, LC.
50. J. O. Bloss to TW, December 1, 1860, TW Papers (1st quotation); Aaron Young and George Taylor to Benjamin Wade, December 28, 1860, Benjamin Wade Papers, LC (2d quotation).
51. J. P. Sanderson to Leonard Swett, December 7, 1860, AL Papers, LC (1st quotation); Wade to Trumbull, November 14, 1860, Trumbull Papers, LC (2d quotation); Chandler to Lyman Trumbull, November 15, 1860, Trumbull Papers, ALPL (3d quotation); *NYTR*, November 19 (4th quotation), December 31 (5th quotation), 1860.
52. Sanderson to Swett, see note 51 above; J. A. Andrew to Montgomery Blair, December 4, 1860, Blair Family Papers, LC (1st and 2d quotations); Henry Hardy to Richard Yates, November 19, 1860, AL Papers (3d quotation); Kirk H. Porter and Donald Bruce Johnson, comps., *National Party Platforms, 1840–1964* (Urbana, IL, 1966), 32 (4th quotation).
53. W. A. Pursavant to Cameron, December 4, 1860, Cameron Papers, LC (1st quotation); James Myers to AL, December 10, 1860, AL Papers (2d quotation); Z. Phillips to John Sherman, December 15, 1860, John Sherman Papers, LC (3d quotation).
54. Tho. Richmond to Trumbull, December 14, 1860 (1st quotation), W. H. Herndon

to Trumbull, December 21, 1860 (2d quotation), Trumbull Papers, LC; J. O. Bloss to TW, December 1, 1860, TW Papers (3d quotation); Charles Cooke to WHS, December 3, 1860, and William Russel to WHS, December, nd, 1860, WHS Papers.

55. King to TW, December 19, 1860, TW Papers.
56. William Cullen Bryant to AL, December 25, 1860 (1st quotation), Thomas Dudley to David Davis, December 7, 1860 (2d quotation), C. J. Jack to AL, December 5, 1860, James Myers to AL, December 10, 1860, AL Papers; M. M. Fisher to CFA, December 16, 1860, Adams Family Papers; George Noyes to WHS, November 28, 1860, WHS Papers.
57. B. F. Wade to Trumbull, November 14, 1860, Trumbull Papers, LC (quotation); Ransom Balsam to WHS, December 3, 1860, WHS Papers.
58. Thomas Dudley to David Davis, December 7, 1860, AL Papers (quotation); Charles Cooke to WHS, December 3, 1860, WHS Papers.
59. E. Stafford to Trumbull, December 20, 1860, Trumbull Papers, LC (1st quotation); White to AL, December 22, 1860, AL Papers (2d quotation).
60. Washburne to AL, December 9, 1860, AL Papers.
61. Dixon to Gideon Welles, December 8, 1860, Welles Papers, LC; Curtis Journal, 80, 86–87, Curtis Papers, ALPL; Colfax to Uriah Reavis, December 10, 1860, Reavis Papers, Chicago History Museum (1st quotation); E. G. Spaulding to TW, December 22, 1860, TW Papers (2d quotation).
62. WHS to Home, December 2, 1860, in *Seward,* 2:479; WHS to TW, December 3, 1860, TW Papers.
63. WHS to Home, December 1, 2, 8, 10, 1860, in *Seward,* 2:478, 480, 481; WHS to TW, December 3, 1860, TW Papers.
64. WHS to TW, December 2, 1860, TW Papers (1st quotation); Charles Francis Adams, *Charles Francis Adams, 1835–1915: An Autobiography* (Boston & New York, 1916), 74 (2d quotation).
65. Adams, *Autobiography,* 58; CFA Diary, November 17, December 2, 1860, Adams Family Papers; *CG,* 9–10.
66. *CG,* 112, 158.
67. AL to WHS, December 8, 1860, in *CWL,* 4:148; WHS to TW, December 13, 1860, TW Papers.
68. WHS to AL, December 13, 1860, TW to David Davis, November 17, 1860, and to Leonard Swett, December 2, 1860, AL Papers; *Seward,* 2:481–82; Swett to TW, November 26, 1860, TW Papers; Davis to TW, December 10?, 1860 (photocopy), David Davis Papers, Chicago History Museum (quotation).
69. Henry Adams to C. F. Adams, Jr., December 13, 1860, in *HAL,* 1:206 (1st quotation); George Fogg to AL, December 19, 1860, AL Papers (remaining quotations).
70. *AEJ,* December 17, 1860.
71. For a fascinating account of Weed's visit see *Weed,* 1:604–14.
72. *Words,* 461.

73. AL Resolutions, [December 20, 1860], in *CWL*, 4:156–57; AL to Trumbull, December 21, 1860, in *CWL*, 158; H. Kreis[mann] to Elihu Washburne, December 27, 1860, Elihu Washburne Papers, LC (final quotation).
74. WHS to AL, December 26, 1860, AL Papers. Later in the month, AL obviously changed his mind about any amendment; see text, chap. 3, p. 108 and note 55. I am grateful to Professor Michael Holt for causing me to reconsider the importance of AL's unwritten guidance.
75. David M. Potter, *Lincoln and His Party in the Secession Crisis* (1942; Baton Rouge, LA, 1995), 169–70.
76. H. Stanford to AL, November ?, 1860 (1st quotation), George Waite to AL, December 1, 1860 (2d quotation), Charles King to AL, November 9, 1860 (3d quotation), AL Papers.
77. Nathaniel Pettit to AL, December 10, 1860 (1st quotation), Raymond to AL, November 14, 1860 (2d quotation), Truman Smith to AL, November 7, 1860 (4th quotation), AL Papers; *NYH*, December 17, 1860 (3d quotation).
78. A. Wigard to AL, December 10, 1860 (1st quotation), Schurz to AL, December 18, 1860 (2d quotation), also Gene Gass, December 5, 1860, C. Jack, December 5, 1860, G. North, December 11, 1860, all in AL Papers.
79. Nathaniel Pettit to AL, December 10, 1860, AL Papers.
80. Elihu Washburne to AL, December 9, 1860, Lyman Trumbull to AL, December 4, 17, 1860, Richard Thompson to AL, December 25, 1860, George Fogg to AL, December 17, 1860, Joseph Medill to AL, December 18, 1860, AL Papers.
81. For example, AL to Truman Smith, November 10, 1860, and to Nathaniel Paschall, November 16, 1860, in *CWL*, 4:138, 139–40.
82. *CWL*, 4:141–42 and notes; McClintock, *Lincoln*, 51–52.
83. AL to Henry Raymond, November 28, 1860, in *CWL*, 4:145–46.
84. Michael Burlingame, ed., *With Lincoln in the White House: Letters, Memoranda, and Other Writings of John G. Nicolay* (Carbondale and Edwardsville, IL, 2000), 15; AL to Trumbull, December 10, 1860 (1st quotation), to Kellogg, December 11, 1860 (2d quotation), to Elihu Washburne, December 13, 1860 (3d quotation), in *CWL*, 4:149, 150, 151.
85. See the citations in note 84. The first quotation is from the letter to Trumbull; also see AL to John Defrees, December 18, 1860 (2d quotation), in *CWL*, 4:155.
86. *CWL*, 3:29. For my assessment of Lincoln during the winter, see also my "Where Was Henry Clay? President-Elect Abraham Lincoln and the Crisis of the Union, 1860–1861," in Gary W. Gallagher and Rachel A. Shelden, eds., *A Political Nation: New Directions in Mid-Nineteenth Century American Political History* (Charlottesville, VA, 2012), 126–40.
87. *CWL*, 2:121–32 (quotations on 125, 126, 129); AL to Daniel Ullman, January 1, 1861, in *CWL*, 4:184.
88. *CWL*, 2:130–131 and 3:29, 89, 300–305.

89. Robert Seager II et al., eds., *The Papers of Henry Clay* (10 vols. and supp.; Lexington, KY, 1959–92), 10:658, 664; on Clay and the compromise see Robert V. Remini, *Henry Clay: Statesman for the Union* (New York, 1991), chap. 40.
90. *CWL*, 2:232–33, 241–42, 270 (quotation), 272, 3:119–20.
91. Ibid., 2:461.
92. *Words*, 341.
93. *CWL*, 2:461–69.
94. Biographies of AL cover this—David Herbert Donald's *Lincoln* (New York, 1995) is the best; Michael Burlingame's *Abraham Lincoln: A Life* (2 vols.; Baltimore, 2008) is the most detailed modern treatment. On AL and the pro-Taylor group see Michael F. Holt, *The Rise and Fall of the Whig Party: Jacksonian Politics and the Onset of the Civil War* (New York, 1999), 285–89. No Lincoln scholar has suggested any serious contact. I initially discussed Lincoln and the South in my "The Critical Signpost on the Journey Toward Secession," *JSH* 77 (February 2011), 14–16.
95. *Words*, 341. In the South not all whites agreed on the positive good of slavery, but an overwhelming white consensus did exist on the belief that only they should make decisions about the future of the institution. To them, that prerogative was an essential dimension of their liberty. On this point consult Lacy Ford, *Deliver Us from Evil: the Slavery Question in the Old South* (New York, 2009); Harold D. Tallant, *Evil Necessity: Slavery and Political Culture in Antebellum Kentucky* (Lexington, KY, 2003); William J. Cooper, *Liberty and Slavery: Southern Politics to 1860* (New York, 1983).
96. AL to AHS, November 30, 1860, and December 22, 1860, in *CWL*, 4:146, 160; AHS to AL, December 14, 30, 1860, the former in AL Papers, the latter in AHS, *A Constitutional View of the Late War Between the States . . .* (2 vols.; Philadelphia, 1868–70), 2:267–70. AHS's speech is printed in William W. Freehling and Craig M. Simpson, eds., *Secession Debated: Georgia's Showdown in 1860* (New York, 1992), 51–79 (quotation on 69). For AL's calling AHS "a great man" see Linton Stephens to AHS, February 8, 1861, AHS Papers, Manhattanville College Library, Purchase, NY.
97. See note 81 above.
98. AL to Truman Smith, November 10, 1860 (1st quotation) and to N. Paschall, November 16, 1860 (2d quotation), in *CWL*, 4:138, 140.
99. George Kinkhead (Kentucky) to N. W. Edwards, December 1, 1860 (1st and 2d quotations), All Kentucky to AL, December 2, 1860 (3d quotation), N. Hobson (Tennessee) to AL, November 12, 1860, Edward Samuel (Missouri) to AL, January 1, 1861, all in AL Papers.
100. Daniel W. Crofts, *Reluctant Confederates: Upper South Unionists in the Secession Crisis* (Chapel Hill, NC, 1989), 35, 222–23. There is neither a good biography of Gilmer nor a substantial collection of his papers.
101. Gilmer to AL, December 10, 1860, AL Papers.
102. AL to Gilmer, December 15, 1860, in *CWL*, 4:151–53; on AL's indirect approach see

AL to Montgomery Blair, December 18, 1860, in *CWL*, 4:155. See also Gilmer to AL, December 20, 1860, AL Papers.

103. In judgments reaching across seven decades the closest students of the party—Potter, *Lincoln and His Party;* Sowle, "The Conciliatory Republicans"; and McClintock, *Lincoln*—basically agree with my interpretation.

104. Note 47 has citations on the political success of the territorial issue.

105. TW to Preston King, December 10, 1860, in *Weed*, 2:308 (quotation); Gilmer to AL, December 29, 1860, and Edward Samuel to AL, January 1, 1861, AL Papers; Gilmer to TW, January 12, 1861, and E. Emmons to TW, January 9, 1861, TW Papers; James Cooper to Lyman Trumbull, November 22, 1860, and Horace Cox to Trumbull, November 27, 1860, Trumbull Papers, LC.

106. AL to AHS, December 22, 1860, and to Gilmer, December 15, 1860, in *CWL*, 4:151–53, 160. For the Cooper Union speech see chap. 1, note 10.

107. *Words*, 25 (4th quotation), 193 (final quotation), 245 (3d quotation), 431 (1st quotation); AL to Joshua Speed, August 24, 1855, in *CWL*, 2:320 (2d quotation).

108. Almost every modern AL scholar who comments on AL and slavery comes down on the antislavery side. In many ways the two most nuanced and thoughtful books are George Fredrickson, *Big Enough to Be Inconsistent: Abraham Lincoln Confronts Race and Slavery* (Cambridge, MA, 2008) and Eric Foner, *The Fiery Trial: Abraham Lincoln and American Slavery* (New York, 2010).

CHAPTER THREE: "THE PROSPECTS FOR THE COUNTRY ARE GLOOMY"

1. AL to WHS, December 8, 1860 (two letters), in *CWL*, 4:148–49; WHS to AL, December 13, 1860, AL Papers.

2. *Weed*, 1:606, 608, 611, 2:291–95; WHS to AL, December 25, 1860, AL Papers; Patrick Sowle, "The Conciliatory Republicans During the Winter of Secession" (unpublished Ph.D. dissertation, Duke University, 1963), 114–16; Russell McClintock, *Lincoln and the Decision for War: The Northern Response to Secession* (Chapel Hill, NC, 2008), 91–93.

3. *Weed*, 1:606, 608, 611; Thomas Corwin to AL, December 11, 1860, W. Tabott to AL, November 9, 1860, David Davis to AL, November 19, 1860, J. K. Morehead to AL, November 23, 1860, L. F. Holbrook to AL, November 12, 1860, William Speer to AL, December 26, 1860, all in AL Papers.

4. On the cabinet struggle the following titles are pertinent: William E. Baringer, *A House Dividing: Lincoln as President Elect* (Springfield, IL, 1945), still valuable; Harold Holzer, *Lincoln President-Elect: Abraham Lincoln and the Great Secession Winter, 1860–1861*, Lincoln as omniscient; McClintock, *Lincoln*; John Niven, *Salmon P. Chase: A Biography* (New York, 1995); David M. Potter, *Lincoln and His Party in the Secession Crisis* (1942; Baton Rouge, LA, 1995); Sowle, "Conciliatory Republicans."

For a detailed manuscript record consult the AL Papers as well as the WHS Papers and the TW Papers. Also see specifically W. S. Snethen to Lyman Trumbull, November 21, 1860, Lyman Trumbull Papers, LC, and Frank Blair, Sr., to Frank Blair, Jr., January 5, 1861, AL Papers.

5. *Words,* 253 (quotation); Trumbull to AL, December 18, 1860; Hamlin to AL, December 27, 1860, David Davis to AL, November 19, 1860, all AL Papers; AL to John Defrees, December 18, 1860, and to WHS, December 29, 1860, in *CWL,* 4:155, 164; Springfield *Illinois State Journal,* December 12, 1860, in *CWL,* 4:150; Gilmer to WHS, January 3, 1861, and TW to WHS, January 9, 1861, WHS Papers.
6. WHS to AL, December 26, 1860, AL Papers; WHS to TW, December 2, 1860, TW Papers; CFA Diary, December 2, 1860, Adams Family Papers.
7. CFA Diary, December 27, 1860, Adams Family Papers; TW to David Davis, December 20, 1860, in Sowle, "Conciliatory Republicans," 177.
8. TW to AL, December 23, 1860, AL Papers.
9. Chase used the same phrase in letters to AL, November 7, 1860, AL Papers, to Lyman Trumbull, November 12, 1860, Trumbull Papers, LC, and to Charles Dana, November 10, 1860, in John Niven, ed., *The Salmon P. Chase Papers,* (5 vols.; Kent, OH, 1993–98), 3:32.
10. CFA to M.W. Simpson, December 9, 1860 (1st and 3d quotations), to Richard Dana, December 23, 1860 (2d quotation), to J. Francis Fisher, December 31, 1860 (4th quotation), all in CFA Letterbook and CFA Diary, December 13, 1860 (final quotation), all in Adams Family Papers.
11. *NYH,* December 12, 1860, Philadelphia *Press,* December 27, 1860, in *NEDS,* 1:238, 241.
12. Robert Toombs to AHS, February 10, 1860, in *TSC,* 462; Brown's message quoted in William W. Freehling and Craig M. Simpson, eds., *Secession Debated: Georgia's Showdown in 1860* (New York, 1992), xi-xii.
13. Freehling and Simpson, eds., *Secession Debated,* is superbly edited and invaluable.
14. Freehling and Simpson, eds., *Secession Debated,* 45, 47, 75. There is no first-rate biography of Toombs, as the dearth of his personal papers makes one almost impossible. Even so, William Y. Thompson, *Robert Toombs of Georgia* (Baton Rouge, LA, 1966), the most recent, is serviceable; additionally, Ulrich Bonnell Phillips, *The Life of Robert Toombs* (New York, 1913), still deserves consultation.
15. Thomas E. Schott has a marvelous biography, *Alexander Stephens of Georgia: A Biography* (Baton Rouge, LA, 1988).
16. Freehling and Simpson, eds., *Secession Debated,* xviii.
17. George S. Bryan to JPK, December 26, 1860, JPK Papers, Pratt (1st quotation); Alfred Huger to Joseph Holt, November 12, 1860, Joseph Holt Papers, LC (2d quotation). There are several studies of South Carolina's secession. I have relied chiefly on William W. Freehling, *The Road to Disunion,* vol. 2*: Secessionts Triumphant, 1854–1861* (New York, 2007), part 6, and Lacy K. Ford, Jr., *Origins of Southern Radicalism: The South Carolina Upcountry, 1800–1860* (New York, 1988), part 4; the for-

mer views the railroad coincidence as quite important while the latter sees it as less so. Also see Charles Edward Cauthen, *South Carolina Goes to War, 1861–1865* (Chapel Hill, NC, 1950); Steven A. Channing, *Crisis of Fear: Secession in South Carolina* (New York, 1970); and Manisha Sinha, *The Counterrevolution of Slavery: Politics and Ideology in Antebellum South Carolina* (Chapel Hill, NC, 2000).

18. Memminger to John Rutherfoord, November 27, 1860, John Rutherfoord Papers, DU.
19. C. Vann Woodward, ed., *Mary Chesnut's Civil War* (New Haven, CT, 1981), 82 (the Trescot quotation); Miles to Howell Cobb, January 14, 1861, in *TSC*, 529.
20. Alfred Aldrich to Hammond, November, 6, 1860, and Hammond to Legislature, November 8, 1860, James H. Hammond Papers, LC. For Hammond consult Drew Gilpin Faust's superb biography, *James Henry Hammond and the Old South: A Search for Mastery* (Baton Rouge, LA, 1982), though she does not emphasize his central role in this moment.
21. Woodward, ed. *Mary Chesnut's War*, 4.
22. *CM*, November 12, 1860.
23. JPK Journal, December 21, 1860, JPK Papers (1st quotation) Pratt; Weldon Edwards to G. A. Barksdale, December 21, 1860, Weldon Edwards Papers, VHS (remaining quotations).
24. JPK to Beriah Magoffin, December 25, 1860, Letterbook, JPK Papers, Pratt; Kennedy, *The Border States: Their Power and Duty . . .* (Philadelphia, 1861); Thomas Thomas to William A. Graham, November, 1860, in Max R. Williams and J. G. de Roulhac Hamilton, eds., *The Papers of William Alexander Graham* (8 vols.; Raleigh, NC, 1957–92), 5:195 (final quotation).
25. C. F. Mitchell to Lyman Trumbull, December 10, 1860, Trumbull Papers, LC (1st quotation); Nelson Poe to TW, December 19, 1860, TW Papers; George Kinkead to N. W. Edwards, December 1, 1860 (2d quotation), and N. Hobson to AL, November 12, 1860 (3d quotation), both in AL Papers.
26. Elias Schnabel to SD, January 1, 1861, SD Papers.
27. Chas. Manly to Thomas Ruffin, December 25, 1860, Thomas Ruffin Papers, UNC.
28. W. H. Hurley to SD, December 8, 1860, SD Papers (1st quotation); Charlottesville *Review*, January 4, 1861, in *SEDS*, 389 (2d quotation).
29. *House Reports*, 36th Cong., 2d Sess., No. 31 (Serial 1104), 3, 5, 6, 10, 11, 12; cited hereafter as *House Committee Journal*.
30. Ibid., 9.
31. Ibid., 3, 10 (quotation), 12, 14, passim.
32. Ibid., 10 (quotation), 12, 14, passim.
33. AL to Kellogg, December 11, 1860, in *CWL*, 4:150.
34. *House Committee Journal*, 10, 12, 14, passim; *NYH*, December 22, 1860; Benjamin Curtis Journal, December 28, 1860, Benjamin R. Curtis Papers, ALPL; CFA Diary, December 4, 1860, Adams Family Papers (quotation).
35. *House Committee Journal*, 19.

36. CFA Diary, December 4, 13, 22, Adams Family Papers; Henry Adams to Charles Francis Adams, Jr., December 26, 1860, January 2, 1861, in *HAL*, 1:213, 217. The best biography remains Martin Duberman, *Charles Francis Adams, 1807–1886* (Boston, 1961).
37. CFA to Charles Francis Adams, Jr., December 21, 1860 (1st quotation) and to J. M. Forbes, December 31, 1860, Letterbook (2d quotation), both in Adams Family Papers.
38. On New Mexico see Potter, *Lincoln and His Party*, 292–300, and Allan Nevins, *The Emergence of Lincoln* (2 vols.; New York, 1950), 2:407–10; CFA Diary, December 25, 1860, Adams Family Papers. The 1860 census listed no slaves in New Mexico and only eighty-five free blacks—*Historical Statistics of the United States: Earliest Times to the Present* (5 vols.; New York, 2006), 2:377.
39. *House Committee Journal*, 14, 15, 20, 21; CFA Diary, December 20, 1860 (quotation), Adams Family Papers.
40. CFA Diary, December 25, 1860 (1st quotation), January 5, 1861 (2d quotation), Adams Family Papers; CFA's mail in December and January is filled with anti letters.
41. *House Committee Journal* and *CG* passim.
42. David M. Potter, *The Impending Crisis, 1848–1861*, comp. and ed. Don E. Fehrenbacher (New York, 1976), chap. 8. The addition acquired in 1853 known as the Gadsden Purchase was located in what is now southern Arizona.
43. *CG*, 22–23, 59–62, 190; *House Committee Journal*, 1, 8, 16–17, 19, 20, 21; M. J. Crawford to A. H. Stephens, December 8, 1860, AHS Papers, LC (quotation).
44. *CG*, 19, 24, 28 (2d quotation), 35, 48–53, 55–59, 83, 99 (1st quotation), 112, 117, 158.
45. Ibid., 114.
46. *Senate Reports*, 36th Cong., 2d Sess., No. 288 (Serial 1090), 2; cited hereafter as *Senate Committee Journal*.
47. Ibid.; *CG*, 158.
48. Samuel Butterworth to S.L.M. Barlow, December 2, 1860, S.L.M. Barlow Papers, Huntington Library, San Marino, CA (1st quotation); Reuben Davis, *Recollections of Mississippi and Mississippians* (Boston, 1891), 396; *PJD*, 6:377 (remaining quotations).
49. *PJD*, 1:lxi (first quotation); *NYH*, December 4, 1860 (2d quotation); *Vicksburg Weekly Whig*, December 19, 1860 (3d quotation); Israel Washburne to WHS, December 18, 1860, WHS Papers.
50. *JDA*, 309–10; Varina Howell Davis, *Jefferson Davis, Ex-President of the Confederate States of America: A Memoir by His Wife* (2 vols.; New York, 1890), 1:579–83; Henry Bellows, "Memorandum on Dinner in 1863," Henry Bellows Papers, MHS (I am grateful to Charles Royster for this reference); Sowle, "Conciliatory Republicans," 353–54.
51. *JDA*, 319–20; *CG*, 1391; SD to August Belmont and to Charles Lanphier, December 25, 1860, in Robert Johannsen, ed., *The Letters of Stephen A. Douglas* (Urbana, IL, 1961), 504–5; SD to Millard Fillmore, December 29, 1860, Millard Fillmore Papers, State University of New York at Oswego.

52. Hicks to JJC, December 13, 1860, JJC Papers, LC.
53. Belmont to JJC, December 26, [1860], Winthrop to JJC, December 24, 1860, John A. Dix to JJC, December 22, 1860, Edward Everett to JJC, December 23, 1860, Elisha Whittlelsy to JJC, December 24, 1860, in Mrs. Chapman Coleman, ed., *The Life of John J. Crittenden, with Selections from His Letters and Speeches* (2 vols.; Philadelphia, 1871), 2:317 (1st quotation), 237–39 (2d quotation on p. 239); Van Buren to JJC, December 24, 1860 (copy), Martin Van Buren Papers, LC.
54. Elihu Washburne to AL, December 18, 1860 (1st quotation), George Fogg to AL, December 17, 1860 (2d quotation), Richard Thompson to AL, December 25, 1860 (3d quotation), John Defrees to AL, December 15, 1860, all in AL Papers; Jacob Brinkerhoff to Sherman, December 21, 1860, John Sherman Papers, LC; John Wilson to Richard Yates, January 1, 1861, Richard Yates Papers, ALPL; *NYTR*, December 14, 1860; Elbridge Spaulding to TW, December 22, 1860, TW Papers (final quotation).
55. Green to JB, December 28, 1860, in Philip S. Klein, *President James Buchanan, A Biography* (1962; Newtown, CT, 1995), 385; JB to Royal Phelps, December 22, 1860, in Horatio King, *Turning on the Light: A Dispassionate Survey of President Buchanan's Administration from 1860 to Its Close* (Philadelphia, 1895), 46; AL to Trumbull, December 28, 1860, and to Green, December 28, 1860, in *CWL*, 4:162–63 and n.; Green to AL, January 7, 1861, AL Papers; *NYH*, January 8, 1861; Duff Green, *Facts and Suggestions, Biographical, Historical, Financial and Political, Addressed to the People of the United States* (New York and Philadelphia, 1866), 226–32; M. Adolphe Gravier de Cassagnec, *History of the Working and Burgher Classes*, trans. by Ben E. Green [son of Duff] (Philadelphia, 1871), xii. The only biography of Green, W. Stephen Belko's *The Invincible Duff Green: Whig of the West* (Columbia, MO, 2006) focuses almost exclusively on the pre-1850 years.

    A comment on AL and the amendment—only two weeks transpired between Weed's and Green's visits to Springfield. In that short time, AL evidently changed his mind. The evidence does not permit a definite answer on his shift. Perhaps with Weed he could keep his involvement secret, but with Green his position would become public. The most logical explanation is that he wanted no public identification with a measure that might upset the hard-liners. That concern had shaped other actions. His stance would change again upon his reaching Washington just prior to his inauguration. He then placed his support behind such an amendment. See chapter 6.
56. Elbridge Spaulding to TW, December 23, 1860, TW Papers; CFA Diary, December 22, 1860, Adams Family Papers.
57. *Senate Committee Journal*, 5–8; *NYH*, December 23, 1860; *NYTR*, December 24, 1860; WHS to AL, December 26, 1860, AL Papers; WHS to Home, December 24, 1860, in *Seward*, 2:483 (quotation).
58. *Senate Committee Journal*, 2–3, 8–17; SD to AHS, December 25, 1860, AHS Papers, LC; Douglas to Belmont, December 23, 1860, in Johannsen, *Letters of Stephen Douglas*, 505; SD to Fillmore, December 29, 1860, Fillmore Papers, Oswego.

59. *Senate Committee Journal,* 17–19; *CG,* 211 (quotation); Blair to JD, December 30, 1860 (draft), Blair Family Papers, LC (calendared *PJD,* 6:674). In large measure the Republicans probably separated Kansas because back in 1858 they had successfully battled against its admission as a slave state. This time it would come in as a free state and Republican. This also explains why the southerners and their northern allies who had lost the fight in 1858 voted no. Douglas and his congressional forces at that time had sided with the Republicans. On that struggle see Potter, *Impending Crisis,* chap. 12. It could also have been because they knew that the southerners would oppose it, almost guaranteeing the failure of the larger territorial proposal.
60. William J. Cooper, "The Critical Signpost on the Journey Toward Secession," *JSH* 77 (February 2011), 3–16; JD to Frank Alfriend, August 17, 1867, in *JDE,* 393–96.
61. JD to Frank Alfriend, August 17, 1867, in *JDE,* 394; JJC to S. S. Nicholas, December, nd, 1860, JJC Papers, LC; JJC to Jesse Turner, December 29, 1860, Jesse Turner Papers, DU (1st quotation); SD to August Belmont, December 25, 1860, in Johannsen, *Letters of Stephen Douglas,* 505 (2d quotation).
62. James G. Blaine, *Twenty Years of Congress: From Lincoln to Garfield . . .* (2 vols.; Norwich, CT, 1884), 1:267; *NYTR,* January 1, 1861 (1st quotation); Sumner to John Andrew, January 8, 1861, in Beverly Wilson Palmer, ed., *The Selected Letters of Charles Sumner,* (2 vols.; Boston, 1990), 2:41; CFA Diary, January 6, 1861, Adams Family Papers (2d quotation).
63. SD to Charles Lanphier, December 25, 1860, in Johannsen, *Letters of Stephen Douglas,* 504; WHS to AL, December 26, 1860, AL Papers; E. G. Spaulding to TW, December 23, 1860, TW Papers.
64. Potter, *The Impending Crisis,* chap. 19, and Roy F. Nichols, *The Disruption of American Democracy* (New York, 1948), chap. 22, have excellent treatments; my account generally follows them. My citations will be devoted to quotations and explicit statements.
65. Anderson to Edmund Morris, December 19, 1860, Markham Manuscript Collection, Eleanor Brockenbrough Library, Museum of the Confederacy, Richmond, VA (quotation); *Genesis,* 64, 70. Maury Klein, *Days of Defiance: Sumter, Secession, and the Coming of the Civil War* (New York, 1997), is a solid, popular account.
66. *Genesis,* 71–74; the memorandum is printed on p. 73.
67. Ibid., 68, 75; Floyd to Anderson, December 21, 1860, Robert Anderson Papers, LC (quotation).
68. *DAB,* 1:274–75; Adam Goodheart, *1861: The Civil War Awakening* (New York, 2011), 13–14, 145–49; *Genesis,* 61, 65; Anderson to Col. Samuel Cooper, November 23, 1860, Letterbook, Anderson Papers, LC.
69. Nichols, *Disruption,* 387–88.
70. *Genesis,* 62.
71. Anderson to Robert Gourdin, December 11, 1860, in ibid., 69, 101.
72. J. Johnston Pettigrew to Gov. Francis Pickens, December 27, 1860, Samuel Crawford Papers, LC.
73. Gaillard Hunt, ed., "Narrative and Letter of William Henry Trescot . . . ," *AHR* 13

(1908), 531–53, quotation on p. 544; South Carolina Commissioners to Buchanan, December 28, 1860, JB Papers.

74. Hunt, ed., "Narrative of Trescot," and Potter and Nichols accounts.
75. Hunt, ed., "Narrative of Trescot," 549; Trescot to Howell Cobb, January 14, 1861, in *TSC*, 530.
76. Mrs. William Gwin to Mary Ann Cobb, January 5, [1860], Howell Cobb Papers, UGA (1st quotation); *JDC*, 5:6 (2d quotation); JD to Edwin DeLeon, January 8, 1861, in *PJD*, 7:6–7 (remaining quotations).
77. J. A. Campbell to Franklin Pierce, December 29, 1860, Franklin Pierce Papers, LC (quotation); F. P. Blair, Sr., to AL, January 14, 1861, AL Papers; Salmon Chase to Benjamin Wade, November 21, 1860, and to Winfield Scott, December 29, 1860, in Niven, ed., *Chase Papers*, 3:42–43; Allan Nevins and Milton Halsey Thomas, eds., *The Diary of George Templeton Strong* (4 vols.; New York, 1952), 3:103, for the "Old Public Functionary."
78. On the Nullification Crisis the classic treatment is William W. Freehling, *Prelude to Civil War: The Nullification Controversy in South Carolina, 1816–1836* (New York, 1966); but see also Richard E. Ellis, *The Union at Risk: Jacksonian Democracy, States' Rights, and the Nullification Crisis* (New York, 1987), which emphasizes the positive outcome for South Carolina, and Merrill Peterson, *Olive Branch and Sword: The Compromise of 1833* (Baton Rouge, LA, 1982).

CHAPTER FOUR: "UP WITH FOLLY, DOWN WITH WISDOM IS THE ORDER OF THE DAY"

1. *NYH*, December 28, 1860; Edmund Morris to Anderson, December 28, 1860, Robert Anderson Papers, LC (1st quotation); Joseph Sargent to Sumner, December 30, 1860, in J. G. Randall, *Lincoln the President: Springfield to Gettysburg* (2 vols.; New York, 1945), 1:242 (2d quotation); John A. Dix to Horatio King, December 29, 1860, in Horatio King, *Turning on the Light: A Dispassionate Survey of President Buchanan's Administration from 1860 to Its Close* (Philadelphia, 1895), 280–81 (final quotation).
2. For more detailed discussions of JB's decision see *Genesis*, chap. 14, and Roy Franklin Nichols, *The Disruption of American Democracy* (New York, 1948), 431–35. Scott to Secretary of War, December 28, 1860, Samuel Crawford Papers, LC, and to JB, December 30, 1860, JB Papers. Re: Scott: *DAB*, 8:505–11 and Maury Klein, *Days of Defiance, Sumter, Secession, and the Coming of the Civil War* (New York, 1997), 117.
3. Anderson to Samuel Cooper, December 31, 1860 (received January 5, 1861), *OR*, Series I, 1:120 (all other citations in this chapter are to Series I unless otherwise noted); Mrs. William Gwin to Mary Ann Cobb, January 5, 1861, Howell Cobb Papers, UGA.
4. Charles Edward Cauthen, *South Carolina Goes to War, 1860–1865* (Chapel Hill, NC, 1950), 102; *Genesis*, 180.
5. *OR*, 1:132, 136–37; *Genesis*, 187 (quotation); *NYH*, January 13, 1861; Samuel Crawford to "My Dear Brother," January 17, 1861 (copy), Crawford Papers, LC.

6. Holt to Anderson, January 16, 1861, in *Genesis,* 205.
7. Ibid., conveniently reprints the documents, 188–97.
8. Anderson to JJC, January 12, 1861, in Mrs. Chapman Coleman, ed., *The Life of John J. Crittenden, with Selections from His Correspondence and Speeches* (2 vols.; Philadelphia, 1871), 2:253–54 and to W. A. Gordon, January 11, 1861 (copy), Anderson Papers, LC.
9. On secession in the Deep South consult William W. Freehling's authoritative *The Road to Disunion,* vol. 2: *Secessionists Triumphant, 1854–1861* (New York, 2007). But for details and particulars studies of individual states are essential. Notable ones include Lacy K. Ford, Jr., *Origins of Southern Radicalism: The South Carolina Upcountry, 1800–1860* (New York, 1988); Manisha Sinha, *The Counterrevolution of Slavery: Politics and Ideology in Antebellum South Carolina* (Chapel Hill, NC, 2000); J. Mills Thornton, III, *Politics and Power in a Slave Society: Alabama, 1800–1860* (Baton Rouge, LA, 1978); William L. Barney, *The Secessionist Impulse: Alabama and Mississippi in 1860* (Princeton, 1974); Christopher J. Olsen, *Political Culture and Secession in Mississippi: Masculinity, Honor, and the Antiparty Tradition, 1830–1860* (New York, 2000); Michael P. Johnson, *Toward a Patriarchal Republic: The Secession of Georgia* (Baton Rouge, LA, 1977); Anthony Gene Carey, *Parties, Slavery and the Union in Antebellum Georgia* (Athens, GA, 1997); John M. Sacher, *A Perfect War of Politics: Parties, Politicians, and Democracy in Louisiana, 1824–1861* (Baton Rouge, LA, 2003); Donald E. Reynolds, *Texas Terror: The Slave Insurrection Panic of 1860 and the Secession of the Lower South* (Baton Rouge, LA, 2007); and Walter L. Buenger, *Secession and the Union in Texas* (Austin, TX, 1984). There is no book-length study of Florida, but two older articles are helpful: Dorothy Dodd, "The Secession Movement in Florida," *Florida Historical Quarterly* 12 (1933–34), 45–66, and John F. Reiger, "Secession of Florida from the Union: A Minority Decision?" *Florida Historical Quarterly* 46 (1968), 358–68.
10. Jere Clemens to JJC, December 25, 1860, JJC Papers, LC.
11. David Clopton to C. C. Clay, December 13, 1860, C. C. Clay Papers, DU (1st quotation); Mary Jones to C. C. Jones, Jr., November 15, 1860, in Robert Manson Myers, ed., *Children of Pride: A True Story of Georgia and the Civil War* (New Haven, CT, 1972), 627–28 (2d quotation); Augusta *Daily Chronicle and Sentinel,* December 22, 1860, in *SEDS,* 361–63 (final quotation). Democrats had long used the term "Black Republican," which they deemed an opprobrium, in an attempt to paint the Republican party as pro-black. Southerners certainly had no trouble with it. By 1860, it was widely used.
12. On Texas and Houston see Freehling, *Secessionists Triumphant,* 449–52, and Buenger, *Secession and Texas.*
13. James Atkins to AHS, December 10, 1860, AHS Papers, DU; Linton Stephens to AHS, November 26, December 2, 1860, AHS Papers, Manhattanville College. On AHS consult Thomas Schott, *Alexander H. Stephens of Georgia, A Biography* (Baton Rouge, LA, 1988), 311–12 and Freehling, *Secessionists Triumphant,* 442–44.

14. AHS to Linton Stephens, November 21, 1860, AHS Papers, Manhattanville (1st quotation); AHS to J. Henley Smith, November 23, 1860, in *TSC*, 504 (remaining quotations).
15. Sarah Lawton to AHS, January 21, 1861, AHS Papers, LC (1st quotation); *CG*, 310 (2d quotation).
16. Nichols, *Disruption*, 436–37; C. C. Clay to A. B. Moore, January 7, 1861, in *OR*, Series IV, 1:28–29; Cauthen, *South Carolina*, 84–85; W. H. Trescot to Howell Cobb, January 14, 1861, in *TSC*, 531.
17. JD to Pickens, January 20, 1861, in *JDC*, 5:39–40; Pickens to JD, January 9, 1861, Executive Council Journal Letterbook, 1861, South Carolina Archives, Columbia, SC.
18. Nichols, *Disruption*, 448–49.
19. *JDA*, 321–22; C. C. Clay to A. B. Moore, January 7, 1861, in *OR*, Series IV, 1:28 (quotation).
20. Freehling, *Secessionists Triumphant*, 482–86, is good on the occupying of the forts. *OR*, 1:442–44; M. S. Perry to J. E. Brown, January 3, 1861, Telamon Cuyler Papers, UGA.
21. Brown to A. B. Moore, January 5, 1861, Crawford Papers, LC.
22. Moore to JB, January 4, 1861, in *OR*, 1:445.
23. *M & P*, 5:656.
24. Ibid., 658; Senators to Gov. Perry, January 18, 1861, in *OR*, 1:445; Stephen Mallory and David Yulee to Perry, January 20, 1861, in *OR*, 1:445.
25. My discussion of the elections and convention deliberations and votes are based on the excellent treatment in Freehling, *Secessionists Triumphant*, chap. 30, and David M. Potter, *The Impending Crisis, 1848–1861* (comp. by Don Fehrenbacher; New York, 1976), 494–513. Those two should be augmented by the state studies cited in note 9 above. I will make specific citations only for quotations in cases where it is essential.
26. Regarding numbers, I have followed the conclusions of leading scholars of the elections in those states: Charles B. Dew, "The Long Lost Returns: The Candidates and Their Tools in the Louisiana Secession Election," *Louisiana History* 10 (1969), 353–69, and "Who Won the Secession Election in Louisiana?" *JSH* 36 (1970), 18–32; Michael P. Johnson, "A New Look at the Popular Vote for Delegates to the Georgia Secession Convention," *Georgia Historical Quarterly* 56 (1972), 259–75.
27. Herschel Johnson to AHS, January 9, 1861, Johnson Papers, DU.
28. Freehling, *Secessionists Triumphant*, 495 (1st quotation); R. S. Hudson to JB, January 24, 1861, JB Papers (2nd quotation).
29. Foster to Sherman, January 21, 1861, John Sherman Papers, LC.
30. AL to WHS, January 3, 1861, in *CWL*, 4:170.
31. On WHS and TW see chap. 3, pp. 82–84, and WHS to AL, December 25 and 28, 1860, AL Papers; David Davis to AL, November 19, 1860, Hamlin to AL, December 14, 1860, William H. Russell to AL, January 16, 1861, Frank Blair, Sr., to Frank

Blair, Jr., January 5, 1861, W. W. Gitt to Montgomery Blair, January 23, 1861 (quotation), all AL Papers; Wm S. Speer to Lyman Trumbull, January 16, 1861, and W. S. Snethen to Trumbull, November 20, 1860, Trumbull Papers, LC.

32. *Words*, 253.
33. Springfield *Illinois State Journal*, December 12, 1860, in *CWL*, 4:150; AL to John Defrees, December 18, 1860, in *CWL*, 4:155 (quotation).
34. AL to WHS, December 29, 1860, January 12, 1861, in *CWL*, 4:164, 173 (quotation); WHS to AL, January 1, 4, 8, 1861, AL Papers; Gilmer to AL, December 29, 1860, and to WHS, January 3, 1861, AL Papers; Gilmer to TW, January 12, 1861, TW Papers.
35. AL to WHS, January 12, 1861, in *CWL*, 4:173.
36. WHS to AL, January 15, 1861, AL Papers. For detailed treatment of AL, Cameron, and the cabinet see Harold Holzer, *Lincoln President-Elect: Abraham Lincoln and the Great Secession Winter, 1860–1861* (New York, 2008), 146–47, 180–83, 201–08, 431–32.
37. Davis to "My Dear Son," January 14, 1861 (photocopy), David Davis Papers, Chicago History Museum; Harold G. and Oswald Garrison Villard, eds., *Lincoln on the Eve of '61: A Journalist's Story by Henry Villard* (New York, 1941), 47,62.
38. *Words*, 170.
39. AL to James T. Hale, January 11, 1861, in *CWL*, 4:172 (quotation); *Words*, 436.
40. AL to James T. Hale, January 11, 1861, in *CWL*, 4:172 (1st and 2d quotations); "Remarks Concerning Concessions to Secession," in *CWL*, 175–76 (3d quotation); Carl Schurz to His Wife, February 9, 1861, in Joseph Schafer, ed., *Intimate Letters of Carl Schurz* (Madison, WI, 1928), 247.
41. Thomas Bragg Diary, January 31, 1861, Thomas Bragg Papers, UNC (1st quotation); H. Adams to C. F. Adams, Jr., January 26, 1861, in *HAL*, 1:225 (2d quotation); WHS to His Wife, January 23, 1861, in *Seward*, 2:497 (3d quotation).
42. WHS to AL, December 28 (1st quotation), 29 (3d quotation), 1860, January 27, 1861 (2d quotation), AL Papers; Leonard Swett to AL, December 31, 1860, AL Papers.
43. WHS to AL, December 29, 1860, January 4, 1861 (quotations), AL Papers.
44. The preceding paragraphs are based on two long letters from WHS to AL, December 26, 1860, and January 27, 1861, AL Papers.
45. *CG*, 341–44; CFA Diary, January 12, 1861, Adams Family Papers.
46. AL to WHS, January 19, 1861, in *CWL*, 4:176 (1st quotation); Fessenden to Elizabeth Warriner, January 12, 1861, in Robert J. Cook, *Civil War Senator: William Pitt Fessenden and the Fight to Save the American Republic* (Baton Rouge, LA, 2011), 127 (2d quotation); John L. Stevens to WHS, January 28, 1861, WHS Papers (3d quotation); Carl Schurz to His Wife, February 4, 1861, in Schafer, ed., *Intimate Letters*, 242–44; John Bigelow to Preston King, January 14, 1861, in John Bigelow, *Retrospections of An Active Life* (3 vols.; New York, 1909), 1:324; August Belmont to WHS, January 17, 1861, in August Belmont, *Letters, Speeches, and Addresses of August Belmont* (np, 1890), 46–47.

47. Winthrop to JPK, January 16, 1861, JPK Papers, Pratt; "Your friend ever" to WHS, January 12, 1861, and D. A. Kellogg to WHS, January 28, 1861, both in WHS Papers.
48. *NYH,* January 13, 14, 1861 (1st quotation); J. A. Bayard to T. F. Bayard, January 14, 1861, T. F. Bayard Papers, LC (2d quotation); James Ogden to JJC, January 29, 1861, JJC Papers, LC (3d quotation); *CM,* January 31, 1861 (final quotation).
49. J. M. Forbes to CFA, January 11, 1861, Adams Family Papers (1st quotation); Bragg Diary, January 12, 31, 1861 (2d and 3d quotations), Bragg Papers, UNC.
50. James E. Harvey to TW, January 15, 1861, WHS Papers, UR.
51. J. D. McKeehan to AL, November 13, 1860, AL Papers; *NYTR,* January 18, 1861.
52. In the following discussion of AL and race I have relied heavily on two superb books: George M. Fredrickson, *Big Enough to Be Inconsistent: Abraham Lincoln Confronts Race and Slavery* (Cambridge, MA, 2008), and Eric Foner, *The Fiery Trial: Abraham Lincoln and American Slavery* (New York, 2010). Each gives insightful and nuanced treatment to a complex matter. Each also, but especially Foner, provides context.
53. Andrew to Montgomery Blair, February 23, 1861, Blair Family Papers, LC; V. Jacque Voegeli, "A Rejected Alternative: Union Policy and the Relocation of Southern 'Contrabands' at the Dawn of Emancipation," *JSH* 49 (2003), 765–90. On the matter of race generally see the Fredrickson and Foner books cited above in note 52 and Foner, *Free Soil, Free Labor, Free Men: The Ideology of the Republican Party before the Civil War* (New York, 1970), chap. 8; Jean H. Baker, *Affairs of Party: The Political Culture of Northern Democrats in the Mid-Nineteenth Century* (Ithaca, NY, 1983), chaps. 5–6; James L. Huston, *Stephen A. Douglas and the Dilemmas of Democratic Equality* (Lanham, MD, 2007), 31–32, 111, 145–48, 171–72; and Joel H. Silbey, *A Respectable Minority: The Democratic Party in the Civil War Era* (New York, 1977), 27, 70, 80–81.
54. Foner, *Fiery Trial,* 120.
55. JJC to S. S. Nicholas, December [nd, but after the Committee of Thirteen failed], 1860, JJC Papers, LC (1st quotation); JJC and SD to Citizens, in *TSC,* 528n (2d quotation); SD to Millard Fillmore, December 29, 1860, Millard Fillmore Papers, Oswego State University (3d quotation).
56. SD to Millard Fillmore, December 29, 1860, Fillmore Papers, Oswego; SD to August Belmont, December 25, 1860 (1st quotation), and to Charles Lanphier, December 25, 1860 (2d quotation), in Robert Johannsen, ed., *The Letters of Stephen A. Douglas* (Urbana, IL, 1961), 505, 504; SD to AHS, December 25, 1860, AHS Papers, LC (3d quotation); AHS to J. Henley Smith, December 30, 1860, in *TSC,* 526; *Senate Reports,* 36th Cong., 2d Sess., No. 288 (Serial 1090), 8–12; cited hereafter as *Senate Committee Journal.*
57. *CG,* 237.
58. Ibid., Appendix, 38–42.
59. For Republican intransigence see *CG,* December passim; Amos Lawrence to JJC, January 12, 1861, JJC Papers, LC (quotation); that collection has a multitude of such letters; also see Coleman, *Life of Crittenden,* 2:250–51, 254–55, 263–64.

60. *Journal of the Senate,* 36th Cong., 2d Sess., 494–97; *CG,* 282–83, 401–02, 862.; and *Seward,* 2:498.
61. *CG,* 283, 289, 362 (SD quotation), 404, 409.
62. Ibid., 106, 107, 123, 193, 231, 365, 498 (quotation).
63. *House Reports,* 36th Cong., 2d Sess., No. 31 (Serial 1104), passim; cited hereafter as *House Committee Journal.*
64. Ibid., 35–38.
65. Ibid., 39–40.
66. Corwin to AL, January 15, 1861, AL Papers.
67. *House Committee Journal,* 16, 39–40; CFA Diary, December 20 (1st quotation), 25, 26 (3d quotation), 27, 1860, January 5, 1861 (4th quotation), CFA to C. F. Adams, Jr., December 30, 1860 (2d quotation), and to Edward Pierce, January 1, 1861, Letterbook, Adams Family Papers; Henry Adams to C. F. Adams, Jr., December 26, 1860, in *HAL,* 1:213; David M. Potter, *Lincoln and His Party in the Secession Crisis* (1942; Baton Rouge, LA, 1995), 293, n.26. The Adams Family Papers contain numerous anti letters. For census figures, see *Historical Statistics of the United States: Earliest Times to the Present* (5 vols.; New York, 2006), 2:377.
68. For the text see *House Committee Journal,* 39–40.
69. JPK to Robert C. Winthrop, January 9, 1861, Letterbook, JPK Papers, Pratt (1st quotation); Hicks to JJC, January 25, 1861, JJC Papers, LC (2d quotation); Bedford Brown to Rives, January 17, 1861, William C. Rives Papers, LC (3d quotation).
70. E. Emmons to TW, January 9, 1861, TW Papers (1st quotation); William Walker to Hamilton Fish, January 26, 1861, Hamilton Fish Papers, LC; Ira Lucas to AL, January 10, 1861 (2d quotation) and J. T. Lyons to AL, January 22, 1861 (3d quotation), AL Papers, LC. The AL, WHS, and TW Papers have many such letters.
71. Robert Hatton (member of the group) to William B. Campbell, January 24, 31, 1861, Campbell Family Papers, DU; *NYH,* January 6, 1861; *AEJ,* January 5, 7, 1861; *NYT,* January 7, 8, 1861; *NYTR,* January 7, 1861; Journal, January 4, 1861, Samuel Curtis Papers, ALPL (quotation); Patrick Michael Sowle, "The Conciliatory Republicans During the Winter of Secession," (Ph.D. dissertation, Duke University, 1963), 221–27; Daniel W. Crofts, *Reluctant Confederates, Upper South Unionists in the Secession Crisis* (Chapel Hill, NC, 1989), 201–4, 232.
72. *NYT,* January 10, 1861; *NYTR,* January 9, 1861; *AEJ,* January 9, 17, 1861; Swett to AL, nd [but clearly early January 1861], David Davis Papers, Chicago History Museum.
73. *NYH,* January 5, 6 (1st quotation), 7, 1861; Journal, January 4, 1861, Curtis Papers, ALPL; CFA Diary, January 4, 5, 1861 (2d quotation), Adams Family Papers.
74. *CG,* 279–82.
75. Hale to AL, January 6, 1861, and Washburne to AL, January 7, 1861, AL Papers, LC; AL to Hale, January 11, 1861, in *CWL,* 4:172.
76. WHS to AL, January 27, 1861, AL Papers, LC.
77. Cauthen's *South Carolina,* 103–6, has the most complete account of Hayne's mission.

78. *M & P*, 5:656.
79. John Bassett Moore, ed., *The Works of James Buchanan* (12 vols; Philadelphia, 1908–11), 11:109–11.
80. Ibid., 127–28.
81. *CM*, January 16, 17, 18, 19, 31, 1861; Larz Anderson to Joseph Holt [January, 1861], Joseph Holt Papers, LC; *JDA*, 344–45; JD to Pickens, January 20, 1861, in *JDC*, 5:39–40.
82. Philip S. Klein, *President James Buchanan, A Biography* (1962; Newtown, CT, 1995), 394; *OR*, 1:133, 140, 143–44, 150, 153–54, 158, 159 (quotation), 160, 161; Samuel Crawford to "My Dear Brother," February 2, 1861 (copy), Samuel Crawford Papers, LC.
83. Moore, *Works of James Buchanan*, 11:128–131, has the letters.
84. Ibid., 131–41, has the letters.
85. JB to Joseph Holt, January 30, 1861, Holt Papers, LC.

CHAPTER FIVE: "YOU CAN STILL THIS STORM"

1. For example, consult Richard Elliott to CFA, February 9, 1861, Thos. Coldwill to CFA, February 20, 1861, Wm. Gold to CFA, February 9, 1861, all in Adams Family Papers; Sam Hays to Cameron, February 1, 1861, Simon Cameron Papers, LC; A. C. Thompson to WHS, February 12, 1861, J. R. Bailey to WHS, February 11, 1861, Enoch Pratt to WHS, February 23, 1861, Jno. Baxter to WHS, February 24, 1861, Jn. Pendleton to WHS, February 15, 1861, WHS Papers.
2. Barbour to WHS, February 8, 1861, and H. Fauntleroy to WHS, February 12, 1861, WHS Papers.
3. Robert W. Johannsen, *Stephen A. Douglas* (New York, 1973), 828; J. S. Black to C. R. Buckalew, January 28, 1861, in Patrick Michael Sowle, "The Conciliatory Republicans During the Winter of Secession" (Ph.D. diss., Duke University, 1963), 301–2 (quotation); WHS to AL, January 27, 1861, AL Papers. The tenor of letters to WHS in the WHS Papers makes indisputably clear that southern Conservatives saw him as one who respected them and would listen to them.
4. Johannsen, *Douglas*, 827–28 (first quotation); *CG*, 669 (remaining quotations).
5. AL to WHS, February 2, 1861, in *CWL*, 4:183; WHS to TW, February 5, 1861, TW Papers.
6. WHS to AL, January 27, 1861, AL Papers.
7. CFA Diary, February 5, Adams Family Papers; Allan Nevins and Milton Halsey Thomas, eds., *The Diary of George Templeton Strong* (4 vols.; New York, 1952), 3:97.
8. Best on the commissioners is Charles B. Dew, *Apostles of Disunion: Southern Secession Commissioners and the Causes of the Civil War* (Charlottesville, VA, 2001), which informs my account; the quotation is on p. 32.
9. G.W. Newell to Samuel Tilden, February 6, 1861, Samuel Tilden Papers, NYPL;

W. H. Harley to SD, December 8, 1860, SD Papers, UC (1st quotation; all other citations in this chapter are from this collection unless otherwise noted); JPK to Philip Pendleton, February 10, 1861, JPK Papers, Pratt (2d quotation); Campbell to W. P. Jones, December 11, 1860, Campbell Family Papers, DU (3d quotation).

10. [William Pettigrew] to "My dear Brother," December 29, 1860 (marked unsent), Pettigrew Family Papers, SHC; Levi Bowen to JB, January 9, 1861, JB Papers (1st quotation); JPK Journal, December 21, 1860, JPK Papers, Pratt (2d quotation).
11. On Virginia and secession Daniel W. Crofts, *Reluctant Confederates: Upper South Unionists in the Secession Crisis* (Chapel Hill, NC, 1989), which gives detailed coverage to Virginia, is superb; William A. Link, *Roots of Secession: Slavery and Politics in Antebellum Virginia* (Chapel Hill, NC, 2003) is worthy. William W. Freehling, *The Road to Disunion*, vol. 2: *Secessionists Triumphant, 1854–1861* (New York, 2007), chap. 31, also spends time on Virginia. The older Henry T. Shanks, *The Secession Movement in Virginia, 1847–1861* (Richmond, VA, 1934), still has value. They inform my account.
12. Alexander H. H. Stuart to William C. Rives, January 15, 1861, William C. Rives Papers, LC.
13. Thomas Hicks to JJC, January 9, 1861, JJC Papers, LC (all other citations in this chapter are to this collection unless otherwise noted); Levi Bowers to JB, February 3, 1861, JB Papers; T. L. Smith to WHS, January 28, 1861, WHS Papers; R. Hatton to W. B. Campbell, February 4, 1861, Campbell Family Papers, DU (quotation).
14. JPK to John Baldwin, February 12, 1861, Letterbook, JPK Papers, Pratt (1st quotation); Jn. Pendleton to WHS, February15, 1861, WHS Papers (2d quotation).
15. Crofts, *Reluctant Confederates*, is best on North Carolina and Tennessee; on Arkansas see James M. Woods, *Rebellion and Realignment: Arkansas's Road to Secession* (Fayetteville, AK, 1987), and Freehling, *Secessionists Triumphant*, 504.
16. A. C. Thompson to WHS, February 12, 1861, WHS Papers; *NYH*, January 4, 1861, referring specifically to Hicks. On the border states there has been surprisingly little scholarship, and almost all of it is more than a quarter century old. Maryland has the best coverage: Jean Baker, *The Politics of Continuity: Maryland Political Parties from 1858 to 1870* (Baltimore, 1973), William J. Evitts, *A Matter of Allegiance: Maryland, 1850–1861* (Baltimore, 1974), and Frank Towers, *The Urban South and the Coming of the Civil War* (Charlottesville, VA, 2004), chap. 5, on the importance of Baltimore. Amazingly, best on Kentucky is still an unpublished dissertation, Harry August Volz III, "Kentucky and the Coming of the American Civil War" (Ph.D. diss., University of Virginia, 1982). For Delaware consult Harold Hancock, *Delaware During the Civil War* (Wilmington, DE, 1961), and for Missouri, William E. Parrish, *Turbulent Partnership: Missouri and the Union, 1861–1865* (Columbia, MO, 1963) and Mark W. Geiger, *Financial Fraud and Guerrilla Violence in Missouri's Civil War* (New Haven, CT, 2010), which has a fascinating account of the secessionists' financial strategy.
17. Hatton to W. B. Campbell, February 18, 1861, Campbell Family Papers, DU (1st quotation); Barbour to WHS, February 8, 1861, WHS Papers (2d quotation).

18. Gouv. Kemble to Martin Van Buren, January 24, 1861, Martin Van Buren Papers, LC; J. L. Pugh to William Porcher Miles, January 24, 1861, William Porcher Miles Papers, UNC (1st quotation); P. C. Clayton to Cobb, February 11, 1861 (2d quotation), and Henry Benning to Cobb, February 13, 1861, Howell Cobb Papers, UGA; *CM*, January 22, 1861.
19. Wm. Gold to CFA, February 9, 1861, Adams Family Papers; Jn. Pendleton to WHS, February 15, 1861, W. B. Campbell to Robert Hatton, February 12, 1861, Jno. Baxter to WHS, February 24, 1861, Barbour to WHS, February 8, 1861 (quotation), WHS Papers; Bragg Diary, February 5, 1861, Bragg Papers, UNC.
20. William C. Rives to Numerous Men, January 23, 1861, Rives Papers, LC. There had been two prior notable conventions, but both had been geographically restricted: the Hartford Convention of 1814, in which New England Federalists considered secession because of the War of 1812, and the Nashville Convention of 1850, in which a number of slave states discussed their reaction to the territorial question.
21. Lyon G. Tyler, *The Letters and Times of the Tylers* (3 vols.; Richmond and Williamsburg, VA, 1884–1885, 1896), 2:579–80.
22. Tyler to JB, January 23, 25, 28, 1861, JB Papers; Memoranda [January 24 and 25, 1861], JB to Tyler, January 25, 28, 1861, in John Bassett Moore, ed., *The Works of James Buchanan* (12 vols.; Philadelphia, 1908–1911), 11:113, 114, 121; *M & P*, 5:661–63 (quotations).
23. On the convention Robert Gray Gunderson's *Old Gentlemen's Convention: The Washington Peace Conference of 1861* (Madison, WI, 1961), though dated, is a thoroughly researched, detailed treatment; also see Crofts, *Reluctant Confederates*, 207–13. My account follows them. On Tyler: Bragg Diary, February 5, 1861, Bragg Papers, UNC; Julia Tyler to Mrs. Gardiner, February 4, 1861, in Tyler, *Letters of the Tylers*, 2:598. At the end of January, Kansas had been admitted as a free state, increasing the number of states to thirty-four.
24. See text pp. 186ff.
25. Schurz to His Wife, February 4, 1861, in Joseph Schafer, ed., *Intimate Letters, of Carl Schurz* (Madison, WI, 1928), 244 (1st quotation); Gustave Koerner, *Memoirs of Gustave Koerner*, ed. Thomas J. McCormack (2 vols.; Cedar Rapids, IA, 1909), 2:113 (2d quotation); *NYTR*, February 5, 1861 (3d quotation).
26. *NYH*, January 25, 1861; Charles Sumner to Andrew, January 28, 1861, in Beverly Wilson Palmer, ed., *The Selected Letters of Charles Sumner* (2 vols.; Boston, 1990), 2:47; CFA Diary, February 2, 1861, Adams Family Papers; Morton to AL, January 29, 1861, AL Papers (1st quotation); W. Jayne to Lyman Trumbull, January 28, 1861, Lyman Trumbull Papers, LC (remaining quotations).
27. Morton to AL, January 29, 1861, AL Papers (quotations); W. Jayne to Lyman Trumbull, January 28, 1861, Trumbull Papers, LC; Springfield *Daily Illinois State Register*, February 2, 1861, in *NEDS*, 1:307–09.
28. CFA Diary, February 2, 1861, Adams Family Papers; *CG*, 476–762 passim (Cobb's remarks on p. 646) and App. 103–18, 164–67.

29. *CG,* 580–83.
30. For the *NYT* quotation as well as other northern papers see Crofts, *Reluctant Confederates,* 206–7; WHS to AL, January 27, 1861, AL Papers.
31. Again, on the convention consult Gunderson, *Old Gentlemen's Convention.*
32. L. E. Chittenden, *Personal Reminiscences, 1840–1890, Including Some Not Hitherto Published of Lincoln and the War* (New York, 1893), 32–33 (all quotations except the final one); Gouv. Kemble to Martin Van Buren, January 24, 1861, Van Buren Papers, LC (final quotation).
33. Sarah Forbes Hughes, ed., *Letters and Recollections of John Murray Forbes* (2 vols.; Boston and New York, 1899), 1:191 (quotation); E. G. Spaulding to TW, February 14, 1861, TW Papers; P. A. Hackelman to Oliver Morton, February 10, 1861, in Kenneth M. Stampp, ed., "Letters from the Washington Peace Conference of 1861," *JSH* 9 (August 1943), 400; Zachariah Chandler to Austin Blair, February 11, 1861, in Sowle, "Conciliatory Republicans," 382.
34. Chandler to Austin Blair, February 11, 1861, in Sowle, "Conciliatory Republicans," 382; Gunderson, *Old Gentlemen's Convention,* 72–77. No delegates ever appeared from those states.
35. George S. Boutwell, *Reminiscences of Sixty Years in Public Affairs* (2 vols.; New York, 1902), 1:271 (quotation).
36. Barringer to "Dearest Wife," February 4, 6, 8, 9, 13, 1861, Daniel Barringer Papers, UNC; Thomas Ruffin to "My dearest Wife," February 9, 1861, Thomas Ruffin Papers, UNC; JPK Journal, February 12, 15, 1861, JPK Papers, Pratt.
37. *NYH,* February 13, 1861 (1st and 2d quotations); Julia Tyler to Her Mother, February 13, 1861, in Tyler, *Letters of the Tylers,* 2:612–13 (3d quotation); Henry Adams to Charles Francis Adams, Jr., February 13, 1861, in *HAL,* 1:231 (final quotation).
38. L. E. Chittenden, *A Report of the Debates and Proceedings of the Secret Sessions of the Conference Convention . . .* (New York, 1864), 94–96 (Seddon 94), 99, 101 (Boutwell); Boutwell, *Reminiscences,* 1:273.
39. Chittenden, *Report,* 146 (quotation), 149; L. E. Chittenden, *Recollections of President Lincoln and His Administration* (New York, 1891), 55, for the fracas.
40. Phillip S. Foner, *Business & Slavery: New York Merchants & the Irrepressible Conflict* (Chapel Hill, 1941), 268–69 (Dodge); Chittenden, *Report,* 126; Tyler, *Letters of the Tylers,* 2:625; Gunderson, *Old Gentlemen's Convention,* 68.
41. Chittenden, *Report,* 294 (Barringer); Boutwell, *Reminiscences,* 1:274.
42. Gunderson, *Old Gentlemen's Convention,* 88.
43. CFA to J. Palfrey, February 22, 1861 (copy), Adams Family Papers.
44. *Philadelphia Inquirer,* February 23, 1861, in *NEDS,* 1:283–87.
45. Lawrence to Pierce, January 27, 1861, Franklin Pierce Papers, LC.
46. A. T. Stewart to TW, February 20, 1861, in *Weed,* 2:318–19.
47. For the businessmen in Washington see Foner, *Business & Slavery,* 250–51, 256–57; all the quotations are from there.
48. Bragg Diary, January 12, 1861, Bragg Papers, UNC; JD to Clement Clay, Novem-

ber 12, 1875, Clement Clay Papers, DU, and to William Walthall, November 21, 1875, William W. Walthall Papers, Mississippi Department of Archives and History, Jackson, MS; *OR,* ser. 1, 1:442–44, ser. 4, 1:28–29.

49. AHS to Samuel Glenn, February 8, 1861 (copy), AHS Papers, LC. On Montgomery, I have relied heavily on the excellent, detailed account by William C. Davis, *"A Government of Our Own": The Making of the Confederacy* (New York, 1994); also consult George C. Rable, *The Confederate Republic: A Revolution Against Politics* (Chapel Hill, NC, 1994), chap. 3. The Confederate Constitution is reprinted on pp. 135–51 of Marshall DeRosa, *The Confederate Constitution of 1861: An Inquiry into American Constitutionalism* (Columbia, MO, 1991).

50. Howell Cobb to "My Dear Son," February 10, 15, 1861, Cobb Papers, UGA, and to His Wife, February 6, 1861, in *TSC,* 537; also see Thomas R. R. Cobb to Marion, February 11, 1861, Thomas R. R. Cobb Papers, UGA, and David Yulee to JD, February 13, 1861, JD Papers, DU.

51. Cobb to "My dear Son," February 10, 1861, H. Cobb Papers, UGA; AHS to "Dear Brother," February 23, 1861, AHS Papers, Manhattanville College; Thomas R. R. Cobb to Marion, February 6, 1861, T. Cobb Papers, UGA; Davis, *"Government of Our Own,"* chap. 5.

52. Cobb to His Wife, February 6, 1861, in *TSC,* 537; *JDA,* 327–28. Davis in *"Government of Our Own,"* chap. 5, tries to make the election suspenseful, but I do not find his speculation persuasive.

53. Bragg Diary, February 10, 1861, Bragg Papers, UNC; *NYH,* February 14, 1861.

54. *JDA,* 328–29.

55. *JDE,* 198–203, has JD's inaugural.

56. William P. Miles to Howell Cobb, January 14, 1861, in *TSC,* 529 (1st quotation); Bragg Diary, February 10, 1861, Bragg Papers, UNC (2d quotation); Howell Cobb to A. R. Wright, February 18, 1861, AL Papers.

57. Hatton to W. B. Campbell, January 31, 1861, Campbell Family Papers, DU (1st quotation); *NYH,* February 14, 1861 (2d quotation); *AEJ,* February 12, 1861; *Utica Morning Herald and Daily Gazette,* February 20, 1861, in *NEDS,* 2:614 (3d quotation); *New York Evening Post,* February 18, 1861, in *NEDS,* 608–9 (4th quotation).

58. JD to Varina Davis, February 20, 1861, in *PJD,* 7:54. In addition to the previously cited books by Davis and Rable, I have borrowed extensively from *JDA,* 355–60.

59. Cobb to "My Dear Son," February 15, 1861, H. Cobb Papers, UGA.

60. JD to Pickens, January 20, March 1, 18, in *JDC,* 5:40, 58–59, 60–61, and on February 20, 22 (quotation), in *PJD,* 7:55, 57–58; Pickens to William P. Miles, February 7, 1861, Miles Papers, UNC, and to JD, February, 27, 1861, in *JDC,* 5:58.

61. *NYH,* January 7, 1861; David M. Potter, *Lincoln and His Party in the Secession Crisis* (1942; Baton Rouge, LA, 1995), 254–55; WHS to AL, December 29, 1860, AL Papers; Charles Sumner to John Andrew, January 28, 1861, in Palmer, ed., *Selected Letters of Sumner,* 2:47–48; CFA Diary, January 29, 1861, Adams Family Papers; Layne S. Cannon, "Lieutenant-General Winfield Scott During the Secession Crisis: A Thread

of Continuity Through a Time of Change" (unpublished seminar paper, Louisiana State University, 2007), 9–10; Adams to Charles Francis Adams, Jr., December 29, 1860, in *HAL*, 1:216.

62. Cannon, "Winfield Scott," 9–10; Potter, *Lincoln and His Party*, 255; Elihu Washburne to AL, January 30, 1861, AL Papers.
63. *CWL*, 4:190. Harold Holzer's *Lincoln President-Elect: Abraham Lincoln and the Great Secession Winter, 1860–1861* (New York, 2008), chaps. 9–11, has a detailed account of AL's journey. For an exemplary discussion of the speeches consult Ronald C. White, Jr., *The Eloquent President: A Portrait of Lincoln Through His Words* (New York, 2005), 16, 34, 40–42, 45–46, 54, 57.
64. John Nicolay to Therena Bates, February 11, 15, 17, 1861, in Michael Burlingame, ed., *With Lincoln in the White House: Letters, Memoranda, and Other Writings of John G. Nicolay, 1860–1865* (Carbondale and Edwardsville, IL, 2000), 27–28; Harold G. and Oswald Garrison Villard, eds., *Lincoln on the Eve of '61: A Journalist's Story by Henry Villard* (New York, 1941), chap. 4; Norman Judd to Lyman Trumbull, February 17, 1861, Trumbull Papers, LC.
65. *CWL*, 4:190–247, has all, from prepared addresses to impromptu remarks; the quotation is on p. 195.
66. Ibid., 207.
67. Ibid., 193 (1st, 2d, final quotations), 234 (3d quotation), 236 (4th quotation).
68. Ibid., 241–42.
69. Ibid., 211 (1st three quotations), 237 (next three quotations), 245 (final two quotations).
70. Ibid., 198–99. This part of the speech was set off in quotation marks to show that the words were the same as back in 1856.
71. *NYTR*, February 13, 16, 1861; E. Hunn to WHS, February 23, 1861, and TW to WHS, February 21, 1861 (quotation), WHS Papers; CFA Diary, February 11, 1861, Adams Family Papers.
72. Sherrard Clemens to John Underwood, February 18, 1861 (2d quotation), WHS Papers; James Barbour to William C. Rives, February 18, 1861 (1st quotation), William C. Rives Papers, LC; CFA Diary, February 19, 1861, Adams Family Papers.
73. For detail see Holzer, *Lincoln President-Elect*, 390–96.
74. David Herbert Donald, *Lincoln* (New York, 1995), 279–80; Russell McClintock, *Lincoln and the Decision for War: The Northern Response to Secession* (Chapel Hill, NC, 2008), 192–93; Crofts, *Reluctant Confederates*, 245–47, and "A Reluctant Unionist: John A. Gilmer and Lincoln's Cabinet," *CWH* 24 (1978), 225–49; Gilmer to AL, February 21, 1861, AL Papers; Bragg Diary, February 26, 1861, Bragg Papers, UNC; CFA Diary, February 28, 1861, Adams Family Papers.
75. *Weed*, 1:316; TW to WHS, February 19 (1st quotation), 21 (2d quotation), WHS Papers.
76. Gunderson, *Old Gentlemen's Convention*, 84–85 (quotation); Donald, *Lincoln*, 279–80.
77. *Words*, 8.

78. The only contemporary accounts come from Morehead, both in 1862: a letter to JJC and a speech he gave in England. By then he had become a Confederate and had been imprisoned for a time by federal authorities; in fact, the letter to JJC was written while he was in prison on Staten Island. Thus, caution is called for, though Morehead claims he made notes immediately after the interview. In addition, two other sources in which AL refers to the meeting and corroborates Morehead add to his credibility. The first occurred in conversation with a European diplomat while he was still president-elect; the second took place in the fall of 1861 in the presence of his private secretary. The letter dated February 23, 1862, is in Mrs. Chapman Coleman, ed., *The Life of John J. Crittenden, with Selections from His Correspondence and Speeches* (2 vols.; Philadelphia, 1871), 2:337–38; for the speech see David Rankin Barbee and Milledge L. Bonham, Jr., "Fort Sumter Again," *MVHR* 28 (June 1941), 63–73; all quotations are from here, except the Clemens letter. The two Lincoln references are from Ralph Haswell Lutz, "Rudolph Schleiden and the Visit to Richmond, April 25, 1861," *Annual Report of the American Historical Association for the Year 1915* (Washington, 1917), 211, and Michael Burlingame and John R. Turner Ettlinger, eds., *Inside Lincoln's White House: The Complete Civil War Diary of John Hay* (Carbondale and Edwardsville, IL, 1997), 28. On the dating of the meeting consult McClintock, *Lincoln*, 318–19, n. 18. Sherrard Clemens to Unknown, nd, in William E. Baringer, *A House Dividing Lincoln as President Elect* (Springfield, IL, 1945), 313. Congressman Clemens specified that the meeting he attended along with others was held on February 26, and he was writing only days thereafter. Thus, because there is no record of any other such meeting during those few days, it seems almost certain that he was talking about this assembly.
79. Lutz, "Rudolph Schleiden," 211. It is puzzling that no follow-up seems to have occurred.
80. A. R. Boteler, "Mr. Lincoln and the Force Bill," in *The Annals of the War Written by Leading Participants North and South* (Philadelphia, 1879), 220–27 (quotations on 226); *CG*, 1031–33, 1097–98, 1201–02, 1225–32, 1335–38, App. 231–35.
81. *CWL*, 4:246–47.

CHAPTER SIX: "FRATERNITY IS THE ELEMENT OF UNION"

1. *CG*, 1331–33: CFA Diary, March 2, 1861, Adams Family Papers; Hiland Hall to WHS, February 23, 1861, AL Papers.
2. *CG*, 1254–55, 1269–70, 1305–18 (Baker on 1314), 1342–50, 1403–05.
3. AL to WHS, February 1, 1861, in *CWL*, 4:183.
4. *CG*, 1326–27.
5. Ibid., 1264; CFA Diary, February 27, 1861, Adams Family Papers.
6. *CG*, 1284–85; David Rankin Barbee and Milledge L. Bonham, Jr., "Fort Sumter Again," *MVHR*, 28 (June, 1941), 68 (1st quotation); *CWL*, 4:270 (2d quotation).

7. *CG,* 1305–18, 1338–39, 1342–56, 1359–1405; *NYH,* March 4, 1861; *NYTR,* March 5, 1861.
8. Marc Engal, *Clash of Extremes: The Economic Origins of the Civil War* (New York, 2009), 248–50; James L. Huston, *The Panic of 1857 and the Coming of the Civil War* (Baton Rouge, LA, 1987), 266–68; Kenneth M. Stampp, *And the War Came: The North and the Secession Crisis, 1860–1861* (Baton Rouge, LA, 1950), 162–64; *CG,* 1065, 1195–1201. For the Republican platform statement on the tariff see Kirk H. Porter and Donald Bruce Johnson, comps, *National Party Platforms, 1840–1964* (Urbana, IL, 1966), 33.
9. *CG,* 641, 763–68, 1005, 1205–8, 1334–35; the Epilogue in Christopher Childers's *The Failure of Popular Sovereignty: Slavery, Manifest Destiny, and the Radicalization of Southern Politics* (Lawrence, KS, 2012).
10. *CG,* 1391 (Douglas quotation).
11. James G. Blaine, *Twenty Years of Congress, From Lincoln to Garfield* . . . (2 vols.; Norwich, CT, 1884) 1:271–72.
12. *CG,* 1205–8 (Douglas on 1205).
13. On JJC see the Prologue; *NYH,* March 5, 1861. The Senate was sitting because JB had called a special session to handle executive appointments.
14. AL to George Prentice, February 2, 1861, in *CWL,* 4:184; Ronald C. White, Jr., *The Eloquent President: A Portrait of Lincoln Through His Words* (New York, 2005), 67–68. White in chap. 3 has a fine discussion of the preparation and content of the inaugural.
15. *CWL,* 4:249–61, has the first draft.
16. White, *Eloquent President,* 96; *Words,* 391 (quotation); Patrick Michael Sowle, "The Conciliatory Republicans During the Winter of Secession" (Ph.D. diss. Duke University, 1963), 401.
17. Theodore Calvin Pease and James G. Randall, eds., *The Diary of Orville Hickman Browning* (2 vols.; Springfield, IL, 1925), 1:455–56: Browning to AL, February 17, 1861 (with endorsement by AL), AL Papers.
18. Michael Burlingame, ed., *An Oral History of Abraham Lincoln: John G. Nicolay's Interviews and Essays* (Carbondale and Edwardsville, IL, 1996), 47. WHS's response was based on his own reaction plus all his efforts during the winter; see below.
19. See above and chap. 5 for citations; Sowle, "Conciliatory Republicans," 353, has the WHS quotation.
20. F. W. Lander to WHS, February 24, 1861, and WHS to AL, February 24, 1861 (copy), WHS Papers; two memoranda [February 1861] from WHS, AL Papers; *CWL,* 4:249–71, has WHS's line-by-line recommendations and AL's action on each.
21. WHS to AL, March 2, 1861, AL papers. I agree with Sowle and Russell McClintock, *Lincoln and the Decision for War: The Northern Response to Secession* (Chapel Hill, NC, 2008) that concern about secession chiefly motivated WHS, not the makeup of the cabinet. Most scholars emphasize the latter reason. See McClintock, *Lincoln and War,* 318, n. 14.

22. *NYH,* March 5, 1861; CFA Diary, March 4, 1861, Adams Family Papers.
23. *CWL,* 4:262–71 has the inaugural.
24. *NYTR,* March 5, 1861; *AEJ,* March 5, 1861; *NEDS,* 2:618–24 passim, 629–31, 638–42 (quotations 623 and 639).
25. *NYH,* March 5, 1861 (1st quotation); *NEDS,* 2:624–29, 631–38; Black to JB, March 11, 1861, JB Papers (2d quotation); Stanton to P. D. Lowe, March 4, 1861, Edwin Stanton Papers, LC (3d quotation).
26. *CM,* March 5, 1861 (1st quotation); Cobb to "My Dear Son," March 5, 1861, Howell Cobb Papers, UGA (2d quotation; all other citations in this chapter are from this collection unless otherwise noted); Thomas Bragg Diary, November 15, 1861, Thomas Bragg Papers, UNC (3d quotation; all other citations in this chapter are from this collection unless otherwise noted).
27. *SEDS,* 478 (1st quotation); Graham to David Swain [March 1861], Max R. Williams and J.G. de Roulhac Hamilton, eds., *The Papers of William Alexander Graham,* (8 vols.; Raleigh, NC, 1957–92), 5:241 (2d quotation); Edward Tayloe to B. O. Tayloe, March 9, 1861, WHS Papers; John Brockenbrough to John Rutherfoord, March 5, 1861, John Rutherfoord Papers, DU.
28. White, *Eloquent President,* 96; CFA Diary, March 4, 1861, Adams Family Papers.
29. Allan Nevins and Milton Halsey Thomas, eds., *The Diary of George Templeton Strong* (4 vols.; New York, 1952), 3:106.
30. AL to Scott, January 11, 1861, and to Wool, January 14, 1861, in *CWL,* 4:172–73, 175; AL to Elihu Washburne, December, 21, 1860, in *CWL,* 4:159; *Words,* 343.
31. M. Smith to Elihu Washburne, March 21, 1861, Elihu Washburne Papers, LC; Sumner to Henry W. Longfellow, March 16, 1861, in Beverly Wilson Palmer, ed., *The Selected Letters of Charles Sumner* (2 vols.; Boston, 1990), 2:59 (1st quotation); *Words,* 375 (remaining quotations). A glance at *CWL,* 4:278–313, reveals just how much patronage absorbed Lincoln in his first weeks as president. Michael Burlingame, *Abraham Lincoln: A Life* (2 vols.; Baltimore, 2008), 2:chap. 21 provides details.
32. *Words,* 344 (1st quotation); AL to WHS, March 4, 1861, in *CWL,* 4:273 (2d quotation); WHS to AL, March 5, 1861, AL Papers.
33. John G. Nicolay and John Hay, *Abraham Lincoln: A History* (10 vols.; New York, 1890), 3:371–72.
34. Anderson to Samuel Cooper (adjutant general of the army), February 28, 1861, AL Papers; JB Memorandum [March 9, 1861], John Bassett Moore, ed., *The Works of James Buchanan* (12 vols.; Philadelphia, 1908–11), 11:156.
35. Anderson to Samuel Cooper, February 28, 1861, AL Papers; the other letters are also there; *Genesis,* 283–84.
36. JB Memorandum [March 9, 1861], Moore, *Works of James Buchanan,* 11:156.
37. Holt and Winfield Scott (Holt secured Scott's endorsement on the letter) to AL, March 5, 1861, AL Papers; AL to Scott, March 9, 1861, in *CWL,* 4:279.
38. Scott to AL, March 5, 1861 (attached to the Holt and Scott letter cited above in note 37), AL Papers.

39. Scott to WHS, March 3, 1861, and WHS to AL, March 4, 1861, both AL Papers; Layne S. Cannon, "Lieutenant General Winfield Scott During the Secession Crisis: A Thread of Continuity Through a Time of Change," (unpublished seminar paper, Louisiana State University, 2007), 10–11.
40. *M & PC,* 1:55–56.
41. Ludwell H. Johnson, "Fort Sumter and Confederate Diplomacy," *JSH* 26 (November 1960), 446–55. This article remains the most detailed discussion of this mission; it informs my account. See also *Genesis,* 319–25 and McClintock, *Lincoln,* 207–9.
42. Undated memorandum signed S.W. [Samuel Ward], WHS Papers; it is printed in Frederic Bancroft, *The Life of William H. Seward* (2 vols.; New York, 1900), 2:542–45.
43. Ibid.; Evan J. Coleman and William M. Gwin, "Gwin and Seward. A Secret Chapter in Ante-Bellum History," *Overland Monthly* 18 (November 1891), 469; Kathryn A. Jacob, *King of the Lobby: The Life and Times of Sam Ward, Man-About-Washington in the Gilded Age* (Baltimore, MD, 2009), 49–50.
44. Martin Crawford to Robert Toombs, March 8, 1861, in Bancroft, *Seward,* 2:109–10, n. 1. Seward's Border included all of the eight slave states still in the Union.
45. Johnson, "Fort Sumter," 450.
46. Ibid., 450–51 (quotation); James A. Bayard to Thomas F. Bayard, March 9, 1861, Thomas F. Bayard Papers, LC.
47. *Genesis,* 325 (quotation); Bancroft, *Seward,* 2:112.
48. *M & PC,* 1:84 (quotation); Johnson, "Fort Sumter," 452.
49. Ralph A. Wooster, *Secession Conventions of the South* (Princeton, NJ, 1962), 231–34. For the Missouri vote see p. 172 above.
50. Ibid., 157–64; James M. Woods, *Rebellion and Realignment: Arkansas's Road to Secession* (Fayetteville, AK, 1987), chap. 9.
51. There are several excellent studies of the Virginia Convention, especially William W. Freehling, *The Road to Disunion,* vol. 2: *Secessionists Triumphant, 1854–1861* (New York, 2007), 504–14; William A. Link, *Roots of Secession: Slavery and Politics in Antebellum Virginia* (Chapel Hill, NC, 2003), 226–40; Nelson D. Lankford, *Cry Havoc! The Crooked Road to Civil War, 1861* (New York, 2007), chap. 4. George H. Reese, ed., *Proceedings of the Virginia State Convention of 1861* (4 vols.; Richmond, VA, 1965), provides a massive documentary record, though lack of an index is a handicap. A brief, invaluable abridgment is William W. Freehling and Craig M. Simpson, eds., *Showdown in Virginia: The 1861 Convention and the Fate of the Union* (Charlottesville, VA, 2010), 106–7 (quotations).
52. Hunter to Cobb, March 15, 1861, Cobb Papers, UGA; G. W. Summers to James C. Welling, March 19, 1861, Blair Family Papers, LC; Alexander H. H. Stuart to Joseph Kennedy, April 1, 1861, and Benjamin O. Tayloe to WHS, March 13, 1861, WHS Papers.
53. G. W. Summers to Montgomery Blair, March 19, 1861, Blair Family Papers, LC.

54. Conrad to "My dear wife," February 18, March 2, 6, 13 (2d quotation), 20, 26, 29 (1st quotation), Robert Conrad Papers, VHS.
55. Reese, ed., *Proceedings,* 1:523–28 (quotation on 526).
56. Leslie Combs to WHS, March 8, 29 (1st quotation), H. E. Thomas to WHS, March 8, 1861, Robt. Twitty to WHS, March 29, 1861, WHS Papers; John M. Harlan to Joseph Holt, March 11, 1861 (2d quotation), Joseph Holt Papers, LC; Norwin Green to AL, March 14, 1861, AL Papers; John Brockenbrough to John Rutherfoord, March 5, 1861, Rutherfoord Papers, DU (3d quotation); Wooster, *Secession Conventions,* 233.
57. *CG,* 1434–46 (Special Session); Robert Johannsen, *Stephen A. Douglas* (New York, 1973), 846–50.
58. Michael Robinson, "James Buchanan, Abraham Lincoln, and the Forts, a Calendar" (research project, Louisiana State University, 2011); Howard K. Beale, ed., *Diary of Gideon Welles: Secretary of the Navy under Lincoln and Johnson* (3 vols.; New York, 1960), 1:3–5; Howard K. Beale, ed., *The Diary of Edward Bates 1859–1866* (Washington, 1933), 177.
59. AL to Scott, March 9, 1861, in *CWL,* 4:279, and Scott to AL, March 11, 1861, AL Papers.
60. Beale, *Diary of Gideon Welles,* 1:5, 8–9, 13–14.
61. *NYTR,* March 11–14, 1861; *NYT,* March 11–13, 1861; *NYH,* March 12–15, 1861; Scott to Anderson, March 11, 1861, AL Papers.
62. F. Blair, Sr., to M. Blair, March 12, 1861, and M. Blair to AL, March 12, 1861, AL Papers.
63. *NYTR,* March 11, 1861 (1st quotation); Neal Dow to AL, March 13, 1861 (2d quotation), and Welles to AL, March 15, 1861 (4th quotation); David Donald, *Charles Sumner and the Coming of the Civil War* (New York, 1960), 386–87; Beale, ed., *Diary of Gideon Welles,* 1:4–5 (3d quotation).
64. Robinson, "The Forts, a Calendar"; CFA Diary, March 12, 1861 (1st quotation), Adams Family Papers; Douglas L. Wilson and Rodney O. Davis, eds., *Herndon's Informants: Letters, Interviews, and Statements about Abraham Lincoln* (Urbana, IL, 1998), 475 (2d quotation).
65. Robinson, "The Forts, a Calendar"; Fox to Winfield Scott, February 8, 1861, with memorandum for the relief of Fort Sumter, in Robert Means Thompson and Richard Wainwright, eds., *Confidential Correspondence of Gustavus Vasa Fox, Assistant Secretary of the Navy, 1861–1865* (2 vols.; New York, 1918–19), 1:7–9; David Detzer, *Allegiance: Fort Sumter, Charleston, and the Beginning of the Civil War* (2001; San Diego, CA, 2002), 226.
66. Fox to Mrs. Fox, March 19, 1861 (1st quotation), in Thompson and Wainwright, eds., *Confidential Correspondence of Gustavus Fox,* 1:9; AL to WHS, March 15, 1861 (2d quotation), in *CWL,* 4:284–85; an identical request went to each cabinet member.
67. WHS to AL, March 15, 1861, AL Papers. William Pitt, the elder, opposed his country's taxing the American colonies in the period leading up to the American Rev-

olution. On Pitt consult Robert Middlekauff, *The Glorious Cause: The American Revolution, 1763–1789* (New York, 1982), 111–12, and Marie Peters, "William Pitt, First Earl of Chatham," *Oxford Dictionary of National Biography* (60 vols.; Oxford, England, 2004), 44:462, 466.

68. Montgomery Blair to AL, March 15, 1861, AL Papers.
69. AL Papers has them all; Welles on March 15, the others on the sixteenth.
70. On Seward and the Confederate Commission, Johnson's "Fort Sumter" remains key, especially pp. 455–61. Additionally consult *Genesis,* 325–32, which also has documents, and McClintock, *Lincoln,* 215–16. Essential for the story are three items from Justice Campbell: Campbell to WHS, April 13, 1861, AL Papers; Campbell to JD, April 3, 1861, in *PJD,* 7:88–89 and 90 n.1; his "Facts of History," in "The Papers of Hon. John A. Campbell," *Southern Historical Society Papers* 72 (New Series—Number 4; October 1917), 30–34; the letter to WHS is reprinted on pp. 38–41. "The Facts" is a postwar recounting of events, but the contemporary letters corroborate it.
71. Campbell, "Facts of History," 31.
72. Ibid., 32. The original of the March 15 letter has not survived, but he refers to it in detail in his letter of April 3 to JD cited in note 70 above.
73. Campbell's note of March 15 is printed in *Genesis,* 330.
74. Johnson, "Fort Sumter," 459.
75. Commissioners to Toombs, March 20, 1861, in *OR,* Ser. I, 1:277 (all other citations in this chapter also come from Ser. I).
76. Commissioners to Beauregard, [March 20, 1861], in ibid., 1:277; Beauregard to Commissioners, March 21, 1861 (quotation), in ibid., 53:136.
77. *Genesis,* 331, has Campbell's note.
78. Ibid., 331 (1st quotation); Campbell, "Facts," 33 (2d quotation).
79. *Genesis,* 331–32, has Campbell's note dated March 22.
80. Ibid., 332; Johnson, "Fort Sumter," 461.
81. L. P. Walker to Beauregard, March 14 and 15 (quotation), 1861, in *OR,*, 1:275–76.
82. JD to Pickens, March 18, 1861, in *JDC,* 5:60–61.
83. WHS to Mrs. Seward, March 18, 1861, in *Seward,* 2:518.
84. McClintock, *Lincoln,* 323–24, n. 18, has a thorough discussion of various views on this matter.

CHAPTER SEVEN: "THE QUICKSANDS THAT ENVIRON OUR SHIP OF STATE"

1. Cameron to Winfield Scott, March 19, 1861, and Anderson to Lorenzo Thomas, March 22, 1861, in *OR,* Ser. I, 1:208–9, 211 (all other citations in this chapter are also to Ser. I unless otherwise noted); Winfield Scott to Fox, March 19, 1861, and Fox to Mrs. Fox, March 19, 1861, in Robert Means Thompson and Richard Wainwright, eds., *Confidential Correspondence of Gustavus Vasa Fox, Assistant Secretary of*

the Navy, 1861–1865 (2 vols.; New York, 1918–19), 1:9–10; *Genesis*, 369–73; John G. Nicolay and John Hay, *Abraham Lincoln, A History* (10 vols.; New York, 1890), 3:389.

2. Hurlburt to AL, March 27, 1861, AL Papers; Michael Burlingame, ed., *An Oral History of Abraham Lincoln: John G. Nicolay's Interviews and Essays* (Carbondale and Edwardsville, IL, 1996), 362–64; Lamon to WHS, March 25, 1861, WHS Papers; Lamon, *Recollections of Abraham Lincoln, 1847–1865*, ed. Dorothy Lamon Teillard (1895; Washington, 1911), 71–79, a clearly embellished, melodramatic account; Pickens to Pierre Beauregard, March 25, 26, 1861, and Beauregard to Anderson, March 26, 1861, in *OR*, 1:281–82, 222. Lamon had no authority to make any statements regarding Fort Sumter; for an excellent analysis of Lamon's possible motives see Russell McClintock, *Lincoln and the Decision for War: The Northern Response to Secession* (Chapel Hill, NC, 2008), 334, n. 55.
3. Michael Robinson, "James Buchanan, Abraham Lincoln, and the Forts, a Calendar" (unpublished research project, Louisiana State University, 2011); Scott to Israel Vogdes, March 12, 1861, in *OR*, 1:360; Howard K. Beale, ed., *Diary of Gideon Welles, Secretary of the Navy Under Lincoln and Johnson* (3vols.; New York, 1960), 1:9; David M. Potter, *Lincoln and His Party in the Secession Crisis* (1942; New Haven, CT, 1962), 359; Nicolay and Hay, *Lincoln*, 3:393–94.
4. Summers to James C. Welling, March 19, 1861 (1st and 2d quotations), Blair Family Papers, LC; George H. Reese, ed., *Proceedings of the Virginia State Convention* (4 vols.; Richmond, VA, 1965), 1:626 (final two quotations); Daniel W. Crofts, *Reluctant Confederates: Upper South Unionists in the Secession Crisis* (Chapel Hill, NC, 1989), 275–76.
5. Crofts, *Reluctant Confederates*, 279 (1st quotation); Quentin Busbee to SD, March 11, 1861, SD Papers; Max R. Williams and J. G. de Roulhac Hamilton, eds., *The Papers of William Alexander Graham* (8 vols.; Raleigh, NC, 1957–92), 5:245 (2d quotation).
6. Benjamin O. Tayloe to WHS, March 16, 1861 (1st quotation) and H. U. Graham to WHS, March 22, 1861 (2d and 3d quotations), WHS Papers; Jeptha Fowlkes to Johnson, March 10, 1861, in Paul H. Bergeron et al., eds., *The Papers of Andrew Johnson* (16 vols.; Knoxville, TN, 1967–2000), 4:379; For a full discussion of a possible national Union party see Crofts, *Reluctant Confederates*, especially chap. 10 for this time period.
7. Summers to James C. Welling, March 19, 1861 (1st quotation), Blair Family Papers, LC; H. U. Graham to WHS, March 22, 1861, and Benjamin O. Tayloe to WHS, March 16, 1861 (2d quotation), WHS Papers.
8. Summers to Montgomery Blair, March 19, 1861 (1st quotation), Blair Family Papers, LC; John Gilmer to SD, March 28, 1861, SD Papers; Jno. B. Gallaher to WHS, April 3, 1861 (2d quotation), WHS Papers.
9. *Words*, 375.
10. Trumbull to J. K. Dubois, March 21, 1861, in McClintock, *Lincoln*, 224.

11. *CG*, 1519 (quotation), 1521, 1526.
12. AL to Chase and Welles, March 18, 1861, in *CWL*, 4:292, 293; Welles to AL, March, nd, 1861, and Chase to AL, March 20, 1861, AL Papers.
13. McClintock, *Lincoln*, 216; Phillip S. Foner, *Business & Slavery, The New York Merchants & the Irrepressible Conflict* (Chapel Hill, NC, 1941), 284, 299, 301–4 (1st quotation on 310, the 2d on 299); Kenneth M. Stampp, *And the War Came: The North and the Secession Crisis, 1860–1861* (Baton Rouge, LA, 1950), 231–38.
14. Scott to AL, nd, in *OR*, 1:200–1. There is an ongoing debate about the proper date of Scott's memorandum. It is undated and in the *OR* accompanies Cameron's March 15 response to Lincoln's query about Fort Sumter. Thus, some scholars prefer that date. Most give it the later date, with which I concur. To me it is inconceivable that Lincoln would have kept to himself this explosive advice. His dealings with Scott changed after the twenty-eighth but not between the fifteenth and the twenty-eighth. McClintock, *Lincoln*, 329–30, n. 9, has a good discussion, historiography included. He and I agree.
15. For Scott as pawn see Gideon Welles, *Lincoln and Seward: Remarks Upon the Memorial Address of Chas. Francis Adams . . .* (New York, 1874), 52ff.
16. Montgomery C. Meigs, "General Montgomery C. Meigs on the Conduct of the Civil War," *AHR* 26 (January 1921), 300 (1st quotation; this article consists of entries from Meigs's diary); E. D. Keyes, *Fifty Years' Observations of Men and Events, Civil and Military* (New York, 1884), 378 (2d and 3d quotations).
17. Welles, *Lincoln and Seward*, 57–60; Beale, ed., *Diary of Gideon Welles*, 1:13–14; Montgomery Blair to Samuel W. Crawford, May 6, 1882, Samuel W. Crawford Papers, LC.
18. Howard K. Beale, ed., *The Diary of Edward Bates, 1859–1866* (Washington, 1933), 180. All the letters, most undated, are filed under March 29 in the AL Papers, with an endorsement by AL that they had been written in the cabinet. Blair's, not endorsed, is filed under March.
19. McClintock, *Lincoln*, 232–33. He underscores that the cabinet shift between March 15 and 29 was not absolute; I concur.
20. AL to Cameron, March 29, 1861, in *OR*, 1:226; Fox's requirements divided between the army and navy are specified on p. 227.
21. "Meigs on the War," 300 (quotation); Keyes, *Fifty Years' Observation*, 380–84.
22. Beale, ed., *Diary of Gideon Welles*, 1:16–18.
23. "Meigs on the War," 301 (quotation); note various AL orders in *CWL*, 4:313–15, 320.
24. WHS to AL, April 1, 1861, AL Papers; also in *CWL*, 4:317–18.
25. Frederick Seward, "After Thirty Years" [1899], WHS Papers.
26. AL to WHS, April 1, 1861, in *CWL*, 4:316–17. McClintock, *Lincoln*, 240, is good on why AL would not dismiss WHS.
27. Robert W. Johannsen, *Stephen A. Douglas* (New York, 1973), 852–54 (quotation on 852).

28. Ludwell H. Johnson, "Fort Sumter and Confederate Diplomacy," *JSH* 26, (November 1960), 463.
29. Ibid., 463–64 (quotation on 463).
30. "The Papers of Hon. John A. Campbell," *Southern Historical Society Papers* 42 (New Series—Number IV; October 1917), 34–35. See also the letter cited in note 31 below and Campbell to WHS, April 13, 1861, AL Papers, and Pierre Beauregard to Leroy Walker, April 4, 1861 (enclosing a telegram from Martin Crawford), in *OR,* 1:283–84. Whether or not WHS actually spoke with AL is uncertain, but Campbell believed that he did.
31. Campbell to JD, April 3, 1861, in *PJD,* 7:88–89.
32. Johnson, "Fort Sumter," 467–68.
33. Commissioners to Toombs, April 2, 3, 5 (1st quotation), 6, in *OR,* 1:284–86, 287; Walker to Beauregard, April 2, 1861, *in OR,* 1:285 (2d quotation); Commissioners to Toombs, April 4, 5, 1861, in *ORN,* Series I, 4:257 (all other citations in this chapter are also to Series I unless otherwise noted).
34. David Herbert Donald, *Lincoln* (New York, 1995), 289; AL to Scott, April 1, 1861, in *CWL,* 4:316.
35. John W. B. Autram to AL, April 2, 1861, AL Papers (1st quotation); Stampp, *And the War Came,* 267 (2d and 3d quotations), 269–70; *NYT,* April 3, 1861 (final quotation).
36. Anderson to Col. L. Thomas, April 1, 1861, in *OR,* 1:230.
37. Summers to WHS, April 1, 1861, WHS Papers; *Words,* 308.
38. Only Baldwin gave a full account, in a pamphlet published in 1866: *Interview Between President Lincoln and Col. John B. Baldwin, April 4, 1861* (Staunton, VA, 1866). This pamphlet contains Baldwin's testimony (the quotations come from it) before a congressional committee in which he recounts the interview. Of course, it is possible that Baldwin might not have his and AL's precise phrasing, but there is no good reason to doubt the accuracy of his thrust. In addition, the pamphlet has corroborating statements from several of Baldwin's colleagues in the convention that confirm his account. It also has the version of John Minor Botts, a Virginia Unionist, who swore that he was told by AL that AL did offer Baldwin to trade Fort Sumter for adjournment. Also see *Words,* 20.
39. Crofts has a judicious, thorough discussion of this history in *Reluctant Confederates,* 301–6, 438–39, n. 39. For the reason I have specified, I agree with Crofts's conclusion regarding Baldwin's veracity. Again, as I said in my text, it is simply inconceivable that Baldwin would have failed to share this bombshell with his allies in Richmond. It would have given them a tremendous victory, which they would have loudly proclaimed.
40. Simon Cameron to Anderson, April 4, 1861, in *CWL,* 4:321–22 (AL drafted the letter which went out over Cameron's signature; see n. 1 to this letter on p. 322). On the sixth the bearer was refused permission to deliver it; see Richard N. Current, *Lincoln and the First Shot* (Philadelphia, 1963), 97–98.

41. Reese, ed., *Proceedings,* 3:163.
42. Crofts, *Reluctant Confederates,* 309–10, 312.
43. Beale, ed., *Diary of Gideon Welles,* 1:9–12.
44. Simon Cameron to Chew, April 6, 1861, in *CWL,* 4:323–24.
45. Campbell to WHS, April 7, 1861, in *ORN,* 4:258–59 (1st quotation); "Papers of John Campbell," 35 (2d quotation). Also, see the letters from Campbell to JD and WHS cited in notes 30 and 31 above.
46. Commissioners to Toombs, April 7, 8, 1861, and Beauregard to Crawford, April 8, 1861, in *ORN,* 4:258–59 (quotation on 258); *Genesis,* 431–42; Johnson, "Fort Sumter," 471.
47. *Words,* 61–62.
48. AL to Fox, May 1, 1861, in *CWL,* 4:351 (1st quotation); *Words,* 62 (2d quotation).
49. Welles to "My Dear Wife," April 10, 1861, Gideon Welles Papers, LC.
50. *CWL,* 4:424–25; Douglas L. Wilson and Rodney O. Davis, eds., *Herndon's Informants: Letters, Interviews, and Statements about Abraham Lincoln* (Urbana and Chicago, 1998), 475 (quotation).
51. The question of whether or not with the expedition to Fort Sumter AL initiated war or hoped for peace is a historical perennial. Books could be written about differing interpretations of his motives and expectations. In fact, half a century ago Richard Current did just that with his *Lincoln and the First Shot.* A new version could easily be done today. McClintock has a good brief discussion in his *Lincoln,* 335–36, n. 64.
52. On Walker and Beauregard see above, note 33; Walker to Governors, April 8, 1861, in *OR,* 1:290–91; Toombs to AHS, April 6, 1861, in *TSC,* 558 (quotation).
53. JD to Bragg, April 3, 1861, in *PJD,* 7:85–86. On the Confederates and Fort Pickens consult Grady McWhiney, "The Confederacy's First Shot," *CWH* 14 (March 1968), 5–14.
54. Pickens and Beauregard to [Walker], April 8, 1861, in *OR,* 1:291.
55. JD to Campbell, April 6, 1861, in *PJD,* 7:92 (quotation); Edward Younger, ed., *Inside the Confederate Government: The Diary of Robert Garlick Hill Kean, Head of the Bureau of War* (New York, 1957), 112–13; Campbell to WHS, April 13, 1861, AL Papers. In the letter Campbell recounted his conversations with Seward and wanted an explanation of what had actually transpired; WHS never responded.
56. JD to John Campbell, April 6, 1861, in *PJD,* 7:92.
57. *New York Citizen,* May 4, 1867; on the point of pride see text chap. 4, page 128.
58. In contrast to the situation for the Lincoln administration, the historical record on the deliberations of the Confederate leadership at this critical moment is exceedingly thin. For my account I have borrowed heavily from my *JDA,* 339–40.
59. On Toombs see *Genesis,* 421, and William Y. Thompson, *Robert Toombs of Georgia* (Baton Rouge, LA, 1966), 168. The evidence for Toombs's statement is slim. His first biographer, Pleasant A. Stovall in *Robert Toombs: Statesman, Speaker, Soldier, Sage . . .* (New York, 1892), 226, made such a claim without providing documentation. Subsequent biographers and most historians have repeated it, still without

any documentation. Toombs evidently said something about the horror of war and shooting first, but his precise words and the details are uncertain. Nothing, however, suggests that he opposed Davis's final decision. The quotations are from AHS to R. Schleiden, April 26, 1861, in *TSC*, 563 (1st) and JD to Bragg, April 3, 1861, in *PJD*, 7:85 (2d).

60. For the messages between Beauregard and his War Department and the dealings between his emissaries and Anderson consult *OR*, 1:13–14, 297, 300–2, 305.

EPILOGUE: "BOTH MARCHING TO THE FIELD OF BLOOD"

1. For excellent accounts of the bombardment see W. A. Swanberg, *First Blood: The Story of Fort Sumter* (New York, 1957), chaps. 27–29, and David Detzer, *Allegiance: Fort Sumter, Charleston, and the Beginning of the Civil War* (2001; San Diego, CA, 2002), chaps. 16–17.
2. *CWL*, 4:330–31.
3. Ibid., 331–32. Two recent books have underscored the powerful force of the concept of the Union in the free states: Liz Varon, *Disunion! The Coming of the American Civil War, 1789–1859* (Chapel Hill, NC, 2008) and Gary W. Gallagher, *The Union War* (Cambridge, MA, 2011).
4. Kenneth M. Stampp, *And the War Came: The North and the Secession Crisis, 1860–1861* (Baton Rouge, LA, 1950), 287 (1st quotation); Allan Nevins and Milton Halsey Thomas, eds., *The Diary of George Templeton Strong* (4 vols., New York, 1952), 3:126 (2d quotation).
5. Edwin Stanton to JB, April 12, 1861, JB Papers (1st quotation); Robert W. Johannsen, *Stephen A. Douglas* (New York, 1973), 868–69 (2d quotation on 868).
6. On these states see the sources cited in chap. 5, notes 11 and 15.
7. On these states see the sources cited in chap. 5, note 16.
8. Albert D. Kirwan, *John J. Crittenden: The Struggle for the Union* (Lexington, KY, 1962), 432–34, 446–48.
9. Gilmer to WHS, April 21, 1861, WHS Papers.

ACKNOWLEDGMENTS

Many people and institutions have helped make this book possible. I am especially indebted to the keepers of manuscripts and books who guided me through their collections. Their number is so large that I must thank them collectively. I also owe an enormous debt of gratitude to the legion of historians who have preceded me in attempting to understand the coming of the Civil War. Throughout my notes I have tried to register my obligations to them. For my entire career my own Louisiana State University has generously supported my research and writing. That generosity has continued with this book.

A number of individuals provided indispensable contributions. When I began this project, Gaines Foster was my departmental chair; prior to completion Victor Stater stepped into that position. Both were most accommodating to my constant calls on them. Additionally, in my department Darlene Albritton gave unstinting aid. I am grateful to Professor Gary D. Joiner of Louisiana State University, Shreveport, for providing the maps. Over the course of my work invaluable research assistance came from several past and present graduate students—Christopher Childers, Spencer McBride, Jennifer Pratt, Michael Robinson, and Ryan Ruckel. Mr. McBride also assisted immeasurably in getting the manuscript ready for publication. Always attentive and helpful, Leslie Levine skillfully shepherded my book through the publication process.

I certainly benefitted from close, careful scrutiny of my manuscript by fellow historians. My colleague Andrew Burstein and my longtime friend Michael Holt read attentively and criticized intelligently. Their thoroughness and candor have made this a much better book.

My wife and my editor stood by me. A stalwart for me, Patricia Cooper has always provided steadfast support. She understood the importance of this book to me. For more than two decades I have been fortunate indeed to have Jane Garrett as an editor. That she could continue to work with me on this book while moving into retirement has meant a great deal to me. As I have said before, I highly value my association with her.

All of the people named in these acknowledgments had a hand in the preparation of this book. Yet, it is mine, and I accept full responsibility for it.

INDEX

Page numbers in *italics* refer to illustrations.